The Glass Church

The Glass Church

Robert H. Schuller, the Crystal
Cathedral, and the Strain
of Megachurch Ministry

MARK T. MULDER AND GERARDO MARTÍ

Rutgers University Press

New Brunswick, Camden, and Newark, New Jersey, and London

Library of Congress Cataloging-in-Publication Data

Names: Mulder, Mark T., 1973– author. | Martí, Gerardo, author.
Title: The glass church : Robert H. Schuller, the Crystal Cathedral, and the strain
    of megachurch ministry / Mark T. Mulder, Gerardo Martí.
Description: New Brunswick : Rutgers University Press, 2020. |
    Includes bibliographical references and index.
Identifiers: LCCN 2019028324 | ISBN 9780813589053 (hardback) |
    ISBN 9780813589077 (epub) | ISBN 9780813589084 (pdf) | ISBN 9781978814257 (mobi)
Subjects: LCSH: Crystal Cathedral (Garden Grove, Calif.) | Big churches. |
    Schuller, Robert H. (Robert Harold), 1926–2015.
Classification: LCC BX9999.G37 M85 2020 | DDC 285.7/79496—dc23
LC record available at https://lccn.loc.gov/2019028324

A British Cataloging-in-Publication record for this book is available from the British Library.

www.rutgersuniversitypress.org

Manufactured in the United States of America

Preface

Robert H. Schuller, a pious farm boy from rural Iowa in a declining mainline Protestant denomination, planted a mission church in Southern California. Through this innovative ministry, he reframed the experience of Sunday morning worship, reoriented the priorities of preaching, and reset the agenda for congregational leadership. Not only did his church grow to an unprecedented scale, but he turned his experience into principles and aggressively advocated spectacular growth as a rational and attainable goal for all churches. Schuller's attractive, cutting-edge vision for a modernized ministry influenced thousands of pastors and emboldened the philosophy of "church growth" that dominated post–World War II Christianity across the United States.

The testing of his approach to pastoral ministry began at an outdoor movie theater in 1955 when he decided to tap into the car-centric culture of greater Los Angeles with a drive-in church.[1] Religious historian Randall Balmer deemed Schuller's auto-accessible strategy "pure genius."[2] Schuller would soon fortuitously locate his expansive church campus within a mile of California's major north-south thoroughfare, Highway 101 (soon renamed U.S. Interstate 5 or the Santa Ana Freeway). In crafting his recipe for success, he borrowed from the religious trendsetters of his day, especially Norman Vincent Peale of New York's Marble Collegiate Church. Schuller also counted Bishop Fulton Sheen and evangelist Billy Graham among his influences. Most importantly, he made ministry growth a manageable and measurable outcome. Schuller maximized a business-inflected approach to pastoral ministry that, for an era at least, allowed him to operate on an unrivaled plane.

And yet, despite the apparent reliability of his methods and the seeming stability of his megachurch, Schuller's ministry abruptly collapsed—a shocking implosion of a vast religious edifice—with his board declaring bankruptcy in October 2010.

In *The Glass Church*, we demonstrate a series of accumulated congregational strains, a mismanagement of core resources obscured by an overoptimistic Possibility Theology, to more fully explain what eventually shattered Schuller's glass church.[3] We use evidence drawn from a rich mixture of data sources, including an array of archival materials, interviews with leaders and members associated with the ministry, and ethnographic observations on site. Our narrative also represents a convergence of the two authors' personal biographies. Much like Schuller, Mulder's formative years occurred within a rural Midwestern Dutch Reformed milieu. Although decades and hundreds of miles separated their childhood experiences in Dutch enclaves, Schuller's Alton, Iowa, and Mulder's Alto, Wisconsin, derived their names from the same Dutch village (Aalten, Gelderland) and fostered similar cultural atmospheres.[4] And akin to Schuller's journey from an Iowa farm to the Southern California megalopolis, Mulder's career has seen him counterintuitively focus on urban and suburban congregations. Martí, on the other hand, grew up in Garden Grove, California, under the looming suburban shadow of the Crystal Cathedral, witnessing firsthand the progressive expansion of the campus. Living ten minutes from "the glass church," he participated in events on site, including youth rallies, Bible studies, high school baccalaureate services, wedding ceremonies, musical productions, and more. The glass church was a busy place, maximizing facilities with dozens of programs and activities every day of the week. But as a Latino whose Cuban parents had migrated to a rapidly diversifying Orange County, he also participated in the demographic trends that subverted the success of the cathedral as it failed to appeal to non-Anglos. We believe our biographies enhance our academic sensibilities toward offering a vivid account of Robert H. Schuller's monumental—yet catastrophic—ministry.

Funding for the research that culminated in this book came from numerous sources. Our thanks to the Van Raalte Institute (VRI) in Holland, Michigan, where Mulder had the opportunity to access church archives as a visiting research fellow. While at the VRI, Mulder enjoyed the hospitality and expertise of folks who knew the Reformed Church in America denomination and Schuller well. With their winsome insights, Elton Bruins, Jack Nyenhuis, Henk Aay, Robert Swierenga, Don Bruggink, Don Luidens, Bill Kennedy, and Nella Kennedy have contributed richly to this volume. In addition, the staff at the VRI—JoHannah Smith, Geoffrey Reynolds, and Lori Tretheway—all offered excellent logistical assistance. Mulder also offers a very special thanks to Dennis Voskuil—whose courageous research charted an initial path toward explaining the phenomenon of Schuller's ministry in the early 1980s. At Calvin University, *The Glass Church* received generous support from the Mellema Program, the Calvin Center for Christian Scholarship, the Department of Sociology and Social Work's Deur Award, the McGregor Fellowship, the Civitas Lab, and the Writing Co-op. Perhaps most significantly, portions of this manuscript were written on the shores of Fox Lake, Wisconsin, during the course of a sabbatical.

From Mark:
For my sons,
Seth and Case

From Gerardo:
For my parents,
Rafael and Caridad Martí

The more successful we became, the more problems I had.
—Robert H. Schuller, *Tough Times Never Last, but Tough People Do!*

The result of action is not an object, which, once it has been conceived, can be produced. The result of action rather has the character of a story, which continues for as long as people continue to act, but the end and the result of which nobody, not even the person who began the story, can foresee or conceive.
—Hannah Arendt, *Freedom and Politics: A Lecture*

Contents

Mulder expresses his gratitude to the Calvin University Board of Trustees for the opportunity. Mulder extends a special gratefulness to Erica Buursma, a student research assistant who provided invaluable support to this project over the course of two years. In Orange County, Jim and Linda Kok's encouragement and networking opened many doors and proved pivotal to the research. Mulder also offers his thanks to Duane Vander Brugge, Eleanor Vander Ark, Shepherd's Grove Church, Don and Martheen (now passed) Griffieon, and his wonderful colleagues in Calvin's Department of Sociology and Social Work. Finally, Mulder reserves his most profound thankfulness for his best friend and wife, Dawn.

Martí is grateful for conversations with family and friends who offered informal reflections on their experience with Schuller and his church. The work also received Faculty Study and Research funding from Davidson College. Mulder and Martí convey their gratitude to their editorial team at Rutgers. Acquisitions editor Peter Mickulas's keen interest, attentiveness, and patience all enhanced the research and writing process. Copyeditor Don Burgard's wisdom, sharp eye, and diligence helped to create a more coherent narrative. And, of course, the texture of this manuscript has been greatly enhanced by the many individuals who knew Robert H. Schuller and the ministry so well. Though most remain unidentified, Mulder and Martí express a special note of thanks for their openness, hospitality, and insights.

For both scholars and ministry leaders, we offer an assessment, but also a warning. The imperative for growth has become foundational to the management orientation of today's megachurch ministries and the ministers who look to apply their template. Schuller directly influenced ministers like John Maxwell—an important figure in the evangelical motivational world—who, in turn, influenced Joel Osteen—one of the preeminent megachurch pastors in the United States today. Indeed, Ronald Keener, editor of *Church Executive*, declared that ministers like Rick Warren of Saddleback Community Church and Bill Hybels (formerly) of Willow Creek Community Church "only stand on the shoulders of Robert H. Schuller." Even now, Schuller's imprint continues to be evident in the building and growth imperatives assumed by pastors across the spectrum of American Christianity today. In relating the story of Schuller's glass church, this book allows them to be more acutely aware of the immense strain that relentless church growth strategies place on their ministry. By avoiding superficial critiques found in many popular discussions of "shallow preaching" or "prosperity theology," we seek to stimulate a more productive dialogue about past consequences and future implications for contemporary Christian congregational ministry. A closer look at the relationship between constituents, charisma, and capital is only the beginning.

Significant Dates for Robert Schuller and U.S. Politics, 1945–2015

1945–1953	Truman administration
1945	Schuller enters Hope College
1947–1991	Cold War
1947	Schuller graduates from Hope College
1947	Billy Graham holds first crusade
1950	Schuller graduates from Western Theological Seminary; he and Arvella get married and move to Illinois
1953–1961	Eisenhower administration
1955	First service held at Orange Drive-in
1958	John Birch Society founded
1961–1963	Kennedy administration
1960	Schuller attends Fred Schwarz School of Anti-Communism
1961	Walk-in–drive-in church opened; designed by Richard Neutra
1962	Francis Amendment appeared on the California election ballot
1963–1969	Johnson administration
1973	*Roe v. Wade* decided
1964	Barry Goldwater campaign
1964	Civil Rights Act passed
1968	Martin Luther King Jr. assassinated
1968	Tower of Hope erected; designed by Richard Neutra
1969–1974	Nixon administration
1969	Leadership institute established
1969	*Hour of Power* begins broadcasting
1972	Schuller's first trip to the Soviet Union

1973	Schuller receives honorary doctor of divinity from Hope College
1974–1977	Ford administration
1975	Willow Creek Community Church founded
1977–1981	Carter administration
1979	Moral Majority founded
1980	Saddleback Community Church founded
1980	Crystal Cathedral opens; designed by Philip Johnson
1981–1989	Reagan administration
1981	*The Glory of Christmas* begins; continues through 2009
1982	Schuller ranked among most prominent religious figures by *The Christian Century*
1982	Schuller publishes *Self Esteem: The New Reformation*
1984	*The Glory of Easter* begins; continues through 2009
1986	Schuller publishes *Your Church Has a Fantastic Future!*
1987	Jim Bakker scandal[1]
1988	Jimmy Swaggart scandal[2]
1988	Pat Robertson runs for president
1989–1993	George H. W. Bush administration
1989	Gorbachev appears on *Hour of Power*; Schuller visits Soviet Union with Armand Hammer
1991	Netherlands trip[3]
1993–2001	Clinton administration
1997	Schuller sits next to Hillary Clinton at State of the Union Address
2001–2008	George W. Bush administration
2001	Schuller publishes *My Journey*
2003	Welcoming Center opens; designed by Richard Meier
2006	Schuller retires; Robert A. assumes leadership
2007–2010	Great Recession
2008–2017	Obama administration
2008	Robert A. resigns from Crystal Cathedral
2009	Sheila Schuller Coleman assumes leadership of Crystal Cathedral
2010	Crystal Cathedral declares bankruptcy
2012	Board sells Crystal Cathedral to the Roman Catholic Diocese of Orange
2013	Bobby assumes leadership of *Hour of Power* and the congregation
2014	Arvella's death
2015	Robert H. Schuller's death

The Glass Church

Schuller preaching from atop the concession stand at the Orange Drive-in. Photo courtesy of the Joint Archives of Holland.

1

Constituency, Charisma, and Capital

I'd rather attempt to do something great
and fail than to attempt to do nothing
and succeed.
—Robert H. Schuller

September 14, 1980, brought yet another beautiful Sunday mornings in Southern California. The sun glinted off automobiles backed up in Garden Grove on Chapman Avenue and Lewis Street for the dedication of the new church building. The staccato static of walkie-talkies echoed off 10,000 panes of glass from the twelve-story-tall Crystal Cathedral as more than two dozen attendants attempted to efficiently solve the placement of so many cars into the parking lot puzzle. Rows of congregants in overflow-seating filled the courtyard outside the sanctuary and quietly conversed over the burbling water from "The Fountains of the 12 Apostles." On the opposite side of the building, two eighty-foot doors silently slid open to reveal the interior of the sanctuary to an eager audience outside who preferred to attend the service from the comfort of their car, a custom cultivated since the first days of the ministry when it had been located at a drive-in theater.[1]

The Reverend Robert H. Schuller had planned a formal, dramatic entry, but his excitement proved too much—he moved to the chancel in his light blue vestment to bear witness as the congregation found their seats. Just prior to the start of the service, a lone woman "emerged from the massive crowd" to "reach out and touch" the minister and experience Schuller's charisma firsthand. Gaining his attention, she gushed, "Dr. Schuller, my name is on a window in this cathedral. I now feel as if I'm *somebody*! I now know that I made a difference! I live on a small income, but my tithe paid off a window in two years!"[2] She had joined the ranks of thousands of donors across the country and throughout the world who subsidized the construction of the cathedral—from $500 window purchases to $1,000,000 gifts.

Aerial cameras above the cathedral captured the magnitude of the star-shaped 414-foot-long church. Inside the building, television equipment streamed the start of the service; a trumpet fanfare, as if heralding a royal court, introduced the first thunderous chords of the custom-designed Hazel Wright organ.[3] A short hymn later, Schuller strode to his massive marble pulpit and boomed his signature salutation, "This is the day the Lord has made; let us rejoice and be glad in it!" The minister described this moment, the official opening of his first cathedral service, as the point when he "finally crested the mountaintop."[4]

After a brief greeting and only four minutes into the service, Schuller took care of business: critics had been grousing about the exorbitant cost of construction, and those in attendance and watching on television needed assurance. Would the cathedral be dedicated debt-free? In a grand and celebratory tone, the minister reported that the board had met the day before and had, in fact, instructed him to announce the good news. And lest anyone mistakenly assume that the board was simply comprised of a few local church volunteers, Schuller slowly called out—and the cameras found—every single board member, titans of banking, industry, insurance, and philanthropy, just like this:

Richard DeVos, president of the Amway Corporation;
Beurt Ser Vaas from Curtis Publishing Company in Indianapolis;
George Johnson, president of the Johnson Products Company in Chicago,
    Illinois;
Henry Block of the Block Brothers Firm in Canada;
Victor Andrews from Southern California;
Vern Draagt from our own church board;
John Crean, chairman of the board from Fleetwood Enterprises;
Lowell Berry of the Lowell Berry Foundation in San Francisco;
Ron Glosser, president of the Goodyear Banks in Akron, Ohio;
Bill Bailey from the legal firm in Boston, Massachusetts who, incidentally,
    along with his brother F. Lee Bailey, have presented to us our new pulpit
    bible and we're very grateful;
Charles Cringle, senior partner of Cringle, Swift, and Grimley, Southern
    California's prestigious accounting firm.

Having identified each board member, each one with a serious expression and wearing suit and tie, Schuller conveyed their message: "After they reviewed the entire Crystal Cathedral financial picture, they drafted the following resolution and have asked me to read it to you: 'We are able to dedicate this Crystal Cathedral this morning to the glory of God with the total cost covered by cash received, pledges and promises in hand, from beautiful and responsible people. Praise God!'"[5] Later in the service, Schuller's son, Robert A. Schuller, read notes of congratulations sent from the U.S. president, Jimmy Carter, and former governor of California Ronald Reagan; in the midst of a presidential campaign against each other, the two candidates made it a priority to publicly demonstrate their close connection to one of the country's premier ministers.[6]

A Church Empire, Skillfully Managed

By displaying his grandest building project, magnificently concluded and ostensibly paid for, Schuller proudly exhibited how he had skillfully braided together the core resources of his impressive ministry—constituency, charisma, and capital—into the premier megachurch in America. He appealed to an audience associated with achievement: younger, mostly white, upwardly mobile, middle-class families, drawn to Orange County for economic opportunity and happy to be aligned with men like Schuller and his high-profile board members. The telegenic cathedral, nothing less than a "religious landmark," embodied the "flush times of Southern California's Orange County" and a "physical representation of the limitless hope of the evangelical community at the time."[7] The building also testified to Schuller's charisma of openness, positivity, and transparency—a bold monument of strength and stability charging into a confident future.

Schuller had originally arrived in Garden Grove, California, in 1955. To that point, the minister had spent his entire life in the Midwest: from Iowa to Michigan and then to Illinois. His migration to Orange County to plant a congregation for his denomination, the Reformed Church in America (RCA), serendipitously coincided with a larger tilt of the country to the Sun Belt.[8] In Southern California, Schuller found a recently migrated, economically aspiring, and white middle class eager to hear his messages based on "Possibility Thinking" and his "Theology of Self-Esteem." When the latter half of the twentieth century brought the rise of high-profile religious men (Billy Graham, Oral Roberts, Jim Bakker, Jerry Falwell, and more), Schuller carved a strategically postured identity that gave him wide appeal. The minister exuded a dynamic charisma. He knew how to raise money and execute successful building projects. His church and television ministry grew dramatically.

Success capitalized on success, and Schuller created a ministry empire. On the surface, it appeared that Schuller had created an unassailable religious industrial complex through skillful management. Every week he appeared on the Sunday morning television broadcast of *Hour of Power*. Thousands of church leaders made the pilgrimage to Orange County to learn the master's principles of church management at the Robert H. Schuller Institute for Successful Church

Leadership. And the campus he built around Garden Grove Community Church (GGCC) featured world-class architecture. In discussing Schuller's landmark capital project, the Crystal Cathedral, one architectural critic remarked that the Orange County minister already had "the low-rent preachers, the Swaggarts, and the Bakkers" largely beaten. The opening of the cathedral, though, "left them for dead, like the greasy spoons trying to compete against the confidence of the McDonald's-style fast-faith corporate steamroller."[9] Capital projects had always injected the ministry with stature and vitality, "leapfrogging Schuller over the heads of his rivals in the increasingly competitive world of televangelism."[10]

Empires, though, need to be fed. Schuller sought to nourish the many branches of his empire with an unremitting emphasis on recurring high-profile projects. Early on, Schuller decided that people only gave money to *successful* causes—success "feeds on the image of success," he insisted.[11] In 1967 he wrote, "Nothing succeeds like success" and "No one likes to follow a loser."[12] Much like a Madison Avenue executive, Schuller concluded that the reputation of his Southern California ministry would drive growth, so the minister decided that his ministry would always be projected as a success—no matter the cost or vulnerability that it might entail. The argument has been made that Schuller himself "introduced marketing to American Christianity."[13] In appealing to a broad audience, Schuller had to assure his followers of the charismatic legitimacy of his methods. Schuller showcased from his pulpit the ability to manage his grand church as a business to millions of people weekly on television, which, in turn, diffused his congregational practices to emulators, offering a trailblazing path for "pastorpreneurs." The spectacular building where he preached before the earnest faces of his members, the Crystal Cathedral, regularly attested to his credibility as a master of growth.

The "gospel of growth" that characterized Schuller's ecclesial approach of more people, more buildings, and more audience, of course, has been an enduring characteristic of evangelicalism in the United States. By definition, evangelicalism emphasizes numeric growth through conversions and, therefore, champions practices that best ensure a "constant harvest," "continual increase," and "expanding churches."[14] Yet the American evangelical megachurch—a set of congregational characteristics that emerged alongside big-box stores, McMansions, supersized meals, and SUVs—became a manifestation of a religious imperative especially fixated on *constant, ongoing*, and *ever expansive* growth.[15] Schuller's Orange County ministry charted a formidable path in demonstrating how to achieve steadfast and dependable church growth. In the process, the minister's approach necessitated a never-ending quest for always broadening the scope of the ministry, always a bit more room (more chairs, more buildings, more parking) for the imagined *future* attenders who had not yet arrived.

In Schuller's vision, a church's capacity must always exceed a leader's projected plan for growth. But as new members arrive, they multiply the diversity of interest groups that must be satisfied, and pastoral messages and ministry programs need to placate more felt needs, placing increasing strain on mobilizing and engaging the loyalty of a wider constituency. Ensuring the credibility for pastoral charisma requires ever expanding infrastructure,[16] which involves increased funding for buildings, programs, and staff. In a continually growing church, these all continue to spiral expansively outward as long as the resources of the ministry can sustain it.

Megachurch Strain

The final sale of all properties comprising the Crystal Cathedral Ministries to the Roman Catholic Diocese of Orange in 2012 represented the symbolic conclusion of a ministry that had spanned more than fifty years. With so much success in meeting growth expectations for so long, why did the ministry implode so quickly and so decisively? Writing to the pastors and leaders of his denomination in 1968, Schuller advised them to "always have something, a new challenge"—revealing the core principle that set the rails of his ministry agenda.[17] Over his long ministry career, the end of one major project signaled the time to initiate a new plan for capital injection. Although he positioned himself as a real estate developer, constantly expanding the church grounds to house more people, the unending string of projects was designed to motivate the flow of fresh capital. Schuller always believed in—and maintained a remarkable transparency about—his strategy of letting his people know that there would always be a need for more money than he had already secured. His campaigns promoted large, idealized projects as concrete needs, all set to be realized in a not-too-distant future.

In 1975, as Schuller ramped up his pitch for the construction of the Crystal Cathedral, he officially described his "philosophy toward capital." He approached the church as a "dynamic business for God" that "would require cash" in order to continually grow. Growth was the goal. Rather than rest on wishful thinking, Schuller planned and enacted the financing of growth, borrowing funds to accommodate a rise in members who would eventually contribute revenue to be used to pay off loans. It was a strategy of rapid growth through aggressive financing. His "philosophy toward growth" appeared in a document that also articulated Schuller's "philosophy of capital debt"—a label that was not only more accurate but also consequential to the burden the founder intentionally placed on his ministry. In describing it, Schuller restated his central strategy, one that he said was present throughout his ministry: a commitment to borrow as much as he could to expand facilities, believing more property would "produce added growth i.e. additional income."[18] At one point Schuller triumphantly asserted, "We borrowed our way into success!"[19]

What Schuller had not comprehended is that deregulation and loosening of domestic and international lending policies in response to the "stagflation" of the 1970s allowed the minister access to unprecedented capital.[20] In these good times, wealthy benefactors happily supported the minster's bold construction projects, and banks willingly loaned considerable sums in anticipation of a healthy return. However, the unique historical circumstance of expansive credit that lasted through the 1980s and 1990s would not endure indefinitely. The terrorist attacks of September 11, 2001, followed by the financial crisis of 2008, would disrupt the assumptions of reliable credit, radically constrict the flow of available capital for ambitious projects, and strain Schuller's church growth model.

At the moment of the financial collapse, the campus encompassed thirty-five acres, seven buildings, and 340,000 square feet of interior space.[21] Schuller remained confident of continued growth even in the final days, assuming that his winning template for church management remained effective, universal, and timeless. The ministry, though, rested on a contingency of monetary structures that, in turn, rested on Schuller's persistent optimism of carrying his charismatic appeal to a wealthy and ever expanding constituency. Schuller's Possibility Thinking (a synthesis of Christianity and mentalism that advocated the power of the mind to change personal circumstances) and Theology of Self-Esteem (an understanding that humans needed affirmation in their dignity rather than criticisms for their sins) both linked to a broader ideology of Christian libertarianism that strengthened his appeal, powered his fund-raising, and fortified his aggressive stance toward financing.[22] But the requirements for continual fresh capital proved unsustainable.

The principles that had been presented and promoted as the state of the art in church management proved dated, rigid, and vulnerable. Building plans and management protocols that had over and over again reaped injections of much needed capital eventually overstrained the ministry. Financial obligations mounted. As the succession of leadership from father (Robert H.) to son (Robert A.) floundered, the cathedral's core constituency faded. And while local evangelical competitor megachurches exploited efficiencies and specializations through market segmentation, Schuller's unswerving model of attracting dollars through *yet another* new capital campaign betrayed the ministry's lack of adaptive resilience.

What we find in Schuller's ministry, and what our narrative describes, are the sources and consequences of *megachurch strain*, a summative concept that indicates how the social imperatives and assured practices inherent to a ministry philosophy of ongoing church expansion increase the risk of resource mismanagement, resulting in congregational collapse.[23] Organizational theorists have long focused on the notion of *organizational strain*, typically defined as discrepancies among structural elements of an organization that threaten its survival.[24] What is most important for understanding the implosion of the Crystal Cathedral is the failure to resolve the dramatic increases in organizational stress on the structural level, specifically, the discrepancy between organizational demands and organizational capacity.[25] Schuller imposed tremendous demands on his ministry by virtue of the priority he placed on continuous and expensive growth, a consequence of his adoption of a church growth perspective combined with his enactment of Possibility Thinking. Regardless of whether the congregation was ready for it or not, the arrangements of the church's infrastructure, which included current constituencies and extended constituencies of wealthy benefactors as well as his own charismatic energy, demanded a continual mobilization toward the goal of ever increasing expansion.

What made the minister so unconcerned about the pressures unleashed by his unceasing growth approach to ministry? Though Schuller created a ministry juggernaut and aggressively promoted his leadership methods, he failed to fully understand the fundamental sources of his ministry's spectacular successes—nor to anticipate its highly publicized collapse. What had been assumed to assure the financial strength of the church instead exposed the ministry to greater vulnerability because of an overdependence on the vagaries of voluntary giving. Indeed, while those associated with the ministry assumed the church progressively built a resilience against financial uncertainty and inevitable economic shocks from the greater environment, Schuller's responses to crises actually reveal a fundamental failure of learning from the shortfalls of the past.

In place of better planning for unexpected pressures or creating greater flexibility and organizational slack for unanticipated emergencies, Schuller insisted on purposefully straining the capacity of the ministry, especially its finances. Rather than securing financial solvency, he extended the fulfillment of debt into an ever longer time frame—assuming that mortgage and maintenance commitments today would be met through an idealized future stream of revenue. Schuller demonstrated a conviction that capital would always appear, almost by miracle, by means of his faith-projecting confidence. After all, the material evidence of impressive buildings and grounds experienced by members and visitors to the campus, printed in books and brochures, and televised every week on *Hour of Power* regularly attested to Schuller's enactment of Possibility Thinking reliably inspiring sacrificial giving from a supportive audience of dedicated admirers and followers—until it didn't.

In presenting our understanding of Schuller's pastorate and its abrupt end, we frame the management of the church as resting on three core components: *constituency, charisma,* and *capital*.[26] These three concepts provide leverage for describing the interrelationship between ongoing structural dynamics of resource management that contributed to both the expansion and the abrupt implosion of the ministry. Constituency, charisma, and capital comprise three core resources that are continually managed in church ministry. Certainly all congregations operate on a mixture of these, yet the structural operations of American megachurches—and the prescriptions proffered for their efficacious execution—heighten the difficulty of keeping interactions among these three components suitably synchronized. At different times in Schuller's congregational career, the level of the resources represented in constituents, charisma, and capital wobbled into an incompatible mismatch. Therefore, megachurch strain results from the fundamental imbalance between available resources, that is, from *resource incompatibility*.[27]

The notion of megachurch strain allows us to grasp the way in which leaders of large churches continually attend to the organizational strain placed on their ministries and how they constantly attempt to manage resources to match congregational *capacity* with congregational *capability*.[28] Stress and strains are dynamic, always present, and continually changing in intensity.[29] One of the core tasks of any organizational leader is to ensure "that demand is not allowed to grow to the point that would overtax the capacity of the organization."[30] So while stresses and strains are not atypical to congregations, the ability to discern and therefore properly manage the mismatch of resources and their compatibility with organizational demands proves crucial for the survival of a congregation over time.

Megachurches are complex organizations with many varied and interrelated processes, and the pursuit of expansion, driven by the imperative for growth often implicit to large church ministries, increases the opportunities for improperly calibrating the complex connections between constituents, charisma, and capital—so much so that the mismatches threaten to implode the entire congregational structure. By examining the church management orientation of Robert Schuller, we come to recognize that organizational stresses of growth-driven megachurches are self-imposed. Megachurch strain therefore results from not only *external* stresses from the economic and social environment but also *internal* stresses imposed by ambitions that leaders place on their own churches. The concept of megachurch strain heuristically draws out the manner in which organizational stress is accentuated due to the demands—by definition—of growth initiatives and the frequent incompatibility of available resources to fulfill those goals.

In short, we suggest that the push for increased size embedded in contemporary megachurch ministries fosters vulnerabilities unspoken by leaders and unseen by members and supporters. Our analysis of the resource management of Schuller's ministry draws on the rise-and-fall arc of the ministry to shed new light on the consequential connections between constituents, charisma, and capital toward explaining the bankruptcy of the cathedral.[31] And while the resources represented by constituents, charisma, and capital are interrelated, a particular focus on sources and flows of funding—the projects and processes for prompting and managing charitable giving—provides the greatest analytical leverage for understanding how weaknesses can amplify so quickly.

Fragility in Constant Growth

In the end, our approach to megachurch strain surpasses a superficial inquiry that centers solely on financial miscalculations or on Schuller's charismatic message or other dynamics that sidestep a finer grained understanding of the structural relationship between constituents, charisma, and the precariousness of managing the flow of capital. As the arc of our narrative moves into later chapters, the focus on capital becomes increasingly indispensable for fathoming the workings of Schuller's church—especially since he based his ministry on what he considered to be sound business practices, managing the growth of his church like a firm. One needs to look no further than the fact that Schuller named himself not *pastor* but *president* of the Crystal Cathedral. He drew on notions of advertising and selling a quality product that would attract clients and investors; they would expand the flow of capital to build the business even further. Schuller borrowed heavily, approaching his ministry as acts of making wise capital investments in the capacity and charismatic attractiveness of his preaching and his church's material infrastructure, believing these would draw out an ever growing constituency, yield increasing revenue, and provide capital for future expansion.

He worked for—and for a time succeeded—in generating a virtuous cycle of growth, spiraling his ministry in expanding waves of marketing, investment, and expansion in an effort to accommodate even more spiritual clients he believed would themselves become loyal investors in the firm. His approach to growth, though, relied too heavily on the attractiveness of new, awe-inspiring capital-intensive projects assumed to serve future constituents and intended to catalyze more revenue. Schuller's ventures required far more resources than current constituents could ever possibly fund. The projects therefore relied on aggressive financing, stacking fiscal obligations on top of a steadily increasing burden of regular operations, which stimulated more and more desperate efforts at finding new paths to generate even more revenue. Schuller's ambition had no end, but his capacity to raise revenue did.

Schuller's church management philosophy appealed to pastors and denominational leaders because he sought to address a fundamental anxiety: congregational survival. In an era increasingly characterized by a greater threat of church closings (especially among mainline Protestant denominations), he promoted surefire strategies to establish stability—a formulaic approach filled with quips and mottos—all illustrated from the experience of his own Garden Grove–based church. Though he offered multiple points of design for church success, perhaps Schuller's most significantly explicit technique expounded the principle that congregations should not be afraid of debt as they strove for growth.[32] On the other hand, it remained mostly unspoken by the minister that for him this strategy included a profound dependence on infusions from a few wealthy donors who were not necessarily members of his church. All the while, Schuller's approach inherently demanded that every church constantly attend to constituents, charisma, and capital. The minister, though, failed to realize both the manner in which he himself exacerbated the strain produced by this demand for growth and how his surefire strategy would financially undermine the ministry.

By orienting our narrative of the collapse of the Crystal Cathedral in the following chapters on these three core components, we suggest that congregational fragility is greatly accentuated in larger churches, a notion we label *megachurch strain*, such that the threat of implosion is significantly heightened by any failure to properly calibrate the interrelationship among these core components. Certainly all churches depend on a mix of constituents, charisma, and capital for the existence of their ministry. Yet the size and ambition of large churches like the Crystal Cathedral exert enormous pressures to continue the stream of people committed to the congregation, to reinforce the spark of charismatic excitement generated by high-profile pastors, and to develop fresh flows of capital funding for maintenance of old projects and launching new initiatives. While congregations often evidence fragility in keeping their doors open, the constant attention to expand constituencies, boost charisma, and stimulate capital among megachurches produces an especially burdensome strain on their ministry. In the case of Schuller's ministry, the dynamism inherent to each of these elements and the context in which they developed are articulated with much greater detail in the succeeding chapters. Closer attention to these components in the history of the ministry allows us to reveal the insidious vulnerability that led to the ministry's collapse. Although Schuller quietly passed away in 2015 with both his profile and his congregation significantly diminished, the growth-oriented, entrepreneurial methods of pastoral leadership adopted by much of today's clergy and the added strain that accompany them live on, tracing back to him—whether ambitious, growth-focused church leaders realize it or not.

Schuller preaching in the hybrid walk-in–drive-in sanctuary. Photo courtesy of the Joint Archives of Holland.

2

The Imperative of
Church Growth

> The church must either grow or perish.
> —Robert H. Schuller

The steady expansion of Schuller's church in Garden Grove, California, stood for decades as a prevailing model of thriving Christian ministry, and the minister enjoyed being hailed as the master of principles for church growth. The iconic all-glass structure of the Crystal Cathedral drew regular attenders and curious visitors. The *Hour of Power* television broadcast, with its mass audience, delivered a worship service that outshined most viewers' local congregations with its polished segues and manicured delivery. More than a façade, the show infused the ministry with cash. Indeed, a journalist in the late 1970s, remarked on the "sophistication" of *Hour of Power*: "The organization is run by a young and energetic staff using modern business and marketing techniques."[1] Further, much like McDonald's proliferated with franchises, the church produced replicas of itself by training thousands of pastors on campus through the Robert H. Schuller Institute for Successful Church Leadership. The Crystal Cathedral manifested itself as a multimodal ministry—each branch designed to feed into the same reinforcing system of ensuring more members, wider notoriety, and healthy cash balances. Its success established the cathedral as a predominant ecclesial paradigm, and church leaders flocked to seize on an elusive certainty for achieving ministerial success.

An assessment of his biography before he moved to California reveals that Robert H. Schuller's ascendance as the social and spiritual architect of the United States' high-profile Crystal Cathedral defies logic. Born and raised in rural Iowa within a strict, conservative religious milieu, what expertise did Schuller bring to his West Coast mission? What tool kit prepared him to employ his strategies in the growing metropolitan—even cosmopolitan—region of suburban Los Angeles? The story remains stranger than fiction: a dour Calvinist farmer revolutionizes the packaging of religion designed to resonate with an economically booming metropolis. Early in his ministry, an interviewer once pressed the minister on his methods: "Tell us about the process. Obviously, you didn't come out of seminary with your head together. How did you learn these things? How did you come to some of these conclusions?" Schuller admitted that he was not sure how to explain it: "I have no way of answering that. I just don't know."[2]

The pastor and his observers were continually caught in explaining the sources of his success. What was the secret of growth? Schuller quickly overcame his early hesitancy to explain his approach to ministry. Through advice books, architectural projects, on-campus training via the leadership institute, and a weekly television broadcast, he regularly demonstrated how to organize pastoral ministry around the imperatives of church growth. C. Peter Wagner, a chief proponent of church growth at Fuller Theological Seminary, provided a laudatory foreword for Schuller's best-selling *Your Church Has a Fantastic Future*, writing, "As a professor of church growth, I am personally indebted to Robert Schuller for much of what I know and teach."[3] Schuller eventually labeled himself "the founder of the church growth movement."[4]

The positive framing of the pastor and the wariness of his critics surprisingly agreed on one thing: whatever Schuller was doing was founded on *strategic calculation*. Schuller brought together several recognizable developments in contemporary ecclesiology and is commonly described as playing "a pioneering and influential role in the twentieth- and twenty-first-century redefinition of Protestant culture." With his ingenuity in capturing the California preoccupation with mobility, celebrity, and entertainment, Schuller fashioned a "wholly new kind of church" that found significance beyond America's West Coast.[5] Schuller's ardent faith in capitalism and the free market meant that he also believed that the economy provided abundant avenues for those with the courage and skill to create their own opportunity and subsequent wealth. He translated those optimistic, growth-oriented economic assumptions onto American congregational life. Viewing the church as a firm, Schuller overlaid his ministry with the rationality of a business plan. And the more the new church leaned on businesslike principles of marketing and management, the more the ministry became obsessively fixated on growth.

If pressed to summarize key aspects of Schuller's church growth principles and how they were exemplified in his ministry, they might be summarized under the subheadings below.

Advocate for Principles of Church Growth

Throughout his pastoral career, Schuller steadfastly advocated for continuous congregational growth. Persistent growth signaled a thriving ministry ("Anything that lives, grows"), while *stasis*, even what was euphemistically called a "plateau," threatened to be an indication of *decline*. Schuller had already adopted this perspective before arriving in California. At his first pastorate in the Chicago suburbs, the minister reported that he actively gauged his "audience" response with a simple test: "If the congregation grew, I was succeeding. If it didn't grow—or, God forbid, if it went down in numbers—then I was failing."[6]

In many ways, "church growth" constitutes a distinct religious orientation among a wide swath of pastors, seminary professors, church consultants, and denominational leaders within American Christianity.[7] This growth disposition pivots on the implementation of deliberate techniques designed to fulfill the imperative of expanding congregational attendance and the buildings and funding needed to accommodate anticipated future growth.[8] Religious historian Kip Richardson argues that "'church growth' became a fixture of the evangelical world."[9] Among megachurch leaders and those who model their high-profile strategies, "bigness, growth, and expansion" became "conscious, deliberate goals." As institutions, they foster "identities around their size and scale," and their "overflowing churches" are testimonies to the "premier marker of ministerial success."[10]

Schuller fully endorsed growth as a goal and would become prolific in promoting his methodology. And despite his Midwest roots, he epitomized the "Sun Belt creed" by which entrepreneurial pastors started new congregations and experimented their way into growing a successful church. The Southern California pastor eventually leveraged his accomplishments into global celebrity. By the mid-1970s, some Sunday mornings would see the freeway backed up with cars waiting to get into the church parking lot.[11] One visiting journalist reported on the minister's productive tactics, "His critics contend that Schuller has done for Jesus what Colonel Sanders has done for chicken, that he offers a kind of fast-food franchise salvation bearing the same relationship to the Christ of the Cross that the plastic automaton Abraham Lincoln at Disneyland does to the American Civil War."[12] Other journalists remarked that Schuller represented "the Henry Ford of organized religion"[13] in his ability to manufacture a "marriage of religion and the Sears, Roebuck corporate ethos."[14] Where others shied from synthesizing religion and the market, Schuller demonstrated little restraint in developing a church-industrial complex dependent on retailing savvy. At one point, the pastor declared himself as the earliest advocate of "the marketing approach in Christianity."[15]

Pragmatic enterprises, though, require results. In promoting the reliability of his pastoral techniques, Schuller often touted concrete numbers as evidence of their efficacy. In 1981, he made it known that Nielsen television ratings revealed that *Hour of Power* reigned as the highest-rated religious television broadcast in the United States, Canada, Australia, and on the Armed Forces Television Network.[16] That same year, the ministry reported having received 1.5 million letters.[17] Quantitative markers like these proved persuasive, so Schuller often discussed his ministry in terms of membership figures, television ratings, best-seller lists, and square footage. Because the church included so many wide-ranging branches of ministry, Schuller eventually created an in-house public relations department to promote them all. Management of the minister's singular reputation became a fundamental ministry operation itself. Michael Nason, the hired head of that effort, described Schuller's assertive marketing posture in this way: "[He] purposely paints a picture that is in every word true but that doesn't necessarily give the whole impression. He doesn't see this as being deceitful; it's just that he's so great with the adjectives and the positive way he views things, he's describing them as he feels they are."[18] At one point Schuller himself attested that "you don't have to tell the whole truth" and that the "total truth" has an elusive quality that no one could ever truly capture.[19] Schuller assured himself that growing his church required finding strategies to continually boost his charisma, nurturing a reputation that would lead to greater loyalty and greater financial support among both his church attenders and more distant broadcast viewers, which would expand the ministry further.

For Schuller, ministerial legitimacy required that people be impressed with vivid indicators of a vibrant church. Perhaps the counterintuitive nature of Schuller's success in Southern California motivated the pastor to put the ministry's accomplishments on display. Even in the first years of his ministry, he noted his "intense interest" in "publicity and promotion" for the church.[20] Impressive buildings, millions of viewers, and the thousands of pastors streaming to Garden Grove, California, all became totems of the ministry's success. Though feeding the ravenous requirements of a highly visible charisma would eventually prove problematic, by the mid-1980s Schuller's multimodal ministry enjoyed high status within American Christianity.

Schuller believed he deserved respect because he viewed Southern California as a fiercely competitive religious marketplace, one that he had conquered and from which he had learned to excel, and because in doing so, he had become an expert on church growth and management. For most of his career, the minister could simply survey his campus and point to the profitability of such financial risks to ministry by displaying his own tangible evidence of achievement. Though he also considered himself a leading theologian, he used his eponymous leadership institute to teach pastors how to excel in their own context, promulgating techniques for them to organize their congregations into success. Using illustrations from his own ministry, Schuller promoted a form of church leadership that prized entrepreneurship, mimicking the rational management principles of ambitious business enterprises. His protocols for church growth appeared as a set of formulaic guidelines, often phrased as straightforward requirements that ensured increased attendance alongside the increased funding needed to fuel even more growth. Schuller proudly asserted that because of his advice, numerous churches had extended themselves to purchase "acres of land in prime locations."[21]

Smart marketing was a cornerstone of his approach, and Schuller welcomed how attractive graphics and pithy quotes boosted his charismatic image. The church had come a long way from Schuller's self-penned press release in 1955 for his first service at the Orange Drive-in theater. The scattered one hundred attenders—nearly half of whom had been specifically invited by Schuller to serve as a guest choir—had been told to consider themselves "fortunate to be part of an exciting church."[22] That first year, the mission church operated on a meager budget of $12,500.[23] Twenty-five years later, the Goodyear blimp, known for appearances at nationally broadcast sporting events such as the Super Bowl, circled overhead during the 1980 dedication service of the Crystal Cathedral.[24] At a luncheon in Los Angeles with a group of extremely selective invitees from a list curated by Queen Elizabeth of England, boxer Muhammad Ali approached Schuller to ask for the *minister's* autograph. Journalist Bella Stumbo of the *Los Angeles Times* reported that Schuller found himself consistently "besieged by wide-eyed fans who want his autograph, his handshake or merely an encouraging word." The journalist also described a flight with the minister: "Aboard the plane, dozens of passengers descended upon Schuller; even the pilot came out of his cockpit to personally shake hands with his celebrated passenger."[25] Stumbo concluded by noting that, while the Crystal Cathedral was likely the "most controversial Protestant Church in America," its minister was now a "nationally recognized celebrity."[26]

Some of the "controversy" around Schuller occurred because of the minister's aggressive marketing. From his vantage point as Schuller's long-time executive assistant and personal PR manager, Nason described the minister's 1982 book, *Self-Esteem: The New Reformation*, as a "bomb-shell." A Chicago insurance magnate and Schuller enthusiast had read the book and believed the minister had unlocked the key to the modern psyche, providing spiritual insights that would stimulate a new American religious awakening. With that, W. Clement Stone decided that all ministers in the United States should have their own copy of *Self-Esteem*. Schuller waived his royalties, and Stone bought copies directly from the publisher, sending thousands (250,000, in fact) to pastors across the country, hoping they would take on Schuller's innovative theology. As a result, *Self-Esteem* became a provocative religious touchstone. Some pastors raved; others railed. Either way, Schuller's innovative message was discussed in pulpits all over the nation. From Nason's perspective, it represented a watershed moment for the minister's reputation. No matter their perspective on Schuller, receiving the book caused pastors nationwide "to sit up and pay attention to this guy out in California." Nason pointed to its distribution as the moment when the Orange County minister became "the magnet" with which fellow pastors, whether they liked it or not, had to have some familiarity as a sign of their own relevance.

With Schuller's developing fame, a 1985 profile in *Newsweek* described the sophisticated image management inherent to every Sunday service: "Fountains spurt. Birds chirp. Organ music swells. The camera pans slowly upward, revealing a white cross against an azure sky." Perhaps more importantly, the magazine realized that production values had been perfected: "No television director could ask for a more inspirational opening." Finally, the minister emerged: "When the blue-robed, silver-haired Rev. Robert Schuller appears, there is no doubt about it: the star has arrived."[27] Schuller's celebrity reached the White House when, after having advised President Bill Clinton for years, the minister sat in a position of honor next to First Lady Hillary Rodham Clinton during the 1997 State of the Union address.[28]

With its scale, Schuller's television ministry cast a large shadow on the actual church. By the mid-1980s, the program claimed more than 2 million viewers from 170 markets. *Hour of Power* became the only television ministry carried on the Armed Forces Network. Conservative media mogul Rupert Murdoch had personally seen to it that the program would air in Europe via his Sky Channel.[29] *Eternity* magazine testified to the profile that Schuller and the Crystal Cathedral had attained in the early 1980s: "The Soviet Union apparently considers Schuller's ministry to be such a totem of God'n'Country American civil religion that they have featured a display of the Garden Grove Church, complete with photographs of its pastor, in the Soviet Museum of Atheism in Leningrad."[30]

Overall, Schuller was not just a promoter of church growth; he was constantly affirmed as its greatest exemplar. His ministry routinely demonstrated what appeared to be the cornerstones of growing a strong, healthy, resilient church—an approach that provided the bases of building expansive congregations with large campuses and steadily climbing membership numbers. Schuller intentionally and prominently displayed the central church management principles guiding the development of the American megachurch.

Attract a Constituency

Schuller's focus on growth underscored that the competitive market of churches demanded a relentless attentiveness to the potential patron. The minister pursued customer satisfaction. Rather than assuming attenders appreciated the service as it stood, Schuller sought feedback, attending to any criticisms in order to respond and improve. A 1960 "Flash Report" disseminated to his Garden Grove Community Church (GGCC) membership mailing list included complaints about a recent service at the drive-in. After each critique, Schuller included an editorial note with a process for improvement. For example, someone commented on "having to strain to hear," and Schuller responded that the sound system would be upgraded from sixty watts to 120 watts the very next week. Another attendee noted that the organ had sounded poor during the offertory, and Schuller had no problem investing in an upgrade: "We won't use this organ for solo work anymore. It has had it. This is the same organ that we have used from the first Sunday. It has been used out of doors under the blazing sun and twice drenched in a storm that blew the covers off! We will have fine organ music this Sunday!"[31] By the following Sunday, Schuller had replaced the organ and offered three methods for hearing the service (high-fidelity field speakers, private drive-in theater speakers, and a GGCC-specific system that integrated the car radio), which ensured that sound would not be problematic again.[32] His responsiveness to his constituents sought to guarantee a constantly improving experience every week. In doing so, according to historian John Curran Hardin, Schuller "shifted the locus of authority from the producer to the consumer" in a type of newfound "customer sovereignty" for the church.[33]

While others might have hedged on the synthesis of religion and business, Schuller had no such misgivings: "We're in the business of retailing religion, and effective business principles should be applied in doing it." Schuller noted, "If I'm shopping for a shirt, I want to know that the store where I stop has the shirt I want—right neck size, sleeve length and color." Beyond that, the church attender, similar to a discerning customer, also had expectations regarding service: "Ultimately, the service department is what will make the retailer succeed. If you purchase an item but find out that the business lets you down when you need it serviced, the odds are that you won't go back there."[34]

According to Schuller, a local congregation would do well to understand itself as a business enterprise centered on gaining more people—an effort that began with attracting their attention. He suggested that churches reserve 5 percent of their budgets for advertising and publicity.[35] Moreover, Schuller once reported to Catholic archbishop and television personality Fulton Sheen that he had spent $20,000 to advertise just one particular service in 1971.[36] Even the content of the minister's messages stemmed from marketing savvy: "In a voluntary society like ours, people will ignore you if you don't give them what they want and need."[37] Indeed, the minister displayed marketing pragmatism: Schuller only settled on "self-esteem" as his defining theological principle when he realized that "self-love" had sexual connotations that catalyzed "people's neurosis," a reference, seemingly, to masturbation.[38] Just as in business, churches had to remain vigilant regarding associations with their products.

Casting the unchurched as customers, the minister sought to design his ministry as tailor-fit to the religious desires of his Orange County audience. Schuller's fame and charisma emanated from a message designed to appeal to lapsed Christians who felt distant or estranged from strict fundamentalist dogma. It oriented the crafting of his tone and influenced a church campus that avoided stuffy steeples in favor of suburban-resonating environments and ease of transportation and participation. In fact, Schuller has been described as "the grandfather of seeker-sensitive megachurches" and the Crystal Cathedral as "a monument to the partnership between megachurch worship and modernism." Historian Molly Worthen asserted that Schuller, in his attempt to remove obstacles to church attendance, "upended the traditional revivalist tactic of rail-ing at sinners until they cried out for redemption."[39] Schuller, though, also defied some of the typical characteristics of other high-profile ministries by resisting adaptation of praise and Pentecostal worship and demurred on ques-tions about end-times prophecy or the inerrancy of scripture. Avoiding thorny issues that might alienate attenders became a primary mode of operation—for both Schuller and his lineage of pastors. And changes that came with the tran-sition into the new millennium would test the robustness of the ministry's template.

To further ensure that the attender-customer returned the next Sunday, Schuller insisted on controlling their experience. One long-time pastor within the ministry recounted his work at the Crystal Cathedral, saying:

> When I had worship hospitality, I had the kiosk workers—the information people at [the front desks]—and the church ushers, the door greeters, shuttle drivers, and translation people. Every one of them—we'd have meetings once in a while with about 150 people——every one of them [had expectations]: Don't ever frown to people; don't ever make them feel stupid that they're asking the wrong question; don't ever, *ever* make anyone feel that they are not welcome. Always a big smile, always a handshake, *unless* they don't seem to be wanting to handshake—some people don't. So don't force it. In every way, [the ministry demanded] absolute perfect conduct. Don't pat people, especially a man with a woman; don't do *that* on the back, unless you know them extremely well. Just don't be too familiar. But, you know, make them feel welcome so that they can come back again.[40]

Schuller strongly advocated for detailed instructions on how to interact with guests in order to routinize warmth, making explicit emotional protocols for drawing guests into their new church home.

Cultivate Charismatic Leadership

Schuller understood that a broad constituency required a carefully cultivated charisma, and he believed he had mastered this quality. This meant eventually honing his ability to attract a steady flow of supporters apart from his affiliation with a denomination. Before escalating to a national profile, Schuller first assured his pastoral legitimacy by emphasizing his connection to his denomination. For a pastor who fixated on growth, the Reformed Church in America (RCA), eth-nically Dutch and the oldest mainline Protestant denomination in the United States, often represented a burden to be jettisoned. Ironically, the grounding of the RCA that kept Schuller from flying as high in his status as he imagined also provided both shelter and mooring whenever turbulence affected the ministry.

Mainline Protestantism began its historic decline just as Schuller began his career, but the Orange County pastor fought to cast his ministry as an outlier in a concerted effort to buttress his charismatic authority.

In assuring his legitimacy, he did not rest on his denominational ordination but always sought to base it on his personal charisma. So Schuller would alternately express pride in the RCA's deep history, which predated the founding of the United States by almost 150 years, or downplay this tradition to present his ministry as historically unprecedented. Schuller framed the relationship between congregation and denomination to be consistent with his retail metaphor. He once related, "The retailers of religion are the local churches, who are supplied and supported by the wholesalers—the denominational headquarters and theological seminaries."[41] For growth purposes, Schuller's strategy assumed that church hierarchies would remain largely in the background. In his mind, Schuller cast himself as the proprietor of a small business—personally managed, with great flexibility and boundless ambition for expansion.

Indeed, Schuller enjoyed a reputation as one of his denomination's most adept church planters.[42] Lynn Japinga, a religion professor at Hope College (Schuller's alma mater), described the Orange County ministry as the denomination's "most creative and well-known church growth effort" and stated that "no one could argue with [Schuller's] success."[43] Schuller's Southern California mission, far from the heart of the RCA's homelands in the Northeast and Great Lakes states, yielded results that no RCA congregation, anywhere, could rival. Although the minister had critics throughout the denomination, Schuller generally enjoyed a stature that brought him both admirers and imitators. Schuller succeeded in setting himself apart by fostering his own distinct charismatic presence, a public persona centered on being an exceptional ecclesial virtuoso.

In 1968, the denomination's communications office requested that Schuller publish an article in the *Church Herald* to demonstrate how denominational investments in church plants like GGCC culminated in a dynamic, growing church.[44] Overall, the idea of growth received widespread support. The details, though, proved thornier. Scrutiny of Schuller's conspicuous development resulted in vigorous debate within the RCA regarding the appropriateness of church growth methods. For instance, Schuller left out "Reformed" in naming GGCC, a tactic some found problematic. Already in 1950, five years before Schuller's move to California, an editor writing in the *Church Herald* lamented a trend toward "Community," rather than "Reformed," churches: "Many of our Churches in new communities where the Reformed Church is little known, have dropped the name entirely, considering it a handicap." The editor went on to offer caution: "Unless we intend and plan to be congregations that are loyal to the Reformed Faith, we will in time be nothing at all. For the so-called Community Church tends to become a sort of religious 'catch-all,' theologically colorless and spiritually impotent." The editor cited Presbyterians and Lutherans who had tested the strategy: "They will tell you that their 'Community Churches' are, generally speaking, the most like a social club, the least missionary-minded, and the least spiritual, among their congregations." Rebuking the early advent of seeker-friendly congregations, the editor contended that strong churches should have the ability to "mold their memberships, not vice versa."[45]

As more and more RCA congregations chose to be known as "community" churches—including GGCC—Schuller hastened to take credit for catalyzing the trend. By generically labeling his congregation as a "community church," Schuller erased some of the insider tendencies of most congregations to draw explicit boundaries on who should attend. Dependence on homophily (attracting members with high similarity and affinity) has the ability to cement tight organizations, but it also inhibits the flow of innovations. When Schuller later opened his leadership institute, that heterophileous label allowed him to span a wide range of religious orientations within Christianity—both socially and theologically. Schuller's heterophileous communication proved crucial to the diffusion of his church growth innovations across dissimilar congregations and denominations. Yet his independence came at a cost to the alliances of deep loyalty and jeopardized the ultimate longevity of his church.

In a letter to a fellow RCA pastor in New York City in 1968, Schuller revealed his feelings regarding the uninspired administrators of his denomination, imploring, "Whatever you do, don't let the impossibility thinkers in high places kill it. They will try." He believed denominational leaders failed to understand the practical challenges of local congregational life as it was happening on the ground "because the chief executives in high administrative positions in church life are so out-of-touch with God's action that they tend to be impossibility thinkers." Moreover, Schuller concluded that the myopia of these denominational leaders inhibited their imaginations—they failed to apprehend the dynamic growth occurring within methodologically progressive congregations like GGCC: "Chief executives in high church positions see their own budgets as struggling. Largely because they are trying to perpetuate old wine skins. Or they are thinking too small."[46]

In perhaps an "old wine skin" strategy, the RCA considered merging with the Southern Presbyterians in the late 1960s. When the vote failed, Schuller seized the moment, seeing the potential for a paradigm shift and casting his vision for a new pattern of ecclesial practices. It would not be the only time Schuller attempted to transform denominational priorities, urging his brethren to follow his methodologies for church growth. In 1969, in the fallout of the failed merger, he wrote an article for the *Church Herald* entitled "We Can Be Strong," in which he argued that the denomination faced strategic choices for the future.[47] By his accounting, "the only hope of long-range success for any denomination or association of Christian churches lies in its ability to win the unchurched." Schuller indicated that he saw little hope within mainline denominations for renewal, citing their atrophied polities, sectarian denominationalism, and "negative thinking preached from the traditional pulpit."

In his characteristically audacious manner, Schuller proposed "a new denomination that could sweep America faster than Holiday Inns or Colonel Sanders' fried chicken." Schuller even offered a name for the new denomination: Christ's Church for America, and listed its priorities:

1 Really believes in living Christ who can miraculously transform human beings.
2 Has roots in the historic evangelical Reformed tradition.
3 Is ecumenical enough in spirit to welcome all who accept Jesus Christ as Lord and Savior (as stated in the Constitution of the RCA).
4 Is characterized by the positive thinking of men like Dr. Norman Vincent Peale.
5 Can conceive of imaginative ministries, such as our successful walk-in–drive-in churches.
6 Encourages the membership to resolve social injustices by actually involving themselves as individuals in the political parties of their choice and avoids having a "right-wing" or "left-wing" political image stamped upon it, frightening away people who need the Gospel.
7 Exalts Christ above any and all theologies.

The list, of course, blatantly suggested the reorganization follow Schuller's GGCC as a blueprint for remaking the denomination in his own image. Only the denomination's obstinance and "impossibility thinking" hindered its realization.

Schuller did not simply insist—he offered his pastoral experience as evidence for his plan's credibility: GGCC claimed a membership of 4,200 members, 3,000 of whom had "come from the ranks of the once indifferent and irreligious." Schuller listed the denomination's assets: preachers such as Norman Vincent Peale, the distinctiveness of "walk-in–drive-in" congregations, a presbyterian church order that offered cohesion, enough congregationalism that new members would not fear that "some bishop will push us around," and the historicity of being the oldest denomination in the country. Schuller predicted that by following his plan, the denomination could develop 100 new walk-in–drive-in churches in the following decade—"propelled by a coast-to-coast television ministry." By his calculation, new members would exceed two million souls.[48]

The minister was convinced that his methods were foolproof. His verified techniques could be routinized and replicated, generating a rationally planned revival. Schuller expressed supreme certainty in the attraction of a new, broad constituency, especially among the irreligious. He did not lack confidence in his methods, and he clearly intimated that the denomination failed to follow his plan at its own peril. In short, the ministry methods established at GGCC, seeded as a "mission church" by the denomination, could become the bellwether for a new breed of RCA churches, if only the leadership demonstrated the willingness to fund this new effort.

To press his point, Schuller, in a letter to an RCA headquarters leader, delighted in pointing to the unparalleled financial return yielded by the denomination's limited investment in GGCC:

> In thirteen years, that [RCA] investment of $2,000 has grown into the Garden Grove Community Church, which thirteen years later in the year 1968 will record an income of over one half million dollars in the general offering. In thirteen years, this young congregation has contributed well over a half million dollars to the denominational and benevolent causes in this country and abroad. This Reformed Church in Garden Grove, California will probably lead all Protestant Churches in the United States of America in winning people to Jesus Christ in the year 1968.[49]

Following Schuller's success, the RCA soon added nine congregations in the West, from Southern California to Arizona, that initiated drive-in services. Between 1968 and 1973, those churches added 2,080 members to the denomination.[50] Thus, while GGCC did not become the template for a new denominational pattern, at least some followed Schuller's prescriptions and found a corresponding measure of growth.

Beyond the implementation of drive-in churches, Schuller must have been pleased to read a 1971 article in the *Church Herald* praising his leadership institute—with the weighty title "New Hope for the Church." The editor of the magazine, Louis Benes, attended the four-day meetings and left impressed. Demonstrating palpable enthusiasm, Benes admitted, "Writing here, some weeks after the Institute, we thought we might be less caught up in enthusiasm, able to write more objectively. No use. So we say it again. Garden Grove has something to give to the churches of America, a secret to share."[51] Benes assured his readers: "There are techniques for successful churches just as there are techniques for successful businesses."[52] Benes endorsed the leadership institute and concluded that "any congregation will be doing its pastor and itself a great favor by sending him and some key laymen to an Institute . . . to make them more efficient in 'the equipping of the saints for the work of ministry' as St. Paul puts it."[53] Thus, the denominational magazine claimed that Schuller's model of ministry offered the boldest hope for the denomination's future. While the RCA failed to establish Schuller's methodology as the new order for its congregations, the leadership institute allowed Schuller to embolden church leaders with his pattern for church growth, without regard to their denominational affiliation or Christian orientation. Schuller did not re-form the RCA. Nevertheless, his leadership institute effectively promoted his methods among an eclectic array of church leaders seeking to reproduce his success.

Harness Media Channels

Schuller's ministry offered a vivid example of the synthesis of religion and entertainment—an amalgamation that he believed enhanced the potency of the message. Though RCA churches had historically broadcast worship services via regional radio, Schuller's foray into national television charted new territory. As a mainline Protestant broadcast among a cohort of Pentecostals and independent evangelicals, *Hour of Power* stood as an odd exception.[54] The American people, though, typically expressed wariness of religious leaders using entertainment as a means for conversion and spiritual uplift, and critics often dismissed the conflation as sordid or crass.[55]

Of course, similar efforts had long been a significant component of American evangelicalism; Schuller stood in continuity with the likes of George Whitefield, who used an almost theatrical, dramatic disposition as the centerpiece of his evangelism.[56] In addition, ministry partners, such as Michael Nason, dismissed critics who felt "that low budgets and amateur programming" better reflected Christian humility, arguing that "Christ must be presented in a *first-class* manner."[57] Schuller forged ahead with a spectacle-filled service to woo the unchurched.

Although Schuller credited Billy Graham with catalyzing the idea of a Sunday morning broadcast of the GGCC worship service in 1969, the Orange County minister had obviously been planning for the frontier of televised ministry since at least the mid-1960s. In fact, his initial efforts to lure the Billy Graham Evangelistic Crusade to Orange County revealed a detailed rationale for producing a Christian worship event at GGCC. A letter urging Graham to visit Schuller's church demonstrated a television-production savvy that would foreshadow *Hour of Power*:

> I envision that closed-circuit television could televise the evening meetings of Billy Graham, projecting them onto the huge Drive-In Theatre screen of the adjacent Drive-In Theatre. As a result, this would be the first Evangelistic Crusade where people would be invited to "bring the aged, the infirmed, and the shut-ins" in their cars to hear the entire service on the giant screen of the adjacent drive-in theatre. It would be the world's first "Walk-In Drive-In Evangelistic Crusade"! This is not to be laughed at! I started our church in this Orange Drive-In Theatre ten years ago and today we have the largest Protestant congregation in Orange County![58]

Similarly, in early 1968, Schuller encouraged Peale to consider using the *Guideposts* magazine apparatus to distribute video of Peale's most recent sermon at GGCC: "I am completely confident that *Guideposts* could take this video tape and show it nation-wide. It is our property, and it is available to *Guideposts*. At no cost, of course, to *Guideposts*. You must have someone in your firm who might be able to line up a sponsor—like Holiday Inn. It would be a fantastic piece of public relations for *Guideposts Magazine*." Schuller saw the appeal of the sermon in Peale's sense of humor: "Every other sentence that you offer is broken up with an enormous audience roar of laughter." Peale's reputation ensured a sizable audience: "It is quite possible that with your connections you could find not a few television stations across the country who would be delighted to show [the worship service] as a public service."[59]

Even as Schuller offered suggestions for a Peale-centered broadcast, he established the foundation for his own television program. After receiving Graham's "suggestion," Schuller set February 1970 as the goal for the first broadcast and approached Peale to write an endorsement of the program to be used for marketing. Schuller, in typical fashion, even suggested the wording: "It would be most helpful if you felt inclined to say that you are thrilled to know that your friends and readers in Southern California could now pack the power of positive thinking into their life by listening to your friend, Robert Schuller, who in your estimation—etc."[60] A press release from the same year outlined the goals of the program: "The *Hour of Power* is a living contradiction to the idea that God is dead ... the church is falling into ruin ... religion is no longer possible." Schuller then acknowledged that viewers might be confused by what they saw: "We may not be preaching evangelistically, but we're helping to awaken unchurched people to their need for a personal relationship with Christ, and we're showing them how to use His teachings as a powerful, positive force in their lives."[61]

The program's high profile and remarkable longevity (it remains on the air today) empowered the ministry—but also demanded its own fuel. Raising the profile of the minister created new stressors for the rest of the ministry. Schuller's grandson Robert (Bobby) V. Schuller eventually credited the show as the lynchpin of the entire church operation. When asked how he explained the overall success of the ministry, Bobby offered a succinct and confident response: "It's just TV, it's just simple, it's just TV." Pressed to elaborate, he noted the relatively barren landscape of early 1970s Sunday morning programming as *Hour of Power* established itself:

> On Sunday morning you'd wake up, and you've got 3 choices, and one of them is Dr. Schuller [chuckles]. And the TV became the sort of fire that people gathered around, like in the caveman days—it's where people gathered to tell stories and hear what's happening. That's where you got your news. He was so far ahead of the curve, nationwide in the 70s, and stayed that way. And people appreciated it. Lots of people [who] couldn't get to church but could [experience it] through their TV set.

Bobby's father, Robert A. Schuller (son of Robert H.), offered a similar explanation that rested on capitalizing on the lack of competitive programming on Sunday mornings:

When we started the *Hour of Power* in 1970 there were three stations on TV. So you turn your TV on. There's no laptops, no iPads, no internet. There's no other distractions. You have a choice of listening to the radio, a lot of stations, or TV. People were watching TV. So they turn their TV on, they go channel 1-2-3, then its bzzz—snow from there on. That was it! If somebody turned their television set on at ten o'clock on Sunday mornings, we had the nation covered at ten A.M. because, when we started in 1970, Sunday morning was considered dead time.

For Bobby, the television ministry not only benefited from access to a mass audience, it also manifested a natural extension of his grandfather's methods:

The TV also was an evolution of the same philosophy as the drive-in church. So the idea is "come as you are in your family car," that not-so-Christian people could put their pajamas on and go to church and not be seen by anybody. That's what TV is—it's church in your pajamas.

The staff of *Hour of Power* routinely underscored that the show maintained qualitative superiority when compared to other religious broadcasts. Schuller initiated *Hour of Power* in the midst of an "electronic church" revolution. Schuller, though, differed from the rest of the cohort in that he constructed a simple repackaging of church worship in a manner that made the service attractive to watch from the family couch. Whereas the competitors tended toward dramatizations, *Hour of Power* offered televised worship that served the "church needs of hundreds of shut-ins across the nation."[62] From the late 1960s to the mid-1980s, the viewership of televangelist broadcasts soared from 5 million to 25 million, and Schuller's program received a large share of that audience, at one point drawing 1.3 million viewers from 156 countries.[63] In other words, Schuller's broadcast offered the "Christian service" of accessible worship and became a potent means for greatly expanding his constituency.

Though *Hour of Power* would not be broadcast until 1970, Schuller had several earlier experiences with multimedia that primed the congregation for televising its services. For example, in 1964, *Great Churches of the Golden West* chose GGCC for filming and broadcast its Easter worship service.[64] Later that same year, Word Records of Waco, Texas, announced that it would record and distribute two of Schuller's sermons as part of *The Great Sermon Recording Series*.[65] As always, the Orange County pastor demonstrated a keen interest in finding new methods for expanding his charismatic reach. According to Nason, the minister seemed "to know instinctively what advertising executives go to school to learn—you've got to keep your product before the public. You must have visibility. It's not that Bob equates the gospel of Jesus Christ . . . with everyday household products such as toothpaste or toilet tissue. It's just that people are people, and they are very predictable most of the time. The same principles that work to sell toothpaste also work to reach the unchurched for Christ."[66]

Schuller never shied away from using pageantry on *Hour of Power*, and a close confidant remarked that he did "everything with a great deal of drama and ceremony." The minister began wearing the vestments because he noted the trend among Presbyterian and Methodist pastors and liked the gravitas that it conveyed. So *Hour of Power* offered viewers a religious spectacle while maintaining a sensible mainline Protestant dignity. Schuller saw a practical side for the robes as well. Robert A. recalled that his father "always wrestled with his weight and [if] the suit didn't fit right, or if he spilled something on his tie, he didn't have to worry about it, he just covers it up with his robe, and he's ready to go." The minister, then, sought to maintain an atmosphere of dignity. A 1981 study of televangelism described Schuller as "the only mainline Protestant in the cast of cathode stars. He doesn't like being confused with the other evangelists on TV, some of whom he thinks are charlatans."[67] Though viewers would eventually receive requests for donations (and trinkets in return), they would never see the pastor debase himself on his knees, in tears, warning that without a miracle of donations, the ministry would be over (although in the midst of a financial crisis in the late 1980s—caused, Schuller would contend, by the misadventures of other televangelists—he would come close).

The business of charisma required careful self-possession, staging, onstage props, and a cooperative system of offstage enablers. A 1983 article in *Eternity* described the production of *Hour of Power*: "Video tapes are carefully screened for sour faces and bad camera angles. Some hymns have been bowdlerized of 'negative' lyrics; for example, in Amazing Grace, 'that saved a wretch like me' is changed to 'a soul like me.' There is no traditional confession in the services, which are fast-paced to avoid silent 'dead-spots.' Special guests are nearly always well-known personalities, from Milton Berle to Gerald Ford. Portions of the service resemble a talk show. Success stories abound. The music is crisp and professional."[68] William Willimon, a prominent Methodist theologian from Duke University, once related that when he preached a sermon at the Crystal Cathedral, he received instructions to smile and thank Schuller for the opportunity to be there that morning. However, Willimon would have to voice his gratitude to an empty chair—Schuller's travels kept him away that morning. Arvella Schuller spliced in video of Schuller graciously nodding his acknowledgment of Willimon's remarks in postproduction.[69]

Hour of Power provided Schuller an opportunity to invite celebrities who would lure in both viewers and attenders, a strategy he had utilized since the earliest days of the church. As he "was building his base," Schuller utilized known personalities such as Norman Vincent Peale to visit and speak at the drive-in. Schuller frequently noted that he "built his church on three Peales and two Sheens [i.e., Bishop Fulton Sheen]" and that "basically, that's how he grew his church in the beginning." In short, the minister believed that "if you want an audience, invite popular guests."[70] *Hour of Power* gained status from celebrities such as Art Linkletter, Tony Orlando, and Burl Ives, who discussed their life and faith with Schuller. The church's proximity to Hollywood allowed access to a broad pool of high-profile telegenic personalities.

Schuller would eventually shift his strategic use of celebrity. While he continued to entice attenders and viewers with the promise of celebrity appearances, he also leveraged his own fame to further legitimate himself. Schuller described the broadcast as "very much a personality centered operation" that "could very easily have a life span that is tied with my own life span." He also insisted that the "church is not dependent upon television."[71] That assessment, though, would be tested when the popularity of *Hour of Power* caused the sanctuary of GGCC, a hybrid walk-in–drive-in structure that would eventually be called the Arboretum, to be inadequate for seating both members *and* curious tourists. Schuller himself would eventually argue that the Crystal Cathedral needed to be constructed to house all the weekly visitors drawn by the television program and the luminaries they might glimpse. After the completion of the cathedral, its architect, the renowned Philip Johnson, marveled at Schuller's television instincts, remarking on the massive doors that opened for the drive-in audience outside of the sanctuary: "They're 80 feet high and 12 feet wide. And the opening of those doors will look great on TV. Dr. Schuller knows exactly what he's doing."[72] The cathedral itself presented an impressive background for *Hour of Power*, highlighting and testifying to the financial success of Schuller's ministry.

Everything about the broadcast, including the spectacular staging of the cathedral, sought to impress the audience. Schuller claimed that he and Arvella designed the program to appeal to those for whom walking into a church sanctuary represented an obstacle: "I'm trying to reach the unchurched. I asked my wife to prepare the services for television because she knows what a worship service is and the television people don't. She is responsible for the unified composition of the service, its elements and pace." He acknowledged that he and his production team designed *Hour of Power* to avoid the drudgery of staid mainline Protestant services, dismissing "the drag that sets in in the typical church service" as "abominable." He even offered an example: "Take the scripture reading. You wait for 30 seconds while the minister steps from his chair, takes four leisurely steps to the pulpit; you wait while he opens the Bible, he adjusts his specs, he lifts his head, he lowers his head, he lifts his head once more and begins to speak. You know what I mean?"[73] In making traditional worship more lively, Schuller and the *Hour of Power* staff remained unapologetic in crafting a seamless drama every Sunday morning. Nason, heavily involved in production at the time, wondered aloud to the *Orange County Register* in 1978: "People criticize us for being too slick and professional, but why should churches use ditto machines and staples when they can use color, sound, and motion to deliver their message?"[74]

In 1993, Schuller himself credited his international profile to his consistent, weekly presence on television—across the globe: "We are the only church and

I'm the only minister of any religion that speaks every Sunday morning on channel one out of Moscow." *Hour of Power* was beamed over Sputnik and appeared on the only broadcast received in "all fifteen" Soviet republics. Schuller shared his viewing numbers, noting that "over ten million people will be listening out of the 300 hundred million who can tune it in—and they will be tuning in Iraq, Iran, and Israel, over Sputnik. This is the only television thing of its kind."[75] The international presence of *Hour of Power* widened the reach of the ministry while further bolstering Schuller's charismatic legitimacy.

Establish a Niche

Just as a corporation might build its reputation by highlighting a strategic distinctiveness, Schuller carved a unique place for his ministry on highly competitive airwaves.[76] Harnessing his image in opposition to his undignified brethren, though, would prove difficult. In speaking with a journalist in 1987, he noted that he resisted tracking statistics related to audience size because it could lead to vanity: "If I did, I might be human enough to want to be No. 1 in both Nielsen and Arbitron." Even worse, though, vanity might reduce him to the level of disreputable competitors: "I could be No. 1 if I did it [Jimmy] Swaggart's way."[77]

Schuller's instincts to maintain distance between himself and other television ministers proved prescient. In 1987, Jim Bakker found himself mired in sexual and financial scandals. The next year, Swaggart confessed to "sinning" with prostitutes. With these maelstroms in the background, the number of households watching Schuller fell from 1,963,000 in early 1986 to 1,215,000 in July 1988, a steep decline that forced *Hour of Power* to lay off 20 percent of its staff. Schuller offered a desperate fund-raising appeal—a last resort that resembled those offered by the same embarrassing televangelists who initially caused the financial spiral. *Hour of Power* viewers saw Schuller on screen holding his thumb and index finger half an inch apart, saying, "We are that close, so close, to losing *Hour of Power*—today, you must do something, or we will die."[78] During the fallout, though, Schuller's ability to maintain 61 percent of his audience looked encouragingly robust when compared to his colleagues: Oral Roberts, Jerry Falwell, and Pat Robertson all maintained only about 40 percent.[79]

In an end-of-year report in 1988, Schuller sought to calm any anxiety among his board with a direct quote (including a footnote with full citation) from *Time* magazine that their ministry had risen above the fray: "Left personally unscathed in all the turmoil were more churchly TV preachers such as Billy Graham and Robert Schuller."[80] Only Schuller and Graham maintained favorability ratings over 60 percent.[81] Schuller noted, though, that the reputation of the Crystal Cathedral had been tarnished because the church "was exposed to a share of the media hysteria. . . . The mental climate of the past two years has been so 'anti-television ministries' that we were vulnerable to unreasonable, unfair, and damaging attacks."[82] More than that, "media probes continued throughout the year in an effort to expose, through intense scrutiny, presumed problems in this ministry, all of which proved fruitless and vain." However, as the controversies subsided, ratings for *Hour of Power* confirmed that Schuller had retained much of his credibility: in 1990 almost three million Americans and twenty million viewers worldwide in 180 countries watched the broadcast each week.[83]

Still, the ostentatiousness of the Crystal Cathedral highlighted every Sunday on the *Hour of Power* made the Orange County ministry an easy mark for criticism that potentially threatened Schuller's charisma. Schuller typically offered a rationalization for the costs of the cathedral that highlighted the missions-generating work across the globe that would be catalyzed through the church. During an appearance on the *Donohue* talk show, the host, Phil Donohue, pressed the minister specifically about how his church tangibly helped people in places such as New York City. Schuller responded that his ministry had built the Mott Haven Reformed Church and day care center in the Bronx. The statement stretched the truth. In response, the pastor of Mott Haven Reformed publicly stated that the Crystal Cathedral had contributed a mere $1,000 toward the $900,000 cost of the center: "[Schuller] gave the impression that [the Crystal Cathedral] almost built Mott Haven Reformed Church by themselves. I couldn't believe he would make such a statement."[84] In instances like these, Schuller adopted the breadth of service accomplished through RCA and the work of far-flung congregations as part of the good work of his "church"—generously defined.

The RCA connection also allowed Schuller cover for his resistance in joining the Evangelical Council for Financial Accountability (ECFA). Schuller contended that his affiliation with the RCA ensured financial accountability. He also insisted that he could not afford the sliding scale of membership dues. When journalists from the *Orange County Register* pressed Schuller that the ECFA expected only $4,800 from a ministry that reported income of over $35 million, he responded, "That's a lot of money to me."[85]

As fallout from the accountability controversy among television ministries overflowed into 1988, Schuller continued to engage in a project of reputation rehabilitation. In a March 19 letter addressed to John J. O'Connor, the Roman Catholic archbishop of New York, Nason wondered if the archbishop would be willing to participate in a ten-minute video endorsement of Schuller to be sent to television station managers around the country. Nason's explanation for the request revealed critiques and concerns the ministry had been fielding: "Is Dr. Schuller like those other evangelists? Does Dr. Schuller encourage people to attend a local church or parish? Is he a fundamentalist? Does he speak out against the Catholic church?" Nason reminded O'Connor of Schuller's legitimacy: "As you know, Dr. Schuller comes out of a mainline church tradition—one that reflects the same great tradition of your own church affiliation."[86] After approving the letter, Schuller wrote a note in the margins to Nason in pen: "If [O'Connor] doesn't [agree], try the L.A. cardinal—a friend and local." In all things, the ministry sought to control the narrative surrounding Schuller's reputation and protect his niche.

Secure Sources of Capital

Capital projects were continually pursued in Schuller's ministry, especially in the construction of new buildings, as another signifier of reputable standing. The minister described his architectural philosophy: "Beauty generates enthusiasm. Beauty marshals enormous support."[87] Already in his first pastorate outside of Chicago, Schuller so desired an addition to the church that he hired a professional fund-raising firm.[88] For Schuller, prominent buildings did not just demand capital, *building projects stimulated fresh sources of capital.*

In 1961, having outgrown a traditional church building dubbed "the Chapel," GGCC dedicated a new "hybrid" walk-in–drive-in church building designed by world-renowned architect Richard Neutra. As a church structure, this building charted new territory as an "architecturally ambitious incarnation of the megachurch."[89] Schuller made sketches available to promote excitement and wonder for the new edifice. One architectural critic noted that the structure might be better understood as a "designed environment" rather than a traditional building.[90] The Tower of Hope, opened in 1968 and also designed by Neutra, stood as one of Orange County's tallest buildings. When Schuller commissioned Neutra to design the tower in 1966, the building plan "consisted of a stacked series of offices for marriage, interpersonal, and family therapists. The top of the tower housed a twenty-four-hour-a-day telephone-operated counseling service—the phone number was 'NEW HOPE.'" One architectural critic reported that "what Neutra called the 'living exterior world' was now saturated with the gospel of popular psychology, transmitted through the television wires as well as the TV airwaves. Having used psychology to develop for architecture an idea of environment, Schuller literally psychologized the environment itself."[91]

Most significantly, with their aggressive architectural flourishes, the ambitious plans alone—even before these buildings were built—provided tangible evidence of the ministry's success. One historian described the architectural synergy of the two buildings on the church campus, the hybrid sanctuary and the Tower of Hope, as providing Schuller an unparalleled ministerial platform for publicity.[92] Later, Schuller used a handheld model of the innovative structure of the Crystal Cathedral as dramatic evidence of the grandeur and beauty of the proposed structure. The sanctuaries and support buildings constructed by Schuller, even when existing only in the planning stages, offered concrete artifacts that signaled the achievements of his ministry.

For Schuller, the scale and spectacle of this new architecture served as "silent advertising."[93] He was right. The hybrid church (later named the Arboretum) won awards from the *New York Times* and the American Institute of Steel Construction. In addition, periodicals ranging from *Life* to *Art and Architecture* featured the church in articles. The buildings afforded Schuller a modicum of gravitas. Such accolades and publicity, though, demanded significant promotional energy. Schuller dogged Neutra for architectural details for completed submissions to design contests. The minister wrote numerous architectural journals suggesting that they publish a feature about his genre-redefining church.[94]

In 1975, Schuller agreed to write a short statement on his philosophy of architecture for *Moody Monthly*. He indicated that GGCC chose an architectural style atypical for a church because the congregation understood itself as more of a mission than a church. He argued that a traditional church, of course, would create a "sheltered, set-apart, secluded tabernacle" in order to create a hospitable place for the congregation to gather. On the other hand, a mission that seeks the "unchurched" would want to create a sanctuary that fosters a tranquilizing experience wherein minds would be receptive to positive suggestions: "Which is why the Garden Grove Community Church makes extensive use of water, and green grass and clear glass. For David knew that there were two universal, timeless, classical, tranquilizing elements: still waters and green pastures."[95] And Schuller continued to invest in the entire church campus in Garden Grove: new statuary and water features appeared throughout the decades.

The completion of the Crystal Cathedral, though, represented Schuller's boldest victory, speaking to both established church leaders and to irreligious critics of traditional Christianity. The Crystal Cathedral stands as one of the earliest models of the prototypical evangelical megachurch. Of course, no other megachurch would attempt the cathedral's audacious architectural flourishes.[96] However, the manner in which it adapted long-held evangelical strategies—utilizing cutting-edge technology, establishing rooms and ministries for every member of an attending family, and curating buildings "to appeal to a broad middle class"— fixed a prominent benchmark in "offering an attractive religious haven within a turbulent world."[97] When Schuller secured eminent modernist architect Philip Johnson to design the cathedral, the move brought immediate credibility and "helped shift the church away from the perception that it was a marginalized sect."[98] The minister's confidence provided context for a 1980 *Newsweek* article in which a self-satisfied Schuller is described as "snorting" that "doctrinaire architecture" stood as "a major cause for Protestantism's decline."[99] Not so his buildings.

Perhaps because of Johnson's stature, architectural critic Witold Rybczynski, while lamenting the standard forms of contemporary megachurch architecture, reserved praise for the Crystal Cathedral, which he described as "both strikingly modern in its crystalline geometry and its transparency and a throw-back to the medieval cathedral-builders' preoccupation with structure and lightness." Rybczynski noted that few megachurches exhibited Schuller's courage in contracting with world-renowned architects and typically built structures that communicated familiarity, comfort, and ease rather than awe and thoughts of transcendence. He praised Johnson for daring to tread the "knife-edge of kitsch" while producing "a building that was both familiar *and* new, suburban *and* transcendental."[100]

With his patronage of Neutra and Johnson, Schuller received accolades from some architectural critics as "the most formidable ecclesiastical patron of the postwar period."[101] Even the landscaping design of the campus inspired a rhetorical flourish. Environmental studies professor Susan Power Bratton asserted that Schuller's "advocacy for water as calming and welcoming" became widely accepted with the megachurch universe.[102] Schuller invested heavily in his campus, once noting that he lived by the axiom "Just don't ever compromise excellence for mediocrity."[103] Critical success in expanding visible features assured constituents of the value of Schuller's seemingly farsighted charismatic leadership, entrusting him with fresh flows of capital for further future projects.

Because it signaled achievement, Schuller described the cathedral and campus as his "calling card."[104] When thinking about the design for the eventual Crystal Cathedral during the mid-1970s, Schuller remained consistent in his core belief in projecting an image of success. The minister insisted that the new building be "a masterpiece" in order to "attract the money we need to build the structure!" Following Schuller's template, megachurches typically seek "to bring middle-class white Protestants who likely grew up within a church but had abandoned it as adults 'back' to church."[105] Schuller himself intimated that his new building had a particular slice of the demographic in mind as the target audience: "It will have to grab the imagination of sophisticated and successful people!"[106] Schuller's approach to the cathedral manifests how constituency, charisma, and capital were profoundly intertwined in the many projects managed over the history of the ministry.

A Caution against Overextension

The strain that ultimately collapsed his megachurch ministry began with Schuller's overweighted self-confidence in his expertise in growth methods. Despite trailblazing efforts in architecture, broadcasting, and reaching "the unchurched," in 2010 Schuller's ministry declared bankruptcy. Without understanding the full trajectory of both the man and structural complexities inherent to his ministry, we fail to fully comprehend the consequences of a pervasive and underlying strand of contemporary American Christianity. The rest of this book offers our explanation for how the stability and resilience promised by church growth methodology yielded an increased risk of total failure. Assets and achievements could not overcome the excessive organizational fractures that remained largely unseen until the very end.

Caution regarding Schuller's approach to church growth is warranted not only because of the collapse of the Crystal Cathedral but also because Schuller insisted that other church leaders adopt his techniques. Always willing to offer advice and counsel to other ministers, Schuller wrote multiple letters in 1974 to Lloyd

Ogilvie, pastor of Hollywood Presbyterian Church (HPC), to offer tips on advertising after the congregation had held a recent Easter service at the Hollywood Bowl. Considering himself a perfecter of church branding, it would not have been surprising if Ogilvie detected a note of condescension as Schuller remarked that HPC's Easter worship service stood "as the most exciting thing that I have seen in Hollywood Presbyterian as long as I have been in California—and that will be 20 years next February."[107] Schuller then moved on to the point of his letter and offered a pointed critique of their marketing: "I would suggest that next year, assuming that you will again use the Hollywood Bowl (and I surely hope you do!), add to your advertising budget a few hundred dollars for an artist." Demonstrating his discerning eye, Schuller noted, "The half-page ad that appeared in the *Los Angeles Times* looked to me as if it were set up by the 'ad-layout people' in the back room of the *Los Angeles Times*. It obviously did not have much investment in art work." Schuller continued: "Invision [*sic*] a two-toned or multi-dimension art scheme showing the huge Hollywood Bowl with the emotional tone of the open-air, the hills, the new dawning, and in that veiled back drop the photos and the story of what's happening. Undoubtedly, you have accessibility to [a] good artist. We use a few in our work and I can recommend some, if you want recommendations."[108] Schuller's certainty to offer unsolicited advice rested on the "proof texts" of his ministry: its successful growth, broadcast, leadership institute, and campus.[109]

As seen in this letter to Ogilvie, Schuller included growth consultation in his ministry portfolio. He aggressively promoted his techniques, and many followed his approach. The Orange County minister's influence remains so pervasive that emulators continue to borrow from his established templates without realizing their source. A 1997 article in *Christianity Today*'s *Leadership Journal* summarized Schuller's "pioneering" influence, asserting, "It would not be overreaching to say that without Schuller and the Crystal Cathedral, there would likely be no Willow Creek Community Church, no Saddleback Community Church, or the thousands of other seeker-oriented churches around the country."[110] Megachurch expert Warren Bird credits Schuller with being the first to describe his denominational church as a "community church," to call a sermon a "message," to use a nontraditional setting for worship services (a drive-in theater), to conduct door-to-door market research, to train pastors in *leadership*, and to televise a weekly church service.[111]

Echoes of Schuller's legacy reverberate into twenty-first-century American Christianity—beyond the lineage of Bill Hybels's Willow Creek Church and Rick Warren's Saddleback Church. A recent ethnographic study of a Hillsong congregation in Chicago revealed that that church imitates vodka advertisements to bait urban hipsters into worship. Greeters and ushers are expected to abide by the "style packet" that the leadership prescribes. Rather than focusing on modesty, instructions highlight fashions seen in recent glossy magazines. The young pastors of this "Downtown Church" view "potential members as retail consumers," relying on the church growth trail blazed by Schuller half a century earlier.[112] And when another Hillsong pastor from New York, Carl Lentz, openly discusses his relationships with singers (Justin Bieber) and professional athletes (Kevin Durant and Tyson Chandler from the NBA), he taps into a form of charisma and proximity to celebrity that was practiced every Sunday for four decades by Schuller as form of legitimation.[113] These pastors manage their images through social media, projecting a sense of success and cultural awareness. Though they have traded Schuller's vestments for skinny jeans and T-shirts, they stand on the shoulders of the Orange County minister.

Schuller's confidence in his multifaceted ministry attached itself to multiple evidences of success: visible growth in attendance, viewership numbers, supportive donors, and pastoral mimics (*constituency*), an assumed acumen of visionary leadership (*charisma*), and ambitious architectural projects with large budgets (*capital*). While Schuller perfected marketing church success for decades and created a new template, the unremitting focus on growth and success would have profound consequences, placing the entire ministry under considerable strain. Planning and projecting the aura of a growing evangelical empire would become an infrastructure-stressing burden. The apparent success of the ministry obscured the many tensions that often threatened its future. At every turn, the answer to potential crises involved *yet more growth*.

Schuller cultivated a belief that he rationally controlled the workings of constituency, charisma, and capital. In truth, these elements are difficult to manage in congregations of any size. Even in his own ministry, the vagaries of larger economic markets, scandals among other television ministers, the local decline of the core demographic, and the preferences of other churchgoers would all have implications for the Crystal Cathedral. Financial consultants may have advised cutting costs, but Schuller remained entrenched in his techniques, confident that his charisma would draw in still more new constituents and that new capital projects would always stimulate fresh markets and new revenue streams. Schuller underestimated the strain—and overestimated the replicability of his template—by failing to discern the ministry's fragile dependence on the tight linkages between constituency, charisma, and capital.

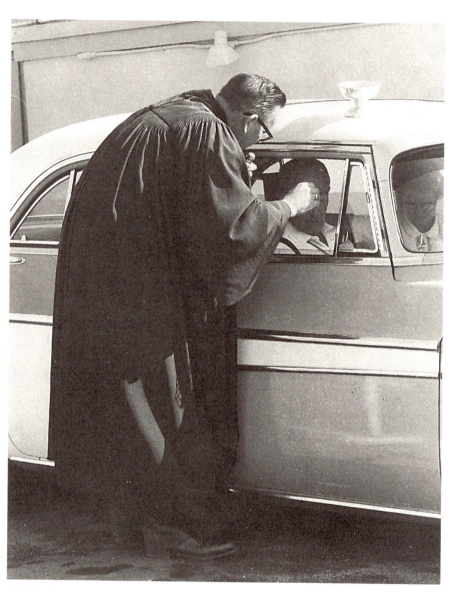

Schuller administers baptism to an infant inside a car at the Orange Drive-in. Photo courtesy of the Joint Archives of Holland.

3

Migrants to Orange County, California

> Winning starts with beginning.
> —Robert H. Schuller

Robert H. Schuller was neither young nor inexperienced when he ventured west to start a congregation in Southern California. Married with two children, he was already ordained in the Reformed Church in America (RCA), having completed his master of divinity degree at Western Theological Seminary in Holland, Michigan, and successfully grew his first RCA congregation from forty to four hundred in suburban Riverdale, Illinois. Yet Schuller had ambition and felt a calling to establish a mission in Orange County. Fueled by a zeal to evangelistically reach the last remnants of the Western frontier, the RCA pastor uprooted from a comfortably traditional mainline Protestant ministry to drive the iconic Route 66 in a car loaded with his family and a mortgaged organ in tow. He would preach, and Arvella would play. All they needed was a place to meet. But where?

Garden Grove, California, became the focus, a bedroom community located about thirty miles south of Los Angeles. When Schuller arrived, the region boasted dramatic growth, and Garden Grove represented the leading age of new development. From 1940 to the mid-1950s, the city grew by 18,000 percent.[1] In just the first five years of Schuller's ministry, the city's population almost doubled from 44,000 people to over 84,000.[2] It had all the ingredients for a successful church plant: a growing suburban population, a burgeoning economy, a range of cheaper housing options, and much land still available to build facilities.

Indeed, all of Orange County grew rapidly after World War II as developers transformed the landscape from farms into grids of suburban, low-density, single-family houses. Historian Darren Dochuk described Orange County as an exemplar of the new suburban America, and included a nod to Schuller: "The virtues of patriotism, entrepreneurialism, localism, and family values assumed conspicuous form in such fantastic creations as Disneyland and Knott's Berry Farm, Walter Knott's brainchild, and such wild innovations as drive-thru restaurants and drive-in churches."[3] The county bubbled with the anticipation of the economic, social, and religious vitality offered by the postwar, car-abetted, and built-up suburban milieu. In addition, 1955 also saw Walt Disney open Disneyland in Anaheim, strategically chosen for its location and about to become a perpetual draw for both locals and tourists.

Equipped only with his wife, the portable organ, and a missionary calling, Schuller began his search for a suitable venue, looking for space to meet, prioritizing where he might be able to start his ministry. At that point, much of Garden Grove remained mostly farmland—broad expanses of strawberry fields and citrus groves—yet for as much land as was available, the minister found it surprisingly difficult to find somewhere to gather for worship services. Schuller worked through a list of potential sites: public schools, warehouses, mortuaries, movie theaters, and synagogues. All of his energies focused on finding a stable place, a property to which he could direct potential members over time. In his words, he "struck out." The region was already becoming thick with new churches. Either space was barred from use (public schools), did not exist (no theaters in town), or other enterprising pastors had beaten him to the spot (Baptists met in the mortuary, Presbyterians in the Seventh-Day Adventist church). His ministry, as he understood it, could not begin without a place to congregate. Then Schuller approached the owner of a local drive-in theater.

There may not have been a better site in the United States for Schuller to establish a car-centric church. Without much intention, Schuller had timed the opening of his drive-in ministry perfectly. Tract homes dotted the landscape for miles around, and a network of roads and highways encouraged people to travel long distances. The year Schuller arrived, Ray A. Kroc teamed with brothers Richard and Maurice McDonald to franchise their chain of drive-in McDonald's restaurants (one in Illinois and, of course, two in California). Americans spent more minutes every day in their cars, prepared to eat in their automobiles but also, apparently, to worship in them as well.[4] Michael Nason, who would become a key staff member and confidante for Schuller, also arrived in February 1955 and recalled being struck by the ubiquity of highway construction: "Everything was about the car."[5] With automobile accessibility, locals equated the drive-in theater with modern, cheap entertainment. Schuller approached the reluctant owner, who expressed confusion about how his theater could be a church. Eventually, though, he agreed to rent it out for $10 a week, only to cover the cost of the unionized sound technician. Schuller then advertised services in the local paper, pulled in the portable organ trailered all the way from Iowa, and invited a large guest choir from another church—urging each one to drive in separate cars to help fill out the empty spaces. (Of the cars in the drive-in that day, nearly half were from the visiting choir members alone.)

In the post–World War II suburban boom, perhaps no other church so aptly captured the burgeoning trends of American culture: a growing middle class, automobile dependence, disdain for city cores in favor of pastoral suburbs, migration patterns following weather and jobs to the Sun Belt, and the enshrinement of the nuclear family. Schuller, always a promoter, used publicity to draw in potential members and issued press releases in the local newspaper. An early church poster added to the local hype, inviting families to "attend Southern California's beautiful drive-in church. Held in the Orange Drive-in Theatre, Santa Ana Freeway (Highway 101) and Chapman Avenue." The ad promised an opportunity to "worship in the shadows of the rising mountains, surrounded by colorful orange groves and eucalyptus trees." Services would feature "storytime for the youngsters, playground nursery for children, outstanding choral singing," and "inspiring preaching." The poster promised easy access when it welcomed everyone to "worship as you are . . . in the family car."[6]

In a region that had no historical roots and few established social networks, creating an effective church meant producing a congregational culture that easily assimilated newcomers. With that, Schuller struck a marketing tone that reverberated in its ability to appeal to its target: young families comfortable spending hours in their car and new enough to the West Coast to enjoy the enchantment of its natural environment. Years later, Schuller's distinguished architect, Richard Neutra, would quip that the appeal of the minister's drive-in church revolved around the fact that the family car in American culture had attained as familiar an intimacy as a second family home.[7]

His church intentionally accommodated for turnstile attendance, and it worked. Garden Grove Community Church mixed a church-planter's ambition to build a dynamic attraction for the "unchurched" with an ability to transform streams of visitors into a cohesive congregational community. Designing the parking, greeting, seating, and responses to attenders with this ethos allowed for audiences of strangers to fit together comfortably—at least comfortably enough for the minister's message to affirm their family, finances, and faith life. The booming economy added to the disposable income his members were able to funnel into his growing ministry.

With his start in the drive-in theater, Schuller established the Garden Grove Community Church (GGCC), a name that shrugged off the ostensibly irrelevant "Reformed" identity of a denomination centered in the Northeast and Midwest and created a mode of congregational life suited to his new California context. Even when Schuller constructed a physical building less than two miles east (dubbed "the chapel"), he would not forego services at the theater, refusing to abandon the faithful people who had called the drive-in their church home. Through cold, wind, and rain, Schuller kept preaching from the top of a snack bar, now seeing the drive-in as the center of his ministry philosophy. In the rapid rise of attendance at both the chapel and the drive-in, the members remained not only loyal to Schuller but also committed to further growth, constantly open to new initiatives that promised to serve greater numbers of grateful people just like them.

Migrants from the South and Midwest

During the first two decades of Schuller's Southern California ministry, Orange County transformed from "scrubland and citrus groves" into the world's "largest suburban population center."[8] Migrants from the South and Midwest found themselves attracted to the area by an expanding economy and more pleasant weather. For most, the arrival to California translated into new lifestyle choices. Previous social and cultural expectations no longer held sway, and the move to Orange County allowed for pursuing novel opportunities amid the "predominantly secular individualism" that pervaded Southern California.[9]

In those early years of the Cold War, the economy of Orange County expanded quickly, a pace one commentator described as "frenetic."[10] Urban historian Kenneth Jackson labeled Orange County as the epitome of suburban, centerless city development. Never having a true core city to serve as the focal point of the economy, the county by 1980 included 26 different municipalities, and not one claimed a population of more than 225,000. Jackson quoted a resident who described the typical Orange County commuter lifestyle: "I live in Garden Grove, work in Irvine, shop in Santa Ana, go to the dentist in Anaheim, my husband works in Long Beach, and I used to be the president of the League of Women Voters in Fullerton."[11] Historian Robert Fishman noted that in Orange County, the absence of a core city translated into a phenomenon in which each residential unit functioned as the "true city of this new city," and from that "central starting point, the members of the household create their own city from the multitude of destinations that are within suitable driving distance."[12]

The region grew into a "multi-centered metropolis" with indiscernible boundaries, shopping centers, and corporate office parks.[13] As the migrants settled in Orange County, they might have noticed this suburban decentralization, where municipal borders offered little differentiation and superhighways served as the connective tissue that kept one corner of the county readily accessible to the other. Just prior to World War II, the county had been dominated by agricultural fields and small, distinct towns. As Schuller built GGCC, though, municipality mattered less, and "Orange County" rose in prominence as "a cohesive spatial unit with a self-definition distinct from neighboring Los Angeles."[14]

Because of its rapid growth, temperate climate, and rising affluence, entrepreneurs of all types felt Orange County represented as good a chance as any locale in the country to turn a profit. Walt Disney, by way of example, did not just happen upon Anaheim. He and his engineers systematically surveyed the country for "the choicest location" and settled on the interior of Orange County. Disney's deliberative analysis turned a quick profit and ushered in a critical mass of attendant hotels and restaurants. By 1963, tourism accounted for 20 percent of all retail sales in the county.[15]

Beyond the service and tourism sector, Orange County received a boost from the defense industry. The specter of the Cold War drove the Department of Defense to issue $228 billion in new contracts during the 1950s (an increase of 246 percent over the course of the decade). Southern California proved to be a singular destination for those defense dollars. In Orange County, the number of employees who worked in defense-related industries went from negligible in 1950 to 31,000 in 1962.[16] With steady growth throughout the 1960s, the county earned a reputation as a hub of the military-industrial complex. All that economic vitality boosted the finances of the families working and residing there. Historian Lisa McGirr described the overwhelmingly white families of the 1960s version of Orange County as a "privileged group" and "an exceedingly strong specimen of a middle class."[17] Schuller had found himself within an increasingly affluent demographic primed to hear his upbeat message within a professionally managed church that extolled the virtues of rising success.

Not only was Orange County economically vibrant, but the people who moved there were conventionally religious, highly churched people. The religious development of Orange County was shaped by the premigration experience of residents who originally hailed from the Midwest, Mid-Atlantic, and South. A snapshot of motor vehicle registrations from 1962 revealed that new residents came from Iowa, Indiana, Ohio, Illinois, Florida, Michigan, Kansas, New York, Pennsylvania, Texas, and Virginia in roughly equal numbers. At 35.5 percent, the Midwest represented the most significant point of origin.[18] Most of these migrants brought with them a sense of the traditional expectation of belonging to a church alongside a newfound openness to consider different forms of religious life. In particular, Garden Grove was (and still remains today) one of the California cities with the most churches per capita. Schuller inadvertently stumbled into a tight cluster of suburbanites looking for a neighborhood congregation. Schuller's church represented a readily convenient option especially welcoming to newcomers in a city already full of churches.

In general, postwar American suburbs have been described as sites for the pursuit of social fulfillment, self-realization, and escape.[19] Places like Garden Grove filled with what sociologist William Whyte described as the "organization man," a largely indistinguishable, rootless middle class of middle managers committed to a relentless pursuit of upward mobility. According to Whyte, the "organization man"—and his family—desired nonoffensive, "useful" churches in their new suburban homes.[20] Thus, the postwar suburbs functioned as geographical primers for seemingly fresh interpretations of religious rituals. Yet by background and by "natural addiction" (according to the editors of *The Christian Century*), 1950s suburban residents exuded a decidedly Protestant ethos. Combining the two, suburbia offered new opportunities for Protestant religious entrepreneurs with a willingness to experiment. In terms of absolute supply, religious buildings had not maintained pace with religious need during the Great Depression and World War II.[21] When denominations rushed to meet demand in the postwar era, most of the construction occurred in places where government policy had subsidized white middle-class homeownership: the suburbs, which necessarily meant that these ecclesial experiments focused on white audiences.[22] Schuller proved to be an affable spokesperson for their aspirations.

As a particularly attractive destination for these upwardly mobile, middle-class, and highly churched families, Garden Grove and the surrounding area became a white evangelical hotbed with its accompanying attitudes and political sensibilities. Eileen Luhr described Orange County in the second half of the twentieth century as a "national symbol of conservatism."[23] Cultural organizations and businesses established strongholds in the area to service the region's conservative Christian population. In 1975 the local KYMS radio station became one of the first in the nation to switch from a secular to a Christian music format. By the end of the 1980s, Orange County ranked as the nation's second-best market for Christian music sales. An area publisher distributed an independent Christian newspaper, the *Christian Times*, and a Christian telephone directory, *Christian Times Yellow Pages*, where businesses often added a logo of a dove or a fish as part of their branding. By the end of the 1980s, residents could navigate the freeways to find a bevy of Christian bookstores and coffee shops. Robert P. Jones, researcher and CEO of the Public Religion Research Institute, described Schuller's destination as particularly primed to the RCA minister's message: "The residents who flocked to live in the region's newly built subdivisions were nearly uniformly wealthy, white, Protestant, and politically conservative. Orange County was ripe for a white Christian conservative awakening."[24] Any assessment of Orange County in the late twentieth century affirms that white evangelicals dominated the political and cultural life of the region.[25]

The geographical and social dislocation of the move to Southern California caused Orange County migrants to seek out the familiarity of church life to find community and belonging. Both mainline Protestant and evangelical congregations flourished. The thickness of the local religious ecology added pressure to carve out a unique congregational niche.[26] Schuller aspired, then, not to establish another new church but to find a way to *distinguish* his church from others. His drive-in church met that challenge.

Schuller's ability to attract so many people to the drive-in was initially a surprise. With perhaps a too-generous description of its economic and demographic diversity, the minister reported in a 1957 letter that "the congregation comes from every level of society." He elaborated: "There will be young parents with their little babies, old people too feeble to walk into a traditional church, parents with children afflicted with crippling sickness, paraplegics with their wheel chairs in the back seat, besides hundreds who attend because they prefer the privacy of their cars."[27] Schuller shaped the rhetoric so that it seemed that the plan of the drive-in ministry had been designed for those who faced physical, psychological, and spiritual obstacles. But these "benefits" were read back into the ministry as it was happening. Schuller eventually added that the strengths of the drive-in church included the accessibility it allowed for individuals with physical and emotional disabilities. In fact, "accessibility" became an important component of Schuller's ministry and those that followed in its wake. Administering pastoral needs that catered to the physical and emotional needs of congregants became an imperative of the evangelical megachurch universe.[28]

When Schuller became a champion of in-car worship, he never claimed to have strategically chosen the Orange Drive-in for his church in California. Classis California representatives had warned him that it would be "impossible to find an empty hall" in Garden Grove.[29] The theater offered a refuge of almost last resort—the ninth of ten possibilities scribbled on a restaurant napkin at a café outside of Albuquerque on Route 66. A school, Masonic hall, warehouse, mortuary chapel, and Jewish synagogue all ranked higher on Schuller's list—only a tent on "an empty piece of ground" graded lower than a drive-in theater. In his search for a suitable worship venue, Schuller quickly exhausted his first eight options. Settling on the drive-in theater became his only refuge.[30]

Nevertheless, the marriage of happenstance and convenience allowed Schuller to market his church as a progressive form of worship that fortuitously mapped onto the highly mobilized, suburban lifestyle of Orange County. While Schuller often received credit for being the pioneer of drive-in churches, he and Arvella first experienced the concept while on their honeymoon in Spirit Lake, Iowa. Schuller described himself as "fascinated" and "inspired" by the Lutheran pastor who preached from the snack-bar rooftop. Also, in his early years at Ivanhoe Reformed Church in suburban Chicago, he had read a book written by J. Wallace Hamilton about transforming negative emotions into positive ones. Hamilton, it turned out, pastored a drive-in church in St. Petersburg, Florida.[31] Schuller had seen the model, but he had not been committed to reproducing it.

Indeed, Schuller reported that many of the local pastors in Orange County doubted that a ministry with such a questionable venue could ever provide a wholesome foundation for a real church.[32] Many Christians in the mid-1950s dismissed drive-in theaters as "passion pits" associated with licentiousness much more so than hymns and sermons. Worship in a drive-in theater crossed the sacred with the profane in an unseemly manner. An architectural critic described the synthesis of church and theater as the "house of God" domesticating the "optical promiscuity of the drive-in" while "the house of God became a porous screening room for the Ten Commandments seen in Technicolor."[33] One fellow RCA minister, upon seeing the advertisement for the first service at the drive-in, visited Schuller's home to confront and "lambaste" him for the foolish concept.[34] A teenager from a nearby RCA congregation—who would later be ordained as a minister in the denomination—reported feeling a cognitive dissonance attending church where he had previously "watched" movies: "I'd take girls over there to date. You sit there, and you don't watch the movie, you kind of mess with your girl. But then to sit there on Sunday morning and have a worship service—let me put it this way—I struggled with it."

Despite misgivings about establishing a viable church community at a drive-in theater, even within his own denomination, Schuller soldiered on. After all, he had no other options. The drive-in theater initiated his renegotiation of the spatial and liturgical norms of American church life, and he strategized intensely about how to foster a sacred atmosphere. As seen in other innovative congregations, unconventional spaces tend to spur on unconventional practices.[35] At Schuller's drive-in, the bulletin for the first-ever service included these instructions for acceptable participation in the liturgy: "Remove the speaker and place it in your car, adjusting the volume as needed. Pray that God may bless the hour you spend here. Participate in your car. During prayer, bow your head; during the singing of hymns, join in the singing; during the sermon, listen and apply the vital truths to your own life. Return next week with your friends and relatives." At the end of the service, an announcement followed the benediction: "Caution! Be sure that the speaker is returned to the rack before you drive away from the park stand."[36] These protocols surely reveal the development of Schuller's ministry philosophy as he considered member involvement and alternative congregational practices.

By 1969, Schuller had reinterpreted the drive-in church as a universal template for accessible worship, one that provided a wide-open door for the curious and uncommitted. Schuller clung to the open-air ambience of the drive-in theater as the ideal venue, even suggesting the possibility of "a ten-acre facility under domed glass at a major freeway interchange outside of Chicago, Illinois." He fantasized about this architectural marvel: "Under this giant astrodome, in a climatized situation, people would worship in pew arrangements, but also in the privacy of their cars. The same would be true just outside of New York City."[37] Even though Orange County enjoyed a uniquely sunny climate that allowed for services year-round, he admitted that being exposed to the elements often exasperated his patience. Yet Schuller argued that drive-in churches could be successful anywhere in the country, even in places with ice and snow. Schuller cited his amusement park neighbor as a model for his fellow ministers: "If Walt Disney were alive today and an ordained minister of the Reformed Church in America in charge of the National Department of Drive-In Ministry, what kind of plans would he have on the drawing board?" The temperate weather of Garden Grove could not be replicated, but dedicated ingenuity and investment would allow for the method of a drive-in church to be instituted everywhere—regardless of climate. For Schuller, ingenuity and proper disposition could overcome any challenge: "The problem of climate is one that can surely be solved if we are dedicated and imaginative enough."[38]

Schuller mulled over many critiques of the drive-in church concept and concluded that he saw no weaknesses in the "technique." He defended the venue in "The Drive-in Church—A Modern Technique of Outreach," an article for *The Reformed Review*, an RCA journal published by his alma mater, Western Theological Seminary. Not only had he attracted a large group of committed constituents, but he also saw that their liturgical participation looked similar to those found in any other RCA church. Listing the benefits of this modern ministry, Schuller asserted that communion elements could be consumed in cars just as easily as pews, that financial offerings passed through car windows just as effortlessly, and that drive-in worshippers experienced as much fellowship as those who left their cars in the parking lot—limited, according to Schuller, in both venues: "The same families in the drive-in church tend to park in the same spots every week. Windows are rolled down, heads nod greetings, and there is as much fellowship in worship at the drive-in as there is in the sanctuary—which is not very much!" For Schuller, the competitive niche of the drive-in ensured loyal members—with no other similar churches nearby, where else would they attend? And real fellowship was fostered through the additional ministries of the church.[39] Schuller's ability to adapt and reinterpret the drive-in as religious innovation would become foundational to the charismatic authority issuing forth from his Orange County ministry.

Due to the unusual setting, observers have speculated as to the motivation of these car-centric constituents. For example, media professor Erica Robles-Anderson asserted that the drive-in appealed to worshippers because it allowed for a simultaneous experience of "going out and staying in." These worshippers found themselves "separated into subregions and yet connected through technologies that generated an overarching, albeit mediated, event in view." Thus, the GGCC worship service allowed both "privatization and co-orientation." Robles-Anderson likened the drive-in church phenomenon to suburban televisions, since both functioned as "important spatial intermediaries in the postwar era that helped facilitate the shift from public to domestic leisure by offering privatized access to collective life."[40] Just as the suburban lifestyle fixated on the centripetal pull of the single-family home, worship at GGCC affirmed the trend by allowing "public" worship within the privacy of the family car. Unwittingly or not, Schuller's drive-in experiment resulted in a reimagining of the sacred into a spatial vernacular that resonated with suburban conventions, establishing a resourceful synthesis of worship and the "Autotopia" ethos of Southern California.[41]

Highways Deliver Worshippers from Afar

Only after committing to purchase the ten acres of orange grove in Garden Grove for his hybrid church did Schuller learn that the new Santa Ana Freeway would be constructed just east of the new church building. The idea that GGCC would very soon be surrounded by office parks, shopping malls, and elaborate freeway interchanges seemed preposterous at the time. Schuller, at one point, described the property as "deep in the sticks and worthless for sure."[42] However, Schuller also *eventually* understood Garden Grove as an exceptional site, perhaps unparalleled in the United States. The fact that entertainment virtuoso Walt Disney chose a locale just two miles away served as unimpeachable evidence that new automobile routes would inevitably serve his growth goals for the congregation: "The unprecedented and unsurpassed location as far as accessibility is concerned is proven with the fact that Mr. Disney looked at the spot on the Southern California map most easily reached by most freeways projected in the future and chose his present site." Schuller also found that a Major League Baseball team had reached the identical conclusion: "For the same reason the Angels' Stadium has selected this location. For the same reason our church is located in this immediate vicinity."[43] Thus, although accidental, Schuller framed the location at the corner of Lewis and Chapman as an informed decision, which enhanced his charismatic credentials.

Schuller came to understand the advantages of his site, and later, as chair of the Steering and Planning Committee of Protestant Ministers and Laymen in Orange County, he pitched the location as a destination for a Billy Graham Evangelistic Crusade, explaining with certainty why he thought the greater Garden Grove–Anaheim area also functioned as the perfect locale for Graham's objectives. First, the area had become a singular entertainment destination for middle class families who found themselves with more and more discretionary income: "The broadcast of the Gospel of Jesus Christ from the evangelistic meetings held in the Angels' Stadium would mean the old-fashioned Gospel in the heart of the entertainment capitol [*sic*] of the world as Disneyland is so rapidly being labeled." Second, Garden Grove was accessible to major U.S. cities: "The Angels' Stadium is only 30 minutes by the Santa Ana Freeway from downtown Los Angeles and is only 90 minutes from downtown San Diego. It is only 45 minutes from Santa Monica and West Los Angeles via the new San Diego–Garden Grove Freeway." Third, the highway infrastructure brought millions of automobiles in close proximity: "The Angels' Stadium lies next to the 100-acre freeway interchange, the largest freeway interchange in the Nation's largest populated state! More than one million people live within a nine-mile radius of this stadium at the present time." Finally, he offered his enthusiastic belief that local population figures would "jump astronomically before 1967!"[44] In pushing the Angels Stadium as a venue, Schuller anticipated the overflow of new converts from the crusade would stream directly into his church.

Since he had arrived in time to be in on the ground floor of the Southern California religious innovations, Schuller stood as a stark anomaly among the rest of his mainline Protestant brethren who oversaw a precipitous decline in numbers and status. The migration of Americans to Sun Belt locations such as Orange County forced denominations to take notice. In a 1985 *Church Herald* article, Chester Droog, field secretary for the RCA's Particular Synod of the West,[45] reported that he had witnessed this growth firsthand and explained that RCA congregations established in the Southwest had to foster identities to draw new members in a way that looked unfamiliar to those who hailed from the Great Lakes and the Northeast. Because the RCA had very little recognition in the area, building a new constituency would necessitate strategic changes of familiar forms.

Droog implied that the future of the denomination rested on the ability to adopt at least some fresh strategies that fit the new residents of the Sun Belt—in other words, to embrace protocols exemplified in Schuller's growing congregation. For Droog, the GGCC methodology represented the prevailing model, and he even mentioned Schuller by name. Obviously trying to overcome the suspicion and resistance that had already been generated within the RCA by Schuller's unconventional methods, Droog insisted that "community" churches, the use of celebrities, and drive-in worship represented RCA congregations "ever reforming" in their effort "to reach people unfamiliar with the Reformed Church." He wrote that "the rise of evangelical 'possibility thinking' ... had great impact on the preaching in all the RCA congregations"—evidence that Schuller's innovations won his approval and earned his admiration. Droog also reported that "the tremendous growth in population of the Mexican and Asian people has begun to influence the RCA in the Southwest." Although Droog astutely observed the shifting demographics of the region, he also interestingly offered only cursory details regarding the dynamics of this new racial and ethnic diversity. Further, he provided no indications as to whether Schuller's strategies included viable techniques to transcend racial and ethnic differences, an unfortunate omission that came to matter for the future viability of the Garden Grove church.[46]

The success of expanding the constituency of the RCA using Schuller's ecclesiological approach in places like Orange County led at least some prominent RCA leaders to believe that the future of Christian growth in the United States lay in the combination of two things: a focus on areas of population growth, and adoption of new congregational practices that would attract new members. Droog continued to champion Schuller's template in an interview that appeared in the *Church Herald* in 1987. Though never directly mentioned, the success of Schuller's strategies for church growth were, once again, his subject.[47] Droog emphasized the priority of focusing on constituency, including contextual factors such as density of population, growth in population, and a clear, targeted homogeneous group within the larger population. Droog also elaborated on the necessity of a certain type of pastoral charisma to attract a constituency: "For example, church planters must be positive, optimistic, loving people. They must be people with a dream. They must have an incredible desire to succeed, to be risk takers, willing to work, and be motivators of people."[48] In other words, they needed to reflect the Possibility Thinking of Robert H. Schuller. In such a description, Droog clearly identified pastors who would be able to replicate the charismatic force of Schuller's personality. The efficacy of this twin focus on attracting the right constituency with the right charisma implied that the capital funds needed to build such a ministry would naturally result—a financially beneficial arrangement to fuel the further growth of the denomination.

Fitting the Pastor to the People

In explaining why his church plant succeeded, Schuller consistently rejected justifications from those who emphasized the serendipity of his circumstance; instead, he asserted a strategic and visionary self-image. He portrayed his success as calculated, the result of planning and forethought. This persona of intentionality and strategy accentuated evermore when Schuller insisted that his ideas could be repeated everywhere. Abounding confidence in his methods was on display at the very beginning of his West Coast ministry. Just two years after establishing GGCC, Schuller developed plans to create a chain of drive-in churches throughout California. In February 1957 he wrote the owners of the Pacific Drive-In Theatres, Inc., about the possibility of creating a drive-in congregation at their Los Altos location.[49] Schuller insisted that any community of over 50,000 citizens could support a hybrid church. Because of his confidence in the technique, he lobbied the RCA to locate a drive-in church on a "major freeway, tollway, or expressway" in every U.S. city that exceeded a population of 200,000.[50]

Although Schuller believed his successes could be repeated, he always underestimated the unique regional circumstances that shaped his persona in drawing in his constituency. Others noticed, however. An associate pastor at the church described the success of the Garden Grove ministry as being owed to that fortuitous intersection of timing and context: "I just think it's being in the right spot at the right time, and the climate is right." The same minister offered caution about balancing ingenuity with the ability to accommodate to local culture, openly wondering about how much Schuller actually "created." For him, Schuller "saw opportunities and he walked through it."

Ultimately, the fellow minister remarked that Schuller "got a whole new type of individual in Orange County, totally different than Los Angeles County." An official from the RCA denominational office indicated that Schuller's message of self-esteem and Possibility Thinking had a particular resonance for the new arrivals: "There was a kind of a hunger for a religious message of hope and success that wasn't weighed down by a lot of the baggage of guilt and judgment and people wanted to hear a more positive message." In response to the contingencies of the region, Schuller crafted a persona fitted to his local target. The locale proved particularly receptive to Schuller's theology since, according to the same denominational official, "it was a real expression of Southern California culture." Even in Schuller's own region, the early ministry involved such a high level of Orange County–specific niche attraction that it may not have even worked a mere twenty-minute drive north in Los Angeles.

Considerations of local context, though, never dissuaded Schuller from asserting that his own strategic concerns—the unique gift of his charismatic persona—determined the effectiveness of his leadership. Again in 1969, Schuller published an article in which he described the drive-in church as an outreach technique suited to the times, not to a particular geographic context. Always trying to position GGCC's success, Schuller introduced his congregation as the oldest drive-in church in the RCA. He then noted that the ability to adapt to environmental constraints proved pivotal for his ministry: "When we could find no empty hall, no available building to rent, we selected a drive-in theatre in Southern California as a place to begin holding preaching services with the objective of collecting some unchurched people into a Christian fellowship."[51] Schuller also noted that his ability to accommodate the desires of the car-centric Orange County population had afforded him the ability to expand in a new, innovative direction with a walk-in–drive-in hybrid church: "Now, with almost fifteen years of ministry behind us, we conduct services of worship in the sanctuary which is the first of its kind in the world." He went on to explain the ingenuity of the building format that allowed for an integration of historic Christian sanctuary expectations with state-of-the-art technology and mechanization: "It is designed as a traditional sanctuary with pews arranged in the ancient architectural format facing the pulpit and communion table area. The distinction of the church, however, is that huge sections of the wall on one side slide open enabling the minister in the pulpit to look out and communicate with his eye as well as his voice to cars parked in a landscaped, terraced area where people sit in the privacy of their automobiles to join in the spirit of worship with those who sit in the pews in the sanctuary."[52] Taking credit for a pioneering worship methodology, Schuller described his operation as representative of a "modern technique" that had proven wildly successful and, perhaps more importantly, *replicable*: "The drive-in church concept has spread until today there are more than ten such churches in operation in the state of California and Florida within the bounds of the Reformed Church in America."[53]

Schuller's explanations for the use of these techniques always served to reaffirm his own charisma as a farsighted, ingenious leader. He explained that the drive-in format allowed the unchurched to remain comfortable as spectators, seated in a grandstand of sorts, watching as participants performed their "religious exercises." Thus, the drive-in church functioned as a point of first contact in a dynamic relationship that could eventually draw the audience into being committed members of the congregation. Schuller offered evidence of the effectiveness of the model by reporting that GGCC had added 798 members in 1968 alone. Framing drive-in church (which, again, had been a last resort) as a progressive modernization, Schuller offered a rationale for its success, explaining that automobile worship appealed to traveling tourists who failed to pack formal attire, uniformed employees (nurses, police officers) who might need to report to work shortly after worship services, or those who had suffered a "clothing accident" and felt too embarrassed to be seen outside of their vehicle. In addition, "businessmen who networked all week as well as celebrities who crave some anonymity would both be attracted to the drive-in service." Schuller asserted that drive-in churches worked because they met "people on their level." The minister presented himself as an effective evangelist able to connect with his audience: "Too often the church puts itself on a higher pedestal and demands that the people rise to the artificial standards that have been conjured up in the minds of overly dignified churchmen."[54]

Schuller also claimed that the drive-in church presented a less-daunting scenario for the "religiously uncommitted, but curious person" to "window-shop without the danger of making a commitment."[55] With that in mind, the drive-in proved a contrast for the seemingly hostile appearance of the traditional church: "To the non-churched person the sanctuary built of bricks and stones with windows that hide the interior from the gaze of those from the sidewalk, is uninviting, forbidding, though often curiosity-stimulating." In addition, the drive-in church shared none of the burdens that people tended to associate with more traditional churches where "the curious hesitate to enter for fear that someone might put a strong hand on their shoulder, reach for their pocketbook, or ask them to get down on their knees and pray."[56]

With similar arguments, Schuller was among the earliest ministry leaders to advocate for the notion of an "easy access" church (Bill Hybels, founder of Willow Creek Community Church, and other church leaders would use "seeker sensitive"[57]) that prioritizes removing any physical, emotional, or attitudinal obstacles that might keep people from committing to a church. An "easy access" church, then, functions similar to a movie theater crowd: both regularly bring strangers into ad hoc congregations. And what better locale? The Los Angeles region still has one of the highest movie-going populations in the world. Moreover, the conglomeration of nearby amusement parks (Disneyland, Knott's Berry Farm, and a host of subsidiary tourist attractions) draw thousands daily. Disneyland is king of all these industries, setting the standard for capturing attention, crowd control, and keeping attractions continually fresh. The saturated experience of Disney affected many businesses in the region and eventually the rest of the world. Innovative ministries such as Schuller's integrated these paradigms and associated practices earlier than most. At all points, the focus on the growth of the congregation assumed a visionary, broad-based appeal to alternative streams of constituents, one that can be rationally attained by inspired pastors in any setting. Schuller sought an intentional methodology that accommodated the modern and mobile churchgoer that would, in turn, unlock for pastors the mystery of how to attract a greater flow of new members into their churches.

Capital Projects Based on Visionary Foresight

As successful as the drive-in had been, proper ministers still needed proper traditional buildings, and Schuller seemed acutely aware of the pressure toward standard indicators of legitimacy. To become an established "institution" in Orange County, GGCC had to secure a long-term physical presence, as explained by Deyan Sudjic: "The Orange Drive-in was all very well as a base for the early days of the movement, but the area was rapidly turning into a new type of city rather than a suburb, and Schuller wanted to build a church with the appropriate civic presence to match his maturing audience."[58] The inventiveness of the drive-in worked to generate interest and initial enthusiasm, but respectability and durability demanded a more traditional, enduring site. With that in mind, GGCC built a 250-seat "chapel" about three and a half miles west of the drive-in theater.[59]

But such a small and traditional building did not meet the ambition of the ministry. After a tiring five years of multiple services, back and forth, relaying the minister between the traditional church and the drive-in (congregants recalled robes flowing in the wind outside car windows as choir members raced between the two sites), Schuller raised funds to consolidate the ministry and build his "hybrid" church.[60] Designed by Richard Neutra, the innovative walk-in–drive-in church merged the familiarity of the drive-in experience with the advantages of a conventional church building, a process Schuller called "marrying the outside with the inside."[61]

Architectural critics noted that the new hybrid church building deliberately undermined typical church design practices. The sanctuary, in particular, functioned as an extension of the parking lot. Schuller would speak from a raised platform next to sliding glass doors, which would open with a push of a button, allowing the minister to step outside and speak directly to the radiating rows of parked cars gathered for the service. Neutra's GGCC design accommodated the automobile so as to crystallize the significance of the car within the suburban milieu. It was Schuller's desire to "monumentalize" the drive-in feature of his first California church that led the minister to seek an architect of Neutra's stature.[62] Examining proposed renderings for the church, a critic noted, "Rather than spatially privileged or visually memorable in the plan, the nave is simply an extra tier of parking slots rotating around the altar. Similarly, instead of serving as the focal point, the pulpit is a fulcrum negotiating the link between the congregation seated in the traditional pews and the congregation seated in the 'pews from Detroit.'"[63] As such, Neutra and Schuller reconciled a new form of ecclesiastical structure and hierarchy that mapped onto the car-centric culture of his constituents.

The "integrated"[64] form of GGCC had initially been located in "the sticks," but new development accelerated, and the church found itself in an "increasingly urbanized and demographically diverse" sort of downtown as the Orange County "elite and ephemeral suburbs" surrounded its campus.[65] By the mid-1960s, Schuller commissioned Neutra again, this time to design the Tower of Hope for the campus. The tower became a regional beacon, easily spied from the freeways. In fact, the *Orange County Register* pronounced the tower "as familiar a landmark to county residents as Disneyland's Matterhorn."[66] Indeed, Schuller never shied from the allusions to the amusement park down the street. In a 1996 interview, the minister noted that the Crystal Cathedral "became almost like a spiritual and religious dimension of a Disney culture. Positive. Enthusiastic. Beautiful. Fun."[67] In fact, a friend of Schuller's reported that the ministry and the amusement park saw enough synergy in each other that they once considered a tram or monorail to offer a direct link between the two venues.

Though obviously a product of necessity more than ingenuity, Schuller's drive-in church functioned as a symbol of a rapidly suburbanizing country in which restaurants, shopping centers, and even bowling alleys designed themselves to be ever more accessible to the family car. With their service and tourism orientation, the suburbs of Orange County maintained the decentralized features of the postindustrial economy. Rather than simply functioning as bedroom communities for Los Angeles or San Diego, these young municipalities operated as multimodal communities that included not just the home but also work, school, play, shopping, and, of course, worship.[68] Highways functioned as the cartilage holding it all together. And Schuller's hybrid church emerged as the religious emblem of the region. Later, with its ninety-foot doors opening every Sunday to include in-car worshippers, the Crystal Cathedral would continue to serve as a testimony to the place of the automobile within the ministry. One urban planning critic described the Crystal Cathedral's glimmering star-shaped exterior as a "logo of God on the run," the edifice "fronted by parking, its spiritual glitz a hymn to the asphalt Almighty."[69]

The significance of Schuller's mandate for attention-getting buildings and plentiful space for attenders' automobiles should not be underestimated, since attracting members and anticipating the need to accommodate more cars required building for that need ahead of time. As Schuller phrased it, "Successful retailing . . . demands far more than *ample* parking. Successful retailing demands SURPLUS parking! With the development of shopping centers and their acres of *surplus* parking, modern Americans became used to this convenience." Schuller advised churches to avoid being sited in the "heart of the community." Instead, they should seek locations on arterial highways. His notions often assumed a suburban locale filled with car-owning drivers, and his strategy was seen as simply complying with the expectations of American motorists: "As they have become spoiled by easy parking afforded by the shopping centers, they have become more and more disenchanted, impatient, and irritated by the parking congestion they find elsewhere, including that in their own church settings."[70] Schuller's push for more parking also primed the pump of the need for funds needed to accomplish these projects.

Although Schuller bought the land for his grand structures *before* he knew the highways and vast developments would be sited in close proximity, he frequently received credit for his apparent foresight. For example, after the opening of the Crystal Cathedral in 1980, one architectural critic described the location as integral to the success of the church: "The view of the cathedral from the freeway is a critical part of Schuller's strategy for attracting the congregations that are needed to fill the steadily increasing number of seats and parking places."[71] Schuller also received recognition for functioning as a religious complement to the wonder of Disneyland. As drivers navigated the highway through Orange County, just past the Angel Stadium, they glimpsed the Crystal Cathedral campus with its Philip Johnson–designed bell tower: "Slightly detached from the main building, Johnson's chrome-plated paraphrase of a campanile marks out the presence of the complex on the Orange County flatlands, just like the turrets of Disneyland a mile away." The chrome sheen of the bell tower captured the eye, but the ringing never really called any congregants to worship: "There is no danger of actually hearing the bells from the freeway, but Schuller wanted the tower anyway." In a nod to Schuller's integration of the ancient with the innovative, the bell tower acknowledged the traditional notion of a parish being signaled by the clamor of ringing while actually silently capturing the attention of distracted drivers. In essence, the bell tower functioned as "both a signpost and a billboard" for automobile-bound commuters and tourists.[72] In this critic's view, "the diffuse scale of Los Angeles makes the bell tower an essential response to its context, providing an updated version of a very traditional element on the urban skyline."[73]

Being given credit for his supposed prescience in the past provided Schuller a powerful charismatic claim that he was drawing on *a distinctive power of foresight* in calling for funding future projects. Therefore, the imperative imposed on his congregation to meet future (and as yet nonexistent) needs did not just prepare a congregation for attendance growth, but communicating visions of further expansion based on his charismatic expertise as a visionary served as a routinized strategy for stimulating new streams of capital.

Ruptures in the Constituency Pipeline

Schuller eventually encountered unexpected social changes, especially in the nature of the people later moving into Orange County and their religious orientations. Source countries for immigration to the area had already begun changing in the 1970s. In the immediate area surrounding the church campus, the Latin American and Asian population soared with an influx of migrants and refugees.[74] The change only accelerated in the following years: between 2000 and

2009, the white percentage of the population dropped nine points—which included a loss of majority status in the county.[75] Schuller's core constituency had diminished and weakened.

By 2014, Orange County included a population of almost one million foreign-born residents, and almost all came from either Latin America (46.6 percent) or Asia (44.4 percent). With that level of immigration, Latinos and Asian Americans accounted for 33.8 percent and 18.3 percent of the county's total population, respectively.[76] That momentum would continue. One journalist noted, "Garden Grove, where Schuller once preached to young white homeowners in their cars, is now inhabited almost entirely by immigrants and their descendants. The adjacent city of Westminster is home to the world's largest population of Vietnamese outside of Vietnam." And down the road in Santa Ana, reports estimated that over 80 percent of the families spoke a language other than English in the home (primarily Spanish).[77] By 2016, Orange County had become "home to the country's third-largest concentration of Asian Americans, thanks to a growth rate of 41 percent between 2000 and 2009."[78]

Schuller had diplomatically expressed in a 1988 year-end report that "the ministry continues to face the challenge of a changing community in Southern California."[79] More specifically, as the region continued to transition, Schuller described the area as becoming more *urban*. Garden Grove and greater Orange County also experienced a shifting mode of urbanism as business, office, and retail centers displaced residential areas. Schuller wrote, "The church now finds itself in the heart of an urban setting with families moving to outlying regions of this and other counties where housing can be acquired at a lower cost." The availability of relocated, already churched, white, young, and upwardly mobile families, the base upon which the church had grown from its beginnings, was dissipating.

Among the factors leading to the abrupt collapse of the Crystal Cathedral, then, included the church finding itself in a shifting urban ecology as its richest nutrients of white, conservative, and rising-income families moved farther from the church grounds. How would the ministry respond? Adapt to become more attractive to its new neighborhoods? Narrow its identity to establish more niche loyalty from farther-flung families?[80] Schuller's statements on the changing social environment, however, evinced no plan forward and no strategy to adapt. Though he would initiate a side project Hispanic ministry (see chapter 8), the farsighted visionary never planned to accommodate—or fully integrate—such a drastic change in his assumed constituency.

Later in the same report, Schuller remarked on the "concern" related to the fluid dynamics of Orange County. In coded language, the minister discussed the loss of a population that possessed a "Christian memory." Schuller recognized that his ministry had risen on the tide of white Midwestern migrants who brought with them at least the residue of their religiously imbued communities back home. Now, though, he expressed doubt about how his message would translate for a population who might not resonate with those reliable cultural touchstones:

> The Crystal Cathedral is concerned about how it can effectively penetrate a community that is drastically changing from the kind of people who tradition-ally bring with them a Christian memory to the kind of people who move into the community *with no concept of Christian memory whatsoever.* This congrega-tion achieved explosive growth during its first 35 years and almost all persons moving into the exploding suburbia came from the Midwest, or mainstream America, with some memory of Sunday School experiences in their minds. Such is not the case today.[81]

Schuller understood that his successes emerged out of a wave of white migrants with Christian orientations settling into new communities amid a rapidly grow-ing economy.

With the influx of newer immigration to the area, the Vietnamese- and Spanish-speaking populations began to rise—and, of course, that translated into corresponding increases in Catholicism, Buddhism, storefront Pentecostalism, and Islam.[82] Schuller's own concerns indicated that true missionary outreach to these new, nonwhite, and, in some cases, non-Christian populations exceeded his ministry's core capacity.[83] For Schuller, the "unchurched" were, in reality, sim-ply white Protestant Christians with no *current* church membership.

Constituents Respond to Charisma and Provide Capital

Schuller's ambition to start a church in Orange County in 1955 centered on gath-ering a group of people to form a congregation. Then, with his unexpected suc-cess at growing a sizable attendance at an unconventional site with a revised liturgy and supplementary ministry programs, Schuller reframed his *inadvertent improvisations* into *intentional innovations.* Though Schuller demonstrated con-sistent confidence in codifying his ideas for church growth and sharing them with other church leaders, his paradigm for the ministry included an acute—and tenuous—dependence on a historically distinctive context of suburban growth and the particularity of his Midwestern and Southern, white, upwardly mobile, and car-enabled constituency. As one RCA denominational leader noted, "Whatever else you want to say about Bob's ministry, it was highly contextual-ized to the culture.... He was a genius in figuring out how to understand a par-ticular culture and then relate religious life within it." But beneath the veneer of a settled social group, seismic demographic changes eroded his ministry base.

Throughout his later history, Schuller would base further expansions of the church on the growth dynamics that had worked seemingly continuously since 1955, a straight-line trend that had been reliably sustained for a long time. Schul-ler began a church in a low-density, moderately populated suburban area. When he arrived, Orange County had just over 200,000 residents. Over the course of his fifty-five-year ministry, the population grew to three million—making it the sixth most populous county in the nation.[84] But as the white middle class climbed the socioeconomic ladder in Orange County, their discretionary income catalyzed an economy that drew in a changing racial population: "Just as Orange County pioneered a new form of low-rise urbanism, it was also among the first places to experience the demographic consequences." In other words, the same opportunities began to draw a more diverse population. One journalist noted that in "all those planned communities" in Southern California, "their well-paid inhabitants like to eat out, their houses needed cleaning, and their lawns needed trimming." These new service economy jobs drew a new round of migrants to the area: "Beginning in the 1970s, migrants, mostly from Mexico, Central and South America, Southeast Asia, and Korea, began arriving to cook, clean, and mow."[85] With the influx of migrants to fill these jobs, formerly all-white neighborhoods began to grow more racially diverse. Soon, Orange County became "one of the most ethnically, politically, and economically diverse places on the planet."[86]

Even when Schuller realized in the late 1980s that demographic changes posed a challenge to the ministry, his methods lacked flexibility in reaching these different populations. His charisma did not appeal equally to all migrants to the area. Even if he could attract these new migrants, the financial strain increasingly characterized by Orange County families meant that their incomes likely would be too limited to subsidize the ministry. In time, the financial commitments made to serve *a future tithing membership* failed to materialize and, ultimately, Schuller's inability to anticipate this failing contributed to the bankruptcy of the ministry.

By the early twenty-first century, the stereotype of Orange County as a monolith of white upper-middle-class families in suburban, single-family detached houses with rising incomes no longer held up to scrutiny. The people with whom Schuller had established so much resonance no longer dominated the population. Not only did the flow of white Southern and Midwestern migrants slow, but their income stalled. Almost one-fifth of the population never graduated from high school. In recent years, 20 percent of the county has not had health insurance. One-third of the county earns less than $50,000 annually.[87] Along with these demographic shifts, the county also saw political modifications. Orange County had earned a reputation as a bastion of white conservatism—voting Republican in every U.S. presidential election since 1936, producing Richard Nixon, and serving as the "cradle of Ronald Reagan's conservatism."[88] Yet the 2016 presidential election demonstrated a loosening grip of conservative politics on the region as Hillary Clinton beat Donald Trump by five percentage points. Two years later, the 2018 congressional election underlined the trend as Democrats captured four Republican-held seats, toppling a "fortress of conservative Republicanism."[89] The momentum of Orange County jumping from red to blue had been building for decades. The *New York Times* described it as a "vast cultural and political upheaval" forty years in the making.[90] In 1990, 52 percent of the county identified as Republican, while 32 percent identified as Democrat. By 2012, the percentage of registered Republicans had fallen to 41 percent. By the 2016 election, only 38 percent of the county's 1.5 million registered voters identified as Republican, while the percentage of Democrats remained fairly steady at 34.[91]

The waning of the core constituency would prove taxing for Schuller's ministry. In his ethnography of Saddleback Community Church, another Orange County ministry, geographer Justin Wilford described how suburban megachurches necessarily engaged in geographic strategies in order to maintain numbers and relevance.[92] Suburban evangelical megachurches, like GGCC and its later incarnation, the Crystal Cathedral, engage in a push-pull relationship with their social and spatial environment. Failure to reckon with geography and demography leads to a fragile congregational life. Without the critical element of an environment that replenishes thick streams of freshly resonant constituency, large congregations must intentionally shrink or inevitably face a crisis of reduced resources for maintaining even the most basic routines of their ministries. However, if the problem of capital can be solved by renting the facilities or drawing on endowments, even a very small congregation can maintain ownership of a large church building for a very long time. The polished veneer of megachurches, though, tends to mask the vulnerability to changes in the urban ecology and demography—until it is too late and the decline has already begun.

Schuller and mentor Norman Vincent Peale participate in groundbreaking ceremonies at the Tower of Hope. Photo courtesy of the Joint Archives of Holland.

4

The Possibility Thinker

What we need is a theology of salvation
that begins and ends with a recognition
of every person's hunger for glory.
—Robert H. Schuller

As a new minister at Ivanhoe Reformed Church in Riverdale, Illinois, Schuller, like other ambitious pastors, graduated from the book-learning of his seminary education to study the techniques of the pastors he most admired. A file of his personal papers containing tracts and radio broadcast sermon transcripts from the early 1950s offers an indication of the influences that informed the direction of his ministry for the next half-century:

1 A 1952 broadcast from the *Temple Time* radio show of the Reformed Church in America by Reverend Harry Bast: "How to Find Inner Security."
2 An undated sermon from G. Ernest Thomas: "Pathways to Power," from The Good Tidings Tract-of-the-Month Club out of Nashville.
3 A 1956 sermon from Norman Vincent Peale: "How to Adjust to People."
4 A 1954 broadcast from *Temple Time* by Bast: "Formulas for Stress and Strain."
5 A 1954 sermon from Peale: "Getting a Lift When You Are Depressed."
6 A 1951 broadcast from *Temple Time* by Reverend Harland Steele: "The Problem of Gambling."
7 A 1954 sermon by Peale: "Things Go Better When You Pray."

8 An undated broadcast from *The Back to God Hour* radio show of the Christian Reformed Church by Reverend Peter Eldersveld: "Don't Worry."

9 A 1950 broadcast from *The Back to God Hour* by Eldersveld: "Don't Be a Quitter."[1]

The titles foreshadow Schuller's eventual emphasis on a therapeutic approach to Christianity. Of all these ministers, though, Schuller's strongest affinity resided with the exciting pastor of Manhattan's Marble Collegiate Church, Norman Vincent Peale.

Peale was, without a doubt, the exemplar for Schuller's own preaching. Although Schuller often claimed his Reformed roots, the manner of his preaching and the substance of his messages evinced Peale far more than John Calvin. Schuller's files reveal he continued doing homework in the crafting of messages as a means to cultivate resonance with the culture of the day. Before his first pastorate, there is no evidence of either the "Possibility Thinking" or the "Theology of Self-Esteem" that became his distinctive philosophies. Instead, these indicated an abrupt shift in his thinking, the product of his puzzling through how to be successful at what he understood to be his vocation: preaching to the "unchurched" and initiating the capital-intensive projects he would utilize as lures to attract them.

What accounts for Schuller's unceasing optimism in the face of financial pressures that emerged at different points of his ministry career? The credit he gave Peale in comparison with the mostly dutiful recognition of his denomination is instructive. Whereas his seminary professors only suggested dry "facts," "theories," and "arguments," Peale offered inspirational and motivational "therapy." Only after reading Peale did the young minister converge his "clerical persona" with his "dramatic persona."[2] Schuller clearly valued the singular charismatic power emanating from Peale far more highly than his bureaucratic affiliation with the Reformed Church in America (RCA). The emphasis on the power of individual charisma would have significant consequences for the structure of the ministry. What became Possibility Thinking undergirded the confidence with which he promoted new projects in his church and consequently shaped the advice given to pastors on how to inspire their own fund-raising, later codified through the Robert H. Schuller Institute for Successful Church Leadership. Through Possibility Thinking, Schuller entrusted the force of his singular charisma to attract constituents while motivating them to provide the capital required for attracting future ones.

Norman Vincent Peale

The beginnings of Schuller's theological[3] sensibilities can be found in a 1955 article in the *Church Herald* where he lamented the brokenness of 1950s America, arguing for a biblically based diagnosis: "The sickness of the world is the disease of sinful hearts in selfish men." He elaborated: "Yes, sin is the sickness of the world. And sin is self-centeredness." Schuller offered a prescription that sounded evangelical in its demand for conversion: "The cure calls for a new heart. The root of evil must be transformed, remade, recreated, reborn." Interestingly, the claim that "the heart of a man must be filled with the spirit of Christ rather than the spirit of self" strikes a note that seems antithetical to the Theology of Self-Esteem that Schuller would craft years later. In a rich irony from a person who would write numerous psychology-tinged books, Schuller rebuked psychologists and psychiatrists who offered "too many false prescriptions" in "volumes of cheap, amateur psychological books."[4]

Schuller's theology evolved, then, while he worked in this first pastorate, from his attraction to Peale's Positive Thinking theology. As the minister of the RCA's high-profile Marble Collegiate Church in Manhattan, Peale cast a large shadow on American Christianity. Peale himself had Methodist roots but joined the RCA upon his call to the prestigious church. His dossier included a syndicated television program (*What's Your Trouble?*), a large audience radio show (*The Art of Living*), and a well-circulated magazine (*Guideposts*). His published sermons garnered 150,000 readers at one point, and his syndicated newspaper column drew an audience of ten million. By the early 1950s, Peale's writing manifested evidence of New Thought—a uniquely American phenomenon that advocated the ability of the mind to change personal circumstances.[5]

In 1952, Peale published his most widely known book, *The Power of Positive Thinking*, a synthesis of Christian theology and psychology wherein he argued that spiritual energy could be concentrated on the "attainment of health, self-esteem, or business acumen."[6] With little to no empirical evidence, Peale posited broad claims such as "Fill your mind with fresh, creative thoughts of faith, love, and goodness. By this process you can actually remake your life."[7] *The Power of Positive Thinking* became a blockbuster, selling over 15 million copies by the late 1980s.

Despite numerous religious and secular critics, Peale's immense popularity reveals the resonance of this message throughout an aspirational post–World War II society. He was the RCA's most prominent pastor, though he hardly articulated a Reformed theology. Instead, in his "religio-psychiatry," Peale urged audiences to see Christianity not as a creed to be recited but as a "power to be tapped."[8] With vivid prose that was accessible, direct, and uncomplicated, Peale's "Christian positive psychology transformed the nation's religious landscape."[9] Many potential acolytes borrowed heavily from Peale, some without even knowing it. For instance, historian John Wigger contended that televangelist "[Jim] Bakker knew next to nothing about New Thought, but he nevertheless adopted much of Peale's language."[10] Others within the world of televangelism also demonstrated trace influences of Peale.[11]

Schuller consciously tapped into Peale's popularity over the years and promoted his association with the Manhattan minister as a boost to his own status. He was especially proud of Peale's first letter, a personal endorsement of Schuller's church planting venture, dated January 26, 1955. Peale's words forever offered Schuller a point of indisputable pride and legitimacy:

> I am glad to learn that you have accepted a call from the Classis of Southern California to serve as a Classical Missionary in Garden Grove with the objective of starting a church to serve that growing community.
>
> Let me congratulate you on the opportunity which that territory provides. I am sure the people there will be truly appreciative of your presence and service.
>
> The Reformed Church is not as large as many other denominations, but down through the centuries of our existence in America, it has been a stable, reliable, and trustworthy denomination. You can be proud of your lineage in the faith. Your members will rejoice in their opportunities of service.
>
> May God bless you, and the people associated with you, and great success in the work of Christ's Kingdom.[12]

Schuller frequently shared Peale's warm regards, for example, by printing it numerous times over the years in anniversary publications.

Capitalizing on Peale's gracious letter in 1955, Schuller immediately extended an invitation for the Manhattan minister to offer the sermon at the dedication service scheduled in 1957 for the new chancel at Garden Grove Community Church (GGCC)—trumpeted as constructed from redwood and the first of its kind "at an American Drive-in Church." Peale could expect an audience of thousands in "the heart of Orange County . . . just two miles below Disneyland." Schuller closed by noting that no dedication plans would be made until the church heard from Peale.[13] To the minister's delight, Peale accepted. At one point, however, Peale attempted to back out of his commitment. While Schuller vacationed in Alton, Iowa, his secretary received word from Peale that the visit had become tenuous. Schuller scrambled, giving orders that "published plans" should be prepared immediately, since the event had already been announced in news releases. He then pressed Peale, indicating that Classis California officials had already committed themselves to be present for his sermon and closing the letter by requesting that Peale send along the title of his message.[14] Peale relented and kept the appointment to preach at the dedication.

Peale's appearance on that dedication Sunday at GGCC in June 1957 was always considered by Schuller to be a watershed moment for the fledgling congregation, and it took on a mythical quality in the ministry's creation story. Newspaper accounts at the time estimated that Peale's visit exceeded the highest expectations, drawing 8,000 attenders and 2,000 cars. Schuller sent Peale a letter afterward in which he gushed with gratitude: "I am sure that you have never, in your life, done more collective good in one hour, than you did when you spoke to our Drive-in audience this past Sunday. Your presence and your dynamic message made a spiritual splash which is extending its rippling influence through our County today." Schuller closed by declaring that if the GGCC ever became a "powerful preaching station in Southern California," it would be "largely due to the dignity" brought by Peale on that Sunday.[15]

The young pastor took note of Peale's dynamic appeal on the national stage, and for many years Schuller claimed Peale as a mentor. Peale, for his part, considered Schuller to be a marvelous exemplar of his own principles of Positive Thinking. His 1967 book, *Enthusiasm Makes the Difference*, includes a brief profile of Schuller, proudly referenced as a member of his own RCA denomination ("the oldest denomination in the United States"), testifying that his "great church" was built from nothing but "enthusiasm." In recounting the origins of the congregation, Peale wrote, "Dr. Schuller was as long on enthusiasm as he was short on money."[16] He recalls Schuller sharing his expectations for the church: "I knew then it would be in fact, for it already existed in his mind, and he had the energy, ingenuity, and the faith to bring it to pass."[17] As much as Schuller benefited from Peale's fame, Peale in turn gained from Schuller's growing notoriety. Peale took pride in playing a part in the astounding growth of the church and seeing its ongoing expansion: "I helped turn the earth for the 'Tower of Hope.'" He added that as he was looking on "the glorious church and its lovely gardens, I realized once again the tremendous fact that enthusiasm is indeed the powerful motivation to make things happen."[18] Schuller validated Peale's method for success, specifically his conviction that applying a mindful, positive zeal to any aspiration would surely make it a reality.

As the two ministers developed rapport, Schuller leveraged his connection to Peale to secure funding to advance the ministry. For example, Schuller prevailed upon Peale in 1968 to write a letter to a developer explaining the necessity of the GGCC expansion. Schuller even penned a "suggested letter from Norman Vincent Peale to Edgar Kaiser" that he invited Peale "to reject" or to borrow "in its entirety." The letter strongly intimated that Peale had an official position at GGCC: "That 10-acre parcel is contiguous to a great church that I have been building on the west coast, with the help of Robert Schuller who is my hand-picked pastor. I have been working hard with Rev. Schuller to develop what I believe is going to be the greatest church on the Pacific Coast."[19] The Southern California minister clearly knew that Peale had the social influence to ensure that such a capital-intensive project would be completed.

Schuller credited Peale far more than his denomination as the impetus for success. In early 1970, he suggested an iteration of the leadership institute built around Peale. After all, Schuller argued, no pastor in the world had a better grasp than Peale regarding the "kind of preaching that turns people on."[20] Schuller also routinely credited Peale's affirmations with nurturing GGCC's growth; in fact, he wrote to Peale in 1970 that "your strong endorsement has constantly brought people to our ministry and more than any other single factor is responsible for our success."[21] He even occasionally described GGCC as a West Coast affiliate of Peale's Marble Collegiate Church.

Distance from His Denomination

A lifelong member of the RCA and educated at an affiliated college and seminary, Schuller saw himself within the mainline and thoroughly of the Calvinist Reformed persuasion. A denominational official remarked that despite the critiques and tension, "Dr. Schuller always prided and praised his relationship to the RCA." During their first meeting in Schuller's office, the official remembered having lunch in the Tower of Hope where the minister "had on his wall the framed baptismal gown that he was baptized in in Iowa, and it was the first thing he pointed out to me, and how proud he was of being from the Reformed Church."

Schuller also knew, though, that the denomination retained a fairly narrow—and ethnically tinged—identity that likely had little resonance with his Southern California population. Though historic, the RCA remained largely unknown in much of the country, and few apprehended its mainline Protestant identity and affiliation. Originally incorporated as the Reformed Protestant Dutch Church, the denomination maintained a highly Dutch membership.[22] The ambiguity regarding the RCA was accentuated by the fact that the small denomination's highest profile church (Marble Collegiate) and its pastor (Peale) straddled multiple religious identities. Schuller also pitched his ministry as decidedly nontraditional: "We're a mission station. We have to use the same type of mission station principles used to reach the unchurched people as we do in India or China."[23] Because the pastor encountered migrants with disparate denominational backgrounds, a focus on RCA identity would only serve to alienate the vast majority who had no familiarity with the ethnically Dutch denomination. With that in mind, Schuller decided his congregation would be named Garden Grove *Community* Church, not Garden Grove *Reformed* Church.

In this religious climate, he synthesized new religious patterns, believing his theology to be nothing short of revolutionary (or at least signaling the advent of a New Reformation). Critics, though, saw a thin, lightweight Christianity that ignored the consequences of sin. Well aware of his detractors, Schuller cultivated a religious individuality while attempting to bolster his legitimacy in a longstanding tradition. His ambiguity protected against threats to his charisma, especially in avoiding association with unwanted stigmas and widespread controversies of other televangelist megachurch pastors. And his wobble between "evangelical" and "mainline" labels gave him purchase with some secular audiences willing to accept him as a minister to the masses. For instance, his book *Tough Times Never Last, but Tough People Do!* sold the vast majority of copies in general interest bookstores, not in evangelical bookstores where most Christian writers made their sales.[24]

So while Schuller maintained enough elements of traditional religious themes and practices to resemble "back home," in the burgeoning suburbs of Orange County, no one tradition dominated the religious landscape.[25] The post–World

War II cultural milieu included the advent of new religions, televangelists, secularism, and a rising sense of ecumenism—all of which weakened denominationalism and religious hierarchies.[26] Schuller existed in an American religious ecology where denominations mattered less and less. More recently, sociologists have described the rise of an Independent Network Christianity (INC). Within INC, hierarchies have been replaced by ad hoc, horizontal relationships that offer autonomy with few formalized guardrails of accountability. Because Schuller's status allowed him to operate largely independently from the RCA, he has been suggested as a "prototype" of INC.[27]

The ambiguity of this religious identity allowed for him to stand independent of the spoiled identity often found in mainstream Christianity, yet the same independence resulted in isolation. Schuller stood apart from valuable allies, other church and parachurch ministries, and even his own denomination. Throughout the decades of his ministry, Schuller wrestled with a dueling desire to make his church as openly innovative as possible while maintaining the legitimacy bestowed by membership in his mainline Protestant denomination. As one pastoral staff member related, "Schuller's going to do what Schuller wants to do, even if it meant going against the fabric of the RCA. . . . If he wanted to do it, he was going to do it." It seemed that the denomination offered Schuller legitimacy more than anything: "He didn't really care what the RCA got. He wanted to stay tied to the RCA because that gave him credibility in the actual church community."

Further complicating his religious identity, journalists and commentators frequently identified Schuller as an "evangelical." For example, a 1976 *Newsweek* article announcing plans for the Crystal Cathedral described him as "the country's most successful drive-in preacher, a minister of the *evangelical* Reformed Church in America."[28] Perhaps for the sake of simplicity or perhaps because the popularity and esteem of evangelicalism was on the rise (especially in his own Southern California), the minister embraced that label. Schuller readily identified as an evangelical, even when the GGCC and the Crystal Cathedral retained strong optics that linked the congregation to the Protestant mainline—including Schuller's robes, the preference for traditional hymns rather than choruses or praise music, and the Sunday night service maintaining the rather formal title of "Eventide." Schuller never embraced the increasing informality that marked much of evangelical worship around his own church (like the floral shirts of Saddleback Church pastor Rick Warren). Instead, Schuller's congregation maintained many of the hallmarks of mainline Protestant worship.

Schuller had little patience, though, for those who simply categorized him as indistinguishable from fellow televangelists. In 2006, shortly after Pat Robertson suggested that Israeli prime minister Ariel Sharon's recent stroke should be interpreted as punishment for "dividing God's lands,"[29] Schuller appeared on *Larry King Live* and offered a strong condemnation of Robertson: "I think it's awful. It's non-Christian. It's terrible." Larry King pressed Schuller about whether he and Robertson had disparate interpretations of the Bible. Schuller confirmed that assessment: "I do not interpret it the way [Robertson] does. If I thought he was interpreting it right, I would agree with him." When King wondered whether he derived his interpretative position from the theology of the RCA, Schuller responded affirmatively.[30]

Overall, Schuller's affiliation with mainline Protestantism shielded him somewhat from the bromides absorbed by televangelists such as Jim Bakker, Jimmy Swaggart, Oral Roberts, Pat Robertson, James Robison, and Jerry Falwell.[31] It seemed, though, that Schuller needed a ready arsenal to avoid the careless categorization of him as an indistinguishable purveyor of televangelism. For example, back in 1987, Schuller appeared in Minneapolis to deliver remarks at the funeral for U.S. Senator Hubert Humphrey. CBS television reporter Roger Mudd noted that "eyebrows were raised" in surprise. Why? Because according to Mudd, Schuller's *Hour of Power* sermons exemplified "a fundamentalist Christian-type program."[32] And what U.S. dignitary would want to be associated with fundamentalism? Schuller's executive assistant, Michael Nason, issued a press release in response, rebutting the "fundamentalist" label: "Dr. Schuller is an ordained minister in the Reformed Church of America." Taking his cues from Schuller, Nason referenced the long history of "this prestigious denomination," wondering if Mudd knew "that the Reformed Church of America is the oldest Protestant denomination with unbroken ministry on the North American continent." Moreover, the denomination boasted association with some of America's most famous families, "carried to the New World by the first Dutch settlers in 1628, and the Roosevelts, the Vanderbilts, the blue-blooded stock of the new land worshipped in what was then the Dutch Reformed Church." In addition, Nason noted that all RCA clergy "must meet the highest academic requirements."[33]

Defending Schuller's religious identity was routine—and necessary: in the late 1980s and early 1990s, an epidemic of financial malfeasance swept through the televised ministry world and implicated Jim Bakker, Kenneth Copeland, Paul Crouch, Robert Tilton, and Joyce Meyer.[34] Partly because of these scandals, Schuller shunned terms like "fundamentalist" and "televangelist" as stigmatizing and delegitimizing insults. Nevertheless, pinning down Schuller's actual religious identity would continue to prove difficult.

At least a component of Schuller's murky religious identity can be traced to the decision to start broadcasting services. Rarely has a member or church from mainline Protestantism condescended to involve themselves in the debased and fraught world of televised ministry. And Schuller did not necessarily *want* to offer clarity regarding his theological tradition. To that end, Arvella Schuller recounted that *Hour of Power* catalyzed a shift in the church's hymnody, making a concerted effort to avoid lyrics that might unnecessarily provoke certain segments within the audience. For instance, the leadership removed all sexist language so as not to offend "all the women that listen." Arvella elaborated: "We'd not use 'mankind,' or 'brotherhood,' or 'Faith of Our Fathers.'" Worship leaders also avoided "institutionalized" hymns (Arvella mentioned "Our Church's

One Foundation" and "Rise Up, O Church of God") and changed words to make the hymns more palatable to "unchurched" sensibilities.[35]

Because of the seeming elusiveness within both the worship on *Hour of Power* and his theological positions, Schuller found himself labeled as a member of a sect, an evangelical, a fundamentalist, and even a proselytizer of the New Age. Schuller often resorted to grasping for his RCA identity when convenient in an effort to distance himself from the less dignified televangelists and more marginal spiritual orientations. As the Orange County minister cloaked the denominational affiliation of his church for television audiences and book sales, he also desired to remain in good standing with the RCA.

Despite his technically Reformed identity, Schuller at times intentionally struck a decidedly evangelical tone unfamiliar in other RCA sanctuaries in the Great Lakes and Northeast. The year he arrived in Orange County, the minister published an article in the RCA's *Church Herald* where he wrote that Christ "will come to men's hearts as we make him known by witnessing in personal evangelism to our world, and we can make Him known by our life."[36] The language likely struck some in the denomination as odd. Schuller's lexicon and emphasis on conversion for "personal redemption and social change" allowed some scholars to locate Schuller within a revivalist lineage that descended from Dwight Moody.[37] Indeed, a couple of decades later a fellow RCA pastor, Herman Ridder (who, coincidentally enough, would eventually join the Crystal Cathedral pastoral staff), once remarked to a newspaper reporter that "Schuller is 'Reformed' in that he is still part of the denomination, but he's not 'Reformed' in the character of his preaching."[38]

Also, though technically a member of the Protestant mainline, Schuller's charisma, skill with popular communication, and affinity for cutting-edge technology linked him to evangelical forebears who stretched to the Great Awakening.[39] His legacy also included twenty-first-century giants within evangelicalism: both Rick Warren (Saddleback Church) and Bill Hybels (Willow Creek Church) implemented tools they had learned at Schuller's leadership institute in the 1970s. More than that, Schuller's grandson and eventual heir of the Crystal Cathedral congregation, Robert (Bobby) V. Schuller, remarked that he saw Joel Osteen, pastor of Lakewood Church in Houston as the contemporary minister who had the most in common with his grandfather. In fact, Bobby surmised that the case could be made that Osteen preached a more orthodox version of Christianity than did his grandfather.

Yet Schuller bristled at being described as an "evangelist." He disliked the term because it conjured up a huckster conning people into conversion. Schuller insisted he was better understood as a "churchman with an organized congregation within traditional mainline church life"[40]—rather ironic given his tendency to tout his own innovations. Certainly, part of Schuller's appeal rested on the fact that he defied typical "religious tradition" labels as a component of his charisma. Schuller fostered an attraction that transcended denominational differences—a belief he fostered in his public persona. In 1981 alone, his "Film Workshop" series, a distillation of the leadership institute curriculum that could be purchased and taught regionally, appeared in local congregations of the following denominations: RCA, Assemblies of God, United Methodist, Congregational, Baptist, Church of God, Presbyterian, and Free Methodist.[41]

Just Put Your Mind to It

Much of the confusion regarding Schuller's theological orientation is resolved when one recognizes that the cornerstone to Schuller's religious identity was provided by Peale—specifically when Schuller took the New York minister's "*Positive* Thinking" and rebranded it for Orange County as "*Possibility* Thinking." Observers made many efforts to discern the meaning of these terms. Many, like Dennis Voskuil, a religion professor from the RCA-affiliated Hope College, categorized Schuller as firmly in the camp of the "mentalist" or "New Thought" tradition.[42] He wrote that Peale and Schuller had been caught up in that wave of Cold War–era advocates who taught "techniques of mind cure" so successfully that it dominated the self-help market. Though framed within a "context of faith and prayer," Schuller's gospel of success traced to a foundation that advocated "mind-conditioning and attitude-shaping" as practices necessary for self-actualization. This orientation became important not just to Schuller's preaching but, even more significantly, in his approach to fund-raising.

As Voskuil suggested, Peale, of course, did not invent Positive Thinking from whole cloth. The United States has a long history with movements that championed "mind power." In the post–Civil War years, the country abounded with an ethos of self-mastery. It was during that time that Mary Baker Eddy, the founder of Christian Science, crafted a synthesis of historical Christianity and the era's confidence in the individual's mind. In her 1875 manifesto, *Science and Health*, Eddy argued that Jesus' salvation came not through his divinity but through his demonstration of right thinking. Soon thereafter, a cohort of intellectuals and ideas would coalesce under the umbrella of New Thought. Both building on and diverging from Eddy, New Thought "emerged in the 1880s as the era's most powerful vehicle of mind-power."[43]

New Thought, according to historian Kate Bowler, included three foundational aspects: First, an assumed unity between God and humanity that, in turn, meant a modification of Christian theology wherein New Thought authors framed salvation, rather than being a God-imposed act, as a process of unearthing the full potential of humanity; second, an emphasis on thought over substance, that the material world remained contingent upon the mind; third, a focus on the ability of individuals to shape and manage their reality with their thinking.[44] Early Pentecostals would borrow from New Thought notions of mind-power, which forged the enduring foundation of the "health and wealth" gospel. Bowler argued that New Thought's influence became hard to measure because it so pervaded the larger culture. Though the movement lacked institutional bulwarks, its broad appeal allowed New Thought to seep inconspicuously into popular magazines, "self-help" instruction, psychotherapy, and, of course, religion. After World War II, though, New Thought resurfaced as "positive thinking."[45] As a sign of mentalism's social saturation, historian Donald Meyer argued that much of Ronald Reagan's rhetoric carried influences of positive thinking.[46] Also, during the early 1980s, marketers from Amway (a multilevel marketing company whose founders shared Schuller's Dutch Reformed background) reported that the corporation expected them to read one "positive thinking" book per month.[47]

Schuller's embrace of Positive Thinking vibrated against his stated doctrinal commitments. According to Voskuil, connecting New Thought to conservative American evangelicalism is where we find Schuller's core theological innovation.[48] Voskuil asserted, "Peale was not Reformed. Peale was a good Arminian, a good Methodist Arminian." Peale had only bridged New Thought with the more open and progressive Protestant mainline. Peale built on nineteenth-century "religious reformers, philosophers, and self-help gurus" who came to be collectively labeled as "New Thought," but his framework dismissed "the Calvinist injunction to examine internal vice" and instead "argued that focusing on wholesome, productive ideas was the path to virtue."[49] In contrast, Schuller carried Calvinist theological training credentials. Schuller "did not think of himself as evangelical in the traditional sense." Instead, he "had a background which was Reformed and Christian Reformed in theology and that never washed out."[50] In the end, Schuller's drive "to succeed, to have a market" enticed him to follow *portions* of the Marble Collegiate minister's theology.

In perhaps one of the most striking ironies of Schuller's theology, the minister refused to accept the inherent tension within Calvinism and Possibility Thinking. How does one integrate total depravity and self-help? He accomplished this by rejecting common interpretations of Calvin. In his memoir, Schuller describes that when "poring over the teachings of John Calvin" he found that typical characterizations of Calvin's theology were wrong. Picturing the Christian life as a constant struggle against the fleshly depravity of our humanity is a misreading of Calvin's true teachings. Instead, Christianity involves a distinctive self-mastery, harnessing one's efforts toward giving "our gifts back to God," issuing forth in the good work we were meant to do: "What I would discover in my studies is that this dismal picture of human life was a product of Calvinist *followers*, not John Calvin himself. My reinterpretation of Calvin's teachings revealed a theology of hope and joy, liberating humanity from a shaming, blaming, cowering Christianity, with its railing against the 'sin' of pride, and replacing that view with a God-inspired drive for self-worth. I didn't know it then, but expounding this liberating force would become my life's work."[51]

The Positive Thinking that Schuller inherited from Peale therefore represents not a synthesis with Reformed theology but a *repudiation* of Calvinism's

insistence on acute awareness of personal sin. Schuller legitimated Positive Thinking while inoculating it, to a degree, with his mainline Protestant gravitas, familiar Christian language, and appropriation of Calvin. A Congregational Church
minister from Berkeley, California, commented on the differences between mentor and disciple: "I have never known Peale to grapple with atonement, grace,
and justification. Anyone who completed, even in his student days, a 300-page
topical index to Calvin's four-volume *Institutes of the Christian Religion*—as
Schuller did—is scarcely ignorant of the issues in Reformed theology."[52] Schuller
himself explained his differences with Peale: "I learned a great deal from Peale,
but I went a step further than he ever has—I developed a systematic theology of
self-esteem."[53] By speaking an evangelical code that referenced conversion experiences and "commitments to Jesus Christ" while seeking to retain orthodox
features of sin and salvation, Schuller fashioned a new, unconventional form of
evangelicalism.[54] By elevating humanity as God-inspired beings with inherent self-worth who offer their lives of service to God, Schuller asserted an ego-
centered, agency-driven philosophy as *truly* Reformed.

At Times Reformed, at Times Not

When reviewing the galleys for Dennis Voskuil's *Mountains into Goldmines*, an
analysis of the Orange County ministry, Schuller discovered a manuscript that
raised provocative questions about his theology. For Voskuil, Schuller's "unconventional" evangelicalism had become so pervasive that it was best described as
a "new orthodoxy," synthesizing Christianity and New Thought.[55] Voskuil
argued that "Schullerism" was the culmination of an American evangelicalism
that had long been primed to see religion as a "vehicle to health, wealth, and
happiness."[56] Therefore, Schuller could be traced as a "direct descendant of a
long line of popular religionists who have proclaimed the gospel of this-worldly
well-being through the gospel of positive thinking."

As he examined Voskuil's galleys, Schuller crossed out the claim in black
marker and protested in the margins "—wait a minute!!" Down the page he made
a case in the margins that he claimed a Calvinist theological lineage and all others
would be secondary.[57] Later, Voskuil discussed Schuller's message as a concocted
blend of "evangelicalism and secular Arminianism." Schuller responded by cross-
ing out "secular Arminianism" and writing "no, no, no—classical Calvinism."
Again, when Voskuil claimed that the Crystal Cathedral ministries promoted a
theology largely "incompatible with the tenets of traditional evangelicalism,"
Schuller responded in blue ink: "Be darn sure you're getting Schuller rite [*sic*]."

With threats like Voskuil's book, Schuller aggressively protected the legitimacy of his charisma and expected others to recognize him as having exceptional
status due to the singularity of his person. Simply said, he viewed himself not
only as theologically correct but as unique; he did not want to be lumped in with
others but instead to be recognized for his distinctiveness. To reinforce his

pioneering persona, Schuller preferred to describe his ministry as a mission not a church: "That's the reason we have never been interested, nor have we felt divinely called, to create a place for a lot of Christians to get together and praise the Lord! But rather we are called to build a mission to impress the unchurched people with the reality of Christ's living love!"[58] As such, Schuller felt it necessary to craft a historically legitimate yet distinctly mission-oriented theology. Richard Mouw, president of Fuller Theological Seminary, recalled an exchange with Schuller:

> I said, "You know, you are one of the key contextualizers in theology in North America." He said, "What do you mean?" So I said "You know in missiology we talk about contextualization, if I were going to be a missionary in some village in Africa that's animist, I'd have to study animism and see how do I bring good news to an animist?" I said, "You've done that with Southern California therapeutic self-actualization culture." And he said, "That's right! You, you understand me!"

Schuller's synthesis of therapy and psychology found support among those who sympathized with the need to innovatively contextualize the ancient message of Christianity to contemporary culture.

To that end, one longtime copastor remarked that perhaps Schuller should have been held to a different standard than other RCA ministers: "Dr. Schuller saw the church as a mission." After all, he had been called to Southern California to "establish a mission outpost"—not a traditional RCA congregation. The copastor continued: "As [Schuller] went door to door meeting people, if they already had a church, he blessed them and moved on. He was not looking for people who had a 'Reformed' background. He was looking for people who were broken and needed healing and hope." The copastor also remarked that the rest of the RCA took decades to realize Schuller's vision: "Our denomination did not emphasize the local church being a 'mission' until the early 2000s."

Though he felt he was most often misunderstood, being ahead of his time, Schuller found gratification in a profile feature in a 1984 issue of *Christianity Today*. Its pages included an interview with Schuller and two articles regarding his theology. Theologian Kenneth Kantzer, president of the evangelical Trinity College (now Trinity International University) in Deerfield, Illinois, estimated that Schuller reached "more non-Christians than any other religious leader in America." Kantzer credited Schuller's success to an "unusual sensitivity to the secular mind" and a "handle on modern society that many of his critics do not see."[59] Kantzer continued in his defense of Schuller: "To understand Robert Schuller, you must not think of his television program as a church service planned for faithful worshippers scattered across the nation. It's strictly 'Show Biz.'" Kantzer explained that Schuller's ministry had entered a new stratum of entertainment: "It's competing with the Astrodome and professional sports. It's competing with soap operas and newscasts from Washington, the Middle East, and Central America. It's competing with '20/20,' 'The Little House on the Prairie;' with 'Wild Kingdom' and 'Sesame Street.'"[60] In other words, as an evangelist, Schuller played a whole new game in a much grander arena.

Kantzer declared after his hours-long interview that he found Schuller to be "unequivocally orthodox—a Protestant in the mainstream of the Reformed tradition." Kantzer diagnosed Schuller's overemphasis on positive self-esteem as an idiosyncratic response from having been formed within a Calvinist milieu that found itself singularly distracted by the supposed worthlessness of humans in the notion of total depravity. Nevertheless, in a preemptive riposte to critics who likely still would not be satisfied with Schuller's bona fides, Kantzer rhetorically asked, "What more could anyone ask [of Schuller]?"[61] On the other hand, some argued that a synergy existed between Schuller's Possibility Thinking and Calvinism. Journalist Barbara Ehrenreich noted that while a Calvinist might be preoccupied with monitoring sins like sloth, gluttony, or greed, the disciple of New Thought would engage the same mental energy toward casting aside negative thoughts of doubt or uncertainty.[62] For Ehrenreich, both religious strains functionally became obsessions.

Rather than focus on the cleverness of synthesizing Calvinism and New Thought, perhaps a simpler and more satisfying approach for understanding Schuller's theological foundation is acknowledging his pragmatism in attracting a broad constituency and growing his congregation. Guarding against any negativity as he positioned himself within the broader culture, Schuller highlighted the most affirming aspects of Christianity while actively moving away from parts he believed alienated people and drained from his charismatic authority. In a mixed metaphor where he is both emergency room surgeon and counseling therapist, Schuller explained in 1975 his hesitancy to approach difficult theological issues: "The basic reason I avoid controversial issues is that on Sunday morning I see my role in the pulpit not as a bible teacher, but as a therapist dealing with people that are in an emergency room of a county hospital on Saturday night with stab wounds."[63] He considered himself an expert at staunching the "bleeding" of hurting people: "From my years of experience . . . I've developed new concepts of how to tie off a bleeding artery in a hurry."[64]

At times, necessity forced Schuller to challenge accepted orthodoxy. In 1979, *Eternity* magazine offered a transcription of a conversation it had arranged between Schuller and Lewis Smedes, an ethics professor from Fuller Theological Seminary. Smedes enjoyed significant stature within the larger Reformed community. As the two men discussed theology and love, Schuller began to describe original sin as synonymous with the loss of self-esteem. Smedes cut in: "I would say that the loss of self-esteem is not identical with original sin, it is one of the effects of it." He then elaborated: "It strikes me, Bob, that with original sin, a human being as a sinner isn't capable of being truthful with dealing with sin. I think that Augustine is right when he said the trouble with man—his human frailty—is that he likes himself too much." Undaunted by Smedes' appeal to a church father, Schuller responded: "St. Augustine was wrong at that point. I don't accept that. If your interpretation is right, [Augustine] didn't have the advantage of some of the information available to us today."[65] In his mind, Schuller merely offered a sensible update on Augustine.

It's not that Schuller remained oblivious to thorny ethical issues or tricky doctrinal stances. Rather, he strategically avoided engagement with such issues in order to broaden his charismatic appeal to the widest audience. For example, the doctrine of predestination—that God has chosen those whom he will save—proved to be an exceedingly dangerous issue for the Calvinist minister. Though Schuller indicated that he did, indeed, believe in predestination as a Reformed theological tenet, he also revealed to an interviewer that he worried that the doctrine sounded "so unintelligent" without proper context.[66] In a 1983 interview, Schuller intimated that it would be "dumb" and "opening a can of worms" to preach about predestination—unless he could be in "a classroom situation where people can dialogue and dialogue and dialogue."[67]

His Possibility Thinking and Reformed theology background also inhibited Schuller from engaging in the "end time" or apocalyptic rhetoric that many of his contemporaries found so effective for ratings.[68] While most of his competitors—including "Falwell, Robertson, Robison, Bakker, Swaggart, and most of the lesser lights of gospel broadcasting"—engaged in end-times conjecture, Schuller refrained from speculation regarding the Second Coming.[69] Even though "rapture theology" (the premise of the *Left Behind* books and movies) was popular, Schuller saw it as a highly controversial orientation that provoked endless speculation over doctrinal details that could never be satisfactorily resolved.[70]

Further, Schuller tended to be somewhat cagey on the issue of homosexuality. Consistent with his emphasis on honoring the dignity of all, Schuller demonstrated hesitancy in offering an outright condemnation of homosexuality. When queried about his stance, Schuller suggested that heterosexual relationships and marriage represented the "more excellent way" and expressed his commitment to the "historic Judeo-Christian viewpoint." After describing himself as a conservative, Schuller went on to note, "We've had homosexuals as representatives of our church the last 40 years," and claimed that he possessed no interest in "attacking" homosexuals. Schuller also intimated that what he described as "the gay liberation movement" had high regard for the Crystal Cathedral ministry because he had no interest in "intentionally embarrassing and shaming them."[71]

The issue of sexuality posed a significant test of Schuller's ability to negotiate a nonprovocative theological position in the latter years of the ministry. Over the course of fifty years, rumors and innuendos occasionally registered at ministry meetings. In one instance, leadership relayed concerns about a prominent member of the ministry. A longtime staff member reported that, in response, Schuller slammed "his fist on the table" and exclaimed, "Shut up! I never want to hear a word of this!" The issue and the whispers, though, continued. In 2011, unbeknownst to Schuller as he began to relinquish day-to-day responsibilities, all members of the staff involved as singers and musicians received a document to sign that signaled their affirmation of lifestyles that accorded with the Bible "in every way."[72] Many saw the document as a thinly veiled strategy to remove a certain member of the worship staff. The "Crystal Cathedral Worship Choir and Worship Team Covenant" discussed the perils of living in an era when confusion existed regarding "personal sexuality." It went on to note that the "Crystal Cathedral Ministries teaches that sexual intimacy is intended by God to only be within the bonds of marriage, between one man and one woman."[73] While acknowledging that the document articulated his own personal view, Schuller voiced strong disapproval of the covenant. The minister groused that the document could be interpreted as a "crusade against homosexuals" and certainly represented a dissonance with "the principles of being positive" that had marked "the history of the ministry." Finally, Schuller offered a resounding repudiation of the covenant and a profound summation of the ministry's identity: "We have never been about covenants or definitions. We don't test anyone who comes to our ministry. We don't require them to be Christian."[74]

In the end, Schuller simply ignored certain theological dogmas and controversial issues if it did not suit his purposes. Similar to Billy Graham, the Orange County minister preferred a widening tent of Christianity that accommodated as many as would enter.[75] Such a proclivity allowed for a measure of disagreement and fuzziness on contested issues. After the bankruptcy of the ministry in 2010, an editorial in *Christianity Today* allowed that Schuller's theology deserved to be criticized; at the same time, the editors also insisted that many of the critiques relied on caricatures: "To be fair, [Schuller's theology] was more nuanced than many critics imagine."[76]

Schullerism

Some RCA leaders embraced Schuller (such as Chester Droog; see chapter 3), seeing his church as an exception that the rest of the denomination should emulate. By the early 1970s, the GGCC had become such an intriguing new form of church life that writers from the denominational magazine *Church Herald* identified it as a possible mode forward to secure the RCA's future. Lois Joice, a staff writer for the denomination's Office of Promotion and Communication, wondered, "We hear that the institutional church is losing its appeal, that it is failing to win new followers for Christ, or to even hold its own people. But if this is true, how do you explain Garden Grove?"[77] Joice then contrasted GGCC with more typical RCA congregations: "There are some things you won't find in [GGCC]. No emphasis on guilt and self-abasement, for example. What you *will* find is an atmosphere of victorious, confident Christianity which says more clearly than words could say, 'With God all things are possible.'"

Aware that even the mention of Schuller's name engendered critiques, Joice dismissed them, insisting, "Theologians might argue the pros and cons of this approach. What no one can dispute, however, is that *something is happening there.* The church is gloriously alive, reaching the normally unreachable and restructuring lives." It was a pragmatic appeal: "Whatever they are doing at Garden Grove, it is working." Finally, Joice anticipated skeptical RCA readers disparaging a numbers-driven approach to congregational life: "Garden Grove Church continues to grow at an astonishing pace, but Bob Schuller is less interested in numbers than in the quality of his flock's spiritual life."

Despite apologists like Joice, others in the denomination harbored serious misgivings. As Schuller stood on the precipice of opening the Crystal Cathedral, an RCA pastor from New Jersey, Donner Atwood, argued in the *Church Herald* that television ministries realized only limited influence. While the electronic church had a role in Christian ministry, it could never replace the local congregation: "Television's religious broadcasts generally result in a neglect of the viewer's commitment to other people." He acknowledged that "the local level cannot match the beauty and drama, the wonder and wizardry of the electronic presentation." And somewhat dismissively, Atwood shrugged in noting that the local congregation could not "offer silver and gold anymore than could Peter and John when they were passing through the gate beautiful (Acts 3:6)." However, the local church offered something much more significant in "the reality of the redeeming Lord in the body of believers."[78]

Similar criticisms multiplied. Some accused Schuller of dabbling in New Age religions or, worse, mentalism, and others simply dismissed his personal blend of theology—often dubbed "Schullerism"—as accommodationist, a panacea for anxious, milquetoast Christians who had scant interest in guilt or confession but were yearning for affirmation in their pursuit of wealth. A 1974 issue of the *Calvin Theological Journal* included a review of Schuller's *You Can Become the Person You Want to Be* that concluded the book "would be funny, if it were not so sad." The reviewer expressed a profound concern that Schuller's theology had actually emerged from a pastor within the Dutch Reformed tradition: "Especially in a Reformed journal warning should be raised to expose the shallow, illegitimate, and certainly not Reformed theology that is at work in this book by a Reformed minister." He condemned Schuller for publishing a volume that pandered to modern Americans: "Intellectual and creedal honesty can only vigorously protest the shallowness and worldliness displayed in a slick piece of work like this 'book.' In other words: This is a bad book." Finally, the reviewer lamented the fact that Schuller's book would yield healthy royalty checks: "The writer will probably earn a lot of money with it. But I can think of more honorable ways of earning a living."[79]

Even within his own congregation, a suspicion festered that a theology of Schuller's own ego had supplanted Christianity. In 1975, a congregant wrote in disgust to a secretary at the church that, because of his layers of buffers and sycophants, Schuller himself would not see her missive. She expressed concern that "Schullerism replaced Christ" and that "very few of the Christians who attended GGCC when I joined are still members."[80] The subtext of the letter, then, considered Schuller's brand of Christianity a form of secularized self-help centered around a personality cult.

"Schullerism" emerged as a caricature of the ministry, one prompting severe criticism. On two separate occasions, a consortium of concerned pastors in Grand Rapids, Michigan, issued a pointed recommendation that local television stations cease broadcasting *Hour of Power* "as a public service."[81] In 1975, a group of pastors from the Christian Reformed Church in North America (CRC) attended the leadership institute and secured a private meeting with Schuller. The CRC contingent had been disquieted by Schuller's avoidance of sin in his sermons and publications. Confronting him in the Tower of Hope, they pressed Schuller to defend himself. At least one young pastor from Holland, Michigan, recounted being swayed by Schuller's vivid metaphor: "Listen, when the gardener works in my yard, and he comes to the door, and he wears muddy boots, and I open the door to him and say you can come in, I don't have to tell him he's got to take his boots off when he sees that white clean carpet. He does that, and he does that automatically. You don't have to hammer away at sin."

Even with these defenses, broader critiques followed. Lutheran theologian Martin Marty lamented in a 1978 article the changes that had been occurring within Christianity in the United States. The piece included a photo of Schuller. Marty argued that the growth of evangelicals (at the expense of mainline Protestant churches) centered on an appealing message of experience that trumped rational thought: "The overall impact of the conservative Protestant surge, however, has been on the affections and not the mind. The Bible bookstores are full of volumes touting experience at the expense of reason." Marty then dismissed "the religious radio and television network stars who know they can get their best guffaws when they satirize the learned who try to puzzle out the things of God." Finally, the theologian directed his agitation toward the self-help strain of evangelicalism associated with Schuller: "The accent has been on dieting for Jesus, being an athlete for Christ, losing weight or winning friends thanks to the Holy Spirit, and always feeling saved and feeling good."[82]

Other influential theologians attacked Schuller for perceived cultural accommodations in his interpretation of scripture. As late as 2015, conservative theologian and radio pastor John MacArthur used Schuller as a narrative foil in his keynote address at a conference organized to offer apologetics for biblical inerrancy (the conviction that the Bible is without error or fault). As he opened the "Inerrancy under Attack" meetings, MacArthur recalled that he and Schuller found themselves seated together on a flight out of Chicago in 1978 (just the mention of "Schuller" at the conference elicited guffaws from the crowd). MacArthur, coincidentally enough, had been reviewing Schuller's latest book, *Self-Esteem: The New Reformation*, and had it sitting on his lap. The flight seemed to have been tense for both men. At one point, Schuller turned to MacArthur and offered his tagline, "God loves you, and so do I," with a slight modification: "God loves you, and *I'm trying*." Schuller's departure from character likely arose from the fact that MacArthur labeled his theology as nothing less than "an all-out assault on scripture."[83] For many conservative Christian pastors and theologians, Schuller represented a weak, liberal Christianity that failed to take scripture seriously.

As Schuller's message gained a higher profile, a growing contingent of detractors found plenty of fodder. A 1979 critique of the failures of evangelicalism in America clearly had Schullerism in mind. Nathan Hatch, a prominent history professor then at the University of Notre Dame, worried that evangelical pastors undermined the gospel when they focused on self-esteem rather than the consequences of sin. Hatch critiqued the sentimentality infiltrating churches: "What seems to be in the works today is a convenient marriage of evangelical piety and self-help. This union, moreover, is based on the assumption that it makes little difference if we replace biblical concepts of moral poverty, selfish blindness, and spiritual nakedness with the more fashionable psychological notions of fear, frustration, and anxiety."[84] Taking on Schuller's desire to market an easy-to-access Christianity as widely and attractively as possible, Hatch asserted, "We are so busy going in the opposite direction, removing every possible inconvenience that one might have to becoming a Christian, that the danger of self-righteousness is hardly a fleeting nuisance." With the Crystal Cathedral in the final stages of construction, Hatch wondered if evangelicals like Schuller had fallen too hard in love with their methods, making their version of Christianity overly reductive: "If we could just upgrade the banquet a bit and advertise it better, why wouldn't everyone want to come?"[85]

Even the cathedral's public concerts became evidence that something was amiss. A 1997 review of *The Glory of Easter* performance in *First Things* (a conservative religious journal) drew together several critiques of the Crystal Cathedral ministry. The reviewer noted that the event included an altered version of the Lord's Prayer wherein "Forgive us our sins" had been omitted. Thus, denuded of the necessity of atonement, the drama production, according to the critic, reduced Jesus to nothing more than a "cosmic pixie" in a "fraudulent gospel."[86] In other words, Schuller promoted a therapeutic religion that revolved around feeling good more than embracing orthodox Christianity. At the opening of the cathedral in 1980, another journalist described Schuller's as a "California pulpit" where "what you hear is no ordinary Bible-thumping sermon. There are no references to Satan, sin, or damnation. Nor is there any mention of such social ills as racism, sexism, crime, or corruption. It's all strictly noncontroversial. And references to the Bible itself are rare."[87]

Even public intellectual Christopher Lasch's *The Culture of Narcissism: American Life in an Age of Diminishing Expectations* could be read as an indictment of Schuller's brand of Christianity. In the late 1970s, Lasch lamented that the cultural climate sought therapy over religion and valued "the feeling, the momentary illusion, of personal well-being, health, and psychic security" over personal salvation.[88] Indeed, no less than *Christianity Today* understood it that way, describing Lasch's as a "scathing critique" of the "general cultural mood" in which Schuller had been involved in fostering—a "new therapeutic culture" that left "people trapped and isolated in the self."[89] Often, Schuller's words could be used as evidence against him: He once contested *Hour of Power* as being thought of an "electronic church," suggesting, "Don't call that a church. Call it emotional therapy."[90]

Over his career, Schuller seemed especially stung by the critiques of *Newsweek* magazine's religion editor, Kenneth L. Woodward. In 1987, Schuller wrote Woodward, first complimenting the journalist on his many "splendid articles" and noting that *Newsweek* ranked as his favorite weekly because of its "fair and unbiased reporting." With pleasantries out of the way, Schuller then broached the reason for his letter. During a June 12 appearance on CNN's *Crossfire* program (the same year the cable news network managed to reach over half of America's homes), Woodward described Schuller as a minister "who doesn't preach the gospel, he just preaches positive thinking." Woodward also made the claim that "of all the big-time television preachers—none of them has a theological education." Seeing a threat to his credibility, Schuller took exception to how he had been lumped in with the other television ministers of the era:

> I may indeed be the only one that has an earned undergraduate degree from an accredited college and university: Hope College. Accredited by the North American Association of Colleges and Universities. And then I went on to complete my 3 years of post-graduate studies in theology at Western Theological Seminary in Holland, Michigan. In seminary, for my thesis I compiled the first Topical and Scriptural Index to the *Institutes of the Christian Religion* by John Calvin—a feat never before performed. And this was done under faculty supervision.[91]

Schuller also expressed a strong reluctance to be associated with other television ministries: "I don't like to be painted and tainted simply because ministers and ministries which are 'independent' and 'para-ecclesiastical,' are proving to be most embarrassing to me." Schuller further bolstered his legitimacy by referencing the size of his viewership: "The latest Arbitron ratings still give me the largest market share of 7.4%. Far and away ahead of the second market share personality, Oral Roberts, with 4.1%."[92]

Woodward's critique represented the kind of threat to charisma Schuller worked hard to diffuse. He contended that his ministry maintained a higher level of financial accountability than other religious programs: "You have also made the statement—both on *Nightline* when the two of us appeared together, and again on *Crossfire*—that none of these television ministries is 'accountable.'

I respectfully ask you to recognize and then cease and desist the practice of putting me in the category of others who lack accountability." Schuller went into detail regarding his accountability to his denomination:

> Furthermore, I have for 32 years been accountable to the Reformed Church in America. Upon graduation from Western Seminary I was installed as a minister of this denomination. For 32 years I have been under the aegis of the Classis of California of the Particular Synod of the West of the Reformed Church in America. Every year I have to submit the financial statements of the Crystal Cathedral to this Classis. Every year I have to submit the minutes of the Board Meetings of the Crystal Cathedral to the Classis of California for a review by its committee. At any time they wish to question me about my *private*, or public, or professional activities, they have the authority and the right to do so. The telephone may ring. I may be called to meet with their Executive Committee. And I will have to be responsible and will have to be open in answering any questions, defending my actions, or submit myself to their admonition, rebuke or correction.[93]

When required to protect his image, Schuller identified closely with the RCA, relying on the denomination's long-standing mainline Protestant status: "Our denomination happens to be affiliated with the World Alliance of Reformed Churches; The World Council of the Churches of Christ; and the National Council of the Churches of Christ in America. I am, therefore, the only minister trained, groomed, molded and shaped, and operating with full approval and credentiality [*sic*] in a denomination that can be authentically labeled, 'Mainstream.'" He argued that *Hour of Power* corrected the narrowness of most religious programming and offered a much-needed leavening: "It was one of the reasons I went into religious television. I felt that without our voice, the entire religious presentation to the modern American public would be the one-sided viewpoint of what might be called extreme fundamentalism and sectarianism."[94]

In their continuing exchange of letters, Woodward in 1997 again elaborated on some of his misgivings related to Schuller's theology. "I do not see how the Scriptures in any way support your pages 151–156 in your book, *Self-Esteem*. I most certainly do not regard salvation as 'rescue from shame to glory.' I find a little insecurity does a lot of good, and too much security a major obstacle to salvation." Moreover, Woodward continued, "Jesus teaches us that nothing succeeds like failure, and nothing fails like success. If large churches were a sign of success in God's eyes, popes would be first in the kingdom of heaven." Then, in what surely had to be a wound in Schuller's pride in his self-regard as a foremost expert on Calvinism: "Regarding your history time-line on page 174, only someone who does not know church history would regard the period from 1000 to 1516 as darkly as do you." Woodward also intimated his suspicion that Schuller had "never read Aquinas, Dominic, Bonaventura or any of the great spiritual and learned figures of that great age. Nor would any church historian see the Reformation as anything less than an age of great schism. Your view shows you haven't forgotten all you learned in Calvinist seminary, just the important parts." Having registered his theological critique, Woodward moved to his concerns regarding television ministries: "I also happen to believe, as I told the American Cinema Academy in Hollywood last year, that popular culture, including television, does authentic religion more harm than good." Finally, Woodward offered Schuller a challenge: "My problem, you see, is this: if folks are given a bastardized, self-congratulatory form of religion and then are told that that is Christianity, they will never recognize the authentic article. What's a public platform for—yours or mine—if not for hard theology?"[95] Schuller responded, very briefly. A missive from May 1, 1997, simply thanked Woodward for his "thoughtful letter," noting that his high profile on "public platforms" inhibited his ability to demonstrate just how "hard and heavy" of a theology he had actually developed.[96]

Typically, when his critics dismissed his theology as narcissistic or materialistic, Schuller reacted most strongly. He registered his displeasure with Voskuil's framing of his theology as a "gospel of success": "It is a widely-known fact that narcissism is an attempt to achieve a fulfillment of the emptiness that happens when a person lacks wholesome self-esteem. And narcissism always is attached to materialism. My theology, my philosophy, are all rooted in prayer, in Jesus Christ. Never do I in word or in deed advocate a materialistic solution to our need for self-esteem."[97] The minister once described a recent sermon that he had given on the Beatitudes as nothing less than "magnificent" because of its synthesis of scripture and scientific knowledge. Schuller explained that its persuasiveness rested in its "scientific, psychological, and theological believability."[98]

Despite his insistence on its sophistication and orthodoxy, Schuller's distinct theological synthesis even brought charges of heresy—or worse: dabbling in New Age religion. In a 1988 book, *Understanding the New Age*, Russell Chandler, a religion writer for the *Los Angeles Times*, repeated the contention that both Peale and Schuller in their messages bore a problematic and "striking resemblance" to the teaching of Mary Baker Eddy, founder of the Church of Christ, Scientist. Moreover, according to Chandler, the two RCA ministers found themselves in a lineage that had stretched back over a century and included the "positive thinking" that had appeared in the work of American Transcendentalists such as Henry David Thoreau, Ralph Waldo Emerson, and Walt Whitman.[99] The RCA's *Church Herald* also duly noted the association of two of the denomination's highest profile ministers with New Age religion in a March 1990 editorial, reporting, "We're all affected by the New Age, and it's therefore not surprising that Chandler names two prominent Reformed Church pastors, Norman Vincent Peale and Robert H. Schuller, in his overview of the movement."[100] Though the editor leveled no further accusations, Schuller wrote the general secretary of the RCA, Edwin Mulder (no relation to one of the authors), requesting that he submit a letter to the editor in defense of Schuller and Peale. Schuller expressed his concern: "It is irresponsible 'Religious McCarthyism' on the part of the author and sad that the *Journal of the Reformed Church in America* appears to share in the irresponsible faulty judgement."[101] With no letter forthcoming from Mulder, Schuller responded directly in a May 1990 letter also published in the *Church Herald*, which revealed his frustration with a lack of loyalty from the RCA: "To find that the Reformed Church in America's official publication takes the faulty judgement of an outsider and names our names, Robert Schuller and Norman Peale, as being in the New Age movement, without questioning at all the possible error of judgment or interpretation by a non-RCA, free-lance writer—I find it reckless, damaging, destructive, and divisive."[102] For Schuller, the RCA's "system of theological accountability to a classis" should assure the denomination of his and Peale's orthodoxy. In every instance, Schuller defended the theological soundness of his orientation.

Two years later, a reporter from the *Miami Herald*, Elinor Brecher, received an advance copy of a manuscript, "Peale's Secret Source," that would eventually be published by *Lutheran Quarterly* in 1995. The two ministers who authored the article claimed that Peale's "positive thinking" manifested occult and Freemasonry influences.[103] They indicted Schuller for engaging in the same "New Age heresy" and derisively described him as "the High Priest of think-and-grow-rich capitalism."[104] According to the authors, Schuller's sermons and books included numerous tales of miracles that seemed resonant with "the Hermetic Cult." Brecher requested an interview with Schuller to allow him to respond to the accusations, but instead, Schuller's chief of staff, Larry Sonnenburg, sent Edwin Mulder another letter requesting that the denomination disseminate a written response in defense of the two RCA pastors.[105] Mulder demurred again, and Brecher, in turn, claimed that Schuller himself could not be reached for comment. Instead, Jeffery Japinga, editor at the time of the RCA's *Church Herald*, told Brecher that Schuller in the past had been "saddened, hurt, and shocked" by any insinuations that linked New Age movements to "positive thinking" and "possibility thinking."[106] Later, when Wesley Granberg-Michaelson become general secretary of the RCA, he noted that the relationship between Schuller and the denomination had frayed further because of this exchange.

As Schuller continued his ministry, a flood of other Christian voices expressed consternation regarding the minister's application of Christianity. Theologian Michael Horton facetiously credited Schuller with improving upon Peale's "upbeat message of self-help" that had discarded "the most important aspects of the Christian proclamation."[107] Horton asserted that Schuller packaged this "quintessentially American gospel" in a manner that allowed it to appeal to evangelicals, asserting, "Not only have evangelicals caught up with their liberal rivals in accommodating religion to secular culture, they are now clearly in the lead. No secular self-help guru comes close to the sales of evangelical rivals." Yale theologian George Lindbeck similarly made the case that Schuller expanded the reach of theologies like that of Peale's. Bemoaning the loss of biblical literacy, Lindbeck viewed Schuller as the breakpoint for the ascent of biblical ignorance among conservative Christians: "Playing fast and loose with the Bible needed a liberal audience in the days of Norman Vincent Peale, but now, as the case of Robert Schuller indicates, professed conservatives eat it up."[108] For theologians like Horton and Lindbeck, Schuller's Theology of Self Esteem and Possibility Thinking had corroded biblicism—even among conservative evangelicals.

Criticisms Accrue

Though he often rhetorically played the RCA card when interrogated about issues of accountability or orthodoxy, Schuller's denomination included a contingent of leaders who openly expressed the very same concerns. Schuller's profile and seemingly ubiquitous presence in American media left the minister vulnerable to the development of the cottage industry of "Schuller shooting."[109] Thus, he often found himself in a defensive posture that subverted his messages of Possibility Thinking and the Theology of Self-Esteem. Schuller camped on his uniqueness, distinction, and, often, the superiority of his methods of ministry, assertions that isolated both him as a person and the church as a whole. For more than four decades, this twin-sided independence and isolation served the ministry well. Schuller's calculated distancing from his mainline Protestant identity in the RCA proved prescient.

During the same era that saw GGCC grow dramatically in Orange County, mainline Protestant denominations began to feel the seismic shifts of the 1960s: steep, sudden membership declines that eroded their stature and influence. With his amorphous identity, Schuller hitched himself to evangelical Protestant churches experiencing dramatic growth at the same time.[110] Closely identifying with a dying component of the American religious scene held no appeal for Schuller.

As they felt the religious trends moving away from them in the late 1950s and throughout the 1960s, a number of mainline denominations considered mergers, including the RCA. Always cagey, Schuller publicly described himself as noncommittal to the notion of an RCA union with other denominations. But privately, Schuller revealed in a letter to fellow RCA minister Peale reservations about mergers with Methodists or Episcopalians because they would lead to a nonpresbyterian form of church government. Schuller expressed concerns about his independence, staking the vitality of the church on the freedom to exercise his own style of leadership that was allowed within the RCA's interpretation of church polity. Schuller dreaded "the thought of a Bishop someday appointing a minister to the [GGCC] pulpit—perhaps making the selection because they were fraternity brothers, wonderful friends, etc." If the RCA did engage in a merger, Schuller reported that GGCC would withdraw from any newly formed denomination that instituted an episcopal form of government. The minister recoiled at any scenario that ceded local control of his congregation to a more hierarchical church government.[111]

Schuller knew that RCA polity ensured that it would be prohibitively difficult for his congregation to secede. Still, for him, GGCC had no reason to feel beholden to the RCA, insisting that "the denomination has not contributed to the purchase of the property and the building of this base of operation which has an appraised value of nearly $7,000,000." Schuller reluctantly acknowledged that "the property, for all practical purposes, belongs to the Reformed Church in America. We cannot pull it out—unless we pulled it into another denomination with the approval of this denomination." He then articulated what would become a central concern related to the church polity of the RCA: succession. Schuller imagined a scenario that allowed him to pass the ministry down to his children: "If our constitution was so structured that I could split it off or my descendants could split it off and form an independent congregation, this would be an entirely different matter in my opinion."[112]

The threat of withdrawal demonstrates Schuller's belief that GGCC was a distinctive, independent ministry, with a vibrancy and financial health that would allow it to survive on its own. That tenuous connection with the RCA had manifested earlier when Schuller requested private loans for the construction of the Tower of Hope in 1968. To appeal to investors, Schuller struck a delicate balance regarding the church's relationship to the RCA. A mailer to potential benefactors first indicated that private loans allowed GGCC to remain congregational in its authority structure—likely a problematic statement since RCA polity dictated classical (or regional) control over all church property: "To guarantee that this church will always be owned by the congregation, this church has always been financed by private loans from members and friends of this church." The same postcard, though, also referenced GGCC's affiliation with the RCA as evidence of the church's stability and longevity—and, thus, a safe investment: "Your investment will be secured . . . by the financial strength of the Oldest Protestant Denomination in America's leading Church—Garden Grove Community Church."[113] Thus, the minister attempted to balance the tension of independence and autonomy with tradition and longevity in order to procure reliable streams of capital.

To the dismay of RCA leaders, Schuller displayed few reservations about predicting the demise of his and similar other denominations: "The mainline church in America is in a phase of death, and it still has a lot of dying to do. That is not bad news. It is not bad news if a grain of wheat is dying on the ground because its death must come before it can sprout new life."[114] Moreover, in a 1975 interview on the CBS radio show *The World of Religion*, Schuller remarked that he thought that religious denominations had become anachronistic: "What we have seen in the sixties and seventies are the dying gasps of 'denominationalism.' An age is coming to its death, thank God." His interviewer, Boyd Harvey of KNX in Los Angeles, introduced Schuller as though he had no connections to the RCA: "Dr. Schuller's church is not affiliated with any major Protestant denomination, partly because Dr. Schuller believes denominationalism is dying." Schuller then elaborated: "I don't want to be a front for any denomination. I don't want to be a front for any polarizing group of Protestants or religious people." Denominationalism, according to Schuller, had been eclipsed by the era of church growth, wherein both Protestants and Catholics found unity in pursuing "the untapped market" of the "spiritually empty."[115] The church's strength would be established by the distance it kept from the trappings of the denomination.

Soon after the interview aired, Schuller received a letter from the editor of the *Church Herald*, John Stapert, seeking clarification regarding his dismissive comments.[116] Initially, Schuller had taken time to reply to Stapert but ultimately chose not to send his tersely worded missive, a letter that reminded Stapert of Schuller's ordination in the RCA and the fact that GGCC understood itself as "a fully integrated congregation in a denomination called the Reformed Church in America." Schuller then hedged by reaffirming his statement from the interview: "I do believe that denominations, universally, are more a hindrance than a help in church growth."[117] The minister, though, must have had reservations about provoking the denomination. The unsent message bears a note from Schuller's personal administrative assistant—"Dr. Schuller does not want Mr. Stapert to know that he even saw Stapert's May 29th letter"[118]—and a plan to attribute her boss's silence to seasonal travel outside of the office.[119]

As often happened, Schuller trusted the management of his persona to his in-house public relations team, a department intentionally created by Schuller and headed by his executive assistant, Michael Nason. The task of crafting a response for Stapert fell to Nason, who warned Stapert that he might want to tread lightly: "I sense overtones in your letter of an attitude that might be interpreted by Dr. Schuller as something less than positive. Would you want Dr. Schuller to get that impression? If not, I can protect you from what appears to be an inquisitorial tone." Nason then offered reassurances that "Garden Grove Community Church is affiliated with the Reformed Church in America" and supplied evidence: "I am including a copy of the weekly Church Bulletin. You will see that the Bulletin identifies each and every Sunday to all who come through, the fact that the Garden Grove Community Church is affiliated with the Reformed Church in America." Nason asserted that GGCC likely contributed more financially to its local classis than any other congregation in the RCA and that Schuller himself subsidized scholarship donations at the denomination's Western Theological Seminary.[120]

Stapert, dissatisfied with Nason's response, again wrote to Schuller directly, requesting an explanation from the minister himself: "After all, the editor of the *Church Herald* should be able to obtain a response from one of the RCA's pastors."[121] Schuller, pleading ignorance about the situation, finally wrote back to Stapert, echoing his administrative assistant by indicating that he had only recently discovered the exchanges with Nason after "pressing through piles of correspondence that have accumulated during my weeks abroad." Schuller described himself as satisfied with Nason's response but also finally indicated that he would be happy to sit for an interview with Stapert.[122]

Despite his assurances to Stapert, in a 1983 interview, Schuller again defended his independence by noting that traditional mainline Protestant churches remained "trapped" in their "history and rituals and creeds and language." He explained, "My audience is broader than that. My audience is wider than the National Council of Churches or the National Association of Evangelicals. They think they are all-encompassing, but they don't realize how limited they are."[123] Although he valued the connection to the RCA—for the legitimation it granted him as a trained pastor rooted in the mainline tradition—he harbored misgivings about the future of denominations within U.S. Christianity and believed that to achieve successes in his ministry he required space away from the shadow of his dated home church. Schuller intimated that because GGCC—and, later, the Crystal Cathedral—had a large audience (an "imagined community")[124] through its *Hour of Power* broadcast, the church necessarily served a much broader constituency than the RCA and, thus, should not be subject to the same church order. For Schuller, the strength of the church based on its powerful combination of constituency, charisma, and capital necessitated its independence from the denomination.

Controversy Evaded, with a Little Help

Although his RCA affiliation was often obscured, on several occasions Schuller's Reformed identity rescued his reputation. In a 1981 letter to Voskuil, who had been fielding interview requests from journalists as he wrote his manuscript about Schuller that would be published as *Mountains into Goldmines*, Schuller registered his frustration with the professor. In a recent magazine article, Voskuil's quoted remarks had been somewhat dismissive of the scriptural index to John Calvin's *Institutes of the Christian Religion* Schuller had written while at Western Seminary. Taking umbrage, the minister described the work as a "topical index" that had required him to read the *Institutes* over ten times. Moreover, the end product of the research included over 100 pages, for which Christian publisher Baker Book House had offered a contract.[125] Schuller credited his work on the index as proof of his expertise on Calvinism.

As the decade wore on, concerns over his Calvinist expertise would become less consequential as *Hour of Power* maintained robust ratings, Schuller's stature grew, and the Crystal Cathedral became a popular religious destination. But the peak of Schuller's ministry, unfortunately, coincided with tabloid scandals that shook American Christianity—especially those of the ministries of Jimmy Swaggart and his former friends Jim and Tammy Faye Bakker (Swaggart had attempted to take control of the Bakker's ministry at one point). As a fellow televangelist, Schuller found himself counted as guilty by association.

In that scandalous milieu, accountability became a buzzword, and the *Orange County Register* reported in 1987 that "some officials" from the RCA had been expressing concern that Schuller was overstating the level of financial oversight the denomination practiced with the ministry. During a March 23, 1987, appearance on *Nightline*, Schuller claimed that the RCA held him accountable. Countering an assertion by *Newsweek*'s Woodward that financial indiscretions tended to be a consistent problem for television evangelists, Schuller insisted his denominational affiliation mandated responsibility:

> I happen to belong to the oldest Protestant denomination with an unbroken ministry in the United States of America, the Reformed Church in America. And I have to present a full financial report to the denomination, and we have been in business a long time. I therefore am financially accountable, I'm morally accountable, I'm theologically accountable, I'm ethically accountable. . . . I'm accountable first to the church board, and then I'm accountable to an international board, then I'm accountable to a denomination, and if I fall in error, I can be de-frocked.[126]

Soon after, two representatives from Classis California voiced a concern that Schuller's declaration could be judged as misleading. They would have preferred Schuller to clearly delineate that the Crystal Cathedral congregation and Robert Schuller Ministries (RSM), which produced *Hour of Power*, stood as two distinct entities. Because of that arrangement, the RCA did, indeed, hold Schuller accountable for any *congregational* activities. However, the denomination had no connection to or control over RSM, the substantial and independent entity that produced *Hour of Power* and in 1986 collected over $35 million. The nature of the relationship between the two discrete organizations attracted attention when it became public knowledge that the congregation's board of directors had agreed to sell the entire campus, including church structures, to RSM. The issue of financial accountability also arose when a former employee accused Schuller of lying to financial supporters in a 1981 fund-raising letter.[127]

In the wake of reporting by the *Orange County Register*, John Stapert, still editor of the *Church Herald* and more than willing to interrogate Schuller, directed significant questions regarding the Crystal Cathedral and the RCA's denominational authority. Stapert noted that at the new building's dedication in 1980, the church duly exhibited denominational connections, but since that juncture, the church's affinity for its denomination had become less clear. Stapert also expressed concern about the June 1987 reports that the ownership of the Crystal Cathedral would be transferred to RSM. In turn, the congregation received a ninety-nine-year lease to use the property at one dollar per year while continuing to carry responsibility for a five-million-dollar debt on the property. RCA officials learned of the sale not from the church directly but from reading the *Orange County Register*. Classis California received a request for approval of the sale several months after the church's consistory had made the decision—and then classis officials refused to discuss the decision with the *Church Herald*. In the context of the Jim and Tammy Faye Bakker scandal, Stapert believed that hiding such information engendered suspicion.[128]

Summarizing his thoughts on the inappropriateness of these financial arrangements, Stapert forcefully (and perceptively) concluded:

> One thing I don't believe about this set of transactions is that the resources of Robert Schuller Ministries will, over the long haul, provide more security for the congregation than property ownership and denominational backing would have provided. A denomination with a 359-year history is more likely to be here a hundred years from now than is a television ministry wrapped around an individual personality. Should the denomination outlive Robert Schuller Ministries, I hope the congregation will be able to repurchase its property for last year's selling price. In the meantime, there's probably no need to append "of the Reformed Church in America" to "Crystal Cathedral" when speaking of the building.[129]

As editor of the RCA's *Church Herald*, he argued that the Crystal Cathedral needed the RCA more than the RCA needed the Crystal Cathedral. The assertion that the denomination would live longer than Schuller's ministry foreshadowed the diminishment of not only the television ministry but the entire operation.

Despite the controversy and apparent misgivings within its membership, Classis California formally responded to Stapert with its full support for Schuller. Chester Droog, still a member of Classis California and a Schuller champion, told the *Register* that the classis had "confidence in the board of the Robert Schuller Ministries."[130] In addition, Mark Rozelle, pastor of Parkview Community Church and president of the classis, wrote Schuller a personal letter in May 1987 to clarify the "accountability relationship" of the ministry to the classis. Acknowledging the concerns that had surfaced from the press and from RCA denominational headquarters, Rozelle summarized the (somewhat obsequious) Classis California opinion to Schuller:

> We came out strongly in support of you and without any criticism. . . . We have absolutely no suspicion of wrong doing on your part, we have absolutely no desire to assert ourselves over the Robert Schuller Ministries, we believe the news articles have picked at insignificant matters in a feeble attempt to expose problems in your ministry, we did not hear what you said on "Nightline" and thus have no opinion on whether you overstated your (that is Robert Schuller Ministry's) accountability to us and in fact have no suspicion that you did overstate the matter, we feel that our role is to support you always and to confront you and any other pastor as a loving brother in the event any major wrong doing could be proved.[131]

Rozelle closed by noting that the executive committee of the classis felt very loyal to Schuller because of their confidence in his integrity and believed that the article in the *Orange County Register* had been "regrettable, sensational, and irresponsible." Whatever the denominational leaders at headquarters felt about the Crystal Cathedral and Schuller, it remained clear that the local classis maintained a formal relationship with the megachurch and committed itself to protecting Schuller's reputation, an unmistakable affirmation of his charismatic authority.

Ambiguity and Independence

Schuller drew on a unique combination of Peale's Positive Thinking and Calvin's anthropology of human vocation to craft the charismatic, therapeutic message of Possibility Thinking with enough theological gravitas to resonate with disparate swaths of mainline Protestant and evangelical Christianity. His independence from set doctrine and dogma allowed for an agility in shaping a widely appealing approach that was, in his mind, faithful to orthodox Christianity. Schuller cast himself as a devout Calvinist, yet his theology was for many a therapeutic concoction. Though frequently controversial, as Schuller experimented his way into Possibility Thinking and the Theology of Self-Esteem, he could always point back to his denomination and membership within mainline Protestantism as a guarantor of his legitimacy. Schuller both prized and dismissed his relationship with a historic mainline Protestant denomination. Over time, he became a frustratingly elusive target for standard-bearers of orthodoxy, and the Orange County minister practiced a charismatic caginess in his religious identity. To that end, sociologist of religion James Davison Hunter remarked that Schuller's theology necessarily insinuated that "for nearly 500 years the basic elements of Christian faith have been misunderstood and misapplied." Despite these departures, Hunter concluded that "most evangelicals" had come to share the minister's assumptions regarding the intrinsic value of the self.[132] Schuller, in fact, discovered a theology comprised of both cultural accommodation and Christian orthodoxy in a manner that gave him legitimacy and longevity—to a point.

Schuller's ambiguous religious identity drew a broad and supportive constituency, but it left him vulnerable to attack. Appealing to theological gatekeepers was never a priority. While undeniably attractive to his audience, Schuller's willingness to experiment with how he framed Christianity distanced the minister from possible allies and even his home denomination. The late 1980s' maneuver to extract the cathedral property from typical RCA ownership protocols represented the minister's boldest declaration of autonomy. Ignoring warnings from officials and experts, Schuller embraced the ambiguity of the relationship of the corporation and the congregation to the denomination. His assertion of independence left Schuller without safe harbor. Financial crises would demonstrate the fragility of the ministry's overreliance on continuous infusions of cash in response to his charismatic, idiosyncratic religious identity. Overdependence on the overconfidence that came with Possibility Thinking, an ego-reinforcing "faith" that Norman Vincent Peale himself commended and affirmed, would allow for insidious vulnerabilities that would not be fully appreciated until the ministry found itself in the throes of financial catastrophe.

The nine-story U.S. flag unfurled in the sanctuary of the Crystal Cathedral. Photo courtesy of the Joint Archives of Holland.

5

No Hippies in the Sanctuary

_____

> You have a God-given right to be a
> capitalist.
> —Robert H. Schuller

A memo from Schuller to his ushers sounded an atypical tone from the normally hospitable minister. In the sharply worded note, Schuller exhorted, "Be alert! If any barefooted, or guitar-carrying, or other 'hippie' people arrive, be prepared to *prohibit* their entrance into the sanctuary." In direct contradiction of the church's motto to "come as you are," his ushers received instructions to admonish these visitors: "Advise them that their attire is improper. We have the right to establish these rules. If they don't like it—too bad." Rather than prescribing a welcoming tenor, extending open arms to anyone who would enter and honoring their dignity, Schuller insisted that ushers be prepared to physically bar anyone dressed in such a way from entry: "*Do not let them get into the sanctuary.* Block their bodies with yours. Join hands to form a line if need be." Moreover, it seems that the ministry employed some type of security on the campus, because the minister suggested that "if they become physically difficult, call one of the policemen." In a church that took pride in its organ and music ministry, Schuller ironically insisted, "No musical instruments are permitted in the sanctuary." The traditional organ was fine, but the praise instruments of the hippies or "Jesus People"—the flutes, guitars, and tambourines they often carried—did not belong in a respectable church. Schuller then signed off, "Pray and hope that we have no difficulty."[1]

In the social tumult of the late 1960s, Southern California saw the rise of the "Jesus People," a new group of Christians characterized by informality, emotional intensity, and a youth-oriented Savior who sought to reshape traditional church services.[2] Combining the hippie counterculture with evangelical Christianity, these fervent youth would have a prominent presence in the membership of several growing churches close to Garden Grove Community Church (GGCC), especially Calvary Chapel in Costa Mesa and the Vineyard Christian Fellowship in Anaheim.[3] In 1968, Schuller registered his concern that GGCC worship services might be the target for infiltration by these unconventional, anti-establishment types. So he issued the memorandum to all "head ushers in sanctuary," the guardians of the gates to the building.

Sure enough, shortly after issuing his memorandum, a disruption occurred on a Sunday morning leading to the removal of a group from church grounds. The expulsion drew the ire of a visitor who wrote a letter about the "rudeness" and "anti-Christian" behavior of church staff. Schuller responded, insisting that GGCC undertook the unsavory task of removing the group not because of their "unconforming [sic] dress"; in fact, had the visitor attended services in the last number of years, he "would have seen people in all kinds of unconforming [sic] dress permitted in the sanctuary." Schuller explained:

> The reason this group was asked to leave is because they were in violation of an ordinance [from city government] that prohibits people from sitting on the floor in the Chancel area or in the aisles that could block the exits. We will do this with any people who sit in the aisles or Chancel area. I don't care if they are dressed in tuxedos! I don't care if it is the General of the Army in all his brass uniforms! Had we chosen to evict them from the church, they would have been asked to leave the church grounds. They were permitted to squat and sit on the grass in the Garden of the Good Shepherd area. They are welcome to return any Sunday, as long as 1) they are willing to sit in the pews or chairs provided 2) they will respect our form of worship.[4]

The key phrase to note is that "they will respect our form of worship."

As observed in chapter 3, in the booming suburban expansion after World War II, Southern California became a hothouse of religious intensity.[5] Despite the Crystal Cathedral's greenhouse-like exterior, the church and its minister cultivated a *limited* religious innovation. For Schuller, religious experimentation had constraints and parameters. His attitude toward "hippie Jesus freaks" demonstrated a clear social boundary for what GGCC determined to be acceptable. And as seen in chapter 4, the ministry espoused an upbeat Possibility Thinking message based on a supposition of the rightness of the general political and economic order of the United States. Indeed, the ministry's success did not appeal to cultural outsiders or those challenging the status quo but rather supported a careful mix of capitalism and patriotism. Clearly, "Come as you are" assumed a white, suburban, middle class propriety, one drawn from the dress-up churched cultures of the South and Midwest.

Sociologist Philip Gorski cited Schuller's post–World War II Southern California as the locus of a militaristic version of American religious nationalism because of its role as a center for the defense industry.[6] While working in consonance with this ethos, Schuller persisted in believing that the stance of his church was apolitical, and he diplomatically avoided overt partisanship in his public ministry. Schuller crafted a tactfully obscured political identity that appealed to white middle-class Americans in general and the midcentury residents of Orange County in particular. As Orange County became a focal point of the military-industrial complex, Schuller devised a theology that embraced patriotism, capitalism, and anticommunism. He once described the United States as a "superpower with superpeople who have the superpotential for superproductivity."[7] And, as a complement to his messages, Schuller routinely unfurled a nine-story U.S. flag in the sanctuary for Memorial Day and the Fourth of July—a potent symbol of the amalgamation of Christianity and patriotism.

Schuller's church, then, intentionally promoted a synergy between religion, capitalism, and political conservatism. This alliance bolstered a charismatic resonance between the minister and his supporters. That concoction, though, also demanded constant signals of growth—assurances that Schuller's recipe and affirmation of the status quo remained legitimate. The minister also felt a pressure to showcase his ministry as an ideal manifestation of that synthesis—the most well-produced worship service, the most credible training for pastors, and the most spectacular architecture. Those who attended were expected to conform to the frameworks that buttressed this base of Schuller's charismatic authority. Such efforts incurred costs and demanded a steady influx of people with similar orientations, the intertwined goals of capital and constituency that persisted as an ongoing challenge for the ministry and that his charisma was intended to address.

Possibility Thinking fit well into a seemingly apolitical stance of promoting personal agency in pursuit of personal success. Schuller focused his charismatic authority on the encouragement and uplift of individuals, not prophetic confrontations of intractable systems of inequality and injustice. As a leadership strategy, why should he invest precarious management energy on recalcitrant structural dynamics? Rallying for causes would alienate his base supporters, only dissipating his power to attract people and mobilize new (but similar) constituents for an even larger church. For Schuller, faithful church attendance under a charismatic leader best ensured that individuals would be spiritually affirmed, which motivated their evangelistic actions toward the already familiar social networks of people who are already around them. The church, then, is the instrument of social betterment because it is the place where people hear spiritual

messages. The self-referential nature of the ministry stimulated tithes to be channeled right back into the church to expand the charismatic authority of its minister. Financial giving to the church to support proclaiming those messages and
expand the capacity for more people to hear them, therefore, became the most
tangible means for the faithful Christian to effect social advancement.

Christian Libertarianism

Schuller, of course, knew his context. Southern California has been described
as a "crucible" for conservative politics. When migrants arrived from other parts
of the country, they often carried moderate Democratic political leanings. Soon,
however, they found themselves alienated by what sociologist Lydia Bean called
"California's fragmented culture, militant labor movement, and a Democratic
establishment that despised their old-time religion and feared their provincial"
cultural habits and values.[8] Seizing the opportunity, "California's economic conservatives and intellectual conservatives began working closely with moral conservatives to rally evangelicals behind a consistent small-government agenda."
Bean noted that the new alliance clearly targeted a "domestic 'liberal establishment' as the enemy of patriotic, godly Americans."[9] Having a vivid sense of an
internal enemy galvanized the coalition.

Schuller's Possibility Thinking worldview came to reflect the intertwining of
conservative Christianity with free market capitalism as *Christian libertarianism*, a religious orientation in America that gained significant ground after the
World War I.[10] During that time, mainline Protestant clergy widely supported
the Social Gospel movement, and theologians such as Walter Rauschenbusch
interrogated corporate greed and argued on a biblical basis for the needs of work-
ers. Businessmen tended to fear their teachings as much too similar to those of
socialism. Philanthropically minded corporate titans (including Schuller's fellow member of the larger Dutch Reformed tradition and cofounder of Amway,
Richard DeVos) sought to counter the Social Gospel through a concerted effort
of offering significant financial support to resonant evangelical ministers who
affirmed their business-friendly version of Christian patriotism. The CEOs of
Chrysler, General Motors, and Eastern Airlines did the same, joining eponymous
businesses with names such as Hilton, Pew, and Kraft to throw financial heft into
disseminating their version of a sound Christian faith.[11] Generous donations
sought to promote biblical teachings that endorsed legitimacy for a "Christian
economics" that fully embraced the principles of free market enterprise.[12]

By the end of the twentieth century, Orange County was cited as the locus
where this evangelically inflected capitalism had been perfected. Christian
libertarianism readily aligned with the conservative political and economic
values found in most white-majority churches in Southern California.[13] For
Schuller, though, this framework resourced an identity that appeared to support the values of openness and accessibility while striking resonant notes for

the largely conservative constituency on whom his ministry particularly depended. Christian libertarianism also avoided the exclusivity of fundamentalists and their political causes, which often promoted separatism from worldly affairs alongside explicit Republican partisanship. Schuller explained his ostensibly apolitical orientation in 1983: "I have an irrevocable and unending commitment to strengthen the church without getting involved in the politics and controversies."[14]

In his more than fifty years of ministry, Schuller mastered a largely apolitical pose oriented around Possibility Thinking and his Theology of Self-Esteem that both implicitly and explicitly endorsed limited government and the beneficence of the free market. With claims against the reach of the federal government and a rejection of political solutions to the problems of economic suffering and poverty consistent with libertarian ideals, Schuller joined a cohort of prominent pastors, which included his mentor Norman Vincent Peale (see chapter 4), who refrained from looking toward collective solutions to alleviate systemic issues. Instead, this Christian libertarian framework assumed that the individual had been gifted by God with talent and agency and an ability to enter into the freedoms guaranteed on the assumptions of a free market. Within that schema, the individual exercised the free will to move forward—to step into opportunities, not be discouraged, and trust in the God who provides options, all within a political system premised on the promises of liberty and the pursuit of happiness.[15] As Schuller wrote, "The person who seizes opportunities with passion, persistence, and positive attitudes will always be generously and proportionately rewarded."[16] Only individual initiative matters.

In 2006 Schuller appeared on *Larry King Live*. A caller to the broadcast asked what the minister thought about the George W. Bush administration's apparent mishandling of the Hurricane Katrina aftermath on the Gulf Coast. Schuller first noted that he "did not take political sides," and then explained that he did not see Bush as blameworthy. When King pressed him about the catastrophic consequences of Katrina and whether it shook his faith, the minister demurred. The conversation continued when King pressed the question: "But [God] could have prevented the scene?" Schuller countered by emphasizing personal responsibility:

SCHULLER I don't think so, [not] without eliminating free will among human beings.

KING But free will had nothing to do with a hurricane—free will with a hurricane . . . ?

SCHULLER It had something to do with the people that chose to live there.

KING You blame the people that chose to live there?

SCHULLER I'm not blaming them. I'm saying we have to think—a family is wiped out in a hurricane, and [then] they came to live where they wouldn't be hit by a hurricane.

Schuller cited his own family experience with a tornado in Iowa as an illustration, relating that he had been the "victim of almost a hurricane" and then continuing: "We were wiped out in a tornado. We got in a car, and we ran away and we saved our lives. We lost everything."[17] When King asked if he blamed God for the tornado, Schuller scoffed, "Of course not." Relying on his personal narrative of overcoming a catastrophe, Schuller insisted that, first, neither the government nor God should be blamed and, second, that with enough grit, the survivors of Hurricane Katrina could follow the lead of his family in Iowa when they rebuilt the farm. As Schuller added about his California ministry, "We focus on empowering [people] with faith."

As evidenced here and in many of his interviews, messages, and publications, Schuller unknowingly embraced the ideology of Christian libertarianism, a framework with roots traced back to the Gilded Age of the United States, in which the sociopolitical system is accepted as good and proper—rewarding the talents of hardworking people with opportunity and prosperity.[18] It is the ideology that frames Possibility Thinking and the Theology of Self-Esteem. If problems occur, if obstacles are encountered, Schuller assumed this was only due to individual problems, individual obstacles.[19] Individuals must overcome their own self-limitations, especially their own predilection toward a self-defeating spiral of shame. (Schuller translated this into his Theology of Self-Esteem.) With the confidence of faith, then, nothing can hinder success. Individuals have the capacity to enter into the system of rewards assured by God and available for all. It is a familiar framework of faith that underlay commonsense notions embedded among Schuller's white, upwardly mobile, suburban audience and made his messages viable, resonant, and legitimate.

Patriotic and Anticommunist

Schuller's form of preaching always incorporated a strong dose of patriotic fervor upholding America's political and economic system. Industrialists and ministers like him who prized the economic engine of the free market directed significant devotion toward their vision of a country that fostered unfettered opportunity. In 1972, as signifier of his own allegiance to the United States and its systems, Schuller composed a sermon titled, "I Am the American Flag." As might be expected, the homily praised the virtues of the American capitalist democracy ("Freedom to borrow and build, to buy and sell, to make an honest profit in return for real service sincerely offered").[20] Though Schuller believed himself to be apolitical, he certainly saw himself—and Christianity—as unquestionably patriotic. In unfurling a nine-story American flag in the midst of his Christian sanctuary, Schuller engaged in a rhetorical maneuver that drew on "the emotional reservoirs of both American myth and religious doctrine."[21]

In his early years in Garden Grove, Schuller spent considerable energy equating his form of patriotic Christianity with anticommunism. With Cold War threats looming over—and catalyzing—the growing military economy of Orange County, Schuller experimented with anticommunism as a central tenet of his ministry. In his anticommunism, Schuller added his voice to a well-established and long-legitimized chorus in the United States,[22] an orientation especially relevant to his Cold War audience who lived in an area saturated with industries funded by defense contracts. Six years before Schuller's move to Southern California, Billy Graham had warned a Los Angeles audience that communism cloaked a new version of "religion that is inspired, directed, and motivated by the Devil himself."[23] Graham, though, assured the gathering that through faith in Christ, communism could be defeated. The message resonated with crowds anxious about the advent of the atomic age and haunted by the shadows of the Cold War. Historian Daniel K. Williams described Graham as a little-known fundamentalist before his Los Angeles crusade. Thereafter, he raised his profile as an "emerging national celebrity—a young dynamic speaker who could draw crowds by offering the spiritual antidote to communism."[24] Graham eventually parlayed his staunchly anticommunist message into a status as the most high-profile evangelical in the nation, a pastor and friend to presidents. Schuller considered doing the same.

Thus, a milieu of conservative Christian culture in Southern California that identified anticommunism as an in-group adhesive had already coalesced by the time Schuller strode to the top of the concession stand at the Orange Drive-in. Early in this ministry, Schuller attended a weeklong class sponsored by the Anti-Communist League (his tuition covered by a benefactor of the church) in 1960.[25] Led by Fred Schwarz, an Australian physician, the class featured a curriculum that posed American Christianity as the world's best hope for a remedy to atheistic communism. Though he enjoyed a national profile, Schwarz found his most welcoming audiences in Southern California. Of course, it helped that Schwarz's anticommunist sentiments gained the endorsement of celebrities who ranged from Ronald Reagan to Jimmy Stewart to Nat "King" Cole to Ozzie and Harriet Nelson. Historian Kevin Kruse described Schwarz as "one of the most energetic and effective voices advancing the cause of religious nationalism in the late 1950s and early 1960s."[26] Schuller found himself learning from a master in synthesizing celebrity, Christianity, and civic concern.

After Schwarz's class, Schuller conveyed great alarm regarding the communist menace around the world and in the United States. In a letter, the minister framed communism as insidious: "I am deeply impressed by the fact that the majority of our ministers, churches, and even missionaries in foreign fields do not understand what communism really is and are being subtly brainwashed through publications that come from the radical liberal wing of world religious movements." Moreover, communism represented a threat to religious freedom: "I personally feel that unless we have a great spiritual revival of evangelical Christianity in the United States (2 Chronicles 14) our nation and the world will lose their freedom to speak and write for our religion."[27] In the same letter, Schuller declared that all seminary students should read FBI director J. Edgar Hoover's books and articles on the topic within a class on communism.[28] The minister clearly believed that preaching about the threat of communism in the Christian ministry should be encouraged.

That same year, Schuller, taking his cues from Schwarz, began advocating Christianity as the sole solution to defeat worldwide communism. The minister highlighted a fall sermon series entitled "How You Can Help Defeat Communism." In a marketing pitch to members of GGCC, Schuller warned that active communist agents lived nearby in Orange County and that "they are dedicated, determined, terribly brave, confident of ultimate victory, and will stop at nothing to win!" Schuller counseled his members that the Communist Party wielded enough power to "take over in America" and that they themselves, the members of GGCC, likely had already been duped into "contributing to their cause right now."[29] With that in mind, Schuller promised a sermon that would "outline a program for the defeat of communism," featuring Hoover's "six positive suggestions." An alarmed Schuller expressed a sense that God clearly preferred the current U.S. political system. He exclaimed, "History is a story of the rise and fall of men, empires, and nations. May God forbid that the story should ever record the fall of democratic government. We join this week with Lincoln in praying 'that government of the people, by the people, for the people shall not perish from the earth.'"[30]

Beyond just educating members, Schuller sought to leverage his anticommunist message into higher attendance. In a press release describing the sermon series, GGCC invited everyone from the community to hear about what they could "do to defeat worldwide communism." Schuller promised to outline a plan of action "to preserve [the] American way of life, to preserve the liberties of our children." The press release framed the communist threat as dire and growing, reporting that though the movement had started in 1903 with one leader and seventeen disciples, by 1960 communism claimed one billion adherents and a beachhead only ninety miles from the United States in Cuba. Schuller also stressed how communist leaders planned for worldwide domination and expected the capitulation of the United States by 1973. Finally, the release noted the skillful ways in which communists would target Orange County: "To demoralize America by infiltrating into institutions, organizations, etc., in this country. To remove or reduce to an ineffective state any and all organizations, committees, etc., that hinder their infiltration today. Orange County with its educators, engineers, electronics experts, is a target for subtle, skillful, winsome, deceitful infiltration." Perhaps most alarming, Schuller disclosed, in a preview of his sermon, that perhaps "America has elected its last President."[31]

The concern about communism permeated the ethos of GGCC in the early 1960s. In 1961 Schuller publicly disassociated from the National Council of Churches because of the organization's condemnation of anticommunism.[32] Even at the dedication of the new hybrid walk-in–drive-in church, noted "Positive

Thinker" Norman Vincent Peale cast a pall over what might have been expected to be a celebratory Sunday. During his remarks, Peale disclosed that because of the looming threat of communism, "the Christian church is fighting for its life." Peale continued by detailing the specter of nuclear fallout: "Today we fear the air we breathe. Always we have looked up into God's beautiful sky and have feared nothing and now suddenly we are made to fear the fallout." Peale blamed the vulnerability of the United States on "intellectuals and, God help them, preachers" who have confused the American people "with a lack of confidence in our system." While heralding the event, even GGCC's press release reporting the dedication service duly noted that "Dr. Peale did not paint a completely optimistic picture of the future."[33] GGCC followed the last of the 1960 sermon series by offering a free showing of the U.S. Navy–produced film *Challenge to America*. A press release quoted Schuller: "It is indeed one of the most challenging and constructively disturbing films I have ever seen on the problem facing America."[34]

Schuller's interest in anticommunism further fueled his charismatic presence in Orange County. The California Free Enterprise Association published a "Freedom Study Clubs Guide" that included local resources to better understand the "communist conspiracy." The guide highlighted Schuller as a speaker worthy of invitation.[35] Schuller also served as committee member on the Orange County School of Anti-Communism and joined the Californians' Committee to Combat Communism.[36] His identity as a minister knowledgeable about the threat of communism gave Schuller both religious *and* political legitimacy.

At certain points, the minister utilized larger anticommunist sentiments for rhetorical points to specifically advance GGCC's agenda. In 1964, Schuller decried movements to tax church properties—a change that would cut the flow of capital into his church. In an effort to ostensibly equate taxation of congregations as an un-American practice, Schuller noted that the Communist Party in the United States had been agitating for the same policy change for at least three decades. Schuller argued that in GGCC's case, the church would be liable for a yearly taxation of $22,000 that would negatively impact benevolence budgets and denominational contributions (other expenses such as his salary or production overhead for his broadcast avoided mention). He intimated that perhaps the United States would find itself in a more communist and totalitarian future where it would be "easy to imagine that many congregations would eventually lose their property to the state."[37]

In addition, Schuller's savvy regarding communism offered the potential for enhancing his international reputation. After a trip to Asia in 1970, Schuller reported his hope that *Hour of Power* would eventually be broadcast from Tokyo. He was confident that the show could staunch a possible communist movement among the Japanese: "And on this island, looking across the waters to the mainland Communist China, live the Japanese people with a real ideological religious vacuum. Unless something positive, like Christianity, fills their minds, they will be ready and ripe for the Communist move."[38] In this and other occasions, Schuller cast his religious program as a bulwark in the fight against communism.

In late 1972, emboldened by the profile granted with the anticommunist stance, Schuller discussed the possibility of starting an endeavor he would call Freedom of Religion (FOR). In a letter to Dick Cavett of the *Dick Cavett Show*, Schuller reported that he became concerned about the issue during a recent visit to the USSR. The minister also mentioned that the itinerary for the tour included a stop at Leningrad's Museum of Atheism and Religion.[39] After ensuring that Cavett understood his religious profile by casually mentioning that the museum included a photo of Schuller alongside the pope and Martin Luther King, he made his pitch: "Would you be willing to dialogue with me on this important issue on one of your upcoming television programs?" In an effort to demonstrate the intensity of the need for the FOR, Schuller alluded to the civil rights movement in the United States: "The time arrived—in the late 1960s—when Negroes in the South realized that they had an intrinsic human right to eat, sleep, and ride on buses! The time has come, I declare, when nations must come to realize that any Country hoping to be respected as a Nation in the Community of Nations must allow all religious faiths the freedom to worship; or be called, not a Country in an International Community, but a cult forcibly occupying parochial territory on Planet Earth!"[40] Communism represented not just a political and economic threat but also an existential menace. For Schuller, the communist crisis energized his base, boosting his charismatic appeal by raising the stakes of his message beyond the provincial borders of Garden Grove.

In other instances, a publicly anticommunist position allowed Schuller protection when he interviewed politically controversial celebrities from the pulpit. In 1976, Schuller invited former Black Panther and newly converted Christian Eldridge Cleaver to appear on *Hour of Power*. When he received criticism from viewers and members of the congregation, Schuller vigorously defended Cleaver's presence at GGCC. One member wrote to report that he and his family would be leaving GGCC for "another church home where the person in the pulpit on Sunday morning personifies a true Christian without a recent criminal past,"[41] Schuller responded with a note wondering whether this congregant had heard anything that Eldridge said and listing some of the key elements of Eldridge's appearance: "1) He publicly confessed his sins and errors, 2) he has had a personal experience with Jesus Christ and believes that he has been forgiven, 3) his sincerity is proven by his willingness to return to face the music in court and accept whatever the court decides, 4) he put down Communism and has replaced it with Jesus Christ."[42] For Schuller, then, Cleaver represented a resounding success story for the manner in which Christian faith defeated communism. But the controversy of his appearance before the congregation revealed the conservatism of his members.

The minister maintained his preoccupation with communism into the 1980s. During a tour of the USSR in 1982, Billy Graham reported that he had experienced "total liberty" in preaching sermons while there and disputed the notion that the country allowed for no form of religious freedom.[43] Perhaps because his marketing firm had been seeking venues for raising his profile with the impending release of *Self-Esteem: The New Reformation*, Schuller felt compelled to make a strong statement denouncing Graham's characterization of religious freedom in the USSR. Departing from his typical deference to America's leading evangelist, Schuller described Graham's statements as "incomprehensible." Pointing to his own three visits over the past decade, Schuller contrasted Graham's bearing with his own while in the USSR: "I maintained a low profile and made no public statements. I also made it a point not to be escorted by the communist-appointed state escorts." Schuller also reported that he had witnessed "terrible repression" and that he considered any statements indicating a level of religious freedom in the USSR to be "both misleading and inaccurate."[44] Such a negative critique of an evangelist of Graham's reputation demonstrated the importance of a vehemently anticommunist stance for Schuller.

A Nonpolitical Politicism

Though Schuller clearly favored more conservative ideologies and the free market, he hesitated to further segment his market and therefore refrained from explicit political partisanship. One local journalist described the minister as approaching social and economic issues "with the caution of man treading through a mine field."[45] In a letter to Ruth Peale (Norman's wife) in 1971, Schuller revealed his avoidance of controversial policy by discussing two discordant political figures whom he admired for their strong, inspirational leadership—Martin Luther King and General Douglas MacArthur—but who covered wildly disparate leadership causes and concerns.[46] Later, in a 1983 conversation, the minister lamented that in resisting the hard-right political turn of some other aforementioned high-profile pastors, Schuller had invited scorn for his hesitancy in joining the partisan herd. Schuller's ostensible apolitical stance differed from that of some of his brethren in the electronic church (the so-called Big 8, which included Oral Roberts, Rex Humbard, Pat Robertson, Jim Bakker, Jerry Falwell, Billy Graham, Jimmy Swaggart)[47] who found new profiles as outspoken supporters of the Religious Right. During the 1980 presidential campaign of Ronald Reagan, Schuller refused to join "his theologically more conservative colleagues in their political adventure."[48] In *Mountains into Goldmines*, Voskuil described Schuller as "to the right on the political spectrum," and Schuller responded in the margins of the galleys, "Not true!"[49] Later, Schuller bristled at Voskuil's suggestion that the minister promoted a "*laissez-faire* individualism" and again scribbled, "Not true."[50] Schuller considered himself unimpeachably centrist and insisted that it would be "terribly unfair" to consider him "Rightest."[51] He suggested to Voskuil, "I wouldn't mind if you said, 'While some of his self-help messages might be interpreted as being oriented toward social and political conservatism, Schuller's been caught in the religious stampede of the Religious Right.'" Such discretion also allowed the *Hour of Power* minister the opportunity to maintain an audience that perhaps "went well beyond conservative church folk."[52]

Schuller intended to cloak any political sympathies by portraying himself as above the fray, even when he implicitly conveyed a conservative streak. In a May 25, 1962, letter to the editor in the *Church Herald*, Schuller responded to an article written by John Beardslee III, a faculty member at the RCA-associated Central College in Pella, Iowa. In the wake of Senator Joseph McCarthy's House Un-American Activities Committee (HUAC) hearings, the professor had argued that "Communism is satanic, but 'anti-communism' may also be satanic. Not everyone who 'opposes communism' is serving Christ."[53] Beardslee wrote his article in a context wherein the 1961 RCA General Synod had received two separate overtures concerning the work of the HUAC: "One classis wanted the Committee to be praised for its anti-Communist work; another wanted it to be rebuked for its methods." Schuller, noting that a member of the HUAC attended his church, cautioned against negativity: "And I would rise to the defense of the House Committee on Un-American Activities. I resent sweeping, generalized charges against this committee which cast a cloud over the integrity of every elected American official who makes up this committee!"[54]

Years later, in the heat of the Watergate scandal involving President Richard Nixon, Schuller quietly voiced support for right-wing politicians. In a note, he confided to Norman Vincent Peale his conservative bona fides: "Norman, I do share your trust and affection for our President. I will continue to pray for him."[55] In contrast to his later association with the Clintons, Schuller's evangelical identity largely assumed conservative leanings, even when he pushed back against such characterization.

Nevertheless, Schuller's *public* persona sought to reinforce an ability to span the political spectrum. In the mid-1970s he once shared his GGCC pulpit with the unlikely trinity of a Watergate conspirator, an underground Nazi-resistance worker, and a former Black Panther (Charles Colson, Corrie ten Boom, and Eldridge Cleaver, respectively).[56] Producers of *Hour of Power* always leavened public appearances of "liberal" figures by booking someone with a conservative reputation. As *Hour of Power* grew in stature and profile, Schuller established a strategy for avoiding the appearance of playing political favorites. A local journalist noted, "Not incidentally, Schuller assiduously avoids using his pulpit as a political platform. If his guest one week is a prominent Democrat, he will almost certainly try to feature an equally prominent Republican the next week." Schuller's well-manicured and yet amorphous political profile was what allowed him to sit next to Hillary Rodham Clinton at the 1997 State of the Union Address. Journalists at the time dismissed Schuller and President Bill Clinton as "spiritual soulmates" because while one engaged in ministry and the other in politics, both manipulated "smoke and mirrors" rather than substance in their professional endeavors.[57] For Schuller, though, his appearance represented not an occasion for partisanship but rather an opportunity to further heighten his charisma through proximity to power.

Above partisanship, his apolitical centrism presumed a ringing endorsement of the current order. The minister seemed loathe to take any position that might unalign him with wealthy capitalists, and his upbeat messages offered a comfortingly palatable affirmation to beneficiaries of the status quo. In appealing to his mass audience and soliciting project funds from wealthy patrons, Schuller likely saw little upside in making a concerted effort to stake out more definitive positions on concrete issues of the day. In numerous instances, the minister feared being publicly pigeonholed politically. Even when Schuller dabbled with establishing the Freedom of Religion (FOR) initiative in the early 1970s, he assured possible supporters he had no interest in forming an anticommunist or pro-American "movement."[58] The pastor felt a necessity in striking a strident anticommunist posture while at the same time not sullying his reputation for being above partisan issues by associating with something as undignified and subversive as a "movement."

Schuller's aloofness signaled a restraint that had been more typical of earlier generations of ministers. Sociologist Robert Wuthnow reported that numerous studies from the 1960s and 1970s revealed a pattern: "The more conservative one was religiously, the less likely it was that one would be involved in political activities."[59] One study indicated that Americans during that era tended to find political activity as so incongruous with the ministerial propriety that it was seen as deviant. Even as other high-profile ministers broke with historical precedent and rushed to embrace the Religious Right, Schuller's avoidance of political rhetoric harkened back to a historical template of politically reserved ministers.

A Nonprophetic Church

Schuller also assumed his best-selling books would be interpreted as politically innocuous. Instead, they further catalyzed critiques that Schuller was erring on the side of cultural accommodation. In 1974, theologian John Mulder (no relation) wrote a scathing review of *You Can Become the Person You Want to Be*. Mulder described Schuller's theology as a blend of "social, economic, and political entrepreneurial worship, blessed by the precepts of religion, and tailored to prosperous, aspiring, but anxious middle-class America." Beyond that, Schuller "enthusiastically and blatantly interpreted" success in "material terms."[60] Mulder reported that he found the book "disturbing" for the manner in which it allied "the sanctions of religion with the goal of success." Moreover, Mulder expressed exasperation that "Schuller contributes to the anti-intellectualism in American life which disdains those who ask questions or express doubt about the values by which men live. Politically, 'possibility thinking,' contributes to the repression of dissent, enemy lists, and the injunctions of a President who wants Watergate put behind him and a reaffirmation of what's right with America." Mulder chastised Schuller for his well-worn ambivalence in challenging the status quo. Beyond that, he wondered aloud regarding the minister's complicit silence: "Schuller has little patience with those who ask questions about the means by which success is obtained, the moral compromises involved in any exercise of power, or the barriers of race, poverty, war, injustice, and disease; and when confronted by difficulties, you can always use the time-honored technique of the powerful—manipulate the institutions."[61] Thus, not even an ostensible apolitical stance allowed Schuller to ever truly escape a vivid political identity.

Perhaps because of Mulder's withering rebuke, the next year, 1975, Schuller sought to again boost the charismatic credentials of his position with an article in October entitled "The Church's Prophetic Stance." Therein he argued that the church had lost any prophetic credibility because it offered no unified voice. The deep divisions within the American church muted its message. Both liberal and conservative church leaders tended to fulfill their perceived prophetic obligations "to lash out with inflammatory, judgmental, negative" sermons. To demonstrate the deleterious consequences of strident sermonizing, Schuller alluded to an experience he had in the late 1950s.

The mostly mainline Protestant ministers in the Ministerial Association in Garden Grove expressed alarm because the John Birch Society had been distributing literature condemning the National Council of Churches for harboring pastors acting as either "secret agents" or "dupes" of the "Communist conspiracy." In response, the mainline ministers of Garden Grove (except for Schuller) concluded that they would all preach sermons the following Sunday condemning the irresponsible behavior of the society. Schuller criticized the effort as a mistake ("clumsy and un-Christian") and pointed to his parallel effort: a new sermon series with the theme "Believe the Best about People—Trust Them and Doubt Suspicion."

According to Schuller, his alternate strategy, of course, yielded better results. The anti–John Birch Society sermons by his ministerial colleagues received applause by congregants already in that camp, confused and perplexed members who knew "good people" in the society, and inflamed the society members sitting in the pews—turning them into "vicious enemies." On the other hand, Schuller described the affirmation he received for his more positive approach:

> The few hard-core, neurotic John Birchers in my congregation quietly drifted away because my messages failed to feed their suspicions, their paranoia, their hostility, their hatred, their frustration and their distrust. Borderline John Birchers were turned away from paranoia to healthy thinking. They were filled with positive emotions to the point where they found negative emotion-producing pamphlets, rallies, and indoctrination classes offensive and unpalatable.[62]

He went on to opine, "There are two ways to fight wolves," and explored the metaphor to illuminate the effectiveness of his approach to preaching:

> One is to listen for their call in the night, pick up a stick, run out into the blackness and charge the beast. You might chase him off. On the other hand, you might come back bloody, bleeding, and half dead. True, you might be applauded as a hero! The odds are the wolf would come back once he has tasted blood, and you have done your cause more harm than good. The second way to fight a wolf is a positive approach. Do two things. 1. Withdraw and hide all food, water, and nourishment from them. Leave no food around for their nostrils to catch hold of. 2. Build a fire and keep the flames burning bright! After a while, I submit, the wolf will go where he can find food for he craves food and fears the light.[63]

For Schuller, his sermon demonstrated a triumph of his charismatic power. The minister expressed his pessimism regarding the effectiveness of "prophetic" preaching and advocated instead for social change through individual conversion. Yes, he allowed, "church can succeed in correcting social injustices and sins. The strategy, however, calls for social redemption before social action." Schuller articulated his conviction that ministers should never use their pulpits to address controversial issues in an effort to catalyze social change. Instead, they should "lead people to make a commitment to Christ, to God, and the Word of God which will produce the conscience, which will give rise to a personal desire to fulfill the value system, which will correct the injustices that offend us all."[64]

Thus, Schuller was convinced that the only method for changing structures and systems involved individual conversion—a classic revivalist approach to social problems. Already in 1955, just as he assumed his pastorate in Garden Grove, Schuller wrote an article in the RCA's *Church Herald* that social problems had only one remedy: "The world will only be made right as Christ comes to the hearts of men."[65] He continued: "Yes, the hope of the world is a living, dynamic, witnessing Church of Christ. As each person then dedicates and surrenders his life to Christ, the world is being made better."[66] Schuller uttered an early form of what sociologists Michael Emerson and Christian Smith would later identify as the "miracle motif," the conviction, prevalent among white evangelicals, that individual conversions to Christianity represented the best method for social change.[67]

Within the social turmoil of the 1960s, Schuller reported that he continued to study the "sciences of human behavior." Acutely influenced by the writing of psychiatrist Victor Frankl, Schuller described his personal shift from what he labeled as a "collectivist" orientation to that of "individualism." The minister understood his original collectivism as residue of his Calvinist and Reformed culture that saw salvation as a "holy club" to be born into. Without the personal decision of conversion, collectivism, for Schuller, led to paternalism. Recalling that he had been initially dumbstruck in witnessing a Billy Graham altar call to *personal* conversion, Schuller eventually found himself persuaded by evangelical notions of individual responsibility.[68]

When a mainline Lutheran minister attended the leadership institute in 1975, he queried a GGCC staffer about the church's prophetic responsibilities. The staffer, it seemed, interpreted "prophetic" strictly as regarding end-of-days prophecy and responded that GGCC considered itself a "non-prophetic church." Thinking that his terminology may have been misunderstood, the Lutheran minister reframed his question: "How does the church address social issues of the day?" Even with rephrasing, the staffer maintained his position: "Our people witness on the job by telling others about Christ and the church and by helping heal the hurts of society and by tithing."[69] At GGCC, social justice centered on individuals who interacted evangelistically with others and gave generously to their church. This staff member summarized the ministry philosophy by reiterating, "We are a non-prophetic church."

Schuller frequently asserted that churches should be functionally apolitical, because he not only distrusted their ability to influence policy but, more importantly, believed a focus on policy served as a misguided distraction. The true Christian solution to social problems resulted from individual conversions. Schuller interpreted the call from progressive mainline Protestant churches to "march in the streets" and "fight social injustice" as "near panic" attempts by anachronistic institutions to remain relevant.[70] Bemused and cautioned by their flailing, Schuller decided his books, sermons, and ministry structures all would be oriented around transforming the individual to have the right faith, which would yield the right kind of life.

The distinction manifested itself in a 1966 letter Schuller wrote to the editor in the *Church Herald*. The minister expressed his dismay that the General Synod of the RCA of the same year had spent time debating the admission of "Red China" to the United Nations. Schuller wrote that the church might gain notice for becoming more involved politically, but not without a cost: "It is the considered opinion of [GGCC] that continuing involvement by the church in political pronouncements will only strain to the breaking point the patience of many people in the Church who have heretofore been quietly silent." Beyond that, Schuller expressed concern that political activity by churches would necessarily chill their ability to evangelize: "It is true that if the Church increases its activities in political affairs that it will not be loved. It is also true that it will be noticed and known. But it will continue to be ignored by growing masses of spiritually hungry men and women who will become quite convinced that the Church has no spiritual inspiration for their feeble faith and fainting heart." He suspected that such deliberations would have only insignificant influence: "It is extremely doubtful that all of the political activity will ever change the political machines that grind out policy in our world."[71]

Schuller reckoned that confronting the political and economic status quo would have stirred up unwanted attention, and he forcefully articulated in 1983[72] that he had no interest in antagonizing people: "My contention is never verbalize on the negative until you're prepared to sell positive creative solution. Otherwise all you do is inflame people. And you polarize people." Schuller also reported his concerns about the lack of constructive dialogue inherent in the prophetic approach: "And when you polarize people you create a mental dialogue where creativity of dialogue and hearing and listening doesn't happen. Then you're arguing and when you're arguing you don't even listen to the other person. You're dreaming already up your answer to his argument." Schuller reported that he had no personal inhibitions regarding the healthy exchange of opinion: "I did well in debate at Hope College. I'm good at it. I know that." But he also found that it caused predatory listening in that "when your opponent is up there, they're sure to say an anticipatory rebuttal. That's the trouble with the negative prophetic approach." Schuller also elaborated that being prophetic had little efficacy in a pluralistic society:

> And history has terrible judgment on classical protestant theology of the 20th century. And where do they get it? They get it from what context, where do they get it, you tell me, I'll tell you, from the Old Testament prophets, right? You know the fatal flaw in that argument? The fatal flaw in that argument [is] their prophetic pronouncements were made in the context of a theocratic state. Not in a pluralistic society. And to draw a whole theology of prophetic pronouncements against social injustices and out of context where people are coming out of a theocratic society and to try to apply that in a pluralistic, democratic institution, like the United States is doomed for failure and they failed.

The minister revealed his perception that modern prophetic efforts had been proven futile: "They really have failed. They really have. The record is not good. We still have, well racism has vastly improved, I would give great credit to Martin Luther King on racism. But boy, the other injustices I think are about as deep rooted as we've ever seen them." As an alternative, Schuller suggested a "positive prophetic approach." He also noted that he himself had been prophetic in an individual case—but only as a last resort:

> When the first blacks moved into this community they moved two blocks from my beautiful new stained-glass chapel. Which is before we moved here, you know? And a mob gathered in front of their house. Who went there and broke them up? I did. There was a time when you have to do it, I admit that. But as a general policy as a general strategy as a basic general approach I would say, "no."[73]

Policy modifications would not fix social problems; spiritual transformation did. And Schuller assumed the force of his preaching offered the most effective means to stimulate that transformation.

Sanctifying Free Enterprise

While reticent to assert partisanship, Schuller was not hesitant to elevate the dominant economic system of the United States. As a consistent champion of capitalism over against communism and socialism, Schuller anticipated critiques of the extravagance of his glass church's worship space. Schuller grew tired of disparagements of the $20 million price tag for the Crystal Cathedral—especially when commenters noted how readily that money could have been utilized to serve the impoverished. In the afterglow of the cathedral's recent opening, Hope College professor Dennis Voskuil interviewed Schuller in September 1980 as he conducted research for his book *Mountains into Goldmines*.[74] Voskuil queried the minister about his response to the cost of the cathedral in the context of a world "full of poverty." Schuller dismissed the concern and turned the conversation into an appraisal of the inherent naiveté of socialism: "Oh that's so easy, so easy, to answer because I'm not a socialist you see." Talk of the cost of the cathedral threatened to undermine his charisma, so he leveraged that criticism to strengthen it even further by arguing that the structure should be understood as an emblem of the success of the capitalist system—and socialism became an easy foil. The dedication of the Crystal Cathedral (see chapter 1) included conspicuous nods of appreciation to the civil order under which Schuller's ministry flourished: Boy Scouts with flags and messages of congratulations from President Jimmy Carter and his Republican rival in the upcoming fall election, former California governor Ronald Reagan. The local papers described these cameos in the worship service as a "secular touch," though they may have been better described as a version of civil religion, affirming Schuller's ministry as part of the grandness of the American project.[75]

As the opulence of the cathedral drew attention, Schuller countered forcefully: "I am not a good, beautiful, sincere, intelligent socialist. I am a Christian capitalist." Schuller then, turning hyperbolic, argued that the socialist economic system would undermine all congregational life in the United States: "If I were [socialist], I'd also have to sell my house and this church, and every church would have to sell its property."[76] In an interview with his alma mater's student newspaper, Schuller again remarked, "I'm not a socialist. I never learned to be a socialist at Hope College." Schuller then turned the argument and obliquely wondered about the political and economic orientations of his critics: "If I were a socialist, I would say, 'Let's take all the money and feed the poor.' But if I did that, I would be one of them—then I would be poor. What we need in this world is not the distribution of wealth, but the generation of new wealth."[77]

Schuller explained that the $20 million invested in the cathedral would, in his estimate, generate vast amounts of cash for missionary work—and all because of the utilization of "dynamic, creative, capitalistic principles." Critics should see the cost as an investment that will yield much higher returns: "If I gave away the 20 million dollars that's all [the poor would] get."[78] In contrast, the church will use the new building "to generate new wealth. On the opening Sunday, *we'll take an offering*, which hopefully may have a million dollars, to build a hospital in Chiapas, Mexico" (emphasis added). In a bold prediction, Schuller expected that tithes to the Crystal Cathedral would "generate a minimum of 200 million dollars in the next 20 years and probably up to two billion. B-I-L-L-I-O-N dollars for missionary work." Schuller declared that "the private enterprise system is tremendous" because capitalism "generates money, which builds churches, which sustains missions abroad, while at home it perpetuates the self-confidence without which the poverty and unemployment problems will never be solved!" Moreover, having built the Crystal Cathedral debt-free symbolized "to the nation and the world that capitalism is a fantastic system."

Within his argument lay an embedded message: church members need not feel guilt for their own pursuit of wealth because, when given as tithes to their congregation, they will function as public benefactors for godly causes. For Schuller, then, capitalism was a noble good that functioned as an engine for the betterment of impoverished nations and the general flourishing of Christianity. Integral to this viewpoint, he habitually pursued partnerships with wealthy Christian capitalists, couching their donations to his ministry as fulfilling noble initiatives.

Schuller's conflation of modern Christian faith and capitalism and his alignment with wealthy businessmen represented a larger trend in American Christianity, especially an intertwined history with probusiness sentiments. In the era between the Civil War and World War I, "corporate evangelicals" set themselves about the task of establishing the case that Christianity and modern consumer capitalism had an inescapably synergistic relationship. With a striking deliberateness, men such as Henry Parsons Crowell (president of Quaker Oats) created a corporate evangelical network of institutions like Moody Bible Institute in Chicago to disseminate a framework that blessed business practices and consumer capitalism with a correct faith. According to historian Timothy Gloege, Croswell and his network, however, mostly included individuals who would be best labeled as "fundamentalists."[79] Though Schuller distanced himself from fundamentalist doctrine, he had no inhibitions of jointly carrying forward the message that Christianity and capitalism worked together to fulfill the idea of God's kingdom on earth. Schuller expressed confidence that his church and multilevel marketing corporations like DeVos's Amway represented only slightly different manifestations of the American synergy of Christianity and capitalism.

While Schuller and ministers like him operated as apologists for capitalism, other Christian leaders, including members of his own denomination, wrestled with the inequities of American economic priorities. In 1975, Classis California and the General Synod of the RCA debated concerns related to the economic inequality produced by capitalism. In September of that year, the National Council of Churches convened a four-day meeting regarding hunger and poverty in the United States. At the conclusion of the consultation, the body released a press statement identifying capitalism as "basically unjust" and incapable of eradicating poverty. The current economic system exploited "the many for the sake of the few."[80]

Within a few days, the congregations of the RCA's Classis California offered a subtle retort infused with Schuller's orientation—originating out of a meeting at GGCC and seeming to carry the minister's imprimatur.[81] While acknowledging the social and economic problems of poverty and hunger, the resolution reflected Christian libertarian principles, suggesting that all Christians evaluate their personal lifestyles, be more willing to share with those in need, and eliminate waste. Broad social structures received no mention, and responsibility for social inequality remained the purview of each private individual. Perhaps most pointedly, the document softened the condemnation of capitalism:

> A call not for the abolition of, but the Christianizing of the capitalist economic system, that faulty though it is, is unsurpassed in historical record of lifting people through the self-dignity-producing private enterprise system to a higher level of human welfare—with greater personal freedom—than any other economic system ever devised. We do not believe that the forced equal distribution of all economic wealth worldwide would eliminate the poverty problem. It would in fact eliminate the entire base of economic wealth. We believe that what is necessary is to produce more wealth with a spirit of Christ's loving, sharing attitude seeing the world as one organismic unity.[82]

The distillation of Schuller's paradigm comprised an argument for neoliberalism dressed in a theological gloss.

Messages on the merits of free enterprise in Schuller's congregation even filtered down into the adult education programs at the church. "The Span of the Bridgebuilders," an internal publication distributed to the members of an adult education group, included a reproduced article written by Amway's DeVos that had originally appeared in *Chemtech*, a journal published by the American Chemical Society. DeVos likened *socialism* to *slavery*, while he argued that free enterprise allowed for true liberty. He encouraged readers to achieve their own wealth: "So, the challenge to the achiever is to be as rich, as prosperous, and as productive as we know how to become."[83] In addition to the dissemination of probusiness literature, college students at GGCC could take a class that promised to gird them with the intellectual defenses to resist that hypothetical "junior who's promoting that 'leftist' action group on Campus."[84]

Beyond the church grounds, Schuller also laced his published writings with a Christian libertarian ethos. Any glance through his books on Possibility Thinking provides abundant evidence. For example, Schuller struck a paradigmatically consistent note in *God's Way to the Good Life*: "You have a God-ordained right to be wealthy. You're a steward of the goods, the golds, the gifts, that God has allowed to come into your hands. Having riches is no sin, wealth is no crime. Christ did not praise poverty. The profit motive is not necessarily unChristian."[85] In another book, *Self-Love: The Dynamic Force of Success* (introduced by Norman Vincent Peale), Schuller wrote, "Every person owes it to himself and to society to earn the most money possible in the best possible way if he uses it for a real contribution to society."[86] Moreover, the minister defended success because "the alternative to prosperity could be poverty"—a potential catalyst for radicalization: "How many people in the poverty pockets of our world have opted for dictatorships because they lacked hope of financial independence?"[87]

Beyond his published writings, the very aesthetics of Schuller's church pointed to the sanctioning of wealth and socioeconomic striving. Visitor tours of the campus emphasized expert craftsmanship, the size and complexity of architectural details, and the special purchase of unique construction materials and their exotic origins from across the United States and, sometimes, the world. In his attention to structural and material detail, Schuller joined the lineage of business-minded American Protestants who assumed that architecture fostered a "moral ambience" capable of changing people for the better.[88] Guides also described subtleties of meaning in features. A visitor to the campus in 1976 reported that during a tour, the docent pointed to the brickwork on the exterior of the church and noted that the vertical, rather than horizontal, pattern kept with the ministry's "philosophy of upward mobility."[89] In the protocols of highlighting the intentionality and details of the church grounds (Schuller's preferred term—it was *not* a "campus"), the ministry engaged in what historian Nicole Kirk has described as "aesthetic evangelism": a uniquely Protestant endeavor that "intentionally mobilized architecture, fashion, art, and music to promote morality and conversion."[90]

Schuller, of course, found fertile territory for his procapitalism message in Cold War Orange County, a region filled with aspiring entrepreneurs and ladder-climbing corporate executives. The newfound wealth that "seemed to bubble up from the rich suburban soil itself" elicited a religious discourse that blessed entrepreneurialism and rebuked any big-government "threats to pristine capitalism."[91] Schuller's message assuaged his audience by spiritualizing "American private enterprise and provid[ing] religious sanction for and rationalization of competitive capitalism."[92] Moreover, "suburban evangelicals began to equate spiritual well-being with the health of their finances" and "discovered that good money management was part of Christian devotion" within Christian libertarianism.[93]

As Historian Darren Dochuk related, a "new gospel of wealth reoriented Cold War Southern California's evangelical culture in new ways. Once-hesitant capitalists now celebrated the range of opportunities free market thinking offered them."[94]

Capitalists Can Be Christians

A component of the minister's resistance to prophetic challenges from the pulpit was his faith in the American economic system. Schuller reported on a chance meeting with Jesse Jackson that offered evidence of the overwhelming appeal of capitalism: "I met [Jackson] a year ago in Chicago. He stopped me cold and told me how the television ministry had absolutely turned him around. He's on *our* side. He is now a believer in positive thinking and private enterprise" (emphasis added). Schuller continued: "When our Crystal Cathedral is dedicated in three years, it will make news like no other new structure! It will say, 'Capitalists can be Christians, too!"[95] Schuller's archetype of a wealth-generating, Possibility Thinker rested on his vision of the person who best exemplified his principles, who embodied the ideal fusion of Christianity, capitalism, and patriotism.

As much as the Orange County minister trusted capitalism, he harbored Christian libertarian suspicions regarding big government. In fact, Schuller evinced little confidence in government-supported social safety nets. As he discussed the Crystal Cathedral's community-engagement efforts in the midst of an early 1980s tax imbroglio with the government, Schuller argued, "Social programs that are today met by churches, temples, and synagogues are performed far more economically than if they were passed on to tax-supported institutions." Making his case for continued tax exemption for his ministry, Schuller insisted that "when social services are launched from properties that are tax-exempt and performed by human beings who volunteer their services, and when the motivation behind the social programs is not a salary check but the desire to fulfill the love of God, then we have social services at an unmatchable level of economic efficiency and human dignity."

Consistent with his Christian libertarian ethos, he believed beneficence should be channeled through churches, tapping into members' desire to love their neighbors, and it would be cheaper to do so. Schuller alluded to inefficiencies in the public social safety net, claiming that if a social service performed by the federal government incurred a $10 cost, then it could be safely assumed that that same service would cost $7 at the state level, $5 at the county level, $3 at the city level, and less than $1 when performed by tax-exempt volunteer organizations like his church. Keeping churches tax exempt and allowing congregations to aggressively engage in social service provision would ultimately save the government more money than if it imposed tax revenues on them. However, Schuller did offer a significant caveat regarding his cost analysis: "Obviously, I cannot verify, nor can I document, the above breakdown. I do not pose it as a scientific[ally] reliable report."[96]

Not that churches would simply give money away. Churches modeled after Schuller's Christian libertarian ideal would reassert individual confidence in members' becoming economically self-sufficient, stimulating their own productive autonomy. Schuller advocated hard work and independence. He had little regard for individuals plagued by the "Disadvantage Complex" that blamed the system for their problems.[97] Writing in 1963, the minister reminded readers that they had "no right to expect the state to take care of you." Moreover, Schuller suggested that a little elbow grease would help both financial and mental health: "Here is a major signpost on God's way to good living: The unhappy man is one who is not working. The unemployed, the forcibly retired, the physically handicapped have a constant battle with boredom, monotony, and that feeling of usefulness.... Are you unhappy? How long has it been since you have done a good day's work?"[98]

The upbeat messages and stern admonishment to readers carried the expectation that every person needs to "buck up" in facing their problems and moving forward. In Schuller's 1977 book *Reach Out for New Life*, he informed people why they struggled: "You fail because you deliberately, knowingly, and willingly choose to fail." With that in mind, readers should refrain from playing the game of "Let's Pick Out the Villain." For Schuller, individuals had no excuses because the free enterprise system "allows you the freedom to choose anything your heart desires."[99] Even racial discrimination was exempt from blame. The minister told his readers, "If you live in a community where racial prejudice does, in fact, exist, don't use that as an excuse to keep from trying. Use it as a challenge to hurdle over an obstacle."[100] In the United States, free enterprise allowed all individuals to maximize their potential—for those willing to have the right attitude and work ethic to succeed. Schuller's principles were surely effective in his idealized vision of America.

Moreover, Schuller's winsomeness did not carry the neutrality he assumed. Instead, his Orange County ministry became a high-wattage disseminator of the larger religiocultural movement that grafted a Christian theology onto the American Dream and free enterprise. In 1981, *TV Guide* published a story that examined the messages of the cohort of celebrity television ministers related to matters of economics and politics. The article described Schuller as a supporter of free-enterprise capitalism and quoted him: "Capitalism creates jobs, government makes us dependent."[101] Moreover, Schuller harbored an assumption that too much government support could drift into socialism. In another instance, Schuller assessed that welfare in America had devolved "into a source of mutual distrust between government and the people" because some had come to "equate it with a constitutional right."[102] The minister also strategically cast the government as an adversary. For instance, while attempting to raise funds for the Tower of Hope, Schuller and his ministerial staff sent an "urgent letter" to all "friends and members" of GGCC with a sentence in all caps: "TIGHT GOVERNMENT REGULATIONS HAVE CHOKED OFF THE COMMERCIAL LOAN WE EXPECTED."[103] Governmental interference and overreach, in his mind, threatened the very base of his ministry.

I Have No Position . . .

Schuller consistently demonstrated a public caginess. Only on certain issues would he offer strong opinions. In a 1983 profile in the *Los Angeles Times*, journalist Bella Stumbo queried Schuller about his position on a range of political matters. Of Ronald Reagan, Schuller limited his comments to disdain for the president's jelly-bean habit: "They're bad for the health, they're bad for the teeth, they've got sugar." When Stumbo pushed for an answer on Reagan's cuts to social programs, Schuller indicated that had not "thought about" or "studied the issues thoroughly enough to comment." Similarly, Schuller demurred on the Equal Rights Amendment: "I really don't know what the issues are there." In contrast, he offered his support for increased defense spending in an effort to deter a Soviet nuclear attack. On capital punishment: "I have no position. Well my *heart* has a position . . . that instead of terminating a life we ought to have a person locked up, ineligible for parole in this earthly life, but . . . right now, my *head* is dealing with the kind of society that lets these people out after a few years." On Jerry Falwell and his involvement in politics as a pastor: "I have no doubt that Jerry Falwell sincerely believes God is calling him to what he is doing . . . but the Moral Majority's involvement [in politics] smacks of a basic spirit I resist and resent in religion, and that is that 'I've got the answer and I'm going to make darn sure everybody else converts to my viewpoint.'" On Martin Luther King's civil rights movement: "I never spoke out *against* it because I didn't have a better answer . . . but, in all honesty, I just couldn't feel comfortable with the strategy they used. . . . I was taught from the time I was a child that we did *not* go to the streets, that we did *not* use mass protest . . . that it simply was not the intelligent, educated way to tackle a problem."[104] Schuller also indicated in 1975 that though he never publicly spoke on King's behalf, he had "silently prayed for him."[105]

Despite private sympathies for political conservatism, when Stumbo asked him about being a registered Republican, Schuller first denied the affiliation. When shown the proof in the Crystal Cathedral press packet, Stumbo described Schuller as "appalled" and said that he nearly shouted with disbelief, "That's not possible!" He quickly picked up a telephone to chastise the responsible administrative assistant. Stumbo described the scene with the bemused minister after the phone call: "'I may be a registered Republican,' Schuller declared, openly belligerent, 'but as you *know*, you've got to register one way or the *other* in California! It doesn't mean I'm a Republican! Don't *call* me a Republican! I cross over all the *time*! I voted for [Democratic gubernatorial candidate] Tom Bradley, for instance!'" Stumbo reported Schuller as looking chagrined "the minute he said it," apparently annoyed by his own loss of restraint and composure. Moving on, the minister sighed and relented, explaining that, indeed, he had voted for Bradley because of the politician's "tremendous character," "integrity," and management skills. Most of all, though, Schuller expressed enthusiasm for Bradley as "a *very* positive person. He's a possibility thinker, *absolutely*." Concluding the political discussion, Stumbo revealed that Schuller collected himself and "flatly refused to say if he had voted for Ronald Reagan and, with a sly grin, said he couldn't remember how he voted on California's nuclear arms freeze initiative, thereby avoiding the possibility of alienating current and potential constituents."[106]

In some instances, Schuller's insistence on avoiding controversy became self-defeating. In 1986, the Crystal Cathedral hosted the RCA General Synod (the denomination's governing body) meeting. Previous synods had debated proper responses to apartheid in South Africa. Percolating out of those deliberations, the synod of 1985 voted to extend an invitation to Oliver Tambo, president of the African National Congress (ANC), to address the RCA delegates the following year. When Tambo accepted, the *Church Herald* received letters of concern that Tambo represented a terrorist organization and that the invitation was "unconscionable." Amid that controversy, Schuller decided that he would not be able to host Tambo at the cathedral because of concerns about violent protests and damage to his public persona. A denominational leader described the episode as a "real crisis" for Schuller because Tambo "was regarded as leftist and communist." Despite that, many in the denomination felt honored to have Tambo visit the synod from his location of exile in Sweden because it demonstrated an attractive solidarity with the antiapartheid movement in South Africa. Schuller, though, would not relent. According to RCA historian Lynn Japinga, Schuller's insolence provoked questions of authority: "Did the host church have the right to control the guests of the General Synod?"[107] In the meantime, the United Nations International Labor Organization trumped the RCA's invitation to Tambo, and he ended up in Paris. In Tambo's place, the ANC sent its general secretary, Alfred Nzo. To avoid a costly relocation of the synod, the RCA moved Nzo's speech down the street from the cathedral to the Doubletree Hotel where the delegates roomed. Thus, as Schuller sought to avoid any large-scale controversy that implicated his public image, he agitated his own denomination—causing further fissures in his relationships with the top echelon of RCA leadership.[108]

Schuller's ministry had little inclination to directly challenge unjust political systems and structures. Some interpreted the minister's reticence as an effort to reinforce "the capitalistic hierarchy." For others, Schuller's "careful, deliberate avoidance of the controversial issues which sometimes polarized the country made his message a refreshing and appealing alternative to the more strident voices of other groups."[109] Even when engaging with public figures known for their liberal activism, he intentionally minimized the prophetic aspect of the person's work. For example, in 1975 Schuller corresponded with Jesse Jackson and noted that he felt "highly honored" to count him as a friend. In an invitation to have Jackson join him in a "sermon dialogue" on *Hour of Power*, Schuller offered his appreciation: "Your positive thinking is all-important. Your personal commitment to Jesus Christ is absolutely essential. Your capability of fighting injustice without violence is admirable. And that's commanding our esteem!"[110]

When Schuller crafted arguments that married capitalism and faith, some critics pounced and accused the minister of playing a key role in synthesizing a Christian theology with a corrupt socioeconomic system. They argued that Schuller negotiated a palatable détente that minimized a central tension between the successful, individualistic orientation of the American Dream and the sacrificial, care-for-others orientation of orthodox Christianity. They described Schuller as "located in the tradition of divines who seek to aid and comfort upwardly mobile Americans in their ceaseless strivings toward Heaven on Earth."[111] One critic described Schuller's synthesis: "While the American Dream asserts that the opportunity for success is available to all, Schuller's theology depicts it as an intrinsic element in the divine plan. Personal success is, then, not only a possibility open to all Americans, but also an individual manifest destiny." And a final summation of Schuller's perspective: "Realizing the American Dream is achieving God's plan for one's life."[112]

As Schuller's church reached its apex, a larger cultural development that historian Darren Dochuk described as a "cult of free enterprise" evolved. Southern California, in many ways, functioned as the fulcrum of the movement celebrating the benefits of the unfettered market. Schuller's Orange County, in particular, became a place where "free enterprise economics grew into a pastime for the whole family to enjoy." The county included a "hub of happiness" where "tourists visited Walt Disney's Tomorrowland, where they were whisked through a future promising the perfect union between technology and economic freedom." After that, "families visiting Knott's Berry Farm, in nearby Buena Park, could see the pioneering spirit of the old West come alive at a ghost town, take a patriotic tour that recreated the lives of the founding fathers, or stop in at the Freedom Center to collect free enterprise pamphlets for people back home."[113] And with a short drive over to the Crystal Cathedral, they would receive assurance that, yes, the "happiness hub" resonated with God's desires for them and the nation.

Rather than using the prophetic voice to agitate for social changes, Schuller operated as a proponent of a more relational, individualistic form of societal transformation that dominated American evangelical circles in the latter half of the twentieth century. The giving he solicited for his ministry served to expand that ethos as an individualistic, faithful Christian duty. His charisma was rooted in projecting warmth and intimacy, the persona of a close, trusted friend, which he believed was most effective. Beyond that, both the Theology of Self-Esteem and Possibility Thinking implicitly blessed existing systems and structures and advocated neoliberal principles of free enterprise and personal freedom. Rather than challenging socioeconomic inequality, much of Schuller's messaging assumed limitless opportunity in the present political economy—a Christian libertarian confidence needed by his followers to realize their potential within that structure. Schuller did not invent the milieu of a capitalist-friendly, promilitary, conservative political environment, yet his ministry sacralized an unfettered confidence in the righteousness of the American Dream—as long as individuals funneled their finances into their church's ministry as an outgrowth of their faith. But maintaining that reputation as exemplar of Christian capitalist would also tax and strain the ministry. The logic of capitalism, as an economic system, demands growth. Would Schuller's ministry *always* be in a growth cycle? The advent of the twenty-first century would test the minister's template.

Robert H. Schuller looks over a model of the future Crystal Cathedral in Garden Grove, California. File photo by MediaNews Group/Orange County Register via Getty Images.

6

Dig a Hole, Schuller

Failure doesn't mean you are a failure, it
just means you haven't succeeded yet.
—Robert H. Schuller

In April 1977, Robert H. Schuller found himself in crisis. The Possibility Thinker and bold asserter of supreme self-confidence as the mark of spiritual maturity was overcome by self-doubt about his most ambitious project. He had built other buildings from scratch before, but nothing matched the scale and cost of the Crystal Cathedral. Schuller spent years convincing his congregation and benefactors that the growing ministry needed more space. Philip Johnson, a daring and distinguished architect, had been hired. In recruiting Johnson, Schuller wrote, "We have *no* money. We'll borrow the money we need to retain you, and then you'll have to come up with a design that will inspire the congregation. It will have to be such a masterpiece that it will attract the money we need to build the structure! It will have to grab the imagination of sophisticated and successful people!"[1] And Johnson delivered. The model of the state-of-the-art, glass-clad building was inspiring. Fund-raising events generated enthusiastic contributors, and members had already dedicated thousands of dollars. The excitement was palpable. God was surely moving.

But the costs of the new building and its innovative design proved extraordinary—and they continued to climb. Outwardly, the seemingly affable Schuller continued to meet with builders and to motivate his members to give toward the magnificent structure. Privately, he harbored anxiety that the entire project would have to be abandoned. The initial estimate of the elaborate building—a marvel at the time—began at five million dollars and quickly doubled.[2] Once construction began, costs escalated another 30 percent, edging toward $13 million, and with inflation the figure only looked to increase substantially. Schuller had been creative at raising funds to meet the demand for more money. The most ingenious campaign mobilized supporters to "sponsor" every one of the 10,000 individual window panes at $500 apiece. The clever scheme, though, also caused an unexpected consequence: regular tithing dropped. Contributors, those who provided the majority of funds needed to keep the existing ministry in place, responded to Schuller's plea by diverting current donations, those dedicated to the ongoing ministry's general fund, to this special initiative to support the new building. The flow of money directed to the new Crystal Cathedral that did not yet exist undermined the survival of the church that did. The dream of constructing a new site now threatened to collapse the entire ministry. With a cascade of bad news, Schuller became increasingly agitated, and the urgency of an imminent financial shortfall became plain among the new building's inner circle.

A phone call interrupted Schuller's family vacation at a mountain cabin. Unwilling to discuss the pressing matter over the phone, a friend and an advisor insisted on meeting face to face with the minister. So the next day, with the architect in tow, the men drove up to the cabin and explained to Schuller the dismal developments on cost projections. Bottom line: the estimated cost now stood closer to $15 million, the schedule for more funds had accelerated so as to be needed much earlier than expected, and new sources of funding for the significantly higher price tag remained unknown. Everyone understood Schuller's role as motivator and development strategist, so the weight of the cathedral's completion rested solely on his charismatic energy raising even more capital. They could not move forward without his approval.

Schuller stalked the cabin, sputtering with anger and yelling in his booming voice: "Only eight weeks ago you said that we could still build it for ten million dollars!" Stunned, trembling, and bitterly disappointed, Schuller glared at the three men and groused, "This project is becoming impossible." In his memoir, Schuller recalled that the word echoed and intensified in his mind, "*impossible, impossible, impossible.*"[3] The men were shocked, mouths agape. Schuller, the Possibility Thinker, had uttered the word "impossible." At that moment, he decided to forsake the project entirely. The dream of the Crystal Cathedral had dissolved.

With the word "impossible" reverberating, Schuller had nothing more to say. He excused himself to the tiny bathroom in the cabin to collect his emotions; on coming out, he simply dismissed the men. Alone and resolved, he sat down to compose a news release: "The Crystal Cathedral will be abandoned." He wrote out the rationale for abandoning the project: "As the bids came in, the cost rose from ten million dollars to nearly fifteen million dollars. This exceeds our church's capabilities." Although angry before, he now admitted to feeling an immense sense of relief. He would move on.[4]

The minister rose to place a phone call to John Crean, the wealthy benefactor who had provided the first million dollars to fund the project. "John," he said, "I'm sorry to report this, but I'm going to have to give you back your generous donation. Inflation has pushed up the construction costs, and we have to abandon the project. The bids have all come in, and the Crystal Cathedral will cost nearly fifteen million dollars. We simply can't afford that." Saying it out loud increased his feeling of relief. "How would you like me to proceed in refunding your money?"

In response, Crean instructed, "Schuller, dig a hole." He repeated, "Dig a hole."

Crean, a multimillionaire who had managed his own significant capital projects (he had founded Fleetwood Enterprises, maker of recreational vehicles and a Fortune 500 company) and worked through many of his own financial crises, mirrored back to the minister a possibility that had fled Schuller completely. He continued, "Keep my donation and use it to dig a hole for the foundation. A hole shouldn't cost more than a million dollars. Will it?"

Schuller preached Possibility Thinking. He and the people around him believed the disposition to be the essential core of his charismatic authority. As one associate pastor said, "He just didn't see any situation as not having a solution." But privately, Robert Schuller had doubts, anxieties, and uncertainties rarely glimpsed by those outside his closest circle. Crean understood that sustaining the sources of capital for a major project required continued projection of forward movement. Yes, the finances for the construction of the Crystal Cathedral were precarious, but securing funding required continually projecting the possibility of its completion.[5]

Schuller built his ministry on possibility, providing Bible verses, illustrations, and a general vocabulary for Possibility Thinking; carrying forward a Christian libertarian ideology; and urging others to push forward against outstanding odds. Schuller's success is often attributed to his ability to assure his audience that the abstract idea of Possibility Thinking actually was real for him, an unshakable conviction. Yet his public profession of Possibility Thinking existed alongside private uncertainty. In his memoir, he wrote, "I would recite my Possibility Thinker's Creed again and again, and I would draw strength from the words that God had given me over twenty years earlier: 'I will build My church!'"[6] The pressures of the ministry at times produced excessive strain. At the moment of his greatest challenge, the hope-filled framework was found wanting. He needed others to mirror back to him his own projected self. This would happen many times over the history of his pastoral career.

Roughly twenty years before the Crystal Cathedral's first financial crisis, Schuller had experienced a strikingly similar moment of radical doubt. The minister had moved his young congregation from being content with the inadequate 250-seat chapel and toward building a new "walk-in–drive-in church," the world's first "hybrid church," which would combine the atmosphere of the drive-in theater with the more familiar sanctuary and pews of a standard edifice (see chapter 3).[7] Buoyed by the marketing and attendance success of another Norman Vincent Peale visit to Garden Grove, a confident Schuller made plans and mobilized his people. The minister scouted out ten acres of orange trees, a property he deemed to be "deep in the sticks and worthless for sure." But after signing a contract for purchase, during the waiting period before closing on the land, an announcement came that the new Santa Ana Freeway would be constructed just east of the new church property. Real estate prices in the area immediately doubled. Now aware of a change in the value of the land, the property owner wanted the church to fail in making its down payment, thereby nullifying the sale. In an acute irony, it seemed that the burgeoning development of Orange County that allowed for the initial success of Schuller's ministry might also lay waste to his new plan to progress his church even further.

At noon on the day of the deadline for the $18,000 down payment, Schuller found himself $3,000 short—and he knew he would receive no grace from the property owner. He was miserable. Driving home for lunch, he resigned himself to failing: "I sighed dramatically and said, 'It's over. We didn't make it!" Help came from his wife. Channeling Schuller's own Possibility Thinking back to him, Arvella told Schuller to call a congregant who had already given $2,000 to the cause. Schuller made the call, but only in an effort to return the early contribution from the church member. On the phone, Schuller reported, "I have good news. . . . I can return the $2,000 you gave for the land. Escrow closes today at four o'clock, and we're short $3,000. We're going to lose the property, so you'll get the money back."[8]

But Schuller would be admonished when his own theology was projected back to him. The church member demurred, telling his minister to meet him at the Bank of America on Main Street in Santa Ana. He would withdraw the necessary funds to ensure that the project continued, confident that with evidence of continued progress the rest of the funds for the project would eventually follow. Sure enough, Schuller received the cash and walked one block south of the bank directly to the title company to submit payment—an hour before the deadline.

Both episodes—one involving a deadline and a few thousand dollars, the other involving a deadline and a few million dollars—are among the examples that most dramatically reveal how the Possibility Thinker required others who would consistently mirror back his Possibility Thinking in words and actions, projecting confidence and opening a new avenue for achievement. Schuller, then, experienced profound moments wherein he would struggle to maintain his own grip on Possibility Thinking, demonstrating how his own signature charismatic values were difficult to sustain. Schuller's charisma required other people—and the consistency of larger structures to sustain it—to ensure the continued flow of capital as the ministry grew.

The many buildings and programs Schuller built over the years relied on the faith of benefactors who reflected his own charisma in the form of Possibility

Thinking back to the minister. As the organization developed in size, Schuller depended on an elaborate infrastructure for his ministry and building programs to thrive. Rather than the strength of a strong personality, Schuller's charismatic force depended on a larger organizational structure that extended his own charisma, contingent especially on the generosity of wealthy supporters and an institutional coherence that inspired the confidence of unwavering donors.

Capital and Charisma

Schuller's moments of failure to live up to his Possibility credo reveal more than a critical lapse in the biography of a public leader. Sociologically, these episodes accentuate the dynamics of charismatic authority and its interrelationship with economic capital for sustaining the structures that uphold that authority. In a thick irony, the prophet of Possibility Thinking, the pastor who assured the financial success of those who followed his "biblically based" principles, became shackled with self-doubt and malaise. Crean's call for Schuller to "dig a hole," for example, revealed a delicate mix of public charismatic leadership and private insecurity that demonstrated how followers of charismatic authority often support, reaffirm, and legitimate that authority through financial support. More often than not, *capital is the tangible means for affirming the intangible force of a leader's charisma.*[9] In Schuller, we see how charisma demands an "other" to reflect back inspiration as fuel to further energize the exercise of inspirational authority—with finances providing concrete evidence of confidence in the leader's ideas. As a Reformed Church in America (RCA) denominational leader once remarked about Schuller, "There's a way in which all of Bob's ministry about affirmation, the power of Possibility Thinking, etc., etc., you wonder how much he was at one level preaching to himself."[10] Indeed, early in his ministerial career, Schuller even alluded to his need for affirmation through congregational growth: Without grades from seminary professors, for feedback he had to "rely on the audience." He explained what this meant: "If the congregation grew, I was succeeding. If it didn't grow—or, God forbid, if it went down in numbers— then I was failing."[11]

Schuller, of course, did eventually build his landmark Crystal Cathedral. It demonstrated one of many evidences of his success as a leader. He appeared for forty years on *Hour of Power*. Ministers and lay leaders (and their spouses) flocked to his leadership institute. Indeed, both he and his copastors would quietly insist that Schuller even played a key role in international diplomacy during his visits to the USSR and should have been given more credit for the fall of communism.[12] With all this in mind, Schuller became an exemplar of how an institution might be built upon the charismatic leadership of its founder. Yet a closer reading of the history and events of Schuller's ministry reframes the evaluation of his followers, and even of himself, on how to properly assess the role of his charismatic leadership, in particular, considering the crucial tests of securing capital funding.

Typically, the concept of charismatic authority reflects three critical components. First, followers perceive a charismatic leader as displaying extraordinary abilities. Check: Members and associate pastors who spent the most time around Schuller's frequently commented on his unique "genius." An associate pastor said, "Dr. Schuller had a creative mind like no one I had ever met." What some call Schuller's intelligence is actually the resonant power of his charisma. Second, followers interpret their leader's exceptional abilities as divinely inspired. Check: Schuller's followers certainly believed he had been chosen by God for the work of ministry in Southern California, a sentiment buttressed by the fact that both Schuller's father and uncle predicted that God had a powerful plan for the young boy from Iowa. Third, followers believe their charismatic leader to be highly personal in nature—even without direct contact.[13] Check: A woman who had been a member of the congregation since the 1960s described how Schuller had the ability to make any acquaintance feel known and appreciated: "That man could look in your eyes and he could see your soul. He knew what a soul needed to hear." With a congregation that numbered in the thousands, and millions more through television, attenders and viewers felt they had an intimate connection with Schuller. Much of the charisma attributed to Schuller depended on his verbal ability to cultivate an interpersonal, emotional resonance, and he projected that concern from his platform. A longtime congregant described the minister's aura: "All that love from the pulpit, all the stories, that magnificent heart that wrapped itself around you, changed my life." Schuller's messages were a conduit for divine love. One woman described her devotion: "It really made me think that I am God's child, and I am worth something. Anyway, I was worth something to [Schuller]." It might only be Schuller, but that was enough. Even in his writings, Schuller communicated warmth. Though a machine would eventually replicate his signature on letters with "God loves you, and so do I," the receivers of the correspondence felt an authenticity in the one who dictated the message.

An additional characteristic of charismatic authority, crucial yet often forgotten, is that followers demonstrate their support for the shared values exemplified by the leader through tangible economic support, "through sponsors or through honorific gifts, dues, and other voluntary contributions,"[14] participating in the charismatic community not only to support the basic needs of the leader but also to establish and promote a platform for the leader to gain even more followers. Conversely, threats to legitimacy constitute more than the marring of the leader's public image but also involve the potential loss of revenue needed to sustain and extend the charismatic efficacy of the leader. In short, capital and charisma are intertwined.

Publicly Charismatic

The physicality of the drive-in theater surely played a key role in the development of Schuller's charisma. Of course, charisma only exists if the audience or congregation understands the leader as charismatic. The mythical status of Robert Schuller as a public figure (with qualities of a true showman) began early in his California ministry. Having heard about the young, dynamic pastor that his denomination had called fresh from success in suburban Chicago, a local fellow RCA minister and his wife went to see Schuller at his first worship service at the Orange Drive-in. Schuller seemed to possess a flair for the dramatic: At the start of the service, Schuller, somehow, just appeared on top of the concession stand. The couple marveled, remembering that "all the sudden, there he was" on top of the concession stand. The husband reported being enthralled: "I remember sitting there and watching him because this was a big deal."

After only a couple of years at the theater, Schuller's quirky location had become a destination for the curious around Southern California, and he leveraged his surroundings to support his persona. An architectural critic noted the stylistic cachet of the drive-in theater, remarking, "The image of the humble preacher standing atop the snack bar and surrounded by his flock merged with the image of the heroic movie star silhouetted in a close-up on the big screen."[15] Schuller's growing charisma benefited from sharing space with projected Hollywood celebrities. (The minister would later return to regularly using the proximity of celebrity on *Hour of Power*.) Schuller synthesized the upbeat, feel-good aura of the drive-in theater with a theology to match the open, experimental context. A long-time member characterized it as a "fresh atmosphere of worship." Contrasting with other church experiences, she reflected, "You left not being beaten down by how bad you were, but with God's help, you can make it this week." His preaching mobilized around his person. "He always had stories that fit his charisma."

The power of his public persona remained undeniable. A member at the Crystal Cathedral who also contributed to *Hour of Power* for over thirty years remarked about her first visit to GGCC: "I was blown away." This was not at all like the church she had grown up in. She recalled, "My gosh, I'm someone who turned away from the Baptist Church when I was a youngster because every time I went to church I was told how bad I am—hell, fire, and damnation and all this kind of stuff. I didn't want to go back." She thought church life would remain a part of her past. "I had no intention of returning to organized religion." But Schuller was different. "Low and behold, this young charismatic minister. When I went in, I was mesmerized."

Schuller attracted thousands at his church and millions through television. One couple who would become prominent leaders at the church reminisced that they had waited in line for forty-five minutes just to get into their first service, as palpable excitement built outside the Crystal Cathedral in the mid-1980s. The charisma attributed to Schuller as a person allowed him to exercise control over his RCA congregation in a manner unparalleled in the denomination, a level of management made possible because the ministry generated enough capital to assert its independence. For other ministers, authority extended from their ordination in the denomination, a vocation affirmed through seminary and bounded by roles and responsibilities. In contrast, Schuller manufactured an authority attached to himself—and extended to his family. One former employee described the church as becoming a "family owned and operated business" under Schuller's firm direction rather than under the auspices of a board of elders.[16] Another Crystal Cathedral member expressed reservations about the devotion evident among some parishioners, remarking that "a sort of cult developed around Dr. Schuller."[17]

Reminiscing about the peak of the ministry, one congregant insisted that the entire ministry rested solely on Schuller's charisma, and the ministry would never again achieve the successes of the 1980s without the elder Schuller. For her, even the spectacular facilities held little appeal in Schuller's absence: "If we had some billionaire that bought the cathedral back, and we went back there, we would be very, very, very lost. He's gone! He's gone." The member sighed as she remembered the halcyon days of the church and the inability to ever recapture that era, saying, "I didn't want to leave *that* cathedral, I wanted *that* cathedral"—the cathedral that included Schuller and his dynamism. Without Schuller, no amount of money could solve the compounding problems of the church: "Not even a billionaire could have made that cathedral happen." Even if the congregation had been able to maintain the financial viability of the cathedral, for her, the charismatic source of its greatness was gone. Constituents never defined the ministry by the wealth it accumulated; it rested on Schuller's distinctive charisma.

Privately "Not One of the Boys"

Schuller exhibited the qualities of charismatic leadership as part of his public persona. Yet his outward presentation of self existed alongside a less attractive, less readily engaging, and much less winsome private person. Evidence suggests that Schuller's public and private personas varied. Very early on, Schuller realized the necessity of expertly managing his image. The success of the ministry depended upon it. But the minister could be somewhat cantankerous and insecure in private. Glimpses of that inconsistency could prove problematic for a theological posture built on the optimistic notions of Possibility Thinking and the building of others' self-esteem.

The public/private variation was known best to those who spent time with Schuller away from the spotlight. For example, during a whirlwind tour of the country, Schuller and two copastors went to a restaurant for dinner, where their boss confided that he felt "really bushed." Knowing Schuller, the other two pastors deliberately attempted to "avoid irritating topics," especially since the one who had only started working for Schuller recently had "heard from old-time staffers that Dr. Schuller had a temper when properly provoked." However calm they kept the conversation, they had no ability to control the actions of an adoring public:

Suddenly, out of the dark appeared a little boy. He ran right up to our table and looked at Dr. Schuller squarely in the eye. Behind him was his father, who explained that when his son had heard that Dr. Schuller was sitting across the room, he bolted out to get an autograph. It was panic time! For a moment, Dr. Schuller just stared back at the boy. Our thoughts were racing. How was he going to react?

A tired Schuller with a ready temper was accosted by the boldness of a child. In that instant, the associate pastor witnessed a transformation:

> In a flurry, Dr. Schuller pointed his finger at the young man and said, *in his best television manner*, "You are outstanding, young man. You are going to go far. You know what you want, and you don't settle for anything less. I'm glad to know you, and I'd love to give you my autograph. How would you like it if I said: 'To John, a really great young man who is going places. Your friend, Robert Schuller.'" The boy beamed, shook hands, and left. The father was grateful and bid us a good evening.[18]

Privately, he could be prickly, but publicly he had an ability to turn on the charm, successfully asserting a gregariousness that matched his onstage presence. Schuller showed himself able to mobilize in an instant the qualities of his charisma.

Bella Stumbo, a feature journalist for the *Los Angeles Times*, noted the inconsistency between public persona and private individual after traveling with the pastor. In a profile in 1983, Stumbo described Schuller as somewhat less than charismatic: "The private Schuller—particularly among strangers but even around his faithful staff—is often surprisingly aloof, stiff and uncomfortable, sullen and sour at times, defensive at others." Moreover, Stumbo reported that "in conversation, he is perpetually dominant, both condescending and pedantic. He displays not the slightest trace of spontaneous humor, rarely smiles and never seems to laugh." Similarly, a copastor remarked about Schuller: "As a person, he wasn't a 'one of the boys' type of guy, he was more of a loner, intellectual type person that, you know, he didn't play sports or anything. I think he was more like an egghead." Stumbo, though, admitted the irrelevance of the private version of Schuller the publicly rarely saw, as long as the minister could lift up a distant audience, "the spirits of millions of people who, for whatever reason, would not leave their home to attend church."[19]

Schuller was not always a builder of self-esteem, and those who suffered the most were those closest to him. Stumbo reported that the people who knew Schuller best occasionally revealed a truth about him that he himself probably failed to fully grasp: "Schuller regularly contradicts his best friends, his children, and even his wife." A family member also confirmed that the minister had a temper, describing it in the context of Schuller being a driven man, excusing the anger as "an edge, a ruthless drive to thrive and succeed, and a total passion for doing nothing less than absolute excellence to be the very best at everything." Such an explanation implied that the exacting standards for the ministry were construed as protections of the church through the person of its pastor. Since the ministry was based on Schuller, all needed to be sure to do whatever was needed to follow Schuller's directions, and the people around him sought to avoid offenses that would reflect on his public persona.

Comments from his wife, Arvella, further undermined Schuller's profile as the "self-esteem preacher." She confided to Stumbo that even with all his success and fame, Schuller still suffered from his own lack of self-esteem. Arvella offered the journalist an example: "I can feel his insecurity many times, especially when we're in a room full of strangers." In a private interview with Schuller, Stumbo reported that he looked "irritated" when she related Arvella's assessment: "Even if my wife said that, I would not agree that I am insecure. I would say, instead, that I am merely cautious." Seeming to be pleased with how he had reframed his wife's description, Schuller continued, "Yes, 'cautious.' I don't want to be hurt, and I don't want to hurt others. So, I need (before relaxing) to first figure out where a person is coming from, you know?"[20]

The less public and more intimate the interaction, the more likely to encounter his less than charismatic side. A married couple who had joined GGCC in the late 1960s also remarked about the difference between front stage and back stage for Schuller. The couple had been told that the minister "was actually an introvert and was really at a discomfort one-on-one with people." They also said that not everyone in the congregation found the minister winsome and engaging, relating that some of their friends "were really put off." The wife remembered, "Occasionally, you would go in the Tower [of Hope] and you always have to ride the elevator up, so you'd be on the elevator with him. Just you and him. He would not look at you. He would look the other way, look up." Offering an explanation for Schuller's palpable social discomfort, the husband explained, "His brain was always going ninety miles an hour. He was thinking about other things."

Though this characteristic is not atypical of charismatic leaders, one of Schuller's confidantes described the dissonance between his front-stage and backstage self as his greatest weakness, "an Achilles heel." The minister, he noted, was not an extrovert. Instead, he described Schuller as "an intense Iowa farm boy who had been through tragedy, difficulties, and stresses as a young man. He developed the persona because he had the smart, eclectic personality to recognize that if he wanted to do something significant it had better involve a total package." The friend described the minister as publicly projecting a "wow, superextrovert electromagnet," but "a few people who met him for the first time [one-on-one], were put off" when they glimpsed "the more subdued, not unfriendly, but also not arm-waving, not reach-out-and-give-you-a-big-bear-hug" version of Schuller. In one case, "a very brilliant aerospace engineer from San Diego came off outraged by it, to the point where he never came back" to the church. Schuller's old friend shook his head as he explained that "it wasn't hypocrisy on Bob's part. He was projecting the personality he felt he needed to deliver [to best communicate] the version of the gospel he was espousing." Sociologist Peter Schuurman described the "jarring" dissonance of front-stage versus backstage versions of charismatic leaders as an "alienation effect" that can confuse and disillusion audience members.[21] For Schuller, the massive size of both his audience and his congregation inhibited the opportunity for many to experience the backstage version of the minister.

Even when Schuller "regressed" to his backstage self, though, it generated little-to-no damage to his charismatic authority. Members and staff also found Schuller to be highly demanding as a boss, and many feared not meeting his standards. One congregant indicated that interactions with Schuller carried the burden of exacting expectations, causing anxiety among those who worked in the front offices of the Tower of Hope. If he was anticipated in the building that day, staff would clean off the counters, making sure it would not look messy when he arrived. Even when directions (and corrections) were communicated through Schuller's subordinates, the instructions contained a severity that they could "consciously recognize" as coming from the minister himself. Once understood as carrying Schuller's imprimatur, any directive became nonnegotiable. Some found the atmosphere working for Schuller "stifling," but most staff and members simply shrugged it off, saying, "That's just the way things are."

However they clarified it, members, staff, and associates—Schuller's constituents—went out of their way to explain away a typical aspect of charisma: those qualities are meant for public, not private, consumption. Sociologist Erving Goffman explained that followers of charismatic leaders defend the backstage, underwhelming, and out-of-character interactions with a "plea of forgiveness." That is, they attempt to "soften the disjuncture" that outsiders might encounter in their meeting with the charismatic personality by explaining the introvertedness or distractedness as a necessary component of unique genius. Moreover, the charismatic disconnect functions as a bonding "inside secret" for insiders.[22]

Fortunately for Schuller, he maintained both a faithful cadre of insiders—and his wife, Arvella. During their decades of marriage, she became the most significant manager of the minister's persona. A close friend of Schuller's reported that Arvella "had the smart marketing sense to help Bob craft the persona that he became, and that, of course, is what he affected on television." In the early years, Schuller practiced "in front of a mirror and in front of Arvella, mostly his sermons. He really worked on those so that his presentation, his performance" would be received as "impeccable." Under Arvella's discerning eye, Schuller's charismatic skills were strategically performed, the result of skills honed and perfected over time.

Where Ideas Originate

Schuller attributed his ministry successes to his own talent and intelligence, and the accumulation of so many accomplishments over the years gave the pastor confidence in his own opinions. Yet many of "his" best ideas were cribbed from others around him. Since Schuller believed in the superiority of his own counsel, people working around him learned to present ideas so that he could claim them as his own. For example, a long-time associate pastor noticed that Schuller preferred ideas that he thought originated in his own mind. So this pastor used subtle strategies for framing ideas to allow Schuller to take credit. "I often used to say, 'What's the possibility of . . . ?' There's the word *possibility*. His ears would perk right up." The strategy worked: the pastor frequently threw out targeted ideas with just enough shape to allow Schuller to grasp them. The pastor continued, "Some things he didn't like, he just threw it away, and that's fine. But other things he'd get it, and then we would talk about something else, but I could see he was working on it. Then a few weeks or a month later, he might come back and say, 'I've been thinking . . .' and it would come out." This pastor was not critical of Schuller's taking credit, asserting that Schuller "had a marvelous ability" to refine others' ideas. "As it came from his lips, there was always an angle, an addition, to whatever I might have said. It was enhanced." For this pastor, Schuller "was a tremendous genius."

So in spite of Schuller's being difficult and off-putting on an interpersonal level, there remained admiration for Schuller's success and cleverness that nurtured a devotion still evident in interviews with former congregants and staff. A wealthy supporter fondly recalled, "I got to sit with him in his office and listen to him dream out loud," which she took as an honor. An associate pastor echoed others in saying he felt "really privileged to be in [Schuller's] presence and work with him."

Institutionalizing Charisma

Of course, the success of Schuller's ministry over the years depended on effectively channeling the minister's charisma into a stable organizational structure. By necessity, Schuller concocted a larger infrastructure that mixed religious imperatives and business savvy.[23] Central to the progressive building of his ministry were people who responded to his religious injunctions and gifted their business acumen and wealth to the operations of the church. Among them, he taught that those who had been blessed with great wealth had a special role in the ministry—specifically, by contributing to the God-inspired vision of the church as articulated by Schuller. Wealthy benefactors would be instrumental in institutionalizing Schuller's persona.

Michael Nason, who not only served as Schuller's executive assistant but assumed roles including *Hour of Power* producer and long-time president of the church's in-house public relations agency, opined that the leadership institute represented Schuller's most significant legacy. Established a year prior to *Hour of Power*, the leadership institute never enjoyed the high profile of the television ministry. However, the quarterly sessions where a throng of pastors and volunteer leaders learned Schuller's church growth methodology was significant for ensuring the credibility of his ministry and its legacy. Confidantes of Schuller reported that the institute gave Schuller his greatest joy. It established the ministry's competency, believability, and market leadership—an institutionalization of his charisma.[24] His administrative and organizational style clearly had garnered resonance, as evidenced by Schuller's church gracing the cover of *Church Management* journal in both 1962 and 1967.[25] The eventual creation of the institute provided an opportunity for the distillation and codification of Schuller's principles. The institute routinized the large demand for Schuller's techniques as an expert on congregational growth. And Schuller presented as supremely confident, bearing no misgivings regarding the prescriptions he would disseminate to his eager students. He believed he had devised a foolproof formula for growing ministry. At one point, the minister instructed Wilbert Eichenberger, director of the institute, to "sell" the curriculum with a "money back guarantee."[26]

The first iteration of the institute included over sixty attenders—but only forty paid. Schuller found himself about $2,000 in the red after the event, although he surmised that it would take only about seventy paying attenders at the second institute to cover the losses, so he put his promotional efforts to work.[27] He adjusted his marketing and recruitment and thereby gained far more registrations. An institute mailer included endorsements from Billy Graham ("I highly recommend the Robert Schuller Institute") and Donald McGavran of Fuller Theological Seminary, a leading church-growth expert: "[The institute] is helping turn static middle class American denominations around and start them finding the lost and bringing them Home. Interested in Church Growth? Attend the Schuller Institute."

Over the thirty-five-year run of the institute, "Schuller influenced thousands of pastors and lay leaders." Ministers, elders, and spouses filed in to learn Schuller's methods in person, which included a field trip to the fabled Orange Drive-in ("where it all began"). As the leadership institute promoted its tenth anniversary in 1980, Schuller marketed the newly opened Crystal Cathedral as evidence of the efficacy of the curriculum. In 1981, the institute claimed to have trained over 12,000 pastors and leaders in just eleven years.[28] When his "Film Workshop" series launched to allow the institute to be replayed in local churches, the ministry estimated that within the short span of three years over 16,000 individuals had watched Schuller's five major leadership institute lectures.[29]

Of course, not all participants attended the institute of their own volition. Some were forced by their leadership, and others required significant incentives beyond Schuller's marketing pitch. When the Christian Reformed Church received funds from Amway to send hundreds of pastors and their wives to Orange County to study Schuller's methods, one pastor recalled having no interest in going, feeling mostly disdain for the Garden Grove ministry. He found *Hour of Power* embarrassing: the production with its fountains struck him as cheap and tacky and the messages as trite. But when his wife heard about the possibility of a free trip to Southern California, she changed his mind. In that one short week, Schuller won them over. He mesmerized his audience, as reported by the pastor: "I think the thing that most influenced me was [Schuller's] delivery. It was without notes, and he was always showing and not just telling. I sat there and watched him speak, and there were 360-some people, half of them ministers and the other half spouses, and they were all spellbound." The pastor returned to his congregation in Michigan and changed his sermon style to emulate Schuller's. He convinced his consistory to purchase the vacant house next to the church property; Schuller had insisted that churches should always buy available contiguous space, even if only for future parking. And the pastor's wife, owner of an art boutique, implemented Possibility Thinking into her business practices.

At the institute, Schuller also won over many skeptical mainline Protestant ministers. Browne Barr, pastor of First Congregational Church of Berkeley, California, said he had attended "scores of pastor's conferences, most of them connected with our most prestigious theological schools" but could not "think of a single one that was as directly helpful" to parish ministry as Schuller's institute. He admitted being bemused by Schuller's television personality and viewed the concept of "church growth" to be as "vulgar and plastic as Disneyland" but found himself beguiled by Schuller himself.[30] Writing in *The Christian Century*, Barr counseled his mostly mainline Protestant readership "to be humble enough to learn from a genius like Schuller."[31] *The Economist* described the leadership institute as attracting "crowds of would-be pastorpreneurs who paid handsomely for his insights."[32] Embracing a wider range of traditions within Christianity and a host of other highly charismatic pastors, the institute in its later years included guest teachers like Mark Driscoll of Seattle's Mars Hill, Erwin McManus of Los Angeles's Mosaic Church, Walt Kallestad of Arizona's Community Church of Joy, and Bruce Wilkinson, author of *The Prayer of Jabez*.[33]

Journalists, denominational officials, and seminary professors across the country took even more notice of Schuller and further promoted his ministry method. A Memphis newspaper described the minister as an expert in church growth who insisted that the number-one key to growth is a big parking lot. Moreover, the journalist summarized Schuller's keys for "large successful churches":

1 Never take a church unless you can envision spending the rest of your career there—dreams take a lifetime to fulfill.
2 Don't be controversial in the pulpit. Schuller blames controversy for the membership decline in Protestantism.
3 Sermons should always be positive.
4 Impress the unchurched: "Find out what would impress the non-churched people in your community. Find out what kind of needs exist in the private lives of the unchurched."[34]

By making "principles" like these more accessible through the institute, journalists and others often reduced them to such bullet points, stripped of all history and context—formulaic techniques to be easily adopted, a premise Schuller promoted himself. A 1979 advertisement for the institute included an endorsement from none other than C. Peter Wagner, a prominent church growth movement (CGM) expert and missiologist, declaring the universality of Schuller's principles: "I consider the Institute for Successful Church Leadership to be unsurpassed as a church growth training program available today. One of the things that make it so valuable is that the Institute stresses basic principles of church growth that can be applied anywhere, rather than just saying 'this is the method we use to make it happen here.'"[35]

With so many participants, the institute could promote its efficacy by showcasing a string of famous pastors, indicating that their successes originated from what they learned from Schuller. Over the years, it became easy to note that many participants "became pastors of megachurches and frequent speakers at the Institute, including Charles Blake, Kirbyjon Caldwell, John Maxwell, and Walt Kallestad." These influential pastors would, in turn, credit Schuller and his institute as a pivotal influence, ricocheting their charismatic affinities against each other into a virtuous cycle.

Schuller's most famous mentees, Bill Hybels of Willow Creek Community Church and Rick Warren of Saddleback Community Church, were among those who improvised what they learned in Garden Grove to create two of the most influential megachurches within evangelical Christianity.[36] Hybels attended the institute in 1975 in search of an "exciting" model to create a congregation attractive to the unchurched. Evidently convinced by what he heard and experienced in Garden Grove, Hybels returned the next year with nearly twenty-five staff members and lay leaders from his fledgling suburban Chicago congregation. At one point, the Willow Creek delegation scheduled a private meeting with Schuller in his office in the Tower of Hope. Hybels queried Schuller about buying land. Ever consistent in his message, Schuller encouraged aggressiveness in the land purchase: "Don't buy a thimbleful of land. Buy a fifty-gallon drum."[37] Hybels followed Schuller's advice and eventually even started his own leadership training event, the Global Leadership Summit. One evangelical pastor described Willow Creek as the "mainstreaming of the Schuller concept."[38] Schuller remarked that his two most famous students, Hybels and Warren, "outran their teacher" in crafting successful churches.[39] The achievements of such acolytes also ensured the legitimacy of his ministry.

The fact that thousands of religious leaders trekked to Southern California to learn from Schuller confirmed the appeal of the ministry's institutional logics established in his name, an example of *religious institutional entrepreneurialism*.[40] The institute assumed Schuller's principles could be replicated anywhere. And the books, classes, consultations, seminars, and workshops that flowed through the institute nurtured ever expanding flows of revenue.

The charisma on display through the institute over the years expanded Schuller's constituency to church leaders—a strategy often referred to as "influencing the influencers." Like Warren and Hybels, pastors and volunteer leaders who trained there returned home to spread the minister's methods and give them a try. Though many held their noses when attending the institute, mainline Protestants could not argue with its results. Evangelicals, on the other hand, embraced Schuller's church growth techniques. Theologian Sheila Strobel Smith described the 1974 American Convocation for Church Growth held at GGCC as functionally a "family reunion" for institute leaders and attenders. Over 400 individuals gathered to hear from the dominant names in the church growth community: Schuller, Win Arn, W. A. Criswell, James D. Kennedy, Donald A. McGavran, and C. Peter Wagner.[41] A press release from GGCC reported that the event attracted "the broadest spectrum of Protestantism—from the extreme fundamentalists to the extreme Liberals."[42] Cosponsored by Schuller's leadership institute and Fuller Seminary's Institute for Church Growth, Schuller opened the conference by announcing that it would be the greatest gathering of church growth authorities in history. He promised that everyone attending would be edified by the open disclosure of the "secrets of successful church growth." The strategies shared during the convocation would be universal: they could "be applied by a church in an inner-city section of America, in slum sections of international cities abroad, and in suburban churches of affluent people." Schuller also offered a disclaimer: "We do not believe that church failure will contribute to the immediate or long-range solution of social or spiritual problems." Moreover, attenders should be prepared to embrace the ascendancy of their congregations: "To glorify failure by saluting the loser or putting down the successful individual or institution is to become part of the problem rather than part of the answer. In short, it's time the church released itself from the hang up of negative reaction against 'Success.'"[43]

The leadership institute's attractiveness crossed denominational lines and transcended religious traditions. Though evangelicals likely comprised the largest share of students, Catholic priests and mainline Protestant ministers also made the pilgrimage to Garden Grove to learn Schuller's techniques. In fact, an Episcopal pastor, after attending a 1980 institute, predicted to the *Orange County Register* that Schuller's legacy likely would not be fully recognized until about two centuries into the future. Because of that, the minister suggested that Schuller was "like Bach."[44] All sought to borrow Schuller's charismatic gift, hoping the magic of congregational vitality would transfer to their church. The institute not only diffused the ministry logic of its charismatic leader nationally but also asserted its methodological efficacy on an international scale. For example, Schuller took credit for the South Korean successes of David Yonggi Cho, pastor of Yoido Full Gospel Church (often cited as being the world's largest church), and Sundo Kim, pastor of First Methodist Church in Seoul (the largest Methodist church in the world).[45]

The packaging of Schuller's charisma spawned successive efforts to monetize his approach to pastoral ministry, generating new sources of funding. For example, on receiving accolades from within the church growth community that he had a highly transportable formula, Schuller began to consider new media venues for disseminating his principles of church leadership and growth. In the mid-1970s, Schuller began the "Film Workshop" that promoted the opportunity for congregations to watch lectures from the institute without having to travel to Garden Grove. Herman Ridder described the "Robert H. Schuller Film Workshop" as a distillation of organization and leadership principles that "captains of business" would "pay handsome fees to have delivered at their annual sales meeting." Ridder went on to note that the films relayed "sound management principles" for local congregations. Ridder would soon accept a call to become a pastor at the Crystal Cathedral.[46] This new package not only further demonstrated Schuller's confidence in his method but also expanded opportunities to access the material at different price points.

After viewing the institute's films in a sanctuary or church basement, those attending used a workbook that highlighted key themes. It included the following questions, some more rhetorical than others: "If your church is in need of money, what will specifically begin to attract money to your church? How many doorbells would you be willing to ring, not to evangelize, but to listen to the needs of people in your community? What is the role of your church in your community? Is it to reach people of your own denomination? Is it to reach unchurched people in your community?"[47] The workbook also posed questions that framed churches as businesses: "If there's a market for your product and you're not making it, first check manufacturing. Then check marketing. Then check merchandising. And if you're still in trouble, it's got to be in management." The workshop urged leaders to raise the "visibility" of their church, to remove "provocative material out of the pulpit" and broach sensitive topics "in a classroom setting." The workbook exhorted participants that church growth demanded a willingness to set aside the desires of committed members in order to attract *potential* members: "A church will grow if the decision-making, power-center people are willing to put the spiritual needs of the non-religious people in the community above the spiritual needs of their communicant membership." Finally, participants were encouraged to build agile, responsive congregations: "Are the growth goals of your church based upon the changing social conditions and market situations?" (Ironically, this query would eventually have pointed resonance for Garden Grove as well; see chapter 8.)

Films, surrogates, and written materials allowed a stable public persona to be presented that powerfully reflected the minister's charisma not only to others but also back to himself. For instance, in the early 1980s, the ministry opened the Crystal Cathedral Academy, a school featuring promotional materials that promised Schuller's "dynamics of possibility thinking" would undergird the instruction.[48] In another instance, the Crystal Cathedral sent out a mailer for a conference that promised "A Weekend with Robert Schuller." Hinting at an unlikely intimacy, the brochure included a note from the minister, who expressed his anticipation "to see you, to touch you, to talk to you."[49] Certainly, Schuller did not understand his ministry as about building his own ego. (The minister often remarked to interlocutors that he understood his ministry as an "integrity trip" rather than an ego trip.) He rationalized his own charisma as based on the continuous mission of the church—even when hurt by critiques of his own leadership. His ministry existed within the framework of his Christianity, more specifically, the religious orientation stemming from his own denomination, the RCA. As an international celebrity, Schuller still desired to be embraced by his home denomination. His RCA affiliation remained core to his legitimation. A denominational leader ruminated about Schuller: "He had prime ministers and presidents and kings singing his praises, but he wanted to hear praise and affirmation from the group that really bore him and nurtured him and was his home." The same leader intimated that perhaps the minister needed the Theology of Self-Esteem in an effort to master his own insecurity: "I can't pretend to psychoanalyze Dr. Schuller, but I think he probably had deep needs for people to affirm him as a person, to say he was of value and he was of worth, you know. What he did for so many persons around the world, I think he also needed to hear himself."

In the end, Schuller further capitalized his charisma through the institute, and in the process, his clout only grew. Within the CGM community Schuller's stature expanded, and he earned a reputation as a pioneer who had charted fresh territory in terms of goal-setting as intrinsic to healthy, expanding congregations.[50] In 1980, Dennis Voskuil, then an assistant professor at Schuller's alma mater, Hope College, began shopping a manuscript, "The Schuller Phenomenon," that would become his book *Mountains into Goldmines*. At least one potential publishing house proved somewhat wary of criticizing the Orange County megachurch minister and television personality. Though the editor acknowledged that the fear of Schuller-related backlash preventing publication would be "craven" on the publisher's part, he noted his concern that the evangelical community might not respond well to any criticism of a pastor of Schuller's stature.[51] The strength of Schuller's charisma at one point seemed unassailable. Nevertheless, perceived attacks could end up financially hurting any outlet daring to interrogate the ministry and its methods.

Dependence on Wealthy Supporters

Certainly Schuller could not invent congregational life and growth from scratch, nor was that necessary. However, what became crucial was to project outward a new set of imperatives, eventually implemented into new sets of programs, articulated in transportable training materials, and ultimately encapsulated in all that was represented in the architecture of new buildings. Schuller needed an extraordinary amount of resources to cast a new mold that would channel an innovative set of practices that would usher in the Christianity of a new century. In achieving his vision, Schuller could not wait for the financial stream from constituents who had not yet arrived. He sought to build a ministry structure poised to accommodate them once they did. He also knew regular attenders were not adequate to fund such a vision. For this ambitious effort, he especially courted wealthy benefactors. Schuller once wrote, "Good ideas promoted by good people will always get the attention of people with money."[52]

In raising funding for a succession of building projects, Schuller often explained that he broke down the problem to make it more manageable. For example, in one of his most popular books, *Tough Times Never Last, but Tough People Do!*, Schuller wrote that if he needed a million dollars, then the options were simple. He wrote a list:

1 Get 1 person to give $1,000,000.
2 Get 2 people to give $500,000.
3 Get 4 people to give $250,000.
 . . . etc.[53]

As a pragmatic pastor, Schuller understood that he was unlikely to receive consistently large sums from regular attenders. So his strategy for obtaining adequate funding depended on generous gifts from a few, big-dollar donors. As Billy Graham and other financially shrewd conservative Christian leaders did in the midtwentieth century, Schuller came to depend on the largesse of wealthy corporate givers from across the country.[54]

In fact, when Schuller became anxious about the size of the U.S. national debt, his published solutions revealed a well-worn reliance on wealthy benefactors to remedy almost any situation. First, the minister wondered whether national parks and highways could be named for persons who donated to reduce the national debt. Second, he noted that no law stated that only images of statesmen like George Washington and Abraham Lincoln had to appear on currency. Thus, "in consideration of major contributions of several million dollars, donors could be recognized and thanked by their fellow citizens through an act of Congress so that the donor's face would appear on a determined number of $1, $5, $10, even $100 bills."[55] Schuller assumed that generous patrons could solve almost any problem.

The strategy worked in his ministry. In framing significantly large projects as worth significantly large donations, Schuller was unashamed to nurture relationships with wealthy benefactors such as Richard DeVos and Jay Van Andel, the founders of Amway Corporation outside of Grand Rapids, Michigan. In a letter from December 1976, Schuller reported that fund-raising for the construction of the Crystal Cathedral to that point had reached $8 million in pledges. However, he knew that amount would not cover the full cost. Schuller entreated Van Andel to meet with him: "I would prefer to talk with you personally and privately about this and will be happy to fly anywhere, any time so we can pray about it and finally determine what God wants you to do." Of course, Schuller believed he knew what God wanted.

Schuller had been dogged in his pursuit of Van Andel and DeVos for his most ambitious project to date. Amway generated tremendous revenue by selling household products through interpersonal networks, but more status-conscious religious institutions might have been wary of associating with Amway, a company mocked by some as a low-brow, multilevel pyramid scheme. The pastor smartly drew on an untapped resource.

In May 1976 Schuller had written a four-page letter outlining the desperate need for the cathedral to be built. First, the success of the *Hour of Power* had "lured" such a robust tourist audience that his members had trouble locating seats in the sanctuary (prompting early arrival and waiting in long lines for seats, as much as an hour before the service) and enough room for their children who joined their parents after attending Sunday school. Striking a delicate balance, Schuller promoted the successful growth of the ministry while detailing a dire need, motivating his reason for reaching out: "Unless I can draw national support to solve this problem by building a sanctuary large enough to accommodate the local parents as well as the visiting tourists, I will find myself facing a revolution here at home. So because *Hour of Power* has the highest rating of any religious programming in the following cities: Washington D.C.; New York City; Philadelphia—and the list goes on—it is imperative that we continue to strengthen, sustain, and expand this ministry that is rapidly becoming the No. 1 spiritual influence in the United States."[56] The church no longer remained a *local* ministry but a *national* one and therefore required resources from across the country to sustain its need for further growth. Beyond those tourists and regular attenders who struggled for a seat, Schuller related a story about an "unchurched" young couple who attempted to attend a recent service at GGCC, which would have been the first worship service in their lives. Unfortunately, said Schuller, "they couldn't find a seat. Even the aisles were filled with people standing. It was raining outdoors, so they left! Instead, they went out for Sunday breakfast!!" Schuller lamented being unable to host as many of the "unchurched people in Southern California" as possible. Successfully funding the new cathedral would also pose a strong challenge to any who predicted the decline or failure of the institutional church in the United States. Further expansion offered the only solution.

Moreover, in contrast to his previously built Tower of Hope, Schuller explained to Van Andel and DeVos that the Crystal Cathedral should be seen as housing "4,100 *income producing* seats" (emphasis added), which would generate offerings "to meet the emotional, spiritual, and physical starvation which is destroying lives in America and abroad." Schuller therefore described the new facility as a "money-generating factory." The ostensible success communicated by the confident construction would offer an appealing witness: "People are not going to invest in an organization that's going bankrupt. Unchurched people will not be attracted into the institutional churches if they feel it has no future." Schuller always demonstrated an awareness that the scope of his ambition for the ministry required a healthy flow of revenue that could not be dependent on the continued infusion of special donations. Nor did he want to imply that he would continually demand high dollar contributions. But the need was presented as urgent for now.

Of course, he also quickly noted that any financial windfall would produce funds to support missions programs around the globe. Claiming his affinity with successful business practices, Schuller presented the Crystal Cathedral and Amway as similar in operation: "Even as manufacturing facilities of Amway Corporation in Ada, Michigan aren't simply a place of employment for Western Michigan citizens, but rather a power base making possible tens of thousands of job opportunities around the world, so our Crystal Cathedral is an international manufacturing facility and the products go out in television tapes, printed sermons, pamphlets, etc."[57] Drawing on his charismatic authority, Schuller used value rationality to advocate that Amway support for the Crystal Cathedral would have significant global outcomes that reflected the highest ideals of both organizations. Elaborating on the resonance he saw between his ministry and Amway, Schuller stated unequivocally, "I happen to know that our ministry stands for everything that you, Jay Van Andel, and Richard DeVos and Amway Corporation stand for." Schuller went on to assert that his ministry resonated with the marketing and corporate policies that Van Andel and DeVos had instituted at their company: "Without compromising my deepest convictions one iota, I know how totally we agree on issues and values."

Clearly, Schuller understood the need to mobilize the charisma of the church into a financial vehicle and especially concentrated it through personal meetings with corporate leaders and philanthropists. He did so continually throughout his ministry, and available examples are numerous. For instance, in other correspondence, Schuller prevailed upon the Amway leaders to subsidize the expenses for attenders of the leadership institute. In discussing support for the institute, Schuller expressed to Van Andel his belief that the church and the corporation could be allied for tremendous influence within Christianity: "I want you to know that I'm thrilled that between Amway and Schuller, we've been able to make a difference." Schuller then pivoted to a request to cement that alliance by Van Andel underwriting a Christian Reformed Church (Van Andel's denomination) delegation of pastors to the institute with $145,000: "We could make a final impact that would produce positive results 100 years from now!"[58]

Van Andel and DeVos found Schuller persuasive and became benefactors to the point that DeVos would eventually sit on the ministry's board. Thus, Schuller's ministry, and others like his, became "investments," spiritually inflected ventures, that fulfilled the value imperatives of conservative Christian philanthropists like DeVos and Van Andel while simultaneously fulfilling the practical revenue imperatives of an expanding, ambitious religious organization.

A decade and a half later, at a 1993 Amway distributors event, Schuller reported during a keynote address that his friendship with Rich DeVos and Jay Van Andel could be traced to the very beginnings of Amway. At one point, he described Amway as the world's largest organization of Positive Thinking people and that the Crystal Cathedral, "to a great degree," could be considered "*a ministry of Amway*, unofficially, totally."[59] The growth imperatives of Schuller's ministry depended greatly on the ability to convince wealthy Christians that his church, properly understood, was an extension of their business, a tangible manifestation of the noblest and deepest values they most cherished.

Schuller's dependence on wealthy benefactors was not solely the result of his own singular entrepreneurial strategy. Fortunately for the ministry, his outreach to corporate Christian elites dovetailed with a long-term, nationwide push by conservative Christian businessmen to generously support ministries that aligned with their religious convictions.[60] At the turn of the twentieth century, conservative Christians came to see the power of corporations and funded influential and high-visibility projects consistent with their vision. Corporate board rooms and businessmen donated billions of dollars to church and parachurch ministries, bankrolling a revivalist, biblicist, and free-market-friendly form of Christianity. They sought "a more Christian nation grounded in a more Christian capitalism."[61] The resonance between Schuller's Christian libertarianism (see chapter 5), his embrace of business practices in the management of his congregation, and his willingness to seek advice on the funding and construction of ambitious projects surely aided him in tapping into those elite corporate connections.

Professional Management of Public Charisma

Schuller's church ministry bore a public charisma, and the charisma of the church and its leadership, as a widely broadcast entity, needed to be protected and actively managed, not only for safeguarding the appeal of his audience but also for sustaining the trust of his major donors. Schuller knew he could not manage this alone. It required hiring people who could manage his public impressions as their sole responsibility. To that end, in 1972 he approached Michael Nason, at the time the director of the Orange County office of the Committee to Re-elect President Nixon, to "run a campaign" that would enhance *Hour of Power*'s profile from six television stations to forty. Nason agreed, promising to make the minister a household name within a decade.[62]

Thus began an orchestrated, and successful, marketing of the minister, his methods, and his theology. To do this required multiple approaches. For example, Schuller presented GGCC as a financially lean organization that succeeded because of focused leadership. In a development mailer from the 1970s, he noted that "over 1,500 volunteer lay persons make this mission called Garden Grove Community Church possible." The document also reported that a small staff and minimal budget efficiently systematized all those volunteers: "A staff of 78 are salaried at a total budget of $424,000. They are a dedicated group! The highest salaried person earns less than the average service man making a house call in Orange County today! Because none of these staff persons have received a cost of living increase *in nearly two years*!"[63] Numbers like these attested to the financial efficiency of the church as a complex, well-managed organization. Money was not wasted.

The work of image management was entrusted to established, secular professionals using the best practices of the day. A 1982 memorandum from a hired public relations firm, Cullen & Taylor, Ltd., demonstrated how industrialized the marketing of Schuller, *Hour of Power*, and the Crystal Cathedral had become. Protocols established clear lines of authority and communication in various imaginable scenarios. These included unsolicited press inquiries, emergency press procedures, handling local press, general advertising, and direct mail advertising. Cullen & Taylor described their working procedure: "In order to maximize positive press, minimize negative coverage, and to ensure the projection of a homogeneous image on both the national and local level, Cullen & Taylor recommends the following public relations procedures for an effective relationship with the total Robert Schuller Ministries, including the Crystal Cathedral and *Hour of Power*."[64] The public relations firm blanketed the country with opportunities to interview Schuller and sent personalized letters to media figures, politicians, academics, and businesspeople—all promoting core ideas that appeared in Schuller's latest book, *Self-Esteem: The New Reformation*. Internal documents reported that this campaign sought to position Schuller as a credible "authority on self-esteem."[65] Moreover, the marketing agency explicitly explained to Schuller that it sought to make his "name more of a household word," while maintaining his "image as a statesmanlike religious leader."[66]

The shaping of Schuller's public persona was methodical and outsourced as part of the ministry's budget. Ministry representatives pursued media appearances on network television as a strategy for raising his profile further. At one point, Schuller sent Johnny Carson (*The Tonight Show*), Hugh Downs (*The Today Show*), and David Frost (*The David Frost Show*) the same form letter in which he wondered whether he might be invited as a guest on their respective programs. After detailing when each recipient could watch *Hour of Power* in his respective television market, Schuller described himself as an advocate of Possibility Thinking and surmised that they "would have exciting things to talk about" on their shows. Moreover, Schuller even suggested that the hosts could contact Norman Vincent Peale, Billy Graham, or Doris Day as references, since he regarded all three as "warm and wonderful friends."[67] (The minister often used proximity to celebrity in order to market his stature and general interest. Once, he casually discussed his burgeoning friendship with John Wayne, exhorted Van Andel to pray that the actor make a commitment to Christianity, and then marveled, "What a testimony that could be!"[68]) In these and other ways, image management was routinized into the structure of the church's ministry.

Structure and Charisma

Schuller understood the instability of personal charisma, a familiar problem in the theorizing of Max Weber.[69] Weber described the potency of charismatic authority as centered on intense value commitments, yet followers are fickle, and seemingly fervent bonds are easily severed—especially when the charisma is shown to be manufactured or fake. Sustaining the passionate loyalty of followers demands constant reminders of the authenticity and exceptionality of the leader. Yet even leaders waver in their own self-assessments, which is why charisma requires routinization, an organizational structure that is not continually dependent on an original charismatic individual. Schuller's success, then, rested on more than just unbridled charisma. Even the best circumstances required Schuller to be surrounded by people who could support, affirm, and finance his vision.

For example, Schuller depended heavily on wealthy Possibility Thinkers to mirror back his philosophies for ultimate assurance regarding its veracity and efficacy. These benefactors proved crucial in sustaining the financing necessary to keep the ministry solvent and always growing. In many ways, they actually became the engines of the ministry that supplied both affirmation and capital. With that in mind, the minister sought legitimacy through wealthy patrons, the leadership institute, an in-house public relations firm, and his membership in the country's longest-standing Protestant denomination. His charismatic efficacy found affirmation in the financial support these donors generated to support and extend it over time.

In sum, the humble yet innovative GGCC did not become the religious-industrial complex of the Crystal Cathedral solely on pure charisma. Instead, Schuller crafted a stylized (California blend) concoction of faith, business, and wealth. In order to bring consistency to his new method of church life, Schuller, more than anything, had to implement a new set of institutional logics consistent with and supportive of his public persona. Institutional logics represent established ways of doing things—patterns, behaviors, rituals, and routines—and within contemporary Christianity, institutional logics set a churchgoer's expectations for congregational life and worship. Schuller's techniques tended to breach the institutional logics of American church ministry. In order to establish the plausibility of his apparent violations, Schuller established multiple ways to affirm his legitimacy.

The clout of the institute offered an especially powerful means to establish legitimacy. Schuller gained the entrée to influence church leaders because his ministry offered tangible evidence of success. In fact, the spectacular nature of the campus and the polished professionalism of the television show displayed verification of Schuller's virtuosity. In turn, the attenders became the *virtuosi* of Schuller and normalized his pattern of ministry throughout the United States.[70] Not only did the leadership institute become a must-see among ambitious pastors seeking helps for successful ministry, but Schuller also accurately pointed out that several notable participants had formed *their own* institutes or conferences for church leadership based on their own congregational sites, thereby replicating and enhancing Schuller's pastoral style and influence.[71] Schuller's religious virtuosi diffused the spiritual innovations and abetted their broader adoption into their own pastoral ministries but also mirrored Schuller's methods back to himself.

Moreover, the funding for these activities occurred in the context of a broader movement among conservative Christian corporations and businessmen in the mid-twentieth century to fund a capitalist-friendly faith consistent with their religious convictions.[72] The tenuous promise of church growth techniques as Schuller proposed them rested on the fortuitous historical fact that these benefactors emerged at a particular historical moment to generously support his ministry at just the right time. Future church growth disciples likely would not have such abundant resources available again.

Schuller became a master of bureaucratic impression management and found validation for his theology in the size, status, and success of his ministry. Following theorists such as Charles Horton Cooley, George Herbert Mead, and Erving Goffman, a sociological understanding of the self suggests that even charismatically powerful figures like Schuller depend on their perception of how others perceive them.[73] The church, the institute, and the television program all rested on a calculus (people, media, location, buildings, management) that projected a constant affirmation of Schuller's public persona. The minister's "messages" depended on an audience/congregation that *reflected* back to him that, since they appeared to be successful Possibility Thinkers, he had to be the Possibility Pastor. And yet the minister sometimes simply fell into a malaise, and it would be another person who would channel Schuller's own Possibility Thinking message. That individual, then, would become the spark to catalyze something in Schuller that the minister did not necessarily have in himself. The reflection, then, sustained Schuller's self-understanding. Interpreted in that light, the mirrored glass of the Crystal Cathedral served as continual affirmation of his method—the church as the looking glass self.

The irony of Schuller resided in the fact that while he ably routinized the processes of pastoral ministry for the sake of thousands of other pastors, he failed to routinize his own charisma within his own congregation, making charisma itself an unreliable resource for the long term of the ministry. He had hoped to make the enterprise of his church into its own self-sustaining institution in its own right, one not dependent on his charisma. Unfortunately, we now know that while he accomplished much in his lifetime, Schuller ultimately failed in crafting a sustainable structure for the survival of the church without him, in part due to the failure to recognize charisma itself as a valuable resource whose sustainability must be assured. Moreover, the nature of charisma that had carried the ministry for so long would likely need to change once the ideology of Christian libertarianism buttressing his charismatic authority failed to resonate.

The Crystal Cathedral and the Tower of Hope. Photo courtesy of the Joint Archives of Holland.

7

Always a New Project

You never suffer from a money problem,
you always suffer from an idea problem.
—Robert H. Schuller

Someone as acutely aware of image as Robert H. Schuller knew what people said and wrote about him. A few years after the opening of the Crystal Cathedral, Schuller deadpanned to his congregation one Sunday morning, "Have you heard the latest? They're saying that when Oral Roberts, Billy Graham, and Bob Schuller get to heaven, Graham will convert everybody to Christianity, Roberts will heal them, and Schuller will be out raising money to air condition the place."[1] The joke confirmed that the Orange County minister embraced his reputation for fund-raising savvy. The ostentatious scale and spectacle of the cathedral's glass structure represented a divergence from the restrained tradition of his Dutch Reformed denomination, as noted by Susan Power Bratton: "Schuller's addition of the cathedral, beside what had been an airy and upbeat meeting house [the hybrid Arboretum], was, in itself, a break with Calvinist norms."[2] The more his celebrity grew and the more he built, the more he validated the cost of his religious project. In turn, the pattern authorized Schuller to raise even more capital. In his guidebook to successful church growth, Schuller advised ministry leaders that "big, imaginative, problem-solving ideas really turn people on! Every year you must offer some new challenge in the form of a new program, a new project, a new building, a new addition to the staff, or a new missionary project."[3]

During the 1980s and early 1990s, Schuller's multimodal religious complex had arguably attained the status as the highest-profile church in the United States. *Reader's Digest* testified to the ministry's reputation as a church "power-house." The magazine reported these "staggering" statistics: 10,000 congregational members, 1,000 new members per year, 9,000 ministers (and wives and church leaders) having attended the leadership institute (established in 1969), an annual budget of $2.7 million, and a nationally televised program with an annual budget of $16 million.[4] Obviously, Schuller's message, "a blend of salvation through Christ and a doctrine of self-esteem," had found a receptive audience.[5] The *Los Angeles Times* presented Schuller as "America's leading evangelist," despite his refusal to affiliate with the 950-member National Religious Broadcasters (NRB), one of the most important evangelical organizations of the time. When asked about his reluctance to join, Schuller shrugged and asserted his independence: "It's not the dues—what is it, $200 a year? And I don't want to seem snobbish or stand-offish. It's just that—who *needs* them?"[6] The Orange County minister had carved out his own niche. His books and seminars on church growth represented Schuller's most valuable products, and his viewers and the financial wealth of his ministry served as evidence of its efficacy. Importantly, as a member of the Reformed Church in America (RCA), Schuller viewed himself as having denominational accountability; that made him different from independent evangelicals who lacked validating connections and whose desire for respectability dictated their connection to the NRB.

With his ingenuity and novelty in capturing the California preoccupation with mobility, celebrity, and entertainment, Schuller became an exemplar of how a large church might be built upon the charismatic leadership of its founder. Schuller's message of Possibility Thinking represented his attempt to remove obstacles to church attendance. Rather than engaging in the well-worn revivalist strategy of employing guilt and fear in the service of conversion, he engaged in a therapeutic "pre-evangelism."[7] In the ministry of Schuller, we see how charisma demands an "other" to reflect back inspiration as fuel to further energize the exercise of inspirational authority—with finances providing concrete evidence of the other's confidence in the leader's ideas. Followers of charismatic authority often support, reaffirm, and legitimate authority through financial support. More often than not, *capital is the tangible means for affirming the intangible force of a leader's charisma.*

It appeared on the surface that Schuller had created an unassailable religious-industrial complex, but ensuring increasing streams of revenue remained a constant concern. Schuller believed in the efficacy of his Theology of Self-Esteem (the conception that human beings need to be affirmed in their dignity, not criticized for their sins) and solicited donors to contribute as much as they could to further expanding the platform for his message—his pulpit—based in the physicality of his church. As a pragmatic pastor, Schuller understood he was unlikely

A cartoon that lampooned Schuller's reputation for incessant fund-raising accompanied an article in *The Economist* regarding the minister's death in 2015. Image courtesy of David Parkins and *The Economist*.

to receive consistently large sums from regular attenders. So his strategy for obtaining adequate funding depended not only on fresh efforts at fund-raising but also on generous gifts from a few big-dollar donors. Schuller's charismatic force depended on a larger structure that extended his own charisma, contingent especially on the generosity of wealthy supporters and an institutional coherence that inspired the confidence of unwavering donors.[8] Schuller depended on infusions of capital from wealthy Christian benefactors, obtained in part by promising these spiritual investors that their contribution would further affirm a guarantee of future funding from ordinary, day-to-day givers.

Without access to the broader organizational workings of his ministry, past studies relied largely on Schuller's books and sermons and therefore described the workings of charisma based on his enacting a protoprosperity theology for the growth of his ministry.[9] What this incomplete analysis of charisma misses— and what the recent literature on "the business turn" from American religious historians brings into view[10]—is the dynamics of raising and managing the flow of capital. Even business scholars who used the church's history as case study fodder distilled the ministry's decline as simply the result of overspending, poorly planned succession, and lavish salaries for Schuller family members. Because of its almost exclusive reliance on secondary sources, this scholarship fails to account for the very nature of the church's growth model, which depended on an unwavering and charisma-induced capital inflow and its intrinsic vulnerabilities.[11]

When we ask why the Crystal Cathedral, a seemingly unstoppable juggernaut, failed, our analysis reveals important connections between charisma, religious nonprofit organizations, and capitalism in explaining the ministry's collapse—interrelated dynamics for which the business-turn literature sharpens the focus. More specifically, with its emphasis on "the financing, production, marketing, and distribution of religious goods and services,"[12] this recent scholarship reveals how the business of religion has changed over time and how business interests among conservative Christians and religious entities that align with their vision of a capitalist-friendly spiritual enterprise have become entangled. While scholarship addressing the business turn has noted fund-raising rooted in a Christian libertarian vision at the macro level by tracing out networks and organizational structures that cross regions or states or nations, the case of Schuller's Garden Grove ministry allows us to more closely examine how capital flows are solicited and managed through a message of Possibility Thinking at the local or micro level.

Investigation into the history leading to the implosion of the Crystal Cathedral reveals a long-established pattern of constant, active fund-raising on the part of Schuller and the unsustainable ideational constructs of church growth he created for himself and persuaded others to adopt as the formula for growing ministry in the twentieth century. Our analysis hinges on Schuller's visionary orientation toward fund-raising, demonstrating how he combined the raising of funds and the management of the flow of capital into successive efforts at "new" funding to monetarily feed a growing ministry empire. The need for significant subsidies among some entrepreneurial religious leaders and the availability of sources of funding from scattered benefactors across the country led to intriguing affinities—affinities that became dependencies for churches like Schuller's that lacked any other means to secure infusions of capital. Though he offered multiple points of strategy for church success, perhaps Schuller's most significantly explicit method expounded the principle that congregations should not be afraid of debt as they strove for growth.[13] On the other hand, it remained mostly unspoken by the minister that his strategy also included a profound dependence on significant, almost *ex machina*, infusions from a few wealthy donors.[14] Overall, the minister failed to realize that the manner in which he sought to manage capital flows intensified the fragility of the church. His strategy for growth ironically weakened the entire structure.

Fund-Raising and the Sheen of a New Product

From the beginning of his ministry, Schuller did not just plan for growth—he insisted on it. During his first pastorate in the early 1950s at suburban Chicago's Ivanhoe Reformed Church, he demonstrated a panache for instigating capital development based on increased attendance. In successfully developing this small church in Riverdale, Schuller sent the congregation a letter concerning "the crowded Sunday School" and the "overflow attendance at the morning worship service" and said that, though "splendid," the "growth [presented] problems"—a theme he would revisit throughout his ministry (see Schuller's letter to Jay Van Andel regarding the *necessity* of the Crystal Cathedral in chapter 6).[15] The minister prompted members to consider more generous tithing to allow the church to build to meet its capacity needs. Schuller also delivered a sermon that same week, "Profitable Living," in which he urged congregants to remember two things: "You will never get until you give . . . and you will get only in proportion to what you give." Most importantly for Ivanhoe's building expansion, this "law" also "held true in the church" as well: "The people who get a lot out of the church are the folks who put a lot of their time, talent, tithe, interest, attention, and concern into the church."[16] Schuller framed growth as the antidote to a future problem, pressing congregants to avoid that obstacle with more robust tithing.

After the move to plant a church in Southern California, development became an all-consuming task for Schuller's religious enterprise. Founded at a drive-in theater, his church grew quickly, and the purchase of land and construction of a new building gave the congregation a high profile, which Schuller further promoted. Garden Grove Community Church (GGCC) was built on a reputation for growth and could not afford to slip. Stasis might be interpreted as decline. As the congregation erected yet another new building (mixing the aesthetics of the drive-in church with a traditional "walk-in" church and eventually called the "Arboretum") and Schuller launched a television ministry (*Hour of Power*), the demanding sheen of success required funding for everything from the best television cameras, to elegant robes, to modern-looking facilities. An example of the recurrent call for new giving to the latest challenge came from frequent direct mailings with Schuller's signature. In a 1964 mailer to the members of GGCC, Schuller described the plans for yet another building (the fourth project of his career), dubbed "the Tower of Hope" (a new centerpiece of the ministry that included a chapel, ministerial and psychology staff offices, and ten floors dedicated to classrooms for 500 young people), and entreated investing in bonds for the building: "Here truly your money works for God while it works for you." Schuller promised investors a return of 5 percent, with quarterly disbursements. In doing so, investors would be helping to "build something that is absolutely tremendous for God and for The United States of America!"[17] Schuller fused the desire for accumulating wealth, patriotism, and building God's kingdom in making his ask.

To instigate enthusiastic giving, he would frame capital campaign projects as historically significant. For example, the Tower of Hope offered a physical signal of the ministry's prominence. Promotional materials promised the "tallest and most functional Church Tower in Southern California."[18] Sketches, pictures, and models added visual detail: "When the lights go on in a little over a year, they will never go out in this little chapel in the sky. From Disneyland, Angel Stadium, to the County Hospital, to the freeway, this will be a silent reminder that there is 'an eye that never closes, an ear that is never shut, and a heart that never grows cold.'"[19] At the "Tenth Birthday Dinner Party" in November 1965 (held down the road at the Disneyland Hotel), Schuller unveiled the renderings for the Tower of Hope. A map showed the tower perched at the intersection of the Garden Grove Freeway and the Santa Ana Freeway and described the location as "the highway hub of Southern California." Dinner party brochures included a letter from Schuller in which he described the historical scale of the tower: "It's a tremendous thrill to know that we are picked by God to build this inspiring structure that should stand for more than 1000 years! The pyramids are 500 years old! The Pisa Tower is 500 years old! The London Tower is 1000 years old! And these are towers of Pride, Vanity, and Greed! Now we build God's Tower! A Tower of Hope!"[20]

Amid sweeping, visionary statements, Schuller offered persistently concrete details about the necessary financial commitment. To build the tower, the church needed $1 million. Yet the promotional material helpfully distilled the costs into 520 weekly payments that ranged from $1 to $10 per week. Schuller imagined giving to be like a layaway plan with manageable payments: "A small pledge per week will grow into a large gift!" Wealthy donors were asked for large lump sums, and regular members were taught to see that many repeated smaller contributions over time became just as significant. In return for these pledges, donors providing "pace-setting gifts of over $10 per week" would receive "Founder" wall plaques, while all contributors, regardless of their level of support, would receive "Builders of the Tower" certificates suitable for framing.[21] Once "investors" made their contributions, Schuller followed up with glowing letters to note holders assuring them that the church remained a growing entity about which everyone gushed with praise: "There was hardly a dry eye in the church. Over and over again one heard the expression, 'Never in my life have I experienced such a thrilling religious emotion as I did Sunday morning.'"[22]

Schuller explained his fund-raising strategy for the benefit of all pastors in his denomination in a 1968 article in the RCA's *Church Herald*: "We must constantly offer new challenges in the form of programs or projects: a building program, an addition to the staff, and additional missionary project." By example, Schuller noted that on the day of the Tower of Hope's dedication in 1968, he thought that perhaps the church campus had now been completed. Before the service, the minister relaxed in his office in the new building. As he looked down twelve stories, though, he witnessed a lone automobile circling the parking lot.

The car drove up and down the lanes, searching for an open spot. Finding none, the "car drove out the exit and sped up—and away." Schuller wrote that at that moment he realized that construction "had only just begun." He spied ten acres of adjacent walnut and orange trees that flanked the northern boundary of the church campus and "knew that [the ministry] had to buy it as well!"[23] He pressed his readers to follow his example, crafting new projects to stimulate greater church income.

The 1968 article demonstrated how Possibility Thinking (see chapter 4)[24] provided both the confidence to take on large, capital-intensive projects as well as the fund-raising framework to meet those goals. Schuller initiated his advice with a key principle: *congregations should be honest that they will always need more money than they have secured.* For example, church newsletters over the years would be explicit regarding fund-raising goals and suggested pledges, with deadlines and bold exclamation marks noting the urgency of giving. Indeed, one newsletter included an insert titled "How to Make $385,000 in Ten Minutes" to explain the upcoming tenth anniversary fund-raising dinner.[25] For Schuller, pledges granted permission to move forward on a project. He took his cue from Billy Graham, who told Schuller that if pledges of support came to 50 percent of the annual cost, the project was a go. Quoting Graham, Schuller wrote, "We'd take that as God's order to do it."[26]

But churches should never offer the impression that they have a financial crisis ("Nobody likes to invest in a shaky business," Schuller wrote). Relatedly, "small pickings" like suppers and bake sales waste time and energy. Instead, Schuller advised pastors to tap into members' desires and offer an inspiring project that meets a "human need." ("People love to spend their money. They can't wait to spend it on a new car, a new house, new clothes—anything that excites them or stimulates and inspires imagination.") GGCC's own practices involved a festive dinner where the leadership of the congregation delineated the budget for the next year using projections on big screens: "The entire program of the church from janitor to missionary is emotionalized and dramatized through color graphics."[27]

Schuller argued with evidence from his own ministry that his focus on growth promoted financial stability—a healthy balance sheet—by continually presenting new projects that generated even more capital. Most significantly, his church led "all churches in the Reformed Church in America in income from living donors." Schuller was buoyed by GGCC's "Church of the Year" award announcement from *Guideposts* and had written to his publisher (Doubleday & Co.) in January 1968 with strategies for marketing his recent book, *Move Ahead with Possibility Thinking.* Schuller suggested that timing would be critical: "I would like to request your publicity committee capitalize on the national success image that we now have."[28]

Schuller's high standing demanded an unremitting emphasis on further growth and additional revenue streams. The logic grew from Schuller's earliest years as a pastor and assumed that the ministry could expand its way through any turmoil, shielding the church from the vagaries of environmental chaos, even though the constant, aggressive push produced undue strains. By the mid-1970s, the ministry even included a Department of Planned Giving, offering free classes "for people who sincerely sense the importance of a 'Christ-centered' will and estate plan."[29] Paid staff were charged with eliciting estate plans benefiting the ministry. Once, Schuller lamented that "a staff person had waited too long" to reach out to an aging donor: "When he called on Friday, it was already too late. Only two hours before, my friend the benefactor had died—without a chance to alter his will as he desired."[30]

Just the management of receiving massive flows of capital donations demanded significant effort. By the late 1970s, the ministry received an average of 40,000 letters per week, with three-quarters of the envelopes containing monetary gifts. Upon receiving the mail on the church grounds, staff moved the letters to a secure room and removed the money, wrote a receipt for each donation, and then forwarded the letters to a bank of "readers."[31] An array of computers produced prewritten messages crafted to respond to specific problems mentioned in the correspondence, a marvelous mechanization of Schuller's charisma for monetary purposes. A reporter detailed the process: "The computer quickly assembles the appropriate paragraphs in readable form, and the letter is imprinted with Schuller's signature and mailed. Fast and efficient, a kind of 'Action Line' for the soul."[32]

Franchising a National Chain?

Schuller always demonstrated interest in promulgating his pattern of capital-intensive ministry and focus on architecture, pushing other pastors to dream about their own respective buildings. In late 1968, Schuller encouraged two RCA pastors in New York City to begin plans to design East Coast versions of the Tower of Hope, to be named "Resurrection Tower" and "Bethany Tower." Schuller offered advice on passing resolutions with their councils to aggressively pursue these buildings, even proposing language: "I would suggest that you present this dream and its outline to your consistory and with a recommendation: 'Resolve that the Consistory of Bethany Memorial Reformed Church adopt the Bethany Towers Project as a masterplan of development for this church, allowing God to unfold in our minds the way in which this miracle can occur.'" Schuller then noted that the strategy had proven successful in Garden Grove: "This is the way we operate. It means that we can go on record saying, 'Yes, it is a great idea—we will not stand in God's way, if He wants it, we will help him.'"[33]

With yet more detail, Schuller confidently articulated his vision for one of the potential RCA towers in New York: "I can see in the 21st century the Reformed Church in America on Manhattan Island being the most exciting, progressive, pace-setting church activity in any city in the whole world!" Any such project demanded an architectural rendering to prime the congregations' imaginations: "I would suggest that you find an architectural delineator who could give you a picture of what this 20-story tower would look like. If you do not have the funds for this, I think I might find someone here who could do it certainly for less than $500. And it would look like a picture of the tower itself standing there on the street. It could be done in color, framed, and begin to excite everyone with the fantastic vision." He advised that "Resurrection Tower" be presented as a national-scale denominational mission project: "Forget the money problem. . . . It is my experience that it is easier to raise $1,000,000 or $2,000,000 for a big dream—than it is to raise $1,000 or $2,000 to patch up an old building. I had an awful job to raise $1,800 for a maintenance job on this property." Schuller explained why: "Nobody gets enthused about old ideas. But a big pace-setting, exciting project could win the support of tens of thousands of people across the Country."[34] Of course, an East Coast version of Schuller's church would have significantly validated his own legitimacy. A couple of decades later, he would counsel readers that they should always "colonize" their success: "If you have succeeded, then colonize your success. If you stop where you are now, if you fail to continue to grow, then you will begin to die." As a vivid example, Schuller described how Sam Walton had nurtured his little discount store, Wal-Mart, into a national chain that had made him "America's richest man."[35]

Schuller's formula for fund-raising depended on campaigns for ambitious, vision-rich, and abstract projects, all to be completed several years in the future. He appealed to constituents to agree on the attractiveness of the idea, to seek God's will for the project, and thereby to sanction the call for more capital. Most importantly, large *future* projects would stimulate giving to be used for *past* projects' continual need for maintenance. In 1969, Schuller arranged for GGCC to publish a pamphlet to distribute among RCA congregations promoting innovation among the denomination's congregations on the West Coast: "Walk-in, Drive-in Church News." The pamphlet noted how the walk-in–drive-in congregations reported "phenomenal growth," in contrast to the net loss of members in the denomination overall. Crediting Schuller as the originator of the concept, the pamphlet quoted Norman Vincent Peale extolling the virtues of these hybrid churches: "This is one of the most exciting developments going on in the Protestant world today."[36] Where would funds be obtained? Knowing that the vast majority of RCA members had only distant, if any, connections to the Sun Belt, the pamphlet appealed to "God's plan to use the Midwest Reformed church people to make this great mission succeed," alluding to the denomination's history in international missionary activity. First, a nod to RCA missions field history: "One of the greatest forces for worldwide missions in the history of Christendom has been The Reformed Church in America. No Protestant denomination, however large and lofty, has done more for World Missions than our little Reformed Church in America." Then, an appeal to the RCA's Midwestern center of gravity: "Where did these missionaries come from? And where did the money to support this mission venture come from? Largely from the great Reformed Churches of the Midwestern plains of America. From the solid, dedicated, rural and small towns of Iowa, Illinois, Wisconsin, and Michigan came the bulk of young boys and young girls who became the great missionaries of the Church. And from the heartland of America came also the generous missionary offerings to make this mission a success."[37]

Using a missionary model, established Midwest church members were to provide capital to fund newer Sun Belt churches. As the founder of GGCC, Schuller saw his own church as a primary beneficiary of such mission funding. The pamphlet emphasized that in the twenty-first century, the ostensibly "secular" West Coast of the United States, not a foreign country, would stand as the most significant mission field—but only if churches acted before the "revolutionaries and atheists" started making gains and eventually closed "missionary doors" in this country. Great churches should be built now, while it still remained possible: "Seriously consider taking your savings out of the traditional commercial savings institutions that will not loan your money to build churches—and invest your savings in church promissory notes, and church bonds, where you will earn more interest and know that while your money is working for you, it is building a great mission program in America!" The pamphlet detailed that readers could "choose to join over 1200 of the top investment people in The Reformed Church in America who are investing their savings in the Walk-in–Drive-in Chain of Churches. Here you may invest funds in the amount of $100 up. Interest is paid at the rate of 6% for 'on demand' notes; 7% interest is paid for investments that are left from 5 to 15 years; 7½% interest is paid for investments that are left for a period of from 15 to 20 years."[38]

Clearly, Schuller envisioned "a national chain" of walk-in–drive-in hybrid churches pioneered by his own congregation. He explained a development effort to raise $800,000 from RCA members to solidify the undertaking. His confidence in this wild, blue-sky idea emerged in another pamphlet that described the potential for building walk-in–drive-in churches in the colder climates of the RCA's traditional regions of the Midwest and Northeast, where Schuller added the idea of building giant arenas to enclose these innovative buildings ("If the world can build a dome over a baseball stadium in Houston, Texas to climate control an area, why can't we do the same thing for the Lord?"). The pamphlet also offered details on three "expansion" projects in California: Sacramento, Long Beach, and, of course, at GGCC. According to Schuller, GGCC "found it imperative to expand from their ten acres by purchasing an adjoining twelve acres" so that they could avoid the nagging problem of "unchurched people" driving in "on Sunday mornings only to have to drive out because there isn't a single parking space!" GGCC also considered plans for hosting a West Coast branch of an RCA-affiliated college, expanding a counseling center, and establishing a Christian retirement home. All, of course, would have demanded new construction projects.

Unquestionably, in Schuller's national promotion of church growth strategies for fund-raising, GGCC was the model. He hoped to normalize and legitimize his innovation. And in late 1974, the minister claimed his congregation's status as the "mother of new churches," by which he meant that GGCC provided a rich source of new capital for the expansion of ministry. Schuller pressed his case, insisting that with greater funding, his mission church could accomplish even more. For example, Schuller claimed that since he began preaching at the Orange Drive-in, over fifty other drive-in churches had been founded "through the inspiration, and in many cases, financial support of this Mother Church!"[39] In another letter to promissory note holders, Schuller hailed GGCC as accomplishing the most ministry for the money: "I've been on national boards of many Christian ministries. I've studied the budgets of the so-called greatest missions and Evangelism ministries in the world . . . especially at Billy Graham's Congress in Lausanne, Switzerland, 1974. . . . And I've studied the budgets of 2000 churches that went through our Institute, and the truth is nobody is doing more good for God with dollars than this mission called Garden Grove Community Church."[40] It seemed that perhaps Schuller even used the leadership institute as a reconnaissance tool to study the finances of other ministries. With all this evidence at his disposal, Schuller dismissed a cohort of "unworthy challengers" for donation dollars, arguing for the uniqueness of the impact made possible by contributing to his own church's financial strength.[41]

With these and other efforts, Schuller took unconventional opportunities to campaign for his Southern California ministry, and his creativity in calling for new sources of revenue was both calculated and opportunistic. In a letter expressing regret for missing his twenty-fifth high school reunion in Iowa, Schuller first demurred about reporting his success: "There is not much to say." After a description of his family life, the letter then built to a crescendo with Schuller reporting on his four published books and congregation of 3,500 members. Schuller acknowledged that what followed would be "a little commercial," and then wondered whether his former classmates would be willing to buy his recent book, *Moving Ahead with Possibility Thinking*: "[The publisher is] going into their third printing which means it's a success!" Despite good sales, Schuller would like to see even more: "I can always use a few extra-enthusiastic salesmen so you can talk your friends into ordering it from the bookstore—or you can always write to the Reformed Bookstore in Teaneck, New Jersey." Schuller closed with an invitation for his former classmates to come visit his church: "And if you are ever out in California and visiting Disneyland, remember our church is only a mile from this fabulous fun park. You will have no trouble finding the church. It's the tallest building in Orange County. The Cross on the top of the Tower is 25 stories above ground!"[42]

"Inch by Inch, Anything's a Cinch"

Because of all the success, by the mid-1970s, Schuller grew concerned that the Arboretum, the Richard Neutra–designed space of the walk-in–drive-in structure and the original space for the *Hour of Power* program, was too small—that it lacked the capacity to house regular members and an increased number of weekly visitors. Perhaps more importantly, the structure, not built with television production values in mind, was an overly bland and conventional set for a broadcast. Schuller sketched out a dramatic architectural wonder that would hold a larger audience and provide televised optics, a more stunning backdrop to match a grander scale of broadcast production. Upon its completion, architectural critics viewed the church as designed more as a stage for performance than a traditional space for worship.[43] One critic noted that Schuller's aesthetic choices exhibited an effort to demonstrate "continuing vigor and relevance" in their "violent innovation."[44] Even Schuller admitted that, when completed, the Crystal Cathedral would function as the world's "first church auditorium designed to be a television studio as well as the sanctuary of a worshipping congregation."[45] In a 1975 publication for the twentieth anniversary celebration, Schuller described the dream of a Crystal Cathedral that would be "on the scale of the Great Cathedrals in Cologne, Germany, and the Notre Dame in Paris— even as our Tower of Hope rivals, in size, scale, and impact, the great Cathedral Towers of Europe!" Situating his church in this manner, the minister again signaled the remarkable aspirations of his ministry. Schuller explained that he became ever more convinced about the significance of architecture as he toured the USSR: "The sacred structures dominate the Soviet landscape and still send silent sermons seeping subtly through the secular state."[46]

Mobilizing funding for the cathedral gave Schuller an opportunity to make explicit his "philosophy toward capital." Though he described debt service as "an oppressive burden" and the "toughest and most thankless bill to pay," Schuller clearly understood it as a necessary ingredient in church growth.[47] In a special report written in 1975, his opening gambit for the construction of the cathedral, Schuller impressed upon his consistory that "since the beginning of this Church," he had "known" that to "stimulate and maintain dynamic growth," the congregation would have to be committed to being a "dynamic 'business for God.'" The minister then stated it more bluntly: dynamic growth "would require cash" and "borrowing money."[48] Borrowed funds were required *now* to accommodate the growth in membership that would produce income to pay off the loans *later*. In the statement, Schuller intimated an unequivocal formula for growth: *increased debt produces added growth*. His report expressed urgency to act quickly, since the five million dollars of projected costs could only increase—construction must be initiated now to avoid inflation. Also, currently available land for purchase would be gone. Most starkly, Schuller graphically stated that "prospective customers" would "die before they would have a chance to 'come into a building' to hear The Word." The strategy of rapid growth through financing was not a new one. Schuller reminded the consistory that he had been following a "responsible philosophy of capital debt" for twenty years, which included borrowing "as much as we can—as fast as we can—to do as much good as we can"[49] for "CAPITAL expenditures" because "expanded property or facilities" will "produce added growth i.e. additional income." Within Schuller's protocol, not building the cathedral represented stagnation, decline, and wasted opportunity for growth: "To wait until surplus cash, if ever, was in the church coffers would wait too long."[50]

Schuller also benefitted from historically unprecedented access to borrowed capital. His central philosophy of "borrowing into growth" coincided with policy changes in reaction to the "stagflation" of the 1970s that had crippled the US economy. As a strategic response to high unemployment and inflation, government deregulation freed capital flows both within the United States and between the United States and global markets. The expansion of credit allowed for corporations and assets to grow significantly. At the same time, church bonds offered attractive 7 percent returns of investment.[51] For Schuller, these fiscal policy changes meant that wealthy benefactors had more capital at their disposal (for things like philanthropy) while the ministry benefitted from the ability to offer bonds that provided reliable investment earnings comparable to certificates of deposits from banks. Schuller did not grasp the unique historical contingency of the easy credit he enjoyed, which allowed him to continue to build on his Garden Grove campus. Instead, he assumed that access to easy credit would always be readily available—a posture that would be undermined by the economic instability of the 2000s.

When he publicly announced plans in the late 1970s for a 4,000-seat Crystal Cathedral, Schuller acknowledged that the construction effort would raise the congregation's budget significantly. *The Wittenburg Door*, an evangelical satire magazine, published a scathing indictment regarding the initial cost in a feature titled "How to Spend $15,000,000." The article questioned the integrity of a Christian ministry that spent millions of dollars to build a "big glass church." To demonstrate the scale of the cost of the cathedral, the article calculated the expenditures of hundreds of different social and humanitarian programs targeting the poor around the world to show how much good work could be funded for that price. Suggestions ranged from $180,000 to support ten orphanages in Nairobi for five years, providing food and shelter for 1,000 children, to $2,400,000 for establishing 100 new schools in Haiti in an effort to provide an education for 10,000 children "in a country with only a 19% literacy rate."[52] In response to such indictments, Schuller touted the mission efforts funded by supporters' giving through the church. He also argued for the broader economic benefits of the ministry. A college professor reflecting on a recent tour of the church campus led by Schuller himself noted the minister's focus on the buildings while seemingly remaining oblivious to the murder of six Jesuit priests in El Salvador just days before. Hearing about the professor's concerns, Schuller responded that while he wished he had said something about the killings, he helped people from El Salvador because "an awful lot of [workers] have money this week because of the job opportunities at this building project, some of them from El Salvador."[53] Noticeably, persistent questions involving financial priorities raised the minister's ire, and he repeatedly argued that the economic impact of the ministry should not be oversimplified.

His conspicuous fund-raising and extensive media presence made "Schuller shooting" a highly rewarding hobby for both theologians and cultural commentators.[54] Critics accused Schuller of simply accommodating the white suburban middle class and their infatuation with the nuclear family and the car-centric lifestyle.[55] Detractors equated the ministry with the amusement park just down the highway, both overly dependent on façade and light on substance: "As with Disneyland, the attractions Schuller offers are less important in themselves than for the stage setting they provide for marketing a media image across the rest of the nation."[56] Still other critics pointed to a crass shallowness in Schuller's methods and theology: "In return for their cash, checks and money orders, Schuller's flock receives a sense of community without having to get out of their cars, a feeling of spiritual redemption without having to change their lives."[57] Perhaps most cutting, some fellow Christians decried Schuller's seeming obsession with fund-raising.

Tiring of critiques of his fund-raising efforts, Schuller at one point asserted that he employed only "morally upright" strategies. Though the ostentatious scale made him an easy mark, Schuller argued that his fame offered the best evidence of his integrity: "I'm judged in the marketplace every week by my viewers—just like any other merchant who's accepting money for a product or service. The public will judge you, that's No. 1. And on top of that, we have the judgement of TV stations who carry *Hour of Power*. And they say Robert Schuller is in a class by himself."[58] His growth and success offered a protective shield from those who disparaged the ministry for financial excess. Schuller frequently quipped, "inch by inch, anything's a cinch," emphasizing that even the largest projects could be accomplished if a person broke it up into smaller, manageable tasks.[59] The minister often applied that principle to the financing needed for his large capital projects. Large sums were broken down into smaller schemes for borrowing and fundraising. These combinations of cash, credit, and pledges were used to complete the next phase of a project, leading toward eventual execution.

Schuller tended to discuss the ability to donate lavishly to his ministry as a God-given capacity. He argued that generous giving demonstrated the direct workings of God's Spirit in a person. Abundant givers were spiritually enabled by God to give significantly so that even ordinary people through giving could confirm the unique *charism* (New Testament Greek term meaning "gift") placed on a person's life. Such giving affirmed a person's profound connection to God. Schuller's call for greater giving therefore allowed people to exercise their divine gifting and to discover whether this, indeed, was their "spiritual gift."

For a while, Schuller called spiritually gifted givers "Pillars of Steel," the supports that allowed the glass structure to stand. In a Crystal Cathedral development mailer, the minister described his "Pillars": "These people are unique. They will understand that God calls some people to be windows so his light can shine through them. He calls others to be shining stars, reflecting the beauty of God's great love. And he calls others to be strong, to quietly labor without fanfare or acclaim—to be pillars of steel. I believe God will make it possible for you to send $500 and become a pillar of steel—as he promised the Old Testament prophet: 'I have made you today as an iron pillar' (Jeremiah 1:18)."[60]

To fund the construction of the Crystal Cathedral, Schuller also presented the concept of the "trusting expectation"—a statement of intent to give a specified weekly amount of money to the church. The pamphlet noted that a trusting expectation had no legal obligations and should not be understood as a debt or "an act of resented necessity." Instead, the trusting statement should be seen as an expression of worship, a sacrificial gift, and the "first expenditure" made from "the money God sends." Further empowering the nature of giving as a spiritual investment, the design in the publication included a facsimile of a stock certificate that quoted Malachi 3:10: "Bring the whole tithe into my house and test me now in this way, if I will not open the windows of the heavens, and pour out for you a blessing until there is no more need . . ."[61] The same certificate included the promise of "guaranteed return upon investment." Under the certificate was a final push that sanctioned efforts to increase a family's financial stability: "Trying to get more income for family benefit is a pure motive . . . so even if your only motive would be more income . . . try it . . . prove Him."[62] In this way, Schuller blessed the desire for wealth by offering a scenario in which investors could reassure themselves that their giving was not only for their own individual returns on investment but also for the long-term benefit of their nuclear families.[63]

Still, the demand for capital remained and soon necessitated that members *double their offerings*. With signature calculation, Schuller outlined a plan for those increases in giving, offering a step-by-step process for people to give up more discretionary spending. He suggested, first, eliminating waste: "All of us waste time, money, energy, clothes and opportunities. It's incredible how much money is wasted on food! Most Americans are overweight. In addition, an incredible amount of money is wasted on alcohol, tobacco, and consumption that hurts more than it helps!" He then recommended that individuals consider leaving portions of their estates to the church after death. Third, members might simply consider increasing their income: "Dr. Schuller shared how a 78-year-old woman is planning a direct sales program to earn more money." In a subtle rebuke, he calculated that if every family in the GGCC membership actually tithed, it would produce income of over $5 million.

Most aggressively, Schuller noted that an estimate of the collective net worth of the congregation's 7,500 members likely rose to about $100 million and suggested that some "pioneers" within the church would be tithing from their assets and wealth, not just income: "Many will dip into stocks and savings to double their giving in 1976!"[64] The minister enthusiastically approved of drawing out investment savings to enable a doubling of donations.

Through appeals to wealthy benefactors and expectations of receiving increasing donations from staff, members, and volunteers, the ministry financed the construction of the cathedral through gifts that ranged from John Crean's $1 million (Crean was an Orange County multimillionaire industrialist so generous to the Crystal Cathedral that his grave sits adjacent to the Schullers'; see chapter 6), to $500 gifts for each of the 10,600 windows that sheathed the structure, to faithful tithing, to stray dollars from inspired givers. Rising construction costs and inflation still left Schuller short of development goals, and ticketed events emerged as a new strategy for revenue. Needing a major infusion of capital, the minister booked its most significant event in the history of the church: a major celebrity concert in the not-quite-completed sanctuary.

Monetizing the Cathedral

Opera singer Beverly Sills appeared at a concert for what became the final solo performance of her career—a perfect public relations opportunity. The event was a godsend intended to overcome the growing controversy over the costs of the cathedral. According to Michael Nason, executive assistant to Schuller, the cathedral had attracted massive scorn: "$17 million today is nothing in a building, but then, $17 million—and we were in escalating inflation. Criticism was just huge." It devolved into a media relations disaster that demanded a deflection, something Nason described as "PR 101." To pivot the narrative away from the exorbitant costs, the ministry sought a featured event to celebrate the opening of the cathedral, "but it had to be something bigger and splashier than anything that had ever been done." Fortunately, the concert sold out. Unfortunately, however, the sound quality within the cathedral proved problematic when an unanticipated acoustics issue emerged. Schuller and his leadership team cringed, fearing the media fallout from the poor quality for such an expensive, high-profile event (reserved seats had cost $1,500).[65]

Sills appeared on *The Tonight Show Starring Johnny Carson* the evening after the concert. Carson quipped about needing copious amounts of Windex to keep the cathedral translucent. Sills joked that her voice was likely "still there now, ricocheting from one glass wall to another, trying to find its way out."[66] The comment drew hardy laughs at the expense of the cathedral. Schuller and Nason, though, apparently reveled in the shift in conversation: Sills' remark deflected attention from the costs "to concentrate on the building itself—the Crystal Cathedral was being discussed on national television!" Nason explained. "It became a media sensation for the next several weeks. That was a really big deal. The criticism on the cost of the church stayed within the church community, and the general public just shrugged their shoulders. From then on, the building itself became a great vehicle for [other events like] *The Glory of Christmas* and *The Glory of Easter.*"

The Sills event raised an astounding $4 million.[67] Back in 1965, Schuller had noted with pride that he framed his fund-raising differently from those who debased themselves with their strategies for securing donations: "We have never had to stoop to beg for money from the pulpit, or cheapen our church by selling tickets, selling suppers, or selling bingo games."[68] Schuller maintained a classy effort—fund-raising with dignity. Now, the selling of tickets allowed the cathedral to be built debt-free. So while the Sills event raised questions about the sustainability of fund-raising that targeted wealthy elites instead of committed members of the church, the success of the concert established that ticketed events could become a significant new source of capital—one that elevated the selling of tickets by associating the cathedral with high-quality, high-status entertainment.

In addition, the cathedral served the broadcast ministry as well. Both audience and revenue expanded. Part of the appeal of *Hour of Power* rested in its setting: the spectacle of an all-glass building in perpetually sunny Southern California. The accomplishment of building the Crystal Cathedral itself accentuated how Schuller was not merely an effective communicator but an inventive entrepreneur. He openly described himself as a "religious retailer" and the church campus as a "22-acre shopping center for God."[69] Schuller entered new church growth territory when he embraced economies of scale and a singular focus on customer desires. Moreover, wrote *The Economist*, Schuller "knew that the first rule of marketing is to hold people's attention; so he built his cathedral from glass, installed one of the best organs in the world and invited a constant stream of celebrities, including presidents and film stars. And he understood cross-promotion: his bestselling books promoted his church services, and vice versa."[70]

Building on years of successfully broadcasting *Hour of Power*, and with the relative success of the Beverly Sills concert in the new building, the ministry turned to local theatrical production. In 1980 and 1985, the cathedral began producing *The Glory of Christmas* and *The Glory of Easter*, respectively. Along with the architecture, these events made the church grounds a destination. At one point, the ministry reported that 200,000 individuals attended the two performances annually.[71] In 1982, *Christianity Today* highlighted the grand scale of the *Glory of Christmas* production: 400 cast members, a 120-piece orchestra backing prerecorded in London, 16 live animals, "electronics and lighting [that] would match any Hollywood set for sophistication," $1 million in total production costs, 40 performances, tickets that ranged in price from $6.50 to $12.50, and $10 cassettes for sale.[72] A press release from the RCA in 1982 reported that 56,000 people had attended and that Bob Jani of Walt Disney Productions wrote and produced the performance. The release included a quote from Dan Rather on

CBS Evening News: "It is stunning. A bit of Hollywood, a bit of Broadway, but it is the same beautiful Christmas story."[73]

While lamenting that the exterior of the building resembled a "jazzy corporate headquarters," an architectural critic acknowledged the cathedral's significance as a venue: "The ability of this architecture to excite the average churchgoer is perhaps as interesting as the architecture itself." Further, "if [the Crystal Cathedral] is not the deepest or the most profound religious building of our time, it is at least among the most entertaining—one that will do much more to interest a public that has grown accustomed to thinking of churches as banal works of architecture and not uplifting ones."[74] Journalists noted that the cathedral served as a fitting setting for "spectacles" as a "striking, soaring, light-filled structure justly praised by architecture critics." Some sensed the financial need that prompted its construction: "Like the much beloved, much pilloried Disneyland three miles to the northwest, the Crystal Cathedral is a monument to Americans' inveterate ability to transform dominant cultural impulses—in this case, Christianity itself—into moneymaking enterprises that conquer the world."[75]

Within a few years of the opening of the Crystal Cathedral, the moneymaking capacities of the church would initiate official scrutiny of its tax-exempt status. Perceiving a threat to his charisma, Schuller defended the use of ticketed events. Much as arenas and stadiums today try to generate revenue outside of the local sports team's season with monster truck rallies and concerts, Schuller framed the cathedral as an Orange County cultural center that would host events throughout the week: "Our church has never limited itself only to our congregation. We have always seen ourselves as a place to also serve the secular community, a place to enlighten, to inspire and entertain." Schuller insisted there had been precedent in that: "Historically, churches have always been great centers of culture, of music, and drama." In the end, local residents would feel the loss most acutely: "We should be able to use our church to its maximum facilities, one that can be unselfishly shared with our entire community."[76]

William Grommet, a state Board of Equalization investigator for California, approached the situation differently. Discussing the Crystal Cathedral in 1983, Grommet commented, "This church is commercialized to a much greater extent than I've ever encountered in the state," and then listed specifics: "Our investigation shows that there were in excess of 15 concerts and musical performances, reserved seating $8.50–$15.50; reserved seating for the Glory of Christmas program was $40, $60, $68, and $150; there has been repeated use of the property for profit organizations and by nonprofit organizations that do not qualify for the exemption."[77]

The tax controversy gained national attention. *CBS Evening News* reported, "The word of God is one thing, say California tax officials, but when you throw in everything from Weight Watchers to Lawrence Welk, including aerobic dancing, that's quite another matter." By this time, the cathedral had hosted concerts by Tony Bennett, Victor Borge, the Fifth Dimension, Robert Goulet, and

Fred Waring.[78] Sunday breakfast and brunch were sold starting at five dollars a plate. Sales grew so strong that the church installed its own Ticketron office.[79] Grommet registered his astonishment that the lobby included the Ticketron booth: "You mean you have to buy a ticket to go to church?"[80]

Schuller and his team framed the tax controversy as a test of religious freedom. Herman Ridder, carrying the title "president of the Crystal Cathedral congregation," released a statement that indicated why all religious organizations should be concerned about this episode: "Churches and synagogues will lose the precious right to determine what is religion and what is not. They will lose the right to communicate the love of God to hurting humanity in the way they choose. Some will even lose their ability to exist because they cannot pay the taxes levied. The state ought not to decide such for the church. We should never forget the somber warning of Chief Justice Marshal: 'The power to tax involves the power to destroy.'"[81] Ridder explained that the Board of Equalization likely failed to understand the church's Calvinist theology that understood that "everything in life is religion." Ridder further argued that any event that occurred at the church should "fall under the mantle of religion and should be tax-exempt." Ridder concluded on a defiant note: "We do not plan to be destroyed."[82]

Consistent with the tenets of Christian libertarianism (see chapter 5), Schuller dramatically vowed to litigate any attempts "to tax our pulpit, our choir loft, or our cross and church." He cited support from a range of other faith communities and noted that in that solidarity, "they recognize, correctly, that if the State of California can deny us our tax exemption, it can harass other religious and charitable groups as well."[83] Schuller also suggested that the replacement costs of the social services provided by congregations should never be underestimated:

> Let us not forget that any church that is worth its salt in any community is saving that community an amount of money that surely equals, and very likely exceeds, the tax exemption. I haven't the slightest doubt that the community of Garden Grove, California is $22,000 a year richer because our church is there. If any church is removed from the community, one would see costs rise fantastically in the areas of justice, law enforcement, and welfare. Every responsible church becomes an indispensable service institution in the community, and by a positive constructive program of Christian citizenship it more than pays for its tax-favored position.[84]

Schuller held a press conference and read a more detailed prepared statement. He noted the replacement value services that the church offered the broader community and claimed that without these ministry programs, "millions of dollars would have had to be added to the social service agencies in [Orange County] and [the United States]." He went on: "Only God knows how much we have saved the local taxpayers in what would otherwise have been expanded police services, added welfare costs of unemployed persons, added social services because of marriages that would have been broken, added foster home care for children that would have been abandoned if not hooked on drugs." In arguing for the Crystal Cathedral's tax-exempt status, Schuller asserted, "There isn't a doubt in our mind that whatever tax advantages are extended to churches, synagogues, and temples in this country are far more than offset by untold savings in county, state, and social services."[85]

For a man who had strenuously argued against clergy engagement in political issues (see chapter 4), Schuller forcefully posed the issue as fighting against the potential encroachment of the state in the church's coffers on behalf of all clergy. However, not all clergy came to Schuller's defense on the tax-exemption issue. Fellow television minister Jerry Falwell argued that if "a church competes with free enterprise, it ought to bear the same tax burden the business community bears." A pastor more local to the Crystal Cathedral, Randy Ziegler of Costa Mesa's Calvary Chapel, dismissed the issue with a shrug, noting that the Crystal Cathedral "got what it deserved [from the Board of Equalization.] It is not a church; it is a profitable business."[86]

In the midst of the tax controversy, Schuller wrote what may be his best-known book, *Tough Times Never Last, but Tough People Do!* Perhaps with the California tax code on his mind, the minister advised his readers not to violate the law but also not to "reject an idea because it's illegal," reasoning that "you might be able to get the law changed."[87] To that end, the minister sent a letter to "members and friends" of the Crystal Cathedral urging each of them to contact government officials on the church's behalf. The second page included names and addresses for the Orange County assessor, members of the state Board of Equalization, state senators, and members of the state assembly. Schuller closed by noting that as they waded through the bureaucratic maneuvers, everyone should "pull together" and plan to attend the annual stewardship dinners.[88] All situations could be reframed as an opportunity for capital development.

Despite his optimism, Schuller failed to change the tax code. In a 1982 letter to ticket holders, the ministry indicated that it would not be able to hold the upcoming "Vienna Choir Boys" concert in order "to comply with state and county property tax laws governing non-profit religious organizations." In the spirit of never missing a windfall opportunity, the missive suggested that ticket holders could elect to receive a full refund or simply "make the amount of your ticket(s) a donation to the Crystal Cathedral Endowment Fund."[89] Ultimately, and with a caveat that deemed the state's position a form of "religious harassment," the church paid $473,000 in back taxes in 1983.[90] The ministry would continue to seek out other ways to maintain solvency.

A Theistic Factory

The church infrastructure expanded and grew in complexity. A reporter from Minnesota visiting the Crystal Cathedral in the mid-1980s commented on the organizational scale of Schuller's ministry: "The untold story here is not the television program or the building and grounds. Those are showcases for Schuller's exuberant style. The real success story is the ministry that goes on from week to week through the efforts of other members of the staff." The reporter continued: "Schuller is the image that makes it all possible, but through more than 40 separate ministries, the church meets the needs of virtually every person who walks through the doors."[91] All these ministries required massive capital. In 1985, Robert Schuller Ministries spent $1.2 million on postage alone.[92] Another journalist described the campus as a "vast theistic factory" and marveled at the fact that the ministry employed "190 full-time staff, including 10 assistant ministers, on the campus and in the $1.3 million *Hour of Power* communications center across the street."[93]

The "theistic factory" continued to manufacture more programs and church ministries, and by the late 1980s and early 1990s, there seemed to be almost no limit to the services and opportunities that the church offered. Schuller's infrastructure undergirded a ravenous, wide-ranging ministry that, in its best days, depended on over 400 employees and more than 2,000 volunteers.[94] In a capital campaign for yet another new building, the Family Life Center, the promotional material indicated the need for space for the leadership institute and headquarters for *Hour of Power*—but it promised nurseries, classrooms, and rooms dedicated to exercise and to the performing arts as well.[95] As part of a 1991 pledge drive, the ministry noted that the congregation had "mission and ministry groups for everyone." Indeed, the list included the following:

> Homebuilders, Adult Bible Class, Bridgebuilders, Becomers, Keen-Bereans, Women in the Marketplace, Conquering Compulsive Behaviors, Christian Drama Class, Positive Christian Singles, Korean Singles, Conquering Codependency, Professionals in Transition, Stretch and Walk Time for Women, Women Who Love Too Much, Growing Through Grief, Victors, Survivors of Suicide, Wednesday Night Adult Education, Prison Ministry, Helping Hands, New Members, Women's Bible Study, Men at Peace, Gambler's Anonymous, Family Life, Smoker's Anonymous, Men's Bible Study, Laubach Tutoring, High School Super G's, Conquering Fear of Success, Overeater's Anonymous, College/Career, Parents of Gay Children, Single Mothers, Al Anon, Junior High Friday Night Live, Hightopps Nightclub for Senior Highs, Children of Abuse, Christian Concern for the Environment, Women's Night Out.[96]

These ministries were expected to fit into the increasingly bureaucratized organization of the church. For instance, the bylaws for Positive Christian Singles (a ministry for "single, widowed, and formerly married adults") numbered eleven single-spaced pages and included notes about voting eligibility, censure and dismissal of members, election of officers, impeachment and replacement of officers, creation of subcommittees, and the expectation that all meetings follow parliamentary law.[97]

Bureaucratic procedure pervaded the ministry, which required staffing and active management.[98] The organizational machinery was kept busy, even if only to protect the reputation of the church and its pastor—that is, monitoring threats to the flow of capital. During the tax exemption controversy, members of the Crystal Cathedral staff found themselves tasked with tracking any media mentions of the story. A resulting chart of these mentions included the media source, the headline, the estimated circulation of the publication, and whether the source had a United Press International or Associated Press affiliation.[99] In a "Building Standards" memo, Crystal Cathedral employees received explicit instructions on expectations for their work areas. Guidelines included prohibitions against anything being affixed to windows, outdoor clothing on doorknobs or flung over chairs, and wall displays that utilized glue, staples, or tape.[100] The ministry did not limit formalized expectations only to paid staff members. Explicit expectations were imposed even on regular congregants. Attenders could not become members of the congregation without enrolling in a "comprehensive educational program." The congregation initiated a Center for Advanced Lay Leadership that all prospective members attended, which included evening courses for learning the requirements for participating in an area of service. These requirements were focused on formalizing voluntary roles such as pastoral care, small group leadership, and telephone counseling.[101] For some positions, members needed ninety-eight hours of instruction before they could be commissioned.[102] Tour guides had to be familiar with the history and vision of the Crystal Cathedral.[103] The visitor center guidelines at the cathedral alone numbered fifty-nine single-spaced pages.[104]

Through every level of ministry, the detail on roles and processes for everyone involved in the congregation indicated the lengths to which the church went to ensure a strong, consistent, and positive presentation of the ministry. The "theistic factory" rested heavily on the volunteer labor of thousands of committed members of the church. Labor from all members was expected as part of belonging to the church, which relieved some of the need to hire additional personnel. All were expected to uphold standards of professionalism and quality.[105] Regular tithing and the ongoing support of current capital campaign goals were inherent to their committed service. All were expected to participate in giving to the church.

Clearly, Schuller understood the need to mobilize the charisma of the church into a financial vehicle, yet he especially concentrated it through personal meetings with corporate leaders and philanthropists, which he initiated continually throughout his ministry. During a keynote address at a 1993 Amway distributors event, for example, Schuller reported that his friendship with Rich DeVos and Jay Van Andel could be traced to the very beginnings of Amway. Moreover, because of Amway's use of Positive Thinking material, he surmised to his audience that his church could be the unofficial ministry of Amway.[106] The growth imperatives of Schuller's ministry depended greatly on the ability to convince wealthy Christians that his church, properly understood, was an extension of their business, a tangible manifestation of the noblest and deepest values they most cherished. What would happen, though, if the ministry ever displayed signs of brittle inflexibility?

A Masked Fragility

The success of Schuller's *Hour of Power* proved to be a double-edged sword. The broadcast's popularity translated into a growing number of seats in the cathedral occupied by one-time tourists, often loyal viewers on vacation who managed to schedule a Sunday morning visit. But less than a decade after its construction, overall attendance at the cathedral began to slip.[107] *Hour of Power* revenues maintained the church building and kept other programs going. For many years, the broadcast produced as much as 70 percent of the ministry's revenue.[108] The spending was justified as serving the broadcast constituents—including the live ones sitting in the sanctuary.

Even as attendance declined, Schuller kept on building, using new projects to stimulate more capital while drawing on *Hour of Power*. Almost immediately in the wake of the Crystal Cathedral's dedication, Schuller initiated a quiet development campaign to purchase land for a church conference and retreat center in San Juan Capistrano. By October 1981, letters from the minister to his congregation lamented the "loss of community" caused by the size of the cathedral—"many of us don't see each other as closely as we would like."[109] A little over two weeks later, another letter offered more detail: "Over a period of years, our church has grown and grown, and finally, with the opening of the Crystal Cathedral, the crowds, the press, the media, the celebrated recognition, the hordes of sightseers and security problems . . . has forced me to safety and solitude." Too much success had, again, catalyzed a need for another capital project. In short, Schuller explained that he had a plan he would reveal during a Sunday evening "'fire-side' chat" to rekindle the intimacy within "the wonderful Crystal Cathedral Congregation of happy believers."[110] The next month Schuller revealed the "secret gift" to the members of the church: "the Rancho Capistrano Renewal Center," a venue where congregants could "talk and lunch and enjoy each other without the press of crowds."[111] In 1988, the ministry opened the center, but only with some creative funding: "A ten-million-dollar investment fell only narrowly short of being fully underwritten in cash. The balance was financed with a gift and a low interest loan through the private pension funds of Dr. and Mrs. Schuller which represents a substantial savings to the ministry." (The site also became the location of a Crystal Cathedral church plant led by the Schullers' only son, Robert A. Schuller.) That same year, the ministry expanded its contiguous campus by nearly five acres after buying out homes and relocating eighty-two families.[112]

In anticipation of the 1989 opening of the $25 million Family Life Center (known at one point as the Robert H. Schuller Center), Schuller had requested from the pulpit—and in color brochures—that both members and viewers increase their giving to the ministry *by 25 percent* to cover the predicted costs of increasing maintenance liabilities on the campus.[113] The architectural plans betrayed concern over funding. When critics noted that the 150,000-square-foot Family Life Center looked blandly corporate and was a marked departure from the rest of the church grounds, Schuller insisted that the design had been intentional. The ministry could lease space in the future to local businesses "if the church ever needs money."[114] With these considerations built into the aesthetics, the increasingly tenuous makeup of the ministry's finances shadowed the pastor's thoughts. The financial strain of the megaministry began to escalate, and Schuller seemed somewhat preoccupied with the idea of debt. Though he had been evangelistic regarding debt as a tool of church success, he became so concerned with the national debt of the United States that he published two books on the topic.[115]

Because of budding financial concerns, the ministry continued building, raising capital, and then building again. The sequence of building projects had been unending: from the Chapel to the Arboretum, then on to the Tower of Hope, then the Crystal Cathedral, followed by the Family Life Center, which segued into yet another project. In 1990, the ministry unveiled the 236-foot, $5.5-million Prayer Spire wrapped in polished stainless steel that included a fifty-two-bell carillon (an assembly weighing 50,000 pounds) and a small chapel.[116] Functionally, the spire offered little to the campus beyond symbolic potency. Moreover, its presence quickly became anachronistic as an ascendant form of evangelicalism in the 1990s jettisoned traditional church aesthetics in favor of utility and congregational experience. Schuller, though, reported his feeling that "it had to be built" as the "finishing touch" of the cathedral—an official message that, indeed, the corporate-looking cathedral was a church.

After the Prayer Spire, Schuller again decided that the church needed still more space, this time to host tourists flocking to the church grounds. The land-locked church campus required another ten acres for the proposed facility and its attendant parking, so the ministry gathered funds and bought out the owners of thirty-one nearby houses. Schuller pursued and secured Richard Meier, the renowned designer of the billion-dollar Getty Museum in Los Angeles, as the architect.[117] This project resulted in the $40-million, stainless steel–clad Welcoming Center, which opened in 2003.[118] (Its futuristic architectural style led to its being featured as the twenty-third-century Starfleet headquarters for the film *Star Trek: Into Darkness*.)[119] The second and third floors housed the "DreaMuseum," a series of small exhibits on the "extraordinary history of the Crystal Cathedral Ministry,"[120] including architectural models of past building projects and life-size bronze statues of Billy Graham, Norman Vincent Peale, Fulton Sheen, and Robert H. Schuller himself. To finance the construction, the ministry sold 20,000 optical glass bricks for $500 each to form a translucent wall on the second floor.[121] But fund-raising fell short. By the mid-2000s, the ministry had taken on a debt of between $30 and $40 million.[122]

With more buildings and grounds to maintain and more programs and events to staff, the ministry now ran an annual operating budget of $80 million—only about $10 million less per year than the entire city government of Garden Grove—and that was still too low to meet continually mounting obligations.[123] Schuller had famously quipped, "Nobody has a money problem, only an idea problem."[124] Seeking another infusion of capital, the ministry noted the success of *The Glory of Christmas* and *The Glory of Easter* and decided in 2005 that perhaps a production themed around creation would be successful. The new event required between $13 and $15 million to produce. Local newspapers described the production as "extravagant" with "giant digital screens and elaborate sets."[125] Staged only once, the production ended up losing an estimated $5 million.[126]

Had the fund-raising template of "vision for new projects to raise funds for current needs" been more durable, the Welcoming Center and *The Glory of Creation* might have functioned as two more signals of successful, innovative growth. Instead, both further contributed to financial overextension. For over half a century, Schuller's synthesis of constituents, charisma, and capital had worked, since many contextual factors of the migration and economic boom of the region and sympathy of wealthy Christian businessmen had tilted in his favor. As the strain of harmonizing these elements continued to increase, the strategy of forward-projecting charisma could no longer be trusted to mobilize current constituents to provide ever more capital in anticipation of future constituents. The generosity of wealthy benefactors withered. The veneer of the multiple buildings, programs, and staff members was part of a broad infrastructure that demanded high levels of maintenance. Any tarnishing of the products could be read as contrary evidence.[127] The credibility of the image depended on tangible signs of continued growth. Yet the aggressive and ongoing call to fund future growth became catastrophic in 2005, leading to the declaration of bankruptcy in 2010. Schuller's mandate to produce persistently tangible evidence of growth eventually shattered his glass church.

Fresh Capital Streams Demand New Building Projects

During the 1980s and 1990s, successes and accolades continued. Schuller's church held the profile of the "most striking of a new crop of megachurches that were springing up across America." An article in *The Economist* described Schuller as the "most successful of a new breed of televangelist who realized that technology was their friend."[128] Thinking that he had started a second Reformation, Schuller assumed that his popularity and formula for growth remained universal enough that they transcended both geography and generations. The leadership institute, the architecture, and *Hour of Power* all stood as demonstrations of the successful enactment of the Orange County minister's principles. These products of Schuller's evangelical empire offered viewers, attenders, and fellow pastors a map of the correct path to church success. Schuller's ministry, however, proved less resilient than most observers would have assumed.

Schuller needed an extraordinary amount of resources to channel new practices for ushering in the Christianity of a new century. His religious ambition bent to the logic of capital, the flow of funds required to resource the ministry. Schuller could not wait for the financial stream from constituents who had not yet arrived and sought to build a ministry structure poised to accommodate them once they did. In practice, the minister seemed beholden to a religious version of the "Bilbao Effect," the notion that cultural centers with dramatic architectural flourishes "could deliver enormous returns on huge and often untested investments."[129] Civic leaders often touted these facilities as catalysts of economic vitality for moribund cities. Evidence from a study of 700 of these institutions built between 1994 and 2008, though, revealed that 80 percent became mired in cost overruns—some by nearly 200 percent of early estimates. And more recent indicators reveal significantly limited positive spillover effects. Despite these "fallacies," city leaders clamored to have these centers built because they also were the type of people who were "accustomed to relying on their own judgement and expertise."[130] Similarly, Schuller relied on his own intuition to keep erecting new construction on the campus.

So the ministry continually pursued a string of building projects resulting in the Chapel, the Arboretum, the Tower of Hope, the Crystal Cathedral, the Family Life Center, the Prayer Spire, and the Welcoming Center. For Schuller, prominent buildings did not just demand capital—*building projects stimulated fresh sources of capital*. He knew regular attenders were not adequate to fund his vision, and therefore he especially courted wealthy benefactors. At the same time, Schuller believed their investments would result in a revenue-generating church, a self-sustaining enterprise that never materialized. As the machinery of the ministry experienced greater pressures, it became increasingly difficult to maintain a productive synergy among the core resources of the ministry's constituents, Schuller's charisma, and the necessary capital. At every turn, the answer to potential crises involved *yet more growth*. Apparent successes at expansion obscured the many tensions that threatened its future. And new capital requirements made the Crystal Cathedral inherently fragile. Like the mainline itself, Schuller tried to be everything for everybody; infinite openness, though, requires infinite resources. As Daniel Vaca wrote, "Revenue becomes a concern when voluntary charitable contributions fail to keep pace with the demand to reach a larger audience."[131] To attempt a universal appeal requires unending amounts of capital, an unsustainable imperative. The ministry structure inevitably began to collapse on itself.

The Crystal Cathedral in twilight. Photo courtesy of the Joint Archives of Holland.

8

When the Glass Breaks

Most people who succeed in the face
of seemingly impossible conditions
are people who simply don't know how
to quit.
—Robert H. Schuller

During services at the Crystal Cathedral, two eighty-foot-high glass doors behind the minister majestically opened outward toward parked cars. (Designed with NASA engineers in consultation, they became known around the church as the "Cape Canaveral" doors.) One member described the power of their opening as "inspiring." Another described the experience from the perspective of those outside attending church in their cars: "You could feel a part of the service because the doors had opened. Sometimes Schuller went over to the doors and greeted people in cars. Often we'd hear a car honk if the owner felt positive about a point in the sermon. It really was fun!" The open doors allowed Schuller to be seen by people in their parked cars, harkening back to the drive-in origins of 1955. The climax of the service was defined by Schuller turning around, facing the doors as they slowly widened with his outstretched arms basking in the incoming sunlight—a gesture attesting to the grandeur of the minister's public persona.

Then one day the magnificent doors stopped opening. They operated with expensive mechanisms, and, as one member recalled, "there was much deferred maintenance around the cathedral because of financial troubles." As revenue languished, the need for repairs on the church grounds accumulated. The large sliding glass panels fell into disrepair and failed to open with any consistency.[1] One member noted, "There were frequent maintenance issues on the opening mechanisms through the years, and the doors remained closed a time or two. However, the most recent occasion of them no longer opening was because of maintenance that couldn't be done." By the mid-2000s, when deteriorating maintenance on campus betrayed the increasing fragility of the ministry, the failure of the doors opening stood as emblematic of the undeniable financial vulnerability of the church. Income had so dwindled that the ministry had to forego even routine maintenance.

The decline of the ministry became most evident in 2010 when the iconic 10,000 panes of glass failed to get properly washed. That same year, the ministry sold off properties (including its campus in San Juan Capistrano—which, by that time, included a church, a preschool, and retreat facilities)—laid off employees, and, most notably and publicly, canceled the annual production of *The Glory of Easter*.[2] Beyond the reduction in donations catalyzed by the nationwide financial crisis, the ministry had assumed unprecedented debt in the latest building project: the Welcoming Center. After the failure of a number of pledges to materialize and other fund-raising flops, Robert A. Schuller, who succeeded his father as head pastor from 2006 to 2009, estimated that at the Welcoming Center's completion the church owed roughly $40 million. The ministry had already endured a 24 percent reduction in donations in the previous years. At the point of declaring bankruptcy in October 2010, the ministry projected that it had $50 million to $100 million in outstanding debts. Administrators at first reckoned that they owed perhaps as many as 185 creditors.[3] Further research revealed a more devastating figure: the number of actual creditors exceeded 500.[4]

An editorial in *Christianity Today* referred to the bankruptcy as "a poignant moment in the history of modern evangelicalism."[5] The editors offered a pointed explanation of both a literal and a metaphorical liquidation of this once mighty church-industrial complex:

> Technology moves at such a rapid pace that as soon as you move into the new building, you immediately find yourself stuck with an architecture that is already dated, if only in small degrees at first. It isn't long before another developer announces plans for something even more state-of-the-art. Today both the Crystal Cathedral and the theology that undergird it seem woefully inadequate buildings in which to house the gospel. In an age deeply sensitive to energy conservation, a glass house of worship is a sinful extravagance. In a culture increasingly addicted to the self, the gospel of self-esteem is clearly part of the problem. In short, the Schuller enterprise is filing for bankruptcy on more than one front.[6]

With a sense of "good riddance," the leading periodical of evangelical Christianity in America dismissed the Crystal Cathedral, declaring the failure of finances to be an indictment of the entire ministry. How did it come to this?

Only five years before declaring bankruptcy, the Crystal Cathedral released official numbers that ostensibly indicated a healthy ministry. The council claimed 9,694 total members. That number included 1,000 "confessing members," 4,320 "inactive members," and 4,374 "baptized members."[7] The weekly worship services were estimated to include 4,402 attenders. The year 2005 also saw the church baptize twenty-one infants and thirteen adults. Financially, church leaders reported an income of $8,754,411 and expenses of $8,578,015 (leaving a surplus of $176,396). The church also claimed an indebtedness of only $199,902. But the report included a coded word of caution in discussing "the life and spiritual health of the congregation" by describing the "neighborhood immediately around" the church campus as "changing" and by claiming that the church planned to "reach" these new neighbors.[8] The source of the church's constituency was dwindling.

Even with the demographic shifts noted, the report, though, failed to reveal anything regarding the extent of the capital challenges facing the Crystal Cathedral Ministries. Overextension in the hope of future revenue created a uniquely vulnerable organization. Spokespersons for the ministry frequently cited the economic recession of 2008 for the financial crisis; however, internal documents reveal that the church losses predated the national financial collapse. While most Orange County businesses and nonprofits demonstrated economic vitality in 2006, the ministry lost $6.4 million. In 2007 the losses grew to $7 million and then to $11.5 million in 2008.[9] In short, the financial pressures on the ministry had begun to increase *prior* to the Great Recession.

The losses represented an accumulation of undiscerned sociological forces that undermined the Orange County ministry. As stated in chapter 1, our analysis demonstrates that the success of the ministry rested on the intertwined nature of three core resources: the various participants who comprised its *constituency*, its minister's *charisma*, and the funds for maintaining operational commitments and adequately supporting new projects that comprised its *capital*. As long as these three components worked in concert and remained synergistic, the ministry flourished. But the propulsive imperative of growth embedded in the church resulted in too great a strain on the ministry. As the size of the congregation grew, the consequences of a few missed cycles—charisma stimulating capital to attract constituents and waiting for future capital from future constituents—became more severe. The integrity of the structural engine that had been established to push for continual growth became unsustainable.

When we examine the broad history of Schuller's ministry, with a congregation rooted in relentless commitment toward growth, we find that the fractures from resource incompatibility manifested early on, and that ruptures accelerated alongside the overconfidence of straight-line upward projections. The Crystal Cathedral Ministries demonstrated a limited ability to innovate in appealing to a newer constituency in the American population, especially younger people and racial minorities. Failed leadership transition protocols revealed the vulnerability of a ministry built on a single person's charisma. Compounding the vulnerability of an aging white constituency, Schuller himself had to reckon with the weakening of his charismatic energy with his own aging, which necessitated his retirement. Relatedly, the belief in family succession as a right of inheritance wrongly assumed the capacity of the church to honor a supposedly biologically based charismatic authority. In exerting his independence, Schuller had forged an idiosyncratic and autonomous identity within American Christianity resting on an assumption in the unassailable financial strength of the church. He charmed his congregation but neglected to woo enough allies and establish a supportive network to lean on when the ministry became enmeshed in crises. For a ministry built on a reputation of competency and foresight, even the whiff of instability or negligence would have had a chilling effect on revenue.

The Crystal Cathedral Ministries also depended excessively on always expanding reliable streams of capital by assuming that completed projects functioned as powerful monuments of achievement. Schuller trusted that successive projects and their associated fund-raising campaigns would endlessly motivate donors to dig deeper and give even more, covering loans assumed in anticipation of future revenue. Gifts from wealthy benefactors depended on a delicate balance of demonstrating past success while arguing for even bigger initiatives to meet a future demand, stimulating even more projects. Schuller's Possibility Thinking fueled his fund-raising, but it also kept him persisting in his core financial strategy long past the point of sustainability. Perpetual projects resulted in financial overextension. The need to meet ever larger burdens of debt exacerbated the stresses on the structure of the ministry, undermining the ministry's logic of boundless growth. The failure to meet obligations spiraled beyond solvency. Even the most strenuous Possibility Thinking could not salvage the fundamental fissures of the ministry.

In the end, the failure to effectively mitigate *megachurch strain* collapsed the ministry. Schuller's ministry manifestly demonstrates the extreme pressures that accompany an unremitting focus on growth. The strain of a megachurch like the Crystal Cathedral lies in practices that initially appear to guarantee stability but, in actuality, result in greater weaknesses. Indeed, every congregation encounters difficulty with the management of constituents, charisma, and capital, yet the tension compounds as the scope of congregational activities grow. More specifically, we find the growth and collapse of Robert H. Schuller's ministry as indicative of the dynamics of megachurch strain, meaning *the increased threat of implosion significantly accentuated by constant efforts at managing the resources required to fulfill the demand for congregational expansion and their consequences.* Megachurch strain eventually resulted in implosion because *the work of constant growth provides constant opportunities for accumulating missteps in properly calibrating the relationship among the church's core resources of constituency, charisma, and capital.* In the case of Crystal Cathedral Ministries, then, we conclude that the inability to generate capital to meet the spiral of fiscal obligations, a miscalculation based on an overconfident anticipation of future constituents drawn to the minister's charisma who would generously contribute their own capital, resulted in the irreversible disintegration of the entire enterprise.

A Waning White and Upwardly Mobile Constituency

Religious practices and expectations change. Schuller and the Crystal Cathedral ministry held a profound appeal to a certain constituency. The church had always privileged the notion of accessibility for all the "unchurched"; however, the worship tended to cater to the slice of the white American (and Orange County) population that began to wane at the turn of the century.[10] By the middle of the century's first decade, internal research had indicated that the average viewer of *Hour of Power* was a fifty-three-year-old woman. With that in mind, Schuller's son and heir apparent in the ministry, Robert A. Schuller (RAS), related that he intended to implement new technologies in an attempt to lure younger viewers. Ironically enough, for a ministry built on embracing innovation, "some board members saw [RAS's] high-tech strategies as vague and distracting."[11] At the same time, RAS's examination of congregational records raised questions about the widely cited estimation of 10,000 members. How many were currently committed to the congregation? The younger Schuller reported that his investigation of membership rolls revealed an actual number of closer to 1,000—which meant that the Crystal Cathedral no longer could claim status as a megachurch.

While the Crystal Cathedral perfected a form of worship that clearly targeted an audience that preferred a traditional Protestant style, Orange County and the nation grew more diverse demographically—and religiously. As Latinos and Asians gravitated to the region for its weather and economy, many brought along religious practices incongruent with those offered at the Crystal Cathedral. Schuller's core audience aged, and the minister had difficulty in finding methods to appeal to younger populations. Demographics in the United States and, more specifically, in Orange County trended away from Schuller's marketed core, contributing to the sharp slippage in membership.

For almost fifty years, Schuller's message and style resonated particularly well with his white evangelical constituency. By happenstance, the minister had landed in the right location. His Theology of Self-Esteem and message of Possibility Thinking promoted optimism and individuality for an increasingly affluent membership. Corporations alongside local and federal governments had joined forces in radically expanding available credit, increasing the borrowing power of entrepreneurs and homeowners to finance their dreams while supporting the ambitions of their pastors. Historians have described Orange County as the definitive expression of white, evangelical, and Republican suburbia, one that oriented around the ideology of Christian libertarianism. In fact, some have asserted that 1980, with the election of Ronald Reagan and the opening of the Crystal Cathedral, represented the pivotal moment marking the "emergence of evangelical Christianity as a vocal and influential constituency in America."[12] The ministry and the cathedral "were carefully constructed products of an ascendant conservative Southern California culture, economics, and politics."[13] For two decades, the ministry thrived by drawing support from the sizable contingent of white evangelicals within driving distance of Garden Grove.

But Orange County became a much more diverse place over the half-century of Schuller's ministry there. The attractiveness of the region, even among whites, had dropped over the decades. Overleveraged with derivatives, Orange County declared bankruptcy in 1995. Touring the county in the aftermath, journalist Tom Vanderbilt described it as manifesting a palpable anxiety, as a spate of insolvencies had caused an epidemic of "bankruptcy blues." It seemed that under the sunny surface of Orange County lurked a "gray dystopia of uncertainty and falling property values." Further, as he walked the church grounds, Vanderbilt intuited that the sheen of the Crystal Cathedral itself represented the most striking manifestation of the countywide apprehension.[14] Upon stumbling on Schuller's 1985 book *The Power of Being Debt Free* in a local library, Vanderbilt wondered if the "slim volume" represented "the most ironic piece of the Schuller merchandising empire." (Likely preoccupied by the atmosphere of financial insolvency in the region, Schuller in 1995 published his *second* book regarding the United States' national debt.)[15]

As the decade progressed, good paying work became harder to find in Orange County, and the cost of housing exceeded the means of most young families by the start of the twenty-first century. Loans became harder to access. Some demographers surmised that half of the county's millennials harbored no intentions to remain in the region, noting a flight of 16.3 percent of high-tech jobs after 2008 and a lack of affordable housing. The challenge of jobs and housing both conspired with a reputation for cultural uniformity and blandness to create "an ominous diagnosis: expensive, yet uncool."[16] A Chapman University report colorfully depicted a potential future for the county that mirrors the fate of the Crystal Cathedral: the region could "recede" like an "aging but still attractive dowager, into long-term stagnation and eventual decline."[17] As the county changed, Schuller's ministry, "even with the addition of Spanish-language services," eventually "fell out of sync with the changing demography of Garden Grove."[18] The sheer momentum of the Crystal Cathedral's religious-industrial complex inhibited its ability to be responsive to changing migrations of people.

The Hispanic Ministry Cannot Save the Cathedral

Census data indicates that in the late twentieth century Orange County's white population aged and diminished while the nonwhite population continued to rise. A visitor to the Garden Grove campus in the early 2000s noted, "The gardeners and the maintenance men tending the Crystal Cathedral grounds in the summer heat murmur quietly to one another in Spanish. But the church seems to cater to a different audience."[19] The implicit assertion: Schuller's ministry struggled to appeal to anyone outside of the white middle or upper class. More than that, the municipalities in the vicinity of the cathedral, especially Garden Grove and Anaheim, became sites of some of the most intense shifts. Upon visiting a worship service at the cathedral in 2011, a local journalist found that "broadly speaking, the experience offered by Schuller's ministry was not what these newer residents wanted."[20]

It might be assumed that the ministry forged ahead with its traditional ministry, never taking into account the changing contextual demographics. But Schuller did notice the changes and made a limited effort to respond through a program-based initiative to serve local Hispanics. Back in September 1990, Schuller had prevailed upon Juan Carlos Ortiz, a prominent Latino pastor from Argentina, to initiate a Hispanic ministry at the Crystal Cathedral. Ortiz recalled that Orange County "became flooded with Latinos, and Schuller wanted to evangelize them." Ortiz initially hesitated, telling Schuller that he had witnessed too many instances of Hispanic ministries within Anglo churches being relegated to second-class status. Schuller responded that the Hispanic ministry would have full access to the facility and equipment, and its attenders would be considered full members of the Crystal Cathedral congregation. Though Ortiz continued to have reservations, he found himself persuaded by Schuller's vision and persistence.

Ortiz had been trained within the Assemblies of God denomination in Argentina but happily acquiesced to Schuller's desire for him to become ordained within the RCA. Initial Spanish-language services occurred in the seventy-seat chapel in the Tower of Hope. After a little more than a decade, the Hispanic ministry at the Crystal Cathedral had grown impressively, from thirty-two attenders to over 1,000, becoming one of the largest Latino Protestant ministries on the West Coast.[21] Ortiz's ministry added a motto, "The Crystal Cathedral, a spiritual home for Hispanics," and produced a Spanish version of *Hour of Power* called *Hora de Poder*.[22] The response was enthusiastic, and Easter services exceeded the capacity of the cathedral, with 400 chairs added in the parking lot outside the sliding doors. At its apex, the Crystal Cathedral housed sixty different ministries under its Hispanic Department.[23]

Similar to Schuller, Ortiz developed a strategy to pursue the "unchurched," crafting a statement that described the target audience: "the Catholic Hispanic man who does not attend mass, between 35 and 45 years of age." Ortiz described the worship style during his tenure as "like a Reformed Church." He continued: "I used the robe. I followed the church calendar." More than that, though, Ortiz disclosed that he implemented a "somewhat Catholic liturgy"[24] to make his potential attender more comfortable, "like the sign of the cross, the blessings doing a cross with my hand in the air, did processionals, banners, altar boys and girls, communion with a big silver cup that I elevated."[25] Facing a significant health crisis in 2002, Ortiz resigned from the church. Then in 2008, with the church facing the Schuller family's turmoil of pastoral transition, Ortiz returned as interim pastor of the main congregation. In this role, he recruited Dante Gebel, known as "the youth pastor of Latin America," as the new leader of the Hispanic ministry.[26]

While the Spanish-language ministry had been in place since 1990, the arrival of the charismatic Gebel in 2009 reenergized it, resulting in another explosion of growth. With Gebel's arrival, major stylistic changes occurred in the liturgy, including a much more charismatic, experiential style of worship weighted heavily toward singing and preaching. A typical Sunday saw a line developing outside for the afternoon Spanish-language service, in contrast to a smattering of members and tourists scattered throughout the sanctuary during the fading traditional service. Over Gebel's three years at the cathedral, the Spanish-language service grew to two afternoon worship services with over 5,000 in attendance. The Latino pastor's success encouraged comparisons: "Like Schuller in his prime, Gebel casts a wider net, drawing regular visitors from Bakersfield to Tijuana. He hopes to add a second service this summer and few doubt his ability to fill it."[27] Yet Gebel and Schuller subscribed to different sensibilities within Christianity. Gebel's Pentecostal roots made him much more fundamentalist and charismatic, and the style of worship had little in common with Schuller's "button-down mainline Protestant world of the Reformed Church in America."[28]

Despite Gebel's popularity and ability to fill seats of the cathedral, the revenues associated with the Spanish-language paled in comparison with Schuller's upwardly mobile white population. The Hispanic services only accounted for about $500,000, far too little in relation to the total ministry's budget of $80 million.[29] The comparatively lower incomes of the Hispanic ministries' constituency combined with the lack of a national network of wealthy benefactors who might infuse necessary funding could not sustain the monetary commitments of the cathedral. Unfortunately, the Spanish constituency and its capital were misaligned with the cathedral's fiscal obligations.

It became clear that the Hispanic ministry could not save the cathedral. By late 2011, Gebel distanced himself from ongoing controversies at the cathedral and indicated that the Spanish-language service would be unaffected by any sale of the campus. At one point, he stated emphatically that he had *not* "been called to save the Crystal Cathedral."[30] Gebel cleverly noted that he technically never held a formal staff position at the cathedral and mused that, as an independent contractor, he could leave at any time.[31] By March 2012, while the long-established, traditional morning services routinely included 300 to 400 in attendance, the Spanish-language service continued to grow into the thousands. Gebel decided to leave the cathedral and move his entire ministry over to the Anaheim Convention Center: "We knew that sooner or later we would have to relocate to a larger location, but we asked the Lord that this change be for the better, and he exceeded our expectations. Not only were doors opened for us, but we have the capacity to comfortably seat ten thousand people, which allows us to project and continue to expand."[32]

Attempts to Secure the Ministry's Future

In a study of contrasts, while Gebel enjoyed dynamic growth, Schuller and the traditional ministry wrestled with stagnation and decline. The struggle for Schuller to maintain a sufficiently large, engaged, and financially committed audience proved catastrophic. Schuller had established the ministry's foundation on a reputation of competence, and the dynamics of the minister's charisma demanded signs of continued success. Because the architecture on the campus was interpreted as extensions of the minister's personality, stories of stagnation and financial vulnerability focused on the staggering costs to maintain the facilities. For instance, Judy Hatch, an *Hour of Power* viewer from Waukesha, Wisconsin, had been sending donations to the ministry for fifteen years. Upon hearing about bankruptcy and unpaid creditors, though, she committed no more financial gifts: "I stopped donating to the church the day I heard about what they're doing with the vendors." More pointedly, Hatch registered her frustration that the Crystal Cathedral had failed to maintain its standards as a church: "This is a Christian ministry, not just a business"[33]—a damning comment given that Schuller always projected the church's leadership as based on a sound business model.

The financial vulnerability of the ministry was exacerbated by a bureaucratic shuffling in the financial structure that had been instituted years earlier. These changes sought to increase accessibility to capital—making accounts more efficient yet more flexible. Specifically, in 1988, the two separate boards, Robert Schuller Ministries and the Crystal Cathedral Congregation of the Reformed Church in America, voted to merge under one board: Crystal Cathedral Ministries. Schuller described the merger as an effort toward expediency: "By merging the two boards, efficiency and consolidation, with attendant economic and management advantages, will be fully realized. Both organizations will now jointly own all property and real estate, which will expedite the wise, prudent, and asset-management moves enabling the board to achieve its long range financial goals of the Crystal Cathedral Ministries."[34]

In truth, Schuller had simply shifted ownership of the property from the congregation to the corporate ministry. The congregation sold the facilities to the corporate ministry in return for a ninety-nine-year lease for one dollar annually—although the inability to locate documentation for the agreement would prove problematic some twenty years later. The arrangement gave Robert H. Schuller (and, presumably, any named successor) control of finances from the significant revenue generated from the *Hour of Power* program. The implications of this shift would be momentous.

At that time, concerns about the longevity of Schuller's ministry had started to percolate. Schuller himself wrote that history tended to be cruel to ministries founded by "strong personalities." However, the 1988 year-end report offered no details on leadership transition arrangements. (Schuller himself seemed hesitant to exit. Years later, he established a formal protocol in which he imagined a twenty-year plan that culminated with him delivering his last sermon as he turned 100.[35]) Instead, the document explained plans for financial stability that rested on the assumed continued attractiveness of the message of the *current* messenger and the valuable, debt-free properties that allowed for strategic worldwide marketing. Perhaps most significantly, the document referenced the necessity of financial largess to endure "inevitable dips in fortune during transitions in leadership,"[36] once again indicating dependence on wealthy donors to rescue an inevitable downturn whenever the elder Schuller should step down.

The document again affirmed that Schuller believed his unique charisma generated the capital flows to both the church and the broadcast. Even though he offered no formal plan, by the late 1980s, Schuller realized the necessity of a protocol for succession at the Crystal Cathedral. He anticipated "dips" in income following the appointment of his successor, so he brought the *Hour of Power* and Crystal Cathedral accounts together in the new entity, Crystal Cathedral Ministries, in order to allow for the larger revenue and substantial assets of the television ministry to meet the needs of the church ministry until income could be recovered.

Unfortunately, the plan to merge the two sides of Schuller's capital-intensive ministry failed to consider how much the financial survival of both ministries depended on the elder Schuller's charismatic draw. Yes, the elder Schuller believed the *Hour of Power* might not continue after the founder's departure, but he also believed churches endured as institutions with permanence beyond a single personality. His ecclesiology influenced him to see the church sustaining itself as an instrument of the ministry regardless of who became the new leader. In actuality, while the merger did make it easier to access the accumulated capital from RSM for managing the potential financial shortfalls of the cathedral, Schuller did not anticipate that the shortfalls from both RSM and the cathedral together would be insurmountable. The incoming charismatic leadership of the cathedral could not build up enough capital fast enough.

In the end, the elder Schuller neglected to consider the true impact of charismatic succession on the flow of capital, not simply due to the force of his personality but also because of long-term investments from members and viewers and because of long-established networks of benefactors across the country. As a result of the merger, accessing capital from anywhere in the merged ministry allowed the leadership of the congregation to cover deficits, concealing financial gaps in the hope of new funding, until such actions were unsustainable and it could no longer be hidden from the congregation—and the public.

Even as he combined their financial accounts, Schuller believed that the church and the broadcast remained separate elements—and that charisma particularly undergirded the survival of the broadcast compared to the more secure longevity of the church. Already in 1975 the minister surmised, "The television ministry is unique. It is distinctive. It is separate from Garden Grove Community

Church. [*Hour of Power*] is, of course, very much a *personality centered operation*. And that could very easily have a life span that is tied with my own life span. But this church is not dependent upon television."[37] Given the extensive development of the property, Schuller told *The Christian Century* in 2002 that the Crystal Cathedral's architectural plan ensured that the church would exist in perpetuity. "After I am dead and gone, the real preacher that attracts people and ministry is going to be the structures, the grounds, and the landscaping."[38] He correctly assessed that the ministry desperately needed the constituents represented in the dynamic ratings of the broadcast generated by its charismatic messenger to maintain the entire enterprise. At the same time, Schuller miscalculated the church's resiliency apart from revenues from the broadcast. The church had become too dependent on that income.

An astounding fact that went largely unrecognized at the time is that for many years the broadcast produced as much as 70 percent of the total ministry's revenue.[39] While the program cost as much as $4 million for one hour of weekly airtime, the arithmetic worked as long as *Hour of Power* maintained a baseline of donations. Fluctuations, though, could prove disastrous. End-of-the-year financial reports demonstrated that revenues for *Hour of Power* fell by over 20 percent from 2007 to 2008.[40] Bankruptcy filings indicated that overall donations to the ministry in 2009 fell by 24 percent.[41] Even a small loss from the television ministry sorely impacted the fortunes of the cathedral.

With the downward-spiraling revenues, the transferred ownership of the church campus to the corporate entity loomed with consequences. RAS explained, "What my father had done was transfer all of the properties from the local congregation to the *Hour of Power*." According to RAS, the sale left the congregation "at the complete mercy of the *Hour of Power*." What had originally been perceived as buttressing the church by merging it with *Hour of Power* actually exacerbated the increased fragility of the entire ministry. An executive with the denomination offered a similar assessment: "It's the ministry of the *Hour of Power* that was the driving force. There came a point where this was really a television ministry that had a congregational home, rather than a congregation that had a television ministry."

The spectacle of *Hour of Power* required the dramatic set and production values only afforded by the stunning architecture of the Crystal Cathedral. *Hour of Power* became the tail that wagged the dog. The effects of the camera from *Hour of Power* on the performance of the liturgy in Garden Grove would be difficult to overestimate. Even small details, such as the color of Schuller's robe—better blue than black—were determined by how they would appear on a television set in places like Cedar Rapids, Iowa. RAS described how sartorial choices rested on the television viewers' experience. Initially, Schuller had worn a largely black vestment: "And you can see the contrast, and it just doesn't go well on camera. Today, with the good, high definition cameras, it probably wouldn't be an issue. But back then . . ." Concerned about the color seen on television, RAS remembered that his father experimented until he found the right contrast: "We finally settled on a grey-blue. For camera purpose that worked well. It was all for camera." But the influence of *Hour of Power* on the church extended well-beyond concerns about garment choices.

Congregants acknowledged a palpable tension of "show versus congregation." A member of the church council recalled, "There was a struggle for many, many years of the congregation versus the *Hour of Power*. Which is more important? Who's running the show? Where's the money going? Who's paying for all this?" Beyond that, even longtime congregants expressed confusion about the relationship between the broadcast and the congregation: "And at some points it was proclaimed they were all one; other times they would proclaim they're two separate things. And there was a time when they were definitely two separate things, two separate boards, one for the church and one for the TV." Other congregants discussed their experience sitting in church during the filming. One couple who had been members since the 1960s indicated that the worship service in the Crystal Cathedral left them feeling more like members of an "audience" or "spectators" and less like congregants. Still, the vigor of the elder Schuller kept members like them committed.

Inevitably, though, Schuller aged throughout the 1990s and suffered a number of ailments (for example, an almost catastrophic head injury in 1991 and angioplasty in 1997). He started to consider his own mortality and the future of the ministry.[42] RAS had enjoyed success with his congregation in San Juan Capistrano (established in 1981 on property owned by the Crystal Cathedral; see chapter 7) and seemed like the obvious choice to many. Yet RCA church polity included no provision for a pulpit to just be handed down within a family. And by the middle of the new century's first decade, all five of the Schuller children—and their spouses—would be employed by the ministry.[43] How the next generation of the family would be involved—and who would be the leader—became a primary preoccupation for Schuller.

It appears the Schuller parents engaged in lively discussions about the transition of the ministry to the next generation. One Crystal Cathedral copastor described a conversation overheard in the late 1990s in the Tower of Hope as the couple waited for the elevator:

> I came out of the restroom when I heard them talking. I stopped because I didn't want to be in their presence at that point. Having had a meeting, I knew that they would be hot and bothered, but I heard them. [Schuller] said, "Arvella, the kids need to earn their own way in this world. We should not be handing them everything on a platter." And she said, "No, Bob, this is the family business. This is what it's all for. When we leave, they have this whole thing, a piece of the pie." And so it was that all of them had a different division. That was the idea.

The pastor noted that each of the Schuller children was to eventually receive a "different division" to lead within the ministry.

RAS explained "the family business" as rooted in rural traditions of the Midwest. It reflected his family's history, and he intimated that, as Iowa agricultural stock, Robert and Arvella assumed that a church ministry could perhaps be inherited like a family farm:

> Coming out of the Depression, the farm came first. The farm meant life or death. If they don't have a farm, they don't have a livelihood. They're homeless. They're without food. They don't have anything. As a result, the farm comes first. So, they came out of this farm background, and *the church becomes their farm*. The church is first. That's their livelihood. That's what keeps everybody alive, so it comes first. When parents retire, they move into town, and the farm then takes care of them. That's the way it works. They rent it out until they die, and then it's sold and given to the family members in equal portions. (Emphasis added.)[44]

Churches, however, do not have the same transitive properties as family farms, so the elder Schullers adapted their approach. RAS continued:

> That's the way they saw [the church]. Obviously, they couldn't sell the church and divvy it up among the family members. What they could do is give responsibility to all the family members, which would basically do the same thing. Give them all jobs. Then the church could take care of their kids until they die. Then they've done their responsibility. As far as parents are considered, the farm's done what it's supposed to do.[45]

Likely knowing that the intrafamilial arrangement would raise suspicions while violating RCA church order, the elder Schuller crafted a Christian apologetic for the practice. In 2001 the minister contended that familial legacies in church ministries represented a best practice from both a biblical and a management perspective. In a document titled "The Schuller Family in Ministry," he insisted that "since the beginning of the ministry," the bylaws of the congregation included a section addressing "family policies and procedures." Schuller claimed that the ministry implemented ethical safeguards practiced by "prominent corporate executives." Schuller clarified that his children "inherited, not a corporate dynasty, but a spiritual obligation and calling to carry [the ministry's] distinctive message to their own generations."

All of these organizational maneuvers and their rationalizations indicate that the elder Schuller's transition plan sought to safeguard the financial assets of the ministry for his progeny. Although the minister evinced an awareness that the flow of capital depended on his unique charisma, he hoped that by merging the financial entities of the two broad branches of the ministry (the church and the broadcast), his son—and thereby his extended family—would retain control of all the funds. The strategy was intended to harness the strength of *Hour of Power* revenues to keep the Crystal Cathedral solvent until income rose to meet obligations.

Interestingly, the elder Schuller defended the transition plan in part by claiming that the recent criticisms of nepotism came from nefarious sources that included antiestablishment types who also might not support capitalism (an echo of his early, fervent anticommunism; see chapter 5):

> When we study the history of family in business, it is necessary to remember that the negative attitudes about family crept into society when *left wing liberals and socialists expounding a Marxist philosophy* became more and more vocal about "rich families staying in power, inheriting the wealth and oppressing the poor." Labeled as hegemony they revolted by becoming "anti-family," introducing higher estate taxes and "nepotism" became an n-word. Webster's Dictionary states that "nepotism" (the root comes from "nephew") is favoritism shown to a relative (as by giving an appointive job) on *the basis of relationship.*[46]

Schuller also added that even "nearby universities" taught nepotism as a current business practice.

Not surprisingly, Schuller rooted his argument in scripture, citing numerous instances of "family ministry" in the Bible to support the arrangements at the Crystal Cathedral. These included the genealogies of the Old Testament, Noah's "household" placed on the ark, Jesus' disciples Peter and Andrew being brothers, Jesus being ministered to on the cross by his mother and cousin, and the household baptisms practiced by the early Christian church—among many other examples. Schuller also claimed, "Throughout the centuries, the family has been the supporting unit that has kept the Church of Jesus Christ alive. Today, many families still keep the tradition of ministries operating and functioning as a singular unit."

In a bit of verbal jujitsu, Schuller intimated that there should be less concern about the ministry being inherited by the family. Instead, the congregation should understand the Schuller children as an inheritance that the pastor would leave to the church: "In closing I pray that the lineage of ministry emerging beyond myself will remain the most valuable inheritance I can give to the church: *my children.* I entrust [the congregation] with the protection of this inheritance." In a final declaration of his honorable commitment to passing the ministry on to his children, Schuller described the "family model" as his "code and creed."[47]

Turmoil in the Transition

Schuller had hoped that an obvious and natural transition to his son would occur seamlessly. He began formally introducing RAS in 2004 as the next head of the ministry to large donors at lunches and dinners around the country, and in 2006 RAS took over the pulpit.[48] Upon being named head pastor, RAS took on management responsibilities, attempted to reorganize and streamline the ministry, and met stiff resistance—especially within the Schuller family. In the aftermath, he remarked that his relatives in the ministry "weren't ready to accept [his] leadership."[49] No one had anticipated the conflicts that would ensue, especially the conflict between the elder Schuller and his son.

When the younger Schuller ascended to power, he rankled family members with initiatives to establish better governance, more accountability, and more exacting financial control. Strains based on the management and flow of capital intensified. For example, RAS expressed concerns (rightly, it would turn out) about the fiscal viability of *The Glory of Creation*. In a saga that played out publicly, the *Orange County Register* described the Schuller family as "torn between a revered father, who built the family business and ministry from the ground up and ensured their financial security, and a son, who was eager to change the face of the ministry and take it in a new direction." At one point, RAS's sister, Sheila Schuller Coleman, reported, "We had two pastors in the family who couldn't even talk to each other." The daughters ultimately sided with their father. RAS noted, "They had to pick someone, and I don't blame them."[50]

In the midst of these tensions, the elder Schuller always maintained his position that the ministry should remain in the family. In 2007, he wrote an addendum to his "The Schuller Family in Ministry" document. Under the title "The Trust of the Board of Trustees," Schuller acknowledged that over the "last two years" the family had been perceived as having been "put on the payroll" and "seen only as dollar signs." The explicitness of capital as a motivation was unseemly and threatened all of their claims to charismatic authority. With that in mind, the elder Schuller challenged the board members "to keep and preserve the divine calling to service" that had been "bestowed on the Schuller household." Jarringly, what this meant is that he expected charismatic authority to be extended to the entire family by fiat. He also suggested that the board consider a "resolution to affirm the philosophy of families in ministry" and appoint a committee to annually review "all family units on the Crystal Cathedral payroll."[51] The addendum also included the ministry positions and relevant qualifications for the following Schuller family members: Arvella Schuller (spouse), Sheila Coleman Schuller (daughter), Jim Coleman (son-in-law), Robert A. Schuller (son), Donna Schuller (daughter-in-law), Jeanne Dunn (daughter), Paul Dunn (son-in-law), Carol Schuller Milner (daughter), Timothy Milner (son-in-law), Gretchen Penner (daughter), and James Penner (son-in-law).

The lengthy list of family ties in the addendum revealed the extensive blood and marriage bonds on the payroll throughout the ministry. According to bankruptcy filings, by the late 2000s all of the Schuller children drew salaries from the ministry that totaled almost $1 million—not including housing, cars, or other discretionary accounts.[52]

A pastor on staff at the Crystal Cathedral read Schuller's amended document and offered a pointed commentary. He discerned the document as a thinly veiled attempt to justify transitioning the ministry into a "family owned and operated family business."[53] Moreover, he traced the history of the congregation and noted that it had been initiated as a ministry of the RCA, with a board of elders in accordance with denominational polity. In his view, Schuller "manipulated events and boards" to morph the oversight of the ministry and its properties under an international board that the pastor and his family "basically controlled." The pastor also claimed that while the board restructuring had been completed "legally," the protocols to ensure ethical budgetary oversight were "laughable." According to him, family members experienced almost no scrutiny for their salaries and expenditures. He provided an example: "About ten years ago the Ministry wanted to apply for foundation money that was in the State of Texas. To apply, the Ministry was required to report the wages of the top executives. Knowing that would disqualify them from a successful bid at these funds, they reported only the salaries with all the bonuses, perks, gratuities, etc. cut away, maneuvering the figures to satisfy the foundation." Perhaps most damning, he asserted that Schuller paid little heed to his own advice: "Schuller is infamous in stating excellent principles for keeping yourself debt-free, principles for successful communication, principles for successful church leadership etc. etc. but the fact is, neither he nor his Ministry practice their own principles!" To that end, the pastor offered his—perhaps hyperbolic—estimation that *The Glory of Creation* likely lost close to $25 million.[54]

Transition troubles continued. In July 2008, RAS received word that the board had concluded his preaching was "not anointed." Described by the *New York Times* as a "coup," such an assertion essentially denied RAS's charismatic authority. With that in mind, he would no longer preach on *Hour of Power* but could remain as the senior pastor of the local congregation. RAS would also not be allowed to preach on Sunday mornings.[55] Wounded by the demotion, RAS quit.[56] An anonymous ministry insider reported to *Christian NewsWire* that the younger Schuller had been handcuffed by his family and a board that continued to defer to his father: "Robert A's actions were all carefully regulated to the point of specific limitation by his father and key board members with regard to direction, content, and funding strategy."[57] The insider also commented that RAS had never really been given control. The younger Schuller also remarked that he truly grasped what had occurred when the board elevated his brothers-in-law, Jim Penner and Jim Coleman, to CEO and president, respectively, in July 2009.[58] Control of funds was fundamental to their appointments.

RAS officially departed in January 2009, and the elder Schuller told the church elders that the next senior pastor would not be a "Schuller." Only a few months later, he changed his mind and had his daughter Sheila Schuller Coleman installed as the head of the ministry. Congregants openly wondered about the fit: Schuller Coleman had been a successful educator but came to the position with no experience in leading a church.[59] With the charismatic succession embroiled in dissension, finances suffered, and prominent personalities within the ministry drifted away. Legendary pianist Roger Williams reported that he left the ministry in 2010 due to frustration with the fact that Schuller had mismanaged the succession: "His children had no history of success making it on their own. Bob and Arvella went through tough times and built this church one brick at a time. To me, it's those tough times you had to endure by yourself that make you great. Bob did not give that privilege to his children."[60]

The tumult continued. Non-Schullers on the board mounted an effort to erode the influence of the family. Within two years of the ministry declaring bankruptcy, in February 2012, the board removed Schuller Coleman as CEO and president of the ministry. The next month, the board fired another Schuller daughter, Gretchen Penner, and sons-in-law Coleman and Penner (who had recently been moved to director of creative services and executive producer of *Hour of Power*, respectively). John Charles, who replaced Schuller Coleman as president of Crystal Cathedral Ministries, remarked that the board made the decisions in an effort to "reverse recent declining donations and viewership" of *Hour of Power*.[61] Counterintuitively, it seemed that the board saw the departure of the Schullers as a way to reinvigorate the ministry. They underestimated the intertwined elements of constituency, charisma, and capital, and as these elements went even more radically out of sync with each other, the strain exacerbated the greatly increased fragility of the church.

The Blessing and Curse of Autonomy

Just as the ministry board dissociated itself from the Schullers, some thirty years earlier the minister had found himself in a similar disconnection with his denomination, the RCA. The construction of the Crystal Cathedral became a watershed moment in the church's relationship to the denomination. Not only did many in the RCA distance themselves from the Orange County ministry, but they also initiated a very public critique. So while Schuller's capital projects functioned as extensions of his charisma—both extending and supporting the minister's profile throughout American Christianity—within the RCA, many leaders interpreted the ostentatious cathedral as a definitive monument to Schuller's own ego.

Back in 1977, a mainline Protestant minister had already questioned the church's adherence to polity when he visited the ministry in Garden Grove. Writing in *The Christian Century*, the pastor worried that Schuller had too much authority and warned that the system would not augur well "for the long run."[62] He was right. As Schuller grew in stature among America's pastors and assured himself of his congregation's financial independence, he initiated steps to insulate the Crystal Cathedral from denominational interference. A former executive with the RCA commented that in Garden Grove, "the church and the property were never part of the RCA, which is different from most churches." In an adroitly rhetorical move, Schuller framed the distinct relationship as a method for protecting the RCA: "Way back, Schuller said, 'If this church ever goes down, it will take the entire Reformed Church with it.' So he persuaded them to allow that property and everything else to be in the sole ownership of the local congregation." Schuller also kept Classis California at a distance: "In the RCA, the classis is supposed to own the property. . . . That was not the case; it was all separated through a legal deal. Bob wanted to keep with the classis but he didn't want the classis to control." Another official with the denomination noted that Schuller "was bigger than the classis, and he was bigger than the Synod of the West, and the denomination trembled when he did this or that."

In 1982, as the elder Schuller read the galleys of a book being written by a religion professor at his alma mater, the RCA-affiliated Hope College in Holland, Michigan (see chapter 4), he became agitated. Schuller vehemently disagreed with much of what the author, Dennis Voskuil, had written in his forthcoming *Mountains into Goldmines: Robert Schuller and the Gospel of Success*.[63] In a fit of anger, Schuller called Voskuil on a Saturday evening and threatened a lawsuit over the publication of the book. Voskuil flew to Garden Grove to consider with Schuller the minister's suggested edits. During an orally recorded three-hour meeting, Schuller walked Voskuil through his proposed revisions and corrections.

In discussing the leadership of the Crystal Cathedral, Voskuil had written that the pastor's "grip over a congregation seems contrary to the practice and tradition of the denomination to which he belongs." Schuller responded in the margin in all caps: "WRONG." He followed up with a recommended quote: "[The council] made all decisions. My job is to advise, recommend, and carry out what they decide"[64]—a cleverly coded but ostensible statement. But Schuller's copastors generally agreed with Voskuil's assessment, and they confided that Schuller had a tendency to dominate ministry meetings. One remembered: "We did have a meeting once a week, but when you went to a meeting with Robert Schuller, you don't discuss, you listen. You listen because he would talk the whole time. It was always interesting, he was an interesting guy. He would never say, 'What do you people think? We're thinking about . . .' It was always pretty much a dictatorial style." Voskuil was correct; the ministry in Garden Grove did depart from typical RCA practice in which elders would have ultimate authority. It is likely that the size and complexity of the ministry contributed to church elders and board members ceding control to Schuller, whom they viewed as the positional and God-ordained expert for making decisions about the ministries he himself had grown.

The elder Schuller asserted an unparalleled autonomy that would leave the ministry vulnerable. The church had forged an idiosyncratic path to success. Both in terms of religion and politics, Schuller claimed an amorphous identity that, he hoped, would appeal to the broadest swath of the "unchurched." However, that disinterest in cultivating alliances and formal relationships contributed to the fragility of the ministry. When Schuller's methods began to demonstrate signs of strain, the ministry had few allies or havens. Schuller did highlight his affiliation with the RCA when distancing *Hour of Power* from the embarrassments of the televangelist scandals of the 1980s, but legal arrangements had left the ministry with only a thin, atypical connection with the denomination. Though the weakness of association allowed the church considerable freedom, it also meant that the ministry could not lean on the resources of the denomination in times of crisis. Its continued insistence on independence frayed those ties. As the ministry's status became more tenuous, Schuller had no safe harbor.

Remember that Schuller's plan to have his son, RAS, ascend to the head of the ministry lasted only three years. In a less than amiable reorganization, Schuller's daughter Sheila Schuller Coleman replaced her brother. For many observers, these fraught succession plans likely represent one of the easiest explanations for the diminishment of the ministry. Reliance on RCA polity might have forestalled the painful sequence that saw the Schuller family split over dueling expectations. Following Reformed church order would have prohibited the family succession problems. Classical control over property would have curtailed capital campaign plans in motion and limited the overextension. But by the end of the century's first decade, the ravenous financial appetite for the budget commitments from the many ministry programs, the failure of fund-raising, and the excessive debt from the Welcoming Center (see chapter 7) would have likely foundered the ministry even with the smoothest of transitions for replacing Schuller.

Lack of Checks and Transparency

Even some of Schuller's most loyal congregants and staff began to wonder aloud about authority and transparency. An email from a Crystal Cathedral copastor to Ronald Keener, editor of *Church Executive*, a magazine for large-church leadership, asserted that Schuller had been instructed twice by his board *not* to pursue building the Welcoming Center. As he had done with the cathedral, though, the minister had gone ahead and "dug the hole." The copastor complained: "The money was lost after the hole was dug. They had a choice of filling the hole up or proceeding with its construction. They borrowed the money and built it anyway."[65]

With so many unpaid accounts, it is no surprise that a series of lawsuits ensued. One lawsuit brought against the church argued that the financial peril had really begun in the early 2000s. Court documents revealed allegations that between 2002 and 2009, the ministry borrowed more than $10 million from an endowment meant to pay for specific maintenance items in order to subsidize church expenses and salaries.[66] A longtime member of the *Hour of Power* staff related that many congregants lacked the institutional memory to recall "that Dr. Schuller had an endowment that he had set up so they could continue as a church forever. [Schuller] told me in conversation what he was setting up and going to do because he didn't know if his son or future ministers would be able to keep it functioning." In creating the maintenance endowment, the elder Schuller had demonstrated good foresight. However, financial desperation motivated the ministry to dip into the fund without proper accounting—Schuller's access to those funds allowed him to do so. The sheer size of the ministry limited congregants' ability to fully understand its complexities, so withdrawals from the endowment escaped notice until late in the financial crisis when specific questions emerged and then grew persistent. Making matters even more scandalous, the *OC Weekly* openly suggested that tapping into the endowment to make payroll and support the Schuller family's "generous salaries and perks" bore all the hallmarks of a "Ponzi Scheme."[67]

Stories about the ailing ministry spread, and many in the congregation reading local newspapers began to worry. They gathered together in 2010 before the declaration of bankruptcy to posit formal questions for the church leadership. Homebuilders, an adult education class that had been meeting for decades, sent Sheila Schuller Coleman a list of seventeen questions on topics that ranged from financial oversight to governance to routine maintenance. Their questions demonstrated how little the congregation knew or understood regarding the governance and oversight of the ministry even as the financial decline spiraled. Among the questions asked were these:

1   Who are the current Chairperson and members of the International Board of the Crystal Cathedral Ministries, and what is the process by which a member is selected, added, or dismissed?

2   Most large organizations have a Succession Plan for the top officials in the event one of them is no longer available to do the job. Does the Ministry have a succession plan for the most important leaders (including you and your father)?

3   Would you tell us what Schuller family members are directly or indirectly employed by the Ministry, and would you summarize the job description for each of them?

4   How is the local church governed? Who are the people who report directly to you and could you summarize their job descriptions? How are the decisions made? For example, how is it decided that someone has to be laid off and who it is to be?[68]

The list of questions betrayed the utter absence of knowledge regarding logistical and administrative operations within the congregation just as the church seemed on the verge of collapsing.

The Homebuilders astutely asked more pointed questions about financial management. For example, they wondered about the accuracy of reports in the

Orange County Register that the ministry carried a debt of $55 million. They wondered whether *The Glory of Christmas* lost money. They also requested clarification regarding the relationship between the "Hispanic Church" and Crystal Cathedral Ministries: Had that church's increased attendance "resulted in commensurate increase in payments to the Cathedral?" Moreover, the Homebuilders inquired about the ministry's reluctance to join the Evangelical Council on Financial Accountability and about how much money had been borrowed from the ministry's endowments.[69] Other members of the congregation began to speculate during conversations why the ministry never provided a budget for them to see.[70] After submitting their questions, several members of Homebuilders met with Schuller Coleman on April 25, 2010. They described the disappointing meeting as offering "no answers." Taken as a whole, the questions demonstrated a lack of transparency that left many longtime congregants feeling disoriented by the swirling publicity regarding problems at their church.

Overextension and Bankruptcy

The excessive debt accrued by the ministry—further burdened by new liabilities for new building projects—was taken on because such initiatives were believed to "prime the pump" for further capital. Schuller's longtime strategy had worked in the past, with last-minute efforts yielding just enough funding to keep the ministry afloat. But in these latter days, the efforts failed. In the final months before bankruptcy, the ministry needed to do all it could to staunch the financial hemorrhaging. Its large infrastructure proved ravenous for a flow of capital that had been based on the unsustainable assumption of constant, linear growth.

In an effort to stave off bankruptcy, the ministry sold its San Juan Capistrano property to Hobby Lobby Stores. As an indication of the shifting religious preferences within Orange County, Hobby Lobby promptly leased the property to Saddleback Community Church, whose pastor, Rick Warren, was one of Schuller's highest profile protégés. That church planned to use the new property for athletic fields and a retreat center. Coincidently, while the Crystal Cathedral found itself under an almost insurmountable debt, Warren had beseeched his own congregation just months earlier to donate $900,000 to their church. Within days, the Saddleback congregation exceeded his request, responding with $2.4 million. In an implicit commentary regarding the decline of Schuller's ministry, Johnnie Crean (son of Crystal Cathedral benefactor John Crean; see chapter 7) noted about the Rancho Capistrano lease that "Saddleback is vibrant, and they are closer to this property" than the Crystal Cathedral.[71]

At the same time Warren had asked for increased giving, Schuller also once again engaged in one more public exercise of his own Possibility Thinking, telling his congregation and audience that he planned to raise *$50 million* to pay off the ministry's debts in just *four months* through the "Miracle-Faith Campaign"—a truly outrageous goal. Unsurprisingly, after just two months, Schuller's campaign had only raised $172,755.50. The minister's drive for funds ended quietly when it became clear that the campaign had no chance of success.[72] The efficacy of the elder Schuller's charisma had faded.

By January 2010, the ministry sought to offset another $8 million drop in revenue and announced the cancellation of its hallmark *The Glory of Easter*.[73] Church leaders blamed the moribund U.S. economy, declaring that the audience for *Hour of Power* had aging constituents whose fixed incomes would not allow for extravagant donations. Sociologist Richard Flory agreed and noted that he "couldn't imagine anybody younger than 40 watching some sort of televangelist."[74] No infusion of funds from philanthropists emerged. The well of wealthy benefactors had run dry. By October 2010, desperate measures had proved inadequate, and under the burden of many millions of dollars in debt, the ministry filed for bankruptcy.

In July 2011, members started a frantic petition to "take their church back." The language in the document demanded that the church install a "truly independent board" that no longer included family members, paid staff, or paid contractors. Jim McDonald, an organizer of the petition, noted that many in the congregation also wondered about the role of the denomination: "In my opinion, the [RCA] did not do their job over the years to protect us members." With that in mind, McDonald hoped for 1,000 signatures to present to the RCA to prevail upon it to "help to give the church back to its members" and return it to its "roots" as Garden Grove Community Church.[75] Their mobilization came too late. These efforts failed to stall the eventual sale of the campus.

Ever hopeful, though, the ministry attempted to engineer a sale plan that would allow it to mitigate some debt while controlling the future of the Crystal Cathedral campus. In 2011 the church made plans to sell the campus to Greenlaw Partners, a real estate investment group, with a fifteen-year leaseback plan. In a matter of months, however, Greenlaw withdrew its bid, and creditors threatened suits if the church failed to quickly produce a viable sale plan.[76] When it became obvious that the campus would be sold to the Roman Catholic Diocese of Orange, an eclectic group of business leaders from across the United States made a late pitch to try to raise money through an organization, "Protestant-church.biz," to at least maintain the church as a Protestant entity. The group planned to give the campus back to the RCA. The denomination at that point, though, had no interest in the arrangement. Representatives from the RCA reported that officials had begun a process of formally severing the relationship with the Crystal Cathedral. Scott Treadway, president of the RCA's Classis California, remarked that the "Cathedral's goals and mission, including worship style" no longer matched "those of the denomination." Treadwell's reference to "worship style" obviously hinted at the church's recent shift to contemporary "praise style worship," according to the *Orange County Register*. Moreover, according to Classis California, the relationship became stressed when "there was dissonance in ministry direction, music style, bankruptcy, and risk to the property."[77] At this stage of decline, the singularity of the church—what once had been seen as its distinctive strength and a potential model for the entire denomination—led to its becoming an unwanted outlier.

The Schullers and the Crystal Cathedral Become Estranged

Tensions between the Schuller family and some of the congregants simmered as the ministry seemed to lurch out of control. In November 2011, members of the Crystal Cathedral congregation received emailed instructions not to send any get-well cards to the Schullers as Arvella suffered with pneumonia. Meals, though, would be appreciated for the next few weeks—preferably low sodium with fruit, meats, soup, and egg dishes such as quiche. The guidelines indicated that meals would be picked up by limo drivers in the Tower of Hope lobby at around 4:30 P.M. Congregants expressed offense at the insensitivity of a limo showing up for food donations at the bankrupt church. One fumed that the Schullers had shown "absolutely no remorse" and that they still enjoyed "being chauffeured around in limos" while the congregants had been left with "nothing," since the Schuller family had "completely depleted the church's funds."[78] Another church member explained that the request for meals was odd because the Schullers had been "distant from the congregation" in recent years and wondered why the couple had failed to receive the "support of the many family members who live in the area."[79] Such remarks revealed the disenchantment felt within the ministry's remaining constituency.

In July, the board had removed the elder Schuller from his voting position. It seemed the minister had been trying to add new members to the board in order to gain back a modicum of control. Instead, the board "deposed" Schuller and reassigned him to the nonvoting title of "chairman emeritus." Though the official press release described the move as an effort to give Schuller more time to write and speak, RAS interpreted it as his father being "kicked off" the board and lamented that the elder minister "had to watch his life's work go down the toilet."[80] Later that year, Schuller would have his voting rights restored—only to resign from the board in March 2012 in the wake of a lawsuit he filed against the ministry.

The same month of the filing, Sheila Schuller Coleman made a surprise announcement to the sparse crowd of 400 gathered at the service that she would be taking the congregation out of the cathedral to a new site, as a new church, Hope Center of Christ: "This is the last Sunday we will be worshipping in this building." Schuller Coleman gave the impression that the entire congregation would be moving and then abruptly walked off the pulpit. As she exited the sanctuary, copastor Bill Bennett raced to the front to assure any confused members that services would, indeed, continue the following Sunday and thereafter *at* the cathedral.[81] Members of the congregation now found themselves in the midst of a church schism.

The board confirmed Bennett's announcement in a press release the next day. Moreover, the board expressed enthusiasm that the worship would revert to a more "traditional" style, with hymns and a choir. (After Schuller Coleman had attempted to update the worship with a praise band, alienating some members, one had been heard to grumble that "if I wanted to hear rock 'n' roll, I'd go to a nightclub").[82] The split left congregants with a decision to make regarding where they would attend in the future. Some longtime members expressed jubilation: "We're going to have our church back, with good music and good sermons. They're gone. The Penners are gone. Sheila is gone. [Jim] Coleman is gone. Praise God. We're rid of them. They're the ones who took the Crystal Cathedral down."[83] Pastor emeritus Juan Carlos Ortiz (founder of the Hispanic ministry at the cathedral) initially declined the board's request to fill in as interim pastor: "They asked me and I said, 'No.' It's an embarrassment with what is happening in the church." Eventually, though, Ortiz relented. He would later describe the interim experience as "the saddest nine months of my life." Internal squabbles spoiled any potential joy from the ministry.[84]

For their part, Schuller and Arvella indicated that they commended their daughter for her decision to start a new church, but they would be worshipping at neither location. In fact, the couple had stopped attending the cathedral already in November 2011 as disputes with the board grew untenable.[85] The *New York Times* described the Sunday of Schuller Coleman's dramatic announcement as a watershed moment: "The Schuller family's departure from Crystal Cathedral Ministries ends a stunning decline in fortune for the church's founder, who was one of the most successful preachers in the world, but who has watched in recent years as the church slid toward financial ruin."[86] Perhaps most galling, it seemed that the church gained some momentum with the departure of the Schuller family. Within a month of the schism, John Charles, CEO of the ministry, reported that both congregational size and donations had doubled at the Crystal Cathedral.[87]

Adding injury to insult, in 2011, members of the Schuller family also found themselves being sued by creditors of the Crystal Cathedral. The complaint alleged that Schuller and members of his family received generous salaries, housing allowances, and other benefits while the ministry struggled financially. Moreover, the complaint officially stated what had previously only been whispered: that the ministry borrowed more than $10 million from its endowment to cover operating expenses.[88]

By 2012, Robert and Arvella Schuller, in turn, brought their own lawsuit seeking more than $5 million in damages from the ministry that they had founded. The Schullers claimed that they had established an agreement with the ministry that ensured that the couple would receive $337,000 annually for insurance and housing. The lawsuit also indicated that the ministry had violated the intellectual property rights of the elder Schuller.[89] However, similar to the ninety-nine-year lease between the congregation and Crystal Cathedral Ministries, the Schullers could provide no documentation of legal agreements. The court eventually ruled that the Schullers receive slightly less than $700,000 total. Their daughter Carol Milner described the ruling as a "travesty" that would cause the family to "start liquidating everything." The *Los Angeles Times* pronounced the judgment as marking the "final chapter in the financial unraveling of a ministry that once made Schuller a powerhouse in American Christianity."[90]

The Megachurch Strain of Constituency, Charisma, and Capital

Some confidantes and fellow staff members wondered if the diminishment of the Crystal Cathedral could be traced to an initially innocuous injury back in 1991 that devolved into a life-threatening event for Robert H. Schuller. After bumping his head entering a car in Amsterdam, Schuller failed to show for a meeting. Hotel staff and Schuller's assistant, Michael Nason, discovered the minister collapsed on his balcony. He had suffered a subdural hematoma that required emergency surgery. Recovery proved to be long and arduous. Once, in Rome, he suffered a violent seizure as an after-effect. More than that, some of the individuals who spent time with Schuller in the following years described a changed person—more emotional and yet with less of an edge. They intimated that the minister never fully recovered his dynamism. A fully robust Schuller, they surmised, never would have allowed for his ministry to list into such a fragile and vulnerable state in the early 2000s. Could it be that seemingly minor head bump in Europe led, almost twenty years later, to the bankruptcy of one of the world's most famous churches?

Simple explanations that cast organizational success or decline as wholly contingent on one charismatic personality have a romantic attraction grounded in the tragic mythos of the hero. Schuller, of course, was a force. He used the sensibilities of marketing research and relied on a script that sought to bolster the listener's self-esteem. He stressed the attraction of theater and pageantry alongside the practicalities of parking spaces. Nason, Schuller's close friend, assistant, and biographer, summarized the strategy: "It's just that people are people, and they are very predictable most of the time. The same principles that work to sell toothpaste also work to reach the unchurched for Christ."[91] Yet Schuller was more than a marketing-savvy "feel good" preacher. As an author, builder, and manager, the minister innovated his way into a spectacular array of ministries, and his Possibility Thinking fueled the formation of a vast organizational structure that operated on a complex synthesis of constantly moving components involving constituency, charisma, and capital—each of which required increasingly intricate coordination. The expansion he achieved brought eventual crises, which he (as the Possibility Thinker) believed could always be overcome through even further mobilization toward unrelenting growth.

The route that led Schuller's ministry to declare bankruptcy in 2010 revealed multiple weaknesses that exceeded the declining energy of a single, ailing founder.

More than merely coping with the increasing frailty of their pastor, congregants were blindsided by the fragility of the ministry's financial infrastructure. For example, many had purchased memorial stones that lined the "Walk of Faith." Brochures from the ministry had urged members and viewers to purchase these memorial stones, costing between $2,000 and $2,500, to remember their loved ones. Paperwork indicated that the proceeds would be invested in a "perpetual endowment fund" that would "keep the gardens blooming, the Cathedral glass sparkling, and the waters flowing. The principal will never be depleted." Purchasers could safely assume that the memorial stones would speak silently "through the centuries."[92] Instead, they found that the ministry had drained the endowment. After the sale of the cathedral, the Diocese of Orange announced that, beginning in 2013, all 1,800 memorial stones—emblems of stability, these permanent gifts that were to stand in perpetuity alongside the grounds their purchase had supported—would be removed. Fortunately, the diocese contacted the families associated with the stones. Now many adorn backyard lawns instead of the Crystal Cathedral campus.

In the fallout from the bankruptcy, Crystal Cathedral board member Gary Moore insisted to *Christianity Today* that "it wasn't the bad times" that caused the financial collapse, but "it was the good." The ministry, according to Moore, had extended itself too far and became "over-built."[93] Many congregants agreed and pointed to the construction of the Welcoming Center, completed in 2002. One couple related that the mortgage for its construction had been a fatal break with the ministry's practices: "Everything prior to [the Welcoming Center] pretty much was completed on donor pledges. Maybe there was some swing loans that the bank would do in order to complete construction and that sort of thing, but it was always fully funded by pledges." The ministry's 2008 financial report also hinted at the construction of the Welcoming Center as a mortal blow. It noted that in 2002, "well-meaning individuals could not deliver" on their pledges "due to the '.com bubble burst'"—a reference to the excessive economic speculation related to internet companies that crashed in 2001.[94] Both insiders and observers failed to note that the strategy for continuing capital had rested for decades on the vision—guided by the precepts of Possibility Thinking—of yet *another* new project. The elder Schuller had always insisted that maintenance never motivates, but new vision does.

The financial failure ultimately traces back to the fundamental mismatch between the demands placed on the congregation and the capacity of the congregation by means of its available resources to meet those demands. Schuller appeared surprisingly ill-prepared as an innovator when he refused to alter his "mission church" in response to the changing demographic and religious context around him. The emphasis on Schuller's charisma reinforced by a pervasive Christian libertarianism contributed considerable stability for as long as it represented a valuable resource for attracting the loyalty and generosity of a constituency, but then it played a significant role in the decline of the cathedral when it lacked the ability to draw fresh supplies of new donors. His ministry became encased in a "Crystal Crypt" that inhibited reinvention, instead of a "Crystal Chrysalis" that would have further transformed the ministry into the twenty-first century.[95] A former pastor who visited the cathedral in 2011 reflected on the disrepair and maintenance issues caused by a lack of capital. Former coworkers gathered around him, expressing "fear for their jobs" because the "boat [was] about sunk." In dramatic contrast to the excitement and energy of the cathedral's heyday, they had all morphed into "a depressed, disillusioned, betrayed company of people."[96]

For his part, though, RAS traced the demise to the iconic cathedral itself: "That's the beginning of the [end]." Upon the completion of the grand structure, the sense of community among those who had built it quickly eroded. As RAS surmised, "I think the opening of the cathedral was the death of the local church." For him, the move into the cathedral signaled a shift in ministry emphasis toward the global audience because it was built in service of the ministry's broadcast, not the local congregation: "My parents put the *Hour of Power* so much ahead, they lost sight of things that made the local community what it was." The new image of the cathedral—the charismatic presence of the building itself—demanded a change in staff that would match the scale of the architecture. RAS continued: "With the opening of the Crystal Cathedral, my parents felt like they had to step up to this new level, but they didn't have enough respect for the people who helped them get where they got."

While the religious empire based in Garden Grove seemed, on the surface, too big to fail, the sheer size of Schuller's ministry contributed to its demise. Schuller liked to discuss his penchant for minimizing risk. In *Success Is Never Ending, Failure Is Never Final*, he positioned himself as an expert on risk management. In reinterpreting the cathedral's financial crisis, he discussed the fact that construction had commenced without complete financing. When his board suggested the possibility of a variable rate loan, Schuller had threatened to exercise his veto power. Instead, he pursued more donations from wealthy benefactors: "Thank God! It put pressure on us to raise money and pay cash! This was fortunate, because two years later the prime rate hit 21 percent! Our interest charges would have been $2.3 million a year. That would have made the Crystal Cathedral go bankrupt!"[97] Although Schuller framed the story as a win for his strategic acumen, it again demonstrated his dependence on radical infusions of capital and the confidence that any financial need could be met at the last minute by trusting the fundraising tactics that had worked over and over again in the past.

The ambition of an ever increasing ministry, one that could always accommodate an as-yet unrealized future growth, meant that the church always required greater financing than the current membership could bear. So Schuller relied on the *ex machina* of wealthy benefactors—a factor not always discussed in church growth circles—who gave amounts way above his regular audience to rescue the construction projects from floundering. Narrow escapes in the financing of both the Arboretum and the Crystal Cathedral prompted Schuller to assume an inherent replicability of continuing to place increased demands on his congregation, pushing for other, newer projects. He did not realize that his sequence of ambitious projects fell in line with a broader Christian libertarian movement among conservative Christian corporations and businessmen to fund projects consistent with their own religious desires.

He also relied excessively on the revenue of his broadcast ministry and ended up shaping the imperatives of the ministry around the needs of his mass television audience over his local congregation—yet another element of Schuller's empire not discussed in church growth circles. His accrued "successes" sanctioned the ministry's jettisoning of normal guardrails of church polity and transparency. His ministry was embedded in a larger opportunity structure without which he could not have acted, yet he misunderstood the workings of his own charisma, trusting his own ingenuity, insisting on his autonomy, alienating his denomination, and isolating himself from potential allies.

Moreover, Schuller's historically distinctive pastoral strategies of "church growth"—congregational practices centered on marketing principles and measurable goals of building expansion and membership growth—had all capitalized on vast social changes of the mid-twentieth century. What was attributed to Schuller's charismatic insight turned out to be a contingent pairing of his person and his affluent audience, and once the demographics shifted, his resonance faded. The expected surge of new members never appeared, leaving accumulated debts unpaid, with no new sources of capital emerging. What was left? After all, internal demand for growth by Schuller had already strained the congregation beyond its limits. The number of remaining constituents fell off. The pastoral leadership of Schuller's son, Robert A., and daughter, Sheila, failed to revive the crucial resource of charismatic leadership. When the external circumstance of an economic downturn hampered the ability of supporters to give, all capital flows withered. The strain of the ministry ultimately kept the cathedral from remaining financially solvent.

Schuller's ministry would be interesting in and of itself, but acknowledging that the imperative for growth embedded in the style of his leadership became a powerful model widely adopted by others underscores its significance. His legacy echoes—as noted by *Leadership Journal*—in other high-profile churches, from Bill Hybels's Willow Creek, to Rick Warren's Saddleback, to Joel Osteen's Lakewood, and many others. These congregations did not emerge serendipitously but rather from the strategic work of charismatic pastors using newly institutionalized practices traced back to their progenitor, Robert H. Schuller. Although Schuller claimed his principles were universal—and these ministries have their own books, seminars, and workshops touting their own revised methods—all of them only succeed by constantly improvising on the ever shifting alignments of constituency, charisma, and capital. Their continuity will depend not on the use of "timeless principles" but rather on the manner in which they manage the constant strain of calibrating the mix of constituency, charisma, and capital defining their ministry, a strain that increases tremendously under the internal pressure of continual growth.

Many of today's highest profile megachurch pastors borrow from Schuller's original "open architecture" system of church management, which is designed to appeal to customer preferences.[98] As unsuspecting "students" of his ministry, they have absorbed his guiding principles into their ministry philosophies of growth and have taken the path of obsessive reinvention of their charismatic draw, especially among churches associated with postdenominational evangelicalism (PDE). In his discussion of PDE megachurches, cultural geographer Justin Wilford described how these congregations remain captive to the tyrannical necessity of "meaningful performances" to sustain and grow their churches. Congregational leaders feel compelled to continually reassess every performative element of church life in order to maintain their niche: contemporary relevance.[99] Since their charismatic power rests on resonance with what connects to popular culture, the workings of charisma through speech, dress, props, and ambience demand compulsive monitoring. Whether in rented spaces or permanent facilities, the mobility of their constituency and the demands of continuing streams of capital mean that PDE megachurches "continuously innovate and discard programs, styles, practices, and organizational structures" in their attempt to map their ministries onto the daily rhythms of their attenders' fluid lives.[100] Instead of a singular pattern of familiarity, they "change it up," using the ability to shift music styles, change screen images, start and stop experimental programs. Having succumbed to the priority of image management, the tools of ministry reorient toward improvisation and flexibility. Deep roots are not important; current cultural resonance reigns as *the* indispensable element.

Today's pastors for whom church growth is imperative should take heed. Bolstered by confidence based on large membership, significant television audiences, eager pastors willing to pay for his secrets to success, historic church architecture, and a seemingly healthy balance sheet, Robert H. Schuller's ministry appeared to flourish for a half a century. But his unremitting commitment to growth before it arrived, his strategy of aggressive borrowing for ambitious projects to accommodate anticipated growth, and a lack of institutional checks on current spending based on overconfident projections of future revenue led to its eventual unspooling. Unable to sustain the growth of funds to cover increased obligations, his ministry's debts spiraled, and Schuller's religious empire crumbled.

The sanctuary of the Crystal Cathedral, with its "Cape Canaveral" doors open and Schuller's image appearing on the world's first indoor Sony JumboTron. Photo courtesy of the Joint Archives of Holland.

Coda

Ends and Beginnings

> Every problem holds positive possibilities.
> —Robert H. Schuller

Crystal Cathedral Becomes Christ Cathedral

In the throes of bankruptcy litigation, it became clear that the Crystal Cathedral campus would have to be sold to satisfy creditors. The finalists bidding for the property included Chapman University and the Roman Catholic Diocese of Orange. The university planned to remake the campus as a site for health services offerings, including the possibility of a medical school, and would allow the congregation to lease facilities on campus for local worship and to broadcast *Hour of Power*.[1] In contrast, the Diocese of Orange indicated that the campus would become a proper Orange County cathedral in exchange for an opportunity for the Crystal Cathedral congregation to rent an abandoned Catholic church nearby.[2] By November 2011, the diocese had bid $55.4 million against the university's $51.5 million.

Initially, the cathedral board expressed its preference for Chapman's proposal because it allowed the congregation to remain on the site and perhaps eventually purchase it back. The diocese's offer permitted the congregation to worship on the campus for only three years before moving a mile west to the 1,200-seat-capacity St. Callistus Catholic Church as a rental. In addition, the diocese sweetened the offer by assuring the Schullers that the visitor center would include a library dedicated to the minister and Arvella and that the chapel on the top floor of the Tower of Hope would "remain untouched as an inter-faith place of worship."[3]

As the bidding continued, the university eventually offered $59 million to the diocese's $57.5 million. After consultation with the church's board and the Schullers, the judge in the case picked the diocese's plan.[4] Sheila Schuller Coleman remarked that the Catholic purchase afforded the best possibility for the congregation to continue its "wonderful, beautiful ministries."[5] The elder Schuller also issued a statement clarifying his support for the sale to the diocese because it ensured that the campus would continue to be used for "religious purposes" and "the call of proclaiming Christ's message to humanity."[6] He also confided to friends that he saw the sale to Catholics as a "return to the mother church."

The transition was messy. Though Schuller reconciled himself to the sale of the campus to the diocese, some members of the congregation did not. In early 2012, a contingent from the church attempted to block the sale by asserting that the congregation held a ninety-nine-year lease that it had signed with the Crystal Cathedral Ministries in 1987 (see chapter 3).[7] Longtime member Jim Dawson testified that the congregation had made an arrangement to give the campus to the corporate ministry in return for a payment of one dollar per year on the ninety-nine-year lease. Beyond testimony, though, the members of the congregation failed to produce the records that would have attested to the agreement.[8] The sale to the diocese went through.

On June 9, 2012, the Diocese of Orange rechristened the church as Christ Cathedral—initiating the first time in history that a non-Catholic church would be converted into a Catholic cathedral.[9] The very next day, Schuller's thirty-year-old grandson, Robert (Bobby) V. Schuller, preached to the remnant congregation of the Crystal Cathedral. In 2009, the younger Schuller had started his own congregation, the Gathering Community Church, that had more recently morphed into the Tree of Life Community Church. He had also been a regular guest speaker at the Crystal Cathedral.[10] That Sunday, Bobby acknowledged the sadness attending the loss of the property but also wondered whether it had been a mistake to name a ministry after its campus: "So much of our identity was wrapped up in this beautiful place. How can we survive? Our name is Crystal Cathedral."[11] The young minister channeled his Possibility Thinking grandfather and noted he felt a "sense of hope" as the congregation looked toward making plans to move into the former St. Callistus Church down the street in 2013.

As the younger Schuller spoke, many congregants mourned the sale to the diocese. A board member remarked that the diocese "got a very good deal" only because the Crystal Cathedral congregation had been "under the hammer." The board member claimed that the property that sold for $57.5 million had once been appraised at over $200 million. Another church official remembered that "Dr. Schuller always bemoaned to me that there was a church in New York City, this beautiful RCA church that was torn down and made a parking lot for a shopping center." The minister had confided that he could not bear the thought of that fate for the Crystal Cathedral. The board member continued: "That weighed heavily on his mind, and I think instilled in mine, why he would go with the

Catholic Church bid, to keep it a church. Chapman College wanted to turn it into a campus and use the cathedral—a church—as an entertainment venue."[12]

Some observers wondered whether the diocese knew what it had purchased. Maintenance had become overwhelming, and by the time of its mass of dedication, the diocese estimated that it had spent $77 million in renovations. One consulting architect remarked that the conversion was "a fight with disaster from moment one." The chief operating officer of the renovation also reported that the Tower of Hope required "an exhausting amount of seismic mitigation."[13] One Crystal Cathedral congregant remarked, with a wry grin, that the diocese had no idea what an albatross the cathedral grounds had become. She chuckled when reporting that crows had eaten much of the adhesive grout from in-between the 10,600 glass panels, making them unstable and liable to fall out: "[Does the diocese] know you have to replace that glass?" Indeed, the entire glass exterior had to be recaulked to maintain a measure of earthquake resilience.[14]

Others, though, interpreted the sale as a totem of religious and demographic change—a harbinger of "the end of white Christian America."[15] The transformation of the *Crystal* Cathedral into *Christ* Cathedral represented a symbol of the evolving nature of religion in the United States: "The equipment facilitating Schuller's stagecraft . . . will be ripped out and replaced with a consecrated altar, bishop's cathedra, baptismal font, and votive chapels"—as an embodiment of "a transformation in the nation's spiritual landscape that is only now beginning to be felt."[16] Schuller's nadir, then, portended a religious landscape no longer dominated by white Protestant Christianity.[17]

In a move that testified to the changing demographics of Orange County, the Diocese of Orange announced that as part of the renovation, Christ Cathedral would include shrines to Our Lady of Guadalupe inside and to Our Lady of La Vang outside (for the hefty sum of $25 million). At the announcement of the plans for the shrine to Our Lady of La Vang, the rector and episcopal vicar, Christopher Smith, described the Vietnamese community as "the heart" of Christ Cathedral's larger community. Furthermore, the diocese estimated that 100,000 Vietnamese Catholics resided in Orange County.[18] The shrine not only would draw a new constituency of local Vietnamese, but it was also guaranteed to become an international pilgrimage destination.

In the years after the sale to the diocese, a typical Sunday afternoon on the campus demonstrated changes in American religious and social life. A smattering of tourists walked the church grounds past the stilled cranes on site, equipment used for the $80 million renovation to make the sanctuary liturgically prepared as the bishop's seat. Construction barricades made the cathedral itself unapproachable. In the Arboretum (the original sanctuary and the world's first hybrid church), an overcapacity Spanish-language mass included attenders leaning into the doors, attempting to hear and participate. No one remained seated in their car. In the courtyard between the Arboretum and the cathedral, hundreds of Vietnamese children participated in Eucharistic Youth. The demographic differences between the Crystal Cathedral and Christ Cathedral congregations displayed that afternoon could not have been more vivid. While the new cathedral held ten services a Sunday—in four different languages—Schuller's former congregation, less than a mile away, wrestled with an unsustainable $75,000 per month in rent.

Crystal Cathedral Becomes Shepherd's Grove Church

In 2014, grandson Bobby Schuller's Tree of Life Community Church officially merged with the remaining congregation from the Crystal Cathedral to form Shepherd's Grove Church. The younger Schuller also took the lead role for the *Hour of Power* broadcast. Rebranded as *Hour of Power with Bobby Schuller*, the new version of the program aired on TBN, the Church Channel, NRB Network, and KTLA in Los Angeles.[19] Though never likely to regain the ratings of the late 1980s and early 1990s, the broadcast still garnered almost 150,000 viewers in places like the Netherlands every Sunday.[20] The new version of the show lost "the advantage of that gorgeous, iconic building," according to Bobby. With that in mind, the format shifted to a twenty-five-minute sermon, a hymn, an instrumental rendition, "an inspirational interview," and, ultimately, the "message that the church is not about a building."[21] *World* magazine, a conservative evangelical touchstone, cast grandson Bobby as a potential hero who could salvage the shipwrecked ministry:

> The elder Schuller was often at odds with leaders in his own denomination, the Reformed Church in America, as well as leaders in mainstream evangelicalism. In the mid 2000s, a power struggle ensued within the family. The chaos drove away church members and viewers of the church's TV program, *Hour of Power*. In 2012, the ministry filed for bankruptcy protection. Into this chaotic situation entered young Bobby Schuller, then barely 30 years old. His theology, temperament, and leadership style are far less flamboyant than his grandfather's. Under his leadership, the finances and reach of the *Hour of Power* program have started on an upward trend again. The church also is growing, with attendance of about 1,500.[22]

Though Bobby once described plans to build an architecturally dynamic church, the 2010 bankruptcy problematized borrowing for land purchase and construction. Moreover, the younger minister wrestled with the legacy of ministries overly associated with their buildings: "With the Crystal Cathedral I actually felt, in the brief time I was there, like I was a curator of a work of art. It's a double-edged sword. It draws people. It gives you gravitas as a pastor. It also can be a distraction, where the real value is put in the building rather than in your faith. Not a lot of people did that, but there's always a risk."[23]

With multiple concerns in mind, in late 2017 the congregation approached Irvine Presbyterian Church (IPC)—a congregation within the Presbyterian Church (USA) that had dwindled to about 200 members in a sanctuary built for 600. By April 2018, the two congregations began a process of merging into one church, Shepherd's Grove, meeting in IPC's facilities. All three of Shepherd's Grove's ministers had their ordination transferred to the PC(USA), ostensibly with the Reformed Church in America's blessing. At the same time and for various reasons, all of IPC's pastoral staff departed. With the merger, Shepherd's Grove Church described itself as remaining a "Reformed Evangelical Bible Church."[24]

Shepherd's Grove's move into the PC(USA) denomination reaffirms Robert H. Schuller's paradoxical legacy of a mainline Protestant church in the orbit of evangelical, Pentecostal, and charismatic Christians. Even more, *Hour of Power*'s standing on the Saturday night lineup of TBN also seems somewhat discordant.[25] While fellow TBN stars such as Mike Huckabee and Robert Jeffress capitalize on their proximity to conservative Republican power, Bobby Schuller, like his grandfather, resists any type of political insinuation while on air. Moreover, Bobby proudly discusses the Schuller family legacy (for a few months in 2017, he even wore his grandfather's vestment), while he dispassionately offers an implicit critique in his rhetoric about "going outside the building"[26] and the failures of mass-marketed "Wal-Mart Christianity."[27] Bobby once described his commitment to a "vintage" or ancient form of Christianity that repudiated modern manifestations of "fast food Christianity."[28] When pressed on issues of historical tradition and orthodoxy, Bobby seemed to refute his grandfather's methodology: "One of the big dangers is in the goal of being missional. That's usually where it begins ... reaching people right where they're at. [But] sometimes we slip on our principles. That's constantly a danger, especially for millennials or young pastors [who] want to be accepted." In other words, the missional imperative of "meeting people where they are" can lead pastors to alter the Christian message, not for the purpose of teaching or inspiring but rather to be affirmed as a person.

Bobby carries over a good measure of his grandfather's charisma. However, caution regarding capital projects and expediency—rather than a desire to build an architectural wonder—led the congregation to migrate to Irvine and the PC(USA). Moreover, Bobby has exhibited concerns about institutional oversight. His church joined the Evangelical Council for Financial Accountability (EFCA), which his grandfather eschewed, because Shepherd's Grove wants "to be held accountable." The EFCA accreditation included published audits online, and Bobby noted during an interview that the congregation formed "an actual consistory of elected church members." He noted that some of these practices signaled departures from the template: "All these things are very different from when my grandpa was leading, where the board was just family members basically. There really wasn't a consistory, it was really just a genius with a thousand minions."

Schuller's Mixed Legacy

In April 2015, Robert H. Schuller passed quietly at Artesia Christian Home in Orange County. Arvella had preceded her husband in 2014. Though Schuller had submitted plans for his memorial service ten years earlier,[29] the bankruptcy had left the couple's estate bereft, and a "GoFundMe" online campaign sought to raise $30,000 to cover the minister's funeral expenses.[30] While some longtime viewers and congregants happily donated, others used the crowdfunding page to openly rant about the "mercenary mentality" of the ministry and the "vanity projects" the donations would be redirected toward. The funeral was held on the plaza of the Christ Cathedral campus, where the crowd found itself surrounded by artifacts that testified to Schuller's legacy. Congregants, though, reported a poignancy and cognitive dissonance in the fact that the campus no longer belonged to Schuller's ministry. He was now a guest on the very grounds that he had built.

The minister's name now has an elusiveness on the cathedral grounds. Already, many have forgotten Robert H. Schuller, and the transformation of the cathedral will likely cause most to forget the building was ever a Protestant icon. On the grounds is a small cemetery, a short walk from the place where he preached to millions. Visitors can pay their respects at Schuller's gravesite, where he is buried along with Arvella.

In the early years of the twenty-first century, larger social and religious shifts eclipsed the brand of the Crystal Cathedral—leaving its celebrity-infused theatrics and variety show formula in ever bigger buildings to seem hopelessly stagnant in comparison to competitors' coffee shop worship services and cutting-edge multiracial and multisite ministries. In short, what Schuller had perfected proved difficult to refine to remain relevant in a fluid cultural context. When nimbler, edgier, and more culturally relevant competitors arrived, the Crystal Cathedral suddenly seemed like a relic from an antiquated era of Christianity.

Appendix: Research Methodology

While writing this book, we frequently asked undergraduates in our classes whether any of them recognized the name "Robert Schuller," prompting squints and furrowed brows. So we name-checked other aspects of his Southern California ministry: *Hour of Power*? The Crystal Cathedral? These queries predictably caused one or two sympathetic students to nod, "Yeah . . . that seems . . . kind of familiar . . . maybe my grandma watched him . . . ?" Generations born in the twenty-first century, it seems, possess little awareness of Robert H. Schuller and his influence on American Christianity. Despite his fading profile, archives, newspaper accounts, and vivid personal memories all testify to Schuller's significance over the course of more than half a century. The ministry of Robert H. Schuller influenced Christianity in the United States and inspired pervasive and persistent practices in the manner of preaching, the techniques of attracting and sustaining members, and, most importantly, the financial arrangements encouraged among entrepreneurial church pastors ambitious to grow their congregations.

News of the bankruptcy of the Crystal Cathedral and curiosity regarding the once seeming stability yet eventual collapse of Schuller's extensive ministry prompted our initial questions. Research for this book began in earnest in 2016. Our entrée allowed us access to an array of high-quality sources of data, not only historical records of Garden Grove Community Church and the Crystal Cathedral, but also attenders, volunteers, and paid staff—including associate pastors and intimate advisors—of the congregation. In order to accomplish our archival analysis, we secured access to the forty-four linear feet of material related to Robert H. Schuller and the Crystal Cathedral at the Joint Archives of Holland, Michigan.[1] This archival material includes Schuller's correspondence (including exchanges with prominent figures such as Norman Vincent Peale, Johnny Carson, and Jesse Jackson) as well as advertising, bulletins, church directories, church news-letters, marketing research reports, media coverage, *Hour of Power* VHS recordings, and interoffice memoranda. Among the most important papers were the Eugene Coffin office files, significant because Coffin served as an executive minister for the church from 1967 to 1989. The archival records illuminated the internal processes of design, operation, and management of the ministry as the structure of the church grew, shifted, and transformed. In addition, we secured additional documents from wherever we could find them, the most rele-vant being from archives of the New Brunswick Theological Seminary, the Uni-versity of Notre Dame, and Shepherd's Grove Church. In fact, the leadership of Shepherd's Grove delivered banker's boxes out of storage in Newport Beach for our review in Garden Grove. The boxes included documents and recordings from the leadership institute (which trained pastors in Schuller's "techniques" of church management) as well as bulletins and internal memoranda from the congrega-tion. We reviewed a sample of Schuller's best-selling books, especially for bio-graphical or historical statements, and particularly his memoir, *My Journey*. In addition, we scrutinized secondary sources about Schuller's life, including pub-licly accessible unpublished dissertations and master's theses.

We also received unfettered and generous access to the papers of Dennis Voskuil and Ronald Keener. These sets of documents offered rich vantage points because they focus on Schuller's approach to church management. Voskuil wrote the original scholarly volume on Schuller in 1983 and saved files from his years of research—including two recorded interviews with several hours of audio of him interacting with the minister himself at his office in Orange County. In the first, Voskuil, a young assistant professor at the time, begins the interview by attempting to establish rapport with the famous minister. When Schuller has trouble discerning what Voskuil is asking, he impatiently and curtly inter-rupts, "Question?!" Three years later, while Voskuil's book was in the final pro-duction stages, Voskuil shared his galleys with Schuller. A disgruntled and litigious Schuller invited Voskuil back to Garden Grove for what turned out to be a recorded three-hour meeting in which the minister worked through the manuscript on his knees at a coffee table in his Tower of Hope office with the author. Both interviews reveal the complexity, brilliance, defensiveness, and theological imagination of Schuller. In comparison, Keener, editor of *Church Executive* magazine, closely observed and analyzed the Crystal Cathedral, espe-cially in its latter years, and was particularly fascinated by the management of the ministry as it teetered and eventually fell in 2010. *Church Executive* framed itself as "the first source of information for business administrators of Ameri-ca's largest churches" and had featured the Crystal Cathedral as a cover article multiple times—including November 2005 as the church planned for transition. As the ministry careened downhill thereafter, Keener established correspondence with multiple pastors at the church who conveyed their insider's knowledge. The emails from Schuller's associate pastors revealed internal misgivings and frustrations as the long-term ministry staff worried that the church they loved might cease to exist.

We also pursued people who had direct experience with Schuller and his church, ultimately interviewing thirty individuals associated with the ministry. These included a number of longtime congregants, worship leaders, benefactors, multiple members of the pastoral staff, *Hour of Power* staff members, Reformed Church in America denominational leaders, liaisons from other denominations to the leadership institute, and pastors who trained at the institute. We also interviewed some of Schuller's family members. Despite the fact that the vast majority of our interviewees expressed a willingness to speak on the record, in order to enhance cogency and limit distractions, we earnestly sought to maintain the anonymity of most of our participants except in cases of high-profile, public ministry leaders. While acknowledging Schuller's humanity, members and staff of the former Crystal Cathedral expressed great admiration for both him and his wife, Arvella—and a generous willingness to discuss both the halcyon days and the nadir of the ministry.

In California, our field work stretched from Pasadena in the north to Laguna Beach in the south. Perhaps most importantly, we made multiple visits to what is now Christ Cathedral, from the days of exploring the project up through the final steps in forming our argument. Visits included examinations of historical exhibits of the church's history in the Welcome Center, both at the beginning of the transition of the property to the Diocese of Orange when it represented Schuller's DreaMuseum arrangement and three years later when the exhibit emphasized the refurbishment of the cathedral and plans for new grounds. We received a tour guided by Kymmberly Binnquist, the senior property manager for the campus. Binnquist offered a rich explanation for the transitions necessary to convert the grounds into *Christ* Cathedral. At other junctures, we observed Spanish-language masses in the Arboretum. We walked the grounds, comparing the current site to past incarnations seen in photographs, and visited the gravesites of Schuller and his wife alongside those of major donors to his ministry. In addition, we attended multiple worship services at Shepherd's Grove—including the taping of the 2,500th episode of *Hour of Power*, led by grandson Bobby Schuller. That same Sunday, the adult Sunday school group Homebuilders generously allowed us to present an argument about the workings of Schuller's charisma as a component of our member check (an opportunity for members of the congregation to hear about preliminary findings and offer both challenges and affirmations). Nearby, we searched through the dedicated city history room at the Garden Grove Public Library, where we found a church yearbook that had been part of a fund-raising campaign, which included not only pictures of members but also descriptions of ministries and the earliest (and abandoned) sketches of the Crystal Cathedral. Driving around the area also gave us a feel for the urban makeup of the area, the location of the original drive-in church, and the implications of a commuter-based congregation.

We approached the research and writing of the book somewhat inductively, with no desire to impose preset conclusions or a dominating conceptual framework. At the same time, as experienced sociologists who have dedicated much time to the organizational analysis of contemporary congregations, we brought to this project an analytical perspective attentive to structures of participation and power, comparing the richness of dynamics within this case to others we have studied in the past as well as others found in the existing scholarly literature. In addition to our stance as scholars, we also brought to this study our immersive experiences with the practical workings of congregational management, which involve a bundle of ambitions, budgets, conflicts, recruitment, member and pastor anxieties, internal and external threats to stability, and the consequences of decisions and problem solving. Obviously, a compelling story lay in the dramatic arc of this ministry, guiding our observations toward explaining a known end point. Still, we did not presuppose the nature of the analytical arguments we might make, and we were certain that a simple "rise and fall" narrative was too reductive. Only after almost two years of archival visits, participant observation, in-depth interviews, a member check, significant analysis, and continual dialogue between us did we triangulate and settle on the three critical components of *constituency*, *charisma*, and *capital* as linchpins for approaching the steadily increasing fragility of the Crystal Cathedral Ministries—and American megachurches in general. We think the evidence offered in these pages speaks for itself; however, as sociologists, we also offer an interpretation that we think illuminates the structural mechanisms of Schuller's ministry and implications for the religious landscape of the United States.

Notes

Preface

1 With a March opening, Schuller beat Walt Disney and his Disneyland to the punch by four months.
2 Randall Balmer, "The Genius of Robert Schuller," *Valley News,* April 12, 2015. http://www.vnews.com/opinion/16416917-95/column-the-genius-of-robert-schuller.
3 "Glass" stands as an especially apt metaphor for the Garden Grove ministry: "Glass is not like other products used in buildings. It is clear, fairly rigid providing a lot of strength but can be brittle as well. When glass is under load it will bend and accommodate stress to a certain level and then suddenly fail once its threshold is met. The failure can be sudden and spectacular." https://www.pilkington.com/en-gb/uk/architects/glass-information/functions-of-glass/mechanicalfunctionsofglass/glass-strength.
4 See Elton J. Bruins, "My Town Alto: The First Dutch Immigrant Community in Wisconsin," in *Diverse Destinies: Dutch Kolonies in Wisconsin and the East,* ed. Nella Kennedy, Mary Risseeuw, and Robert P. Swierenga (Holland, MI: Van Raalte Press, 2012), 83.

Significant Dates for Robert Schuller and U.S. Politics, 1945–2015

1 Jim Bakker was convicted of mail and wire fraud and was accused of sexual encounters with his secretary. After the Bakker scandal, the *New York Times* found that 65 percent of Americans had unfavorable opinions about TV evangelists (William Martin, *With God on Our Side: The Rise of the Religious Right in America* [New York: Broadway Books, 1996]).
2 Jimmy Swaggart was found in the company of prostitutes multiple times.
3 While in the Netherlands, Schuller hit his head on a car door, causing a burst blood vessel in his brain. He was in surgery for eight hours and recovered fully.

Chapter 1   Constituency, Charisma, and Capital

1 Robert H. Schuller and James Coleman, *A Place of Beauty, a Joy Forever: The Glorious Gardens and Grounds of the Crystal Cathedral in Garden Grove, California* (Garden Grove, CA: Crystal Cathedral Creative Services, 2005), 110.

2   Robert H. Schuller, *My Journey: From an Iowa Farm to a Cathedral of Dreams* (San Francisco: HarperOne, 2001), 397–398.

3   Hazel Wright, wife of the late Harold D. Wright, president and chairman of the board of Republic Coal and Coke Company, had donated $1,000,000 for the construction of the organ. See Crystal Cathedral Dedication Booklet, September 14, 1980, Shepherd's Grove Church Archive, Irvine, CA.

4   Schuller, *My Journey*, 397–398.

5   Note here that Schuller declared the cathedral "debt free" while adding that this pronouncement included a calculation of "pledges and promises" of funding that had not yet been received.

6   To view the service in its entirety, see https://www.youtube.com/watch?v =IqB39TW4miQ.

7   Heather Adams, "Crystal Cathedral, Home to 'Hour of Power,' Transforms into Catholic Seat," Religion News Service, November 28, 2018. https://religionnews .com/2018/11/28/crystal-cathedral-home-to-the-hour-of-power-transforms-into -catholic-seat/.

8   When convenient, Schuller proudly asserted his and the congregation's membership with the RCA. He especially liked to note the denomination's status as having the longest continuous ministry in the United States. The RCA traced its arrival in America to 1609 and Henry Hudson's ship, *Half Moon*. Less than twenty years later, in 1628, the Dutch West India Company established in New Amsterdam (later to be renamed New York City) the first congregation of what would eventually became the RCA denomination. By the time of the American Revolution, the Dutch Reformed Church (as it was known at the time), numbered ninety-eight congregations and 45,000 parishioners throughout New York and New Jersey. With more immigrants arriving from the Netherlands, the denomination continued to grow—especially in the Middle Atlantic states and in the Midwest (primarily Illinois, Iowa, Michigan, and Wisconsin).

9   Deyan Sudjic, *The Edifice Complex: How the Rich and Powerful Shape the World* (New York: Penguin Books, 2005), 310–311.

10 Sudjic, *Edifice Complex*, 310.

11 Dennis Voskuil, *Mountains into Goldmines: Robert Schuller and the Gospel of Success* (Grand Rapids, MI: Eerdmans, 1983), 14.

12 Robert H. Schuller, *Move Ahead with Possibility Thinking* (Old Tappan, NJ: Spire Books, 1967), 199.

13 John Curran Hardin, "Retailing Religion: Business Promotionalism in American Christian Churches in the Twentieth Century" (PhD diss., University of Maryland, 2011).

14 Kip Richardson, "Gospels of Growth: The American Megachurch at Home and Abroad," in *Secularization and Innovation in the North Atlantic World*, ed. David Hempton and Hugh McLeod (New York: Oxford University Press, 2017), 301.

15 For more on the American preoccupation with bigger and bigger, see Sarah Z. Wexler, *Living Large: From SUVs to Double Ds: Why Going Bigger Isn't Going Better* (New York: St. Martin's Press, 2010).

16 Organizational theorists have long recognized the expansive administrative burden inherent to congregational growth—specifically, how increases in the size of an organization generate differentiation in subdivision responsibilities, which in turn increase the administrative infrastructure required to operate, supervise, and coordinate those subdivisions. See Peter M. Blau, "A Formal Theory of Differentiation in Organizations," *American Sociological Review* 35 (April 1970): 201–218.

17 Robert H. Schuller, "Make Them Want to Give," *Church Herald*, November 22, 1968, 11.

18 A Special Report from Robert H. Schuller to the Consistory, September 23, 1975, Shepherd's Grove Church Archives, Irvine, CA.

19 Robert H. Schuller and Paul David Dunn, *The Power of Being Debt Free: How Eliminating the National Debt Could Radically Improve Your Standard of Living* (Nashville: Thomas Nelson, 1985), xii.

20 David M. Kotz, *The Rise and Fall of Neoliberal Capitalism* (Cambridge, MA: Harvard University Press, 2015); Greta R Krippner, *Capitalizing on Crisis: The Political Origins of the Rise of Finance* (Cambridge, MA: Harvard University Press, 2011); and Gerald F. Davis, *Managed by the Markets: How Finance Re-Shaped America* (New York: Oxford University Press, 2009).

21 Adams, "Crystal Cathedral, Home to 'Hour of Power.'"

22 Gerardo Martí, *American Blindspot: Race, Class, Religion, and the Trump Presidency* (Lanham, MD: Rowman & Littlefield, 2020).

23 In conceptualizing the notion of "megachurch strain," we are influenced not only by older literature on "organizational strain" but also by the rapidly expanding recent scholarship on "organizational resilience." For an entrée into this newer literature, see Timothy J. Vogus and Kathleen M. Sutcliffe, "Organizational Resilience: Towards a Theory and a Research Agenda," *IEEE Systems, Man, and Cybernetics 2007 Proceedings, Montreal* (October 2007): 3418–3422; Kathleen M. Sutcliffe and Timothy J. Vogus, "Organizing for Resilience," in *Positive Organizational Scholarship: Foundations of a New Discipline*, ed. Kim Cameron, Jane E. Dutton, and Robert E. Quinn (San Francisco: Berrett-Koehler, 2003): 94–110; Ran Bhamra, Samir Dani, and Kevin Burnard, "Resilience: The Concept, a Literature Review and Future Directions," *International Journal of Production Research* 49, no. 18: 5375–5393; Deniz Kantur and Arzu İşeri-Say, "Organizational Resilience: A Conceptual Integrative Framework," *Journal of Management and Organization* 18, no. 6 (November 2012): 762–773; Stephanie Duchek, "Organizational Resilience: A Capability-Based Conceptualization," *Business Research* (January 14, 2019): 1–32; C. A. Lengnick-Hall, "Organizational Resilience," in *International Encyclopedia of Organization Studies*, ed. S. Clegg and J. Bailey (London: Sage, 2008): 1160–1161; Miguel Pina e Cunha, Filipa Castanheira, Pedro Neves, et al., "Resilience in Organizations," Working Paper 573 (February 2013); Gerben S. van der Vegt, Peter Essens, Margareta Wahlström, et al. "Managing Risk and Resilience," *Academy of Management Journal* 58, no. 4 (August 1, 2015): 971–980.

24 J. Eugene Haas and Thomas E. Drabek. *Complex Organizations: A Sociological Perspective* (New York: Macmillan, 1973), 239.

25 Haas and Drabek, *Complex Organizations*, 251.

26 Generally speaking, in accomplishing our sociological analysis, these three concepts serve to organize patterns of data based on a host of theoretical sensibilities we have accrued in our development as scholars, attuning us to issues of structure and agency, more specifically in the schemas enacted and the resources made available by agents who deploy social practices that are presumed to create or innovate ongoing social structures. For a classic statement that orients our general analytical orientation, see William H. Sewell, "A Theory of Structure: Duality, Agency, and Transformation," *American Journal of Sociology* 98, no. 1 (July 1992): 1–29.

27 Haas and Drabek, *Complex Organizations*, 244.

28 Haas and Drabek, 247.

29 Haas and Drabek, 259.

30   James D. Thompson, *Organizations in Action: Social Science Bases of Administrative Theory* (New York: McGraw-Hill, 1967), 21.

31   On the use of a more microlevel history to achieve broader historical insight, see Carol V. R. George, *God's Salesman: Norman Vincent Peale and the Power of Positive Thinking* (New York: Oxford University Press, 1993).

32   Robert H. Schuller, *Your Church Has a Fantastic Future!* (Ventura, CA: Regal Books, 1986), 306.

Chapter 2   The Imperative of Church Growth

1   Ron Kirkpatrick, "Pastor Parlays Drive-in Sermon into National Fame," *Orange County Register*, March 5, 1978.

2   "Door Interview: Dr. Robert Schuller," *Wittenburg Door*, no. 25, June–July 1975, 11

3   Robert H. Schuller, *Your Church Has a Fantastic Future! A Possibility Thinker's Guide to a Successful Church* (Ventura, CA: Regal Books, 1986), 16. This sentence from Wagner's foreword is featured on the dustcover of the hardbound edition.

4   Schuller, *Your Church*; and John Curran Hardin, "Retailing Religion: Business Promotionalism in American Christian Churches in the Twentieth Century" (PhD diss., University of Maryland, 2011), 292.

5   Erica Robles-Anderson, "The Crystal Cathedral: Architecture for Mediated Congregation," *Public Culture* 24, no. 3 (2012): 579.

6   Robert H. Schuller, *My Journey: From an Iowa Farm to a Cathedral of Dreams* (San Francisco: HarperOne, 2001), 163.

7   On the notion of a "religious orientation" built on a set of shared practices, see Gerardo Martí and Gladys Ganiel, *The Deconstructed Church: Understanding Emerging Christianity* (New York: Oxford University Press, 2014), 6–8; and Gerardo Martí, "New Concepts for New Dynamics: Generating Theory for the Study of Religious Innovation and Social Change," *Journal for the Scientific Study of Religion* 56, no. 1 (2017): 8.

8   For a multivoiced practitioner's perspective, see Paul E. Engle and Gary L. McIntosh, eds., *Evaluating the Church Growth Movement: Five Views* (Grand Rapids, MI: Zondervan, 2004).

9   Kip Richardson, "The Spatial Strategies of American Megachurches," *Oxford Research Encyclopedia of Religion*, May 2017, 4. http://religion.oxfordre.com/view /10.1093/acrefore/9780199340378.001.0001/acrefore-9780199340378-e-473.

10   Richardson, "Spatial Strategies," 4, 6, and 8.

11   T. D. Allman, "Jesus in Tomorrowland: Blessings to Go," *New Republic*, November 27, 1976, 7.

12   Allman, "Jesus in Tomorrowland," 7.

13   Russell Chandler, "A Bold Experiment in Modern Religion Arrives at a Milestone," *Los Angeles Times*, March 17, 1975.

14   Nicholas Von Hoofman, "Give Me That Drive-in Religion," *Washington Post*, May 14, 1975.

15   Schuller quoted in Gregory A. Pritchard, *Willow Creek Seeker Services: Evaluating a New Way of Doing Church* (Grand Rapids, MI: Baker Books, 1996), 51.

16   "'Hour of Power' Rated Number One," *Cathedral Chronicle*, September 1981, 2 Dennis Voskuil Papers, Holland, MI (hereafter DVP).

17   "RHS Ministries Tops Out at 1.5 Million for '81," *Cathedral Chronicle*, September 1981, 3 (DVP).

18   Quoted in Scott Fagerstrom, "Disputes: They Range from the Great Wall to the Bronx," *Orange County Register*, August 9, 1987.

19 Quoted in Fagerstrom, "Disputes."

20 Robert H. Schuller to George Douma, February 27, 1959, CC-Correspondence, 1956–1959, Robert H. Schuller/Crystal Cathedral Collection (hereafter RHS/CC), box 4, Joint Archives of Holland, Holland, MI (hereafter JAH).

21 Schuller, *Your Church*, 141.

22 Schuller, *My Journey*, 214.

23 Robert H. Schuller and Paul David Dunn, *The Power of Being Debt Free: How Eliminating the National Debt Could Radically Improve Your Standard of Living* (Nashville: Thomas Nelson, 1985), xiii.

24 Pat Morrison, "Dedication Day for Crystal Cathedral," *Los Angeles Times* (Orange County edition), September 15, 1980.

25 Bella Stumbo, "The Time Muhammad Ali Asked for Robert Schuller's Autograph," *Los Angeles Times*, May 29, 1983, http://www.latimes.com/local/california/la-me -schuller-1983-profile-20150330-story.html.

26 Stumbo, "The Time Muhammad Ali Asked for Robert Schuller's Autograph."

27 Richard Stengel, "Apostle of Sunny Thoughts," *Newsweek*, March 18, 1985, 30.

28 Todd M. Kerstetter, *Inspiration and Innovation: Religion in the American West* (Malden, MA: Wiley-Blackwell, 2015), 244.

29 Robles-Anderson, "Crystal Cathedral," 579.

30 Lloyd Billingsley, "The Gospel according to Robert Schuller," *Eternity*, March 1983, 25.

31 "Flash Report! From the Garden Grove Community Drive-in Church," September 22, 1960, CC-Membership Mailings (H93-1188), box 6 (JAH).

32 "Flash Report! From the Garden Grove Community Drive-in Church," September 29, 1960, CC-Membership Mailings (H93-1188), box 6 (JAH).

33 Hardin, "Retailing Religion," 292.

34 George R. Plaegenz, "'Church with Big Parking Lot' Called a Necessity," *Memphis Press-Scimitar*, April 19, 1978, CC-News Clippings, RHS/CC, box 29 (JAH).

35 Schuller, *Your Church*, 24.

36 Letter from Robert H. Schuller to the Most Reverend Fulton J. Sheen, April 24, 1972, CC-Correspondence, 1968–1973, RHS/CC, box 4 (JAH).

37 Quoted in Myron Weigle, "Marketing Religion Is the Goal of the Church," *Chicago Today*, August 23, 1974, CC-News Clippings, RHS/CC, box 29 (JAH).

38 Eileen Beyer, "Robert Schuller: Crystal Persuasion," *News from Hope College*, October 1980, 8 (DVP).

39 Molly Worthen, *Apostles of Reason: The Crisis of Authority in American Evangelical-ism* (New York: Oxford University Press, 2014), 155.

40 Telephone interview, September 2016.

41 Dennis Voskuil, *Mountains into Goldmines: Robert Schuller and the Gospel of Success* (Grand Rapids, MI: Eerdmans, 1983), 44.

42 Lynn Japinga, *Loyalty and Loss: The Reformed Church in America, 1945–1994* (Grand Rapids, MI: Eerdmans, 2013), 84.

43 Japinga, *Loyalty and Loss*, 196.

44 Letter from Robert H. Schuller to James W. Baar, September 20, 1968, CC-Correspondence 1968–1973, RHS/CC, box 4 (JAH).

45 Louis H. Benes, "Community or Reformed Churches," *Church Herald*, November 10, 1950, 6.

46 Letter from Robert H. Schuller to Richard Detrich, November 27, 1968, CC-Correspondence, 1968–1973, RHS/CC, box 4 (JAH).

47 Robert H. Schuller, "We Can Be Strong," *Church Herald*, June 6, 1969, 15.

48 Schuller, "We Can Be Strong," 15.

49 Letter from Schuller to Baar.

50 John Dart, "Gaining Membership," *Los Angeles Times*, June 29, 1973.

51 Louis H. Benes, "New Hope for the Church," *Church Herald*, April 16, 1971, 6.

52 Benes, "New Hope for the Church," 8.

53 Benes, 22.

54 Jeffrey K. Hadden and Charles E. Swann, *Prime Time Preachers: The Rising Power of Televangelism* (Reading, MA: Addison-Wesley, 1981), 87.

55 See Randall J. Stephens, "Culture, Entertainment, and Religion in America," *Oxford Research Encyclopedia of Religion*, October 2017, http://religion.oxfordre.com/view/10 .1093/acrefore/9780199340378.001.0001/acrefore-9780199340378-e-446.

56 See Harry S. Stout, *The Divine Dramatist: George Whitefield and the Rise of Modern Evangelicalism* (Grand Rapids, MI: Eerdmans, 1991).

57 Hadden and Swann, *Prime Time Preachers*, 11.

58 Letter from Robert H. Schuller to Walter Smythe, January 27, 1965, CC-Correspondence, 1965, H93-1188, box 4 (JAH).

59 Letter from Robert H. Schuller to Norman Vincent Peale, January 26, 1968, CC-Correspondence, 1968–1973, H93-1188, 4–32 (JAH).

60 Letter from Robert H. Schuller to Norman Vincent Peale, January 12, 1970, CC-Correspondence, 1968–1973, RHS/CC, box 4 (JAH).

61 *Hour of Power* telecast news release, March 1970, Garden Grove Community Church (DVP).

62 Kirkpatrick, "Pastor Parlays Drive-in Sermon."

63 Kate Bowler, *Blessed: A History of the American Prosperity Gospel* (New York: Oxford University Press, 2013), 104.

64 Press release from GGCC, March 19, 1964, GGCC-News Releases, 1956–1965, RHS/CC, box 6 (JAH).

65 Press release from GGCC, June 9, 1964, GGCC-News Releases, 1956–1965, RHS/CC, box 6 (JAH).

66 Michael Nason and Donna Nason, *Robert Schuller: His Story* (Waco, TX: Word Books, 1983).

67 Hadden and Swann, *Prime Time Preachers*, 31.

68 Billingsley, "Gospel according to Robert Schuller," 24–25.

69 Kate Bowler, "Why Are There So Few Mainline Celebrities?" *Faith and Leadership*, May 30, 2017, https://www.faithandleadership.com/kate-bowler-why-are-there-so -few-mainline-celebrities.

70 Voskuil, *Mountains into Goldmines*, 19.

71 "Door Interview: Dr. Robert Schuller," 19.

72 David Singer, "The Crystal Cathedral: Reflections of Schuller's Theology," *Christianity Today*, August 8, 1981, 28.

73 Jan Roorda, "A Call to Live Joyously: Dr. Robert H. Schuller, TV's Powerhouse of Spirituality, Inspires Legions of Possibility Thinkers with His Vision of God's Belief in Man," *Saturday Evening Post* 250, no. 3 (April 1978): 57.

74 Kirkpatrick, "Pastor Parlays Drive-in Sermon."

75 Transcript, Robert H. Schuller, "Message for Possibility Thinkers at the Meadow Spring Extravaganza '93," March 6, 1993, RHS/CC, box 30 (JAH).

76 Manfred Schwaiger, "Components and Parameters of Corporate Reputation—An Empirical Study," *Schmalenbach Business Review* 56 (January 2004): 46–71.

77 Ronald Campbell, "TV Superstar: 'Hour of Power' Is No. 1 or 2 Religious Show," *Orange County Register*, August 9, 1987.

78 Randy Frame, "Surviving the Slump: Can Religious Broadcasters Overcome Rising

Costs, Competition, and the Lingering Effects of Scandal?" *Christianity Today*, February 3, 1989, 32.

79 Frame, "Surviving the Slump," 32–34.

80 Year End Report of the Crystal Cathedral Ministries, December 31, 1988, Shepherd's Grove Church Archive, Irvine, CA (hereafter SGCA).

81 Campbell, "TV Superstar."

82 Year End Report of the Crystal Cathedral Ministries, December 31, 1988 (SCGA).

83 Roy M. Anker, *Self-Help and Popular Religion in Modern American Culture: An Interpretive Guide* (Westport, CT: Greenwood Press, 1999), 147.

84 Quoted in Fagerstrom, "Disputes."

85 Quoted in Fagerstrom, "Disputes."

86 Letter from Michael Nason to John J. O'Connor, Crystal Cathedral Correspondence, General, 1977–1991, RHS/CC, box 4 (JAH).

87 Schuller, *Your Church*, 77.

88 Schuller, 180.

89 Martin Filler, "Faith in Good Taste," *New York Review of Books*, December 14, 2015, https://www.nybooks.com/daily/2015/12/14/grace-farms-faith-in-good-taste/. For an interesting discussion regarding post–World War II suburban church architecture, see Jane Yong Kim, "The Quietly Dangerous Suburban Church," *New Republic*, December 31, 2015, https://newrepublic.com/article/126778/quietly-dangerous-suburban-church.

90 Sylvia Lavin, *Form Follows Libido: Architecture and Richard Neutra in a Psychoanalytic Culture* (Cambridge, MA: MIT Press, 2004), 119.

91 Lavin, *Form Follows Libido*, 130.

92 Hardin, "Retailing Religion," 281.

93 Dan L. Thrapp, "Size of Church Vital to Success, Pastor Says," *Los Angeles Times*, February 21, 1970.

94 Letters from Robert H. Schuller to Richard Neutra, September 9, 1959; January 12, 1962; and June 15, 1962 (CC-Correspondence—Richard Neutra, 1959–1962, RHS/CC, box 4), JAH. "Local Church Gaining International Attention," news release, September 4, 1962, Crystal Cathedral News Releases, 1956–1963, RHS/CC, box 6 (JAH).

95 Letter with attachment from Robert H. Schuller to Shirl Short, assistant editor, *Moody Monthly*, October 14, 1975, CC-Correspondence, 1975, RHS/CC, box 4 (JAH).

96 In fact, megachurch trends include a tendency to repurpose or mimic familiar suburban architecture—including shopping malls, coffee shops, and schools—resulting in religious buildings with few, if any, distinguishing features.

97 Jeanne Halgren Kilde, *When Church Became Theatre: The Transformation of Evangelical Worship in Nineteenth-Century America* (New York: Oxford University Press, 2002), 215–216.

98 Deyan Sudjic, *The Edifice Complex: How the Rich and Powerful Shape the World* (New York: Penguin Press, 2005), 310.

99 Douglas Davis, Jonathan Kirsch, and Maggie Malone, "The Crystal Cathedral," *Newsweek*, October 6, 1980, 97.

100 Witold Rybczynski, "An Anatomy of Megachurches: The New Look for Places of Worship," *Slate*, October 10, 2005, http://www.slate.com/articles/arts/architecture/2005/10/an_anatomy_of_megachurches.html.

101 Lavin, *Form Follows Libido*, 119.

102 Susan Power Bratton, *ChurchScape: Megachurches and the Iconography of Environment* (Waco, TX: Baylor University Press, 2016), 174.

103 Robert H. Schuller and James Coleman, *A Place of Beauty, a Joy Forever: The Glorious Gardens and Grounds of the Crystal Cathedral in Garden Grove, California* (Garden Grove, California: Crystal Cathedral Creative Services, 2005), 72.

104 Schuller and Coleman, *Place of Beauty*, 109.

105 Kilde, *When Church Became Theatre*, 215.

106 Schuller, *My Journey*, 346.

107 Letter from Robert H. Schuller to Lloyd Ogilvie, May 7, 1974, CC-Correspondence, 1974, RHS/CC, box 4 (JAH).

108 Letter from Robert H. Schuller to Lloyd Ogilvie, April 26, 1974, CC-Correspondence, 1974, RHS/CC, box 4 (JAH).

109 Anker, *Self-Help and Popular Religion*, 153.

110 "How Schuller Shaped Your Ministry: A Conversation with Robert Schuller," *Leadership Journal*, spring 1997, http://www.christianitytoday.com/le/1997/spring/7L2114.html?paging=off.

111 Warren Bird, "How Robert H. Schuller Shaped Your Ministry," *Leadership Network*, April 2, 2015, http://leadnet.org/how-robert-h-schuller-shaped-your-ministry/.

112 Jessica M. Barron and Rhys H. Williams, *The Urban Church Imagined: Religion, Race, and Authenticity in the City* (New York: New York University Press, 2017), 49.

113 Elizabeth A. Harris, "Tattoos, Bieber, Black Lives Matter, and Jesus," *New York Times*, October 26, 2017, https://www.nytimes.com/2017/10/26/books/hillsong-church-carl-lentz-book-justin-bieber.html. For more on pastors as cultural innovators, see Shayne Lee and Philip Luke Sinitiere, *Holy Mavericks: Evangelical Innovators and the Spiritual Marketplace* (New York: New York University Press, 2009).

Chapter 3   Migrants to Orange County, California

1 Lisa McGirr, *Suburban Warriors: The Origins of the New American Right* (Princeton, NJ: Princeton University Press, 2001), 28.

2 Jim Hinch, "Where Are the People? Evangelical Christianity in America Is Losing Its Power—What Happened to Orange County's Crystal Cathedral Shows Why," *American Scholar*, Winter 2014, https://theamericanscholar.org/where-are-the-people/#.WVqaA9PyvR0.

3 Darren Dochuk, *From Bible Belt to Sunbelt: Plain-Folk Religion, Grassroots Politics, and the Rise of Evangelical Conservatism* (New York: W. W. Norton & Co., 2011), 175–176.

4 Kenneth T. Jackson, *Crabgrass Frontier: The Suburbanization of the United States* (New York: Oxford University Press, 1985), 263–264.

5 Telephone interview, January 2018.

6 "The Story of a Dream, 1955–1979," n.d., Shepherd's Grove Church Archive, Irvine, CA (hereafter SGCA).

7 Sylvia Lavin, *Form Follows Libido: Architecture and Richard Neutra in a Psychoanalytic Culture* (Cambridge, MA: MIT Press, 2004), 128.

8 T. D. Allman, "Jesus in Tomorrowland: Blessings to Go," *New Republic*, November 27, 1976, 6.

9 Todd M. Kerstetter, *Inspiration and Innovation: Religion in the American West* (Malden, MA: Wiley-Blackwell, 2015), 193.

10 Dochuk, *From Bible Belt to Sunbelt*, 170.

11 Jackson, *Crabgrass Frontier*, 265.

12 Robert Fishman, *Bourgeois Utopias: The Rise and Fall of Suburbia* (New York: Basic Books, 1987), 185.

13 Sam Bass Warner Jr., *The Urban Wilderness: A History of the American City* (Berkeley: University of California Press, 1995), 136–138.

14 McGirr, *Suburban Warriors*, 22.

15 McGirr, 28.

16 McGirr, 26–27.

17 McGirr, 43.

18 McGirr, 46.

19 John Archer, *Architecture and Suburbia: From English Villa to American Dream House, 1690–2000* (Minneapolis: University of Minnesota Press, 2005), 258.

20 William H. Whyte, *The Organization Man* (New York: Simon & Schuster, 1956), 367.

21 McGirr, *Suburban Warriors*, 48–49.

22 James Hudnut-Beumler, *Looking for God in the Suburbs: The Religion of the American Dream and Its Critics, 1945–1965* (New Brunswick, NJ: Rutgers University Press, 1994), 5–7.

23 Eileen Luhr, *Witnessing in Suburbia: Conservatives and Christian Youth Culture* (Berkeley, CA: University of California Press, 2009), 158.

24 Robert P. Jones, *The End of White Christian America* (New York: Simon & Schuster, 2016), 25–26.

25 Luhr, *Witnessing in Suburbia*, 159–160.

26 Nancy Tatom Ammerman, *Congregation and Community* (New Brunswick, NJ: Rutgers University Press, 1997), and Rodney Stark and Roger Finke, *Acts of Faith: Explaining the Human Side of Religion* (Berkeley: University of California Press, 2000).

27 Letter from Robert H. Schuller to Doris W. Phillips, June 3, 1957, CC-Correspondence, 1956–1959, Robert H. Schuller/Crystal Cathedral (hereafter RHS/CC), box 4, Joint Archives of Holland, Holland, MI (hereafter JAH). Phillips worked as an administrative assistant to Norman Vincent Peale.

28 Jeanne Halgren Kilde, *Sacred Power, Sacred Space: An Introduction to Christian Architecture and Worship* (New York: Oxford University Press, 2008), 193–194.

29 Robert H. Schuller, *My Journey: From an Iowa Farm to a Cathedral of Dreams* (San Francisco: HarperOne, 2001), 198. A "classis" functions as the regional governance for congregations and ministers within Reformed church polity. Each church sends representatives to regular meetings of a classis.

30 Schuller, *My Journey*, 206, and Michael Nason and Donna Nason, *Robert Schuller: The Inside Story* (Waco, TX: Word Books, 1983), 47.

31 Schuller, *My Journey*, 180.

32 Ron Kirkpatrick, "Pastor Parlays Drive-in Sermon into National Fame," *The Register*, March 5, 1978.

33 Lavin, *Form Follows Libido*, 122.

34 Schuller, *My Journey*, 208.

35 Gerardo Marti, *A Mosaic of Believers: Diversity and Innovation in a Multiethnic Church* (Bloomington: Indiana University Press, 2005); Gerardo Marti, *Hollywood Faith: Holiness, Prosperity, and Ambition in a Los Angeles Church* (New Brunswick, NJ: Rutgers University Press, 2008); Gerardo Marti and Gladys Ganiel, *The Deconstructed Church: Understanding Emerging Christianity* (New York: Oxford University Press, 2014).

36 Schuller, *My Journey*, 212–213.

37 Robert H. Schuller, "The Drive-in Church—A Modern Technique of Outreach," *Reformed Review* 23, no. 22 (1969): 50.

38 Schuller, "The Drive-in Church," 50.

39 Schuller, "Drive-in Church," 47.

40 Erica Robles-Anderson, "The Crystal Cathedral: Architecture for Mediated Congregation," *Public Culture* 24, no. 3 (2012): 83.

41 Robles-Anderson, "Crystal Cathedral," 83. Robles-Anderson cites Reyner Banham, *Los Angeles: The Architecture of Four Ecologies* (New York: Penguin, 1971), 17.

42 Schuller, *My Journey*, 244.

43 Letter from Robert H. Schuller to Walter Smythe, January 27, 1965, CC-Correspondence, 1965, RHS/CC, box 4 (JAH).

44 Letter from Schuller to Smythe.

45 Within RCA church order, a "particular synod" is a regional body of classes (a group of congregations, typically bound by geographical proximity). For more, see https://www.rca.org/organized.

46 Chester Droog, "The RCA: Growing in the Southwest," *Church Herald*, June 7, 1985, 16–17.

47 John Stapert, "Lessons from RCA Church Growth: An Interview with Chester Droog, *Church Herald*, May 1, 1987, 16–17.

48 Stapert, "Lessons from RCA Church Growth," 17.

49 Letter from Robert H. Schuller to William R. Forman, February 5, 1957, CC-Correspondence, 1956–1959, RHS/CC, box 4 (JAH).

50 Schuller, "Drive-in Church," 50.

51 Schuller, 22.

52 Schuller, 47.

53 Schuller, 47.

54 Schuller, 48–49.

55 Schuller, 47.

56 Schuller, 47–48.

57 Kimon Howland Sargeant, *Seeker Churches: Promoting Traditional Religion in a Nontraditional Way* (New Brunswick, NJ: Rutgers University Press, 2000).

58 Deyan Sudjic, *The Edifice Complex: How the Rich and Powerful Shape the World* (New York: Penguin Press, 2005), 307.

59 Robert H. Schuller and James Coleman, *A Place of Beauty, a Joy Forever: The Glorious Gardens and Grounds of the Crystal Cathedral in Garden Grove, California* (Garden Grove, CA: Crystal Cathedral Creative Services, 2005), 19.

60 Susan Power Bratton, *ChurchScape: Megachurches and the Iconography of Environment* (Waco, TX: Baylor University Press, 2016), 131.

61 Schuller and Coleman, *Place of Beauty*, 19.

62 Lavin, *Form Follows Libido*, 122.

63 Lavin, 124.

64 Schuller frequently described the walk-in–drive-in innovation as an "integrated" church rather than a "hybrid." See, for instance, Schuller and Coleman, *Place of Beauty*, 19.

65 Bratton, *ChurchScape*, 131.

66 Kirkpatrick, "Pastor Parlays Drive-in Sermon," 43.

67 John Burgess, "The Father, the Son, and the 'Hour of Power,'" *Orange Coast Magazine*, December 1996.

68 Dochuk, *From Bible Belt to Sunbelt*, 171.

69 Jan Holtz Kay, *Asphalt Nation: How the Automobile Took Over America and How We Can Take It Back* (Berkeley: University of California Press, 1997), 272.

70   Robert H. Schuller, *Your Church Has a Fantastic Future! A Possibility Thinker's Guide to a Successful Church* (Ventura, CA: Regal Books, 1986), 246.
71   Sudjic, *Edifice Complex*, 306–307.
72   Sudjic, 307.
73   Sudjic, 307.
74   Year End Report of the Crystal Cathedral Ministries, December 31, 1988 (SGCA).
75   Jones, *End of White Christian America*, 27.
76   Meghann N. Cuniff, "Age, Income, Ethnicity: Latest Census Data Reveals All Facets of O.C." *Orange County Register*, December 29, 2014, https://www.ocregister.com/2014/12/29/age-income-ethnicity-latest-census-data-reveals-all-facets-of-oc/.
77   Hinch, "Where Are the People?"
78   Jones, *End of White Christian America*, 27.
79   Year End Report of the Crystal Cathedral Ministries.
80   For more on the congregational ecology of Reformed congregations, see Mark T. Mulder, *Shades of White Flight: Evangelical Congregations and Urban Departure* (New Brunswick, NJ: Rutgers University Press, 2015).
81   Year End Report of the Crystal Cathedral Ministries; emphasis added.
82   Jones, *End of White Christian America*, 27.
83   A 2017 visit to the Arboretum (the original Neutra-designed hybrid church) as the diocese modified the cathedral revealed carts full of Vietnamese- and Spanish-language hymnals.
84   Cuniff, "Age, Income, Ethnicity."
85   Hinch, "Where Are the People?"
86   Hinch.
87   Cuniff, "Age, Income, Ethnicity."
88   Seema Mehta, Christopher Goffard, and Anh Do, "Hillary Clinton Turned Orange County Blue. Minorities and College-Educated Women Helped Her," *Los Angeles Times*, November 9, 2016, http://www.latimes.com/politics/la-me-oc-clinton-20161109-story.html.
89   Adam Nagourney and Robert Gebeloff, "In Orange County, a Republican Fortress Turns Democratic," *New York Times*, December 31, 2018, https://www.nytimes.com/2018/12/31/us/orange-county-republicans-democrats-demographics.html.
90   Nagourney and Gebeloff, "Republican Fortress Turns Democratic."
91   Mehta, Goffard, and Do, "Hillary Clinton Turned Orange County Blue."
92   Justin G. Wilford, *Sacred Subdivisions: The Postsuburban Transformation of American Evangelicalism* (New York: New York University Press, 2012), 3.

Chapter 4   The Possibility Thinker

1   Crystal Cathedral—Christian Inspiration, Robert H. Schuller/Crystal Cathedral (hereafter RHS/CC), box 30. Joint Archives of Holland, Holland, MI (hereafter JAH).
2   Robert H. Schuller, *My Journey: From an Iowa Farm to a Cathedral of Dreams* (San Francisco: HarperOne, 2001), 171.
3   On the methodological sensibilities brought to the analysis of Schuller's theology, see Gerardo Marti, "Found Theologies versus Imposed Theologies: Remarks on Theology and Ethnography from a Sociological Perspective," *Ecclesial Practices* 3, no. 2 (2016): 157–172.
4   Robert H. Schuller, "What's Wrong with the World?" *Church Herald*, February 11, 1955, 16, 23.

5 Kate Bowler, *Blessed: A History of the American Prosperity Gospel* (New York: Oxford University Press, 2013), 55–56.

6 Bowler, *Blessed*, 57. It should also be noted that Peale himself originally intended for the book to be titled *The Power of Faith* and only allowed the retitle with reluctance. See Christopher Lane, *Surge of Piety: Norman Vincent Peale and the Remaking of American Religious Life* (New Haven, CT: Yale University Press, 2016), 82.

7 Norman Vincent Peale, *The Power of Positive Thinking* (New York: Prentice-Hill, 1952), 108, 173.

8 "Dr. Peale Sees Faith as a Source of Power," *New York American*, February 3, 1936, quoted in Lane, *Surge of Piety*, 12.

9 Lane, 17–18.

10 John Wigger, *PTL: The Rise and Fall of Jim and Tammy Faye Bakker's Evangelical Empire* (New York: Oxford University Press, 2017), 67.

11 And some, it should be noted, came to New Thought without any help from Peale. Barbara Ehrenreich lists John Osteen (father of Joel), Kenneth Hagin, and Fred Price as examples: *Bright-Sided: How Positive Thinking Is Undermining America* (New York: Picador, 2009), 134.

12 "The Story of a Dream, 1955–1979," Shepherd's Grove Church Archive, Irvine, CA (hereafter SGCA).

13 Letter from Robert H. Schuller to Doris W. Phillips, May 8, 1957, CC-Correspondence, 1956–1959, RHS/CC, box 4 (JAH).

14 Letter from Robert H. Schuller to Doris W. Phillips, June 14, 1957, CC-Correspondence, 1956–1959, RHS/CC, box 4 (JAH).

15 Letter from Robert H. Schuller to Norman Vincent Peale, July 3, 1957, CC-Correspondence, 1956–1959, RHS/CC, box 4 (JAH).

16 Norman Vincent Peale, *Enthusiasm Makes the Difference* (Englewood Cliffs, NJ: Prentice-Hall, 1967), 151–152.

17 Peale, *Enthusiasm Makes the Difference*, 152.

18 Peale, *Enthusiasm Makes the Difference*, 152.

19 Letter from Robert H. Schuller to Norman Vincent Peale, November 27, 1968, CC-Correspondence, 1968–1973, RHS/CC, box 4 (JAH).

20 Letter from Robert H. Schuller to Norman Vincent Peale, January 4, 1970, CC-Correspondence, 1968–1973, RHS/CC, box 4 (JAH).

21 Letter from Robert H. Schuller to Norman Vincent Peale, January 12, 1970, CC-Correspondence, 1968–1973, RHS/CC, box 4 (JAH).

22 See https://www.rca.org/resources/rca-basics/brief-outline-rca-history.

23 "Door Interview: Dr. Robert Schuller," *Wittenburg Door*, no. 25, June-July 1975, 10.

24 John P. Ferré, "Searching for the Great Commission," in *American Evangelicals and the Mass Media: Perspectives on the Relationship between American Evangelicals and the Mass Media*, ed. Quentin J. Schultze (Grand Rapids, MI: Zondervan, 1990), 112.

25 Todd M. Kerstetter, *Inspiration and Innovation: Religion in the American West* (Malden, MA: Wiley-Blackwell, 2015), 195.

26 For more on the waning significance of denominations, see Robert Wuthnow, *The Restructuring of American Religion: Society and Faith since World War II* (Princeton, NJ: Princeton University Press, 1988).

27 Brad Christerson and Richard Flory, *The Rise of Network Christianity: How Independent Leaders Are Changing the Religious Landscape* (New York: Oxford University Press, 2017), 122–123.

28 Susan Cheever Cowley, "Park and Pray," *Newsweek*, May 10, 1976, 105; emphasis added.

29 "Robertson: Sharon's Stroke Is Divine Punishment," *USA Today*, January 5, 2006, http://usatoday30.usatoday.com/news/nation/2006-01-05-robertson_x.htm.

30 *Larry King Live*, January 23, 2006, http://transcripts.cnn.com/TRANSCRIPTS /0601/23/lkl.01.html.

31 Donald Meyer, *The Positive Thinkers: Popular Religious Psychology from Mary Baker Eddy to Norman Vincent Peale and Ronald Reagan* (Middletown, CT: Wesleyan University Press, 1988), 370.

32 Jan Roorda, "A Call to Live Joyously: Dr. Robert H. Schuller, TV's Powerhouse of Spirituality, Inspires Legions of Possibility Thinkers with His Vision of God's Belief in Man," *Saturday Evening Post* 250, no. 3 (April 1978): 54.

33 Roorda, "Call to Live Joyously," 54–55.

34 Douglas J. Swanson, "From 'Hour of Power' to 'Days of Demise': Media Portrayals of Crisis and Fractured Social Order within Robert Schuller's Crystal Cathedral Ministry," *Case Studies in Strategic Communication* 1 (2012): 129, http://cssc .uscannenberg.org/wp-content/uploads/2013/10/v1art8.pdf.

35 "Arvella Schuller Interview," *Creator*, January 1980, 17.

36 Schuller, "What's Wrong with the World?," 23.

37 Razelle Frankl, *Televangelism: The Marketing of Popular Religion* (Carbondale, IL: Southern Illinois University Press, 1987).

38 Mary Kramer, "Possibility Thinking: Good News from Garden Grove?" *Grand Rapids Press*, March 15, 1975.

39 Randall Balmer, *Evangelicalism in America* (Waco, TX: Baylor University Press, 2016), 79. For a detailed history on an earlier minister who spoke in new ways to large crowds, see Harry S. Stout, *The Divine Dramatist: George Whitefield and the Rise of Modern Evangelicalism* (Grand Rapids, MI: Eerdmans, 1991). The term "evangelical" remains contested. For a thorough discussion, see Stephen V. Monsma, "What Is an Evangelical? And Does It Matter?" *Christian Scholars Review* 46, no. 4 (spring 2017): 323–340.

40 Les Lindeman, "The View from the Crystal Pulpit," *50 Plus*, April 1986, 21.

41 "Schuller Institute Goes on the Road," *Cathedral Chronicle*, September 1981, 4 Dennis Voskuil Papers, Holland, MI.

42 Dennis Voskuil, *Mountains into Goldmines: Robert Schuller and the Gospel of Success* (Grand Rapids, MI: Eerdmans, 1983), 117.

43 Bowler, *Blessed*, 13–14.

44 Bowler, 14.

45 Bowler, 36.

46 Meyer, *Positive Thinkers*.

47 Stephen Butterfield, *Amway: The Cult of Free Enterprise* (Boston: South End Press, 1985), 100.

48 Though not likely due to theological differences, *Los Angeles Times* journalist Bella Stumbo intimated in 1983 that a rift may have developed between Schuller and Peale. She noted that "despite several invitations," Peale had not returned to Schuller's church in over a decade. Stumbo described Schuller as "looking sad-dened" when discussing Peale and wondering aloud whether the New York minister had grown jealous: "It's unfortunate, but, well, I think maybe he *has* had some trouble dealing with it; but it would be presumptuous of me, of course, to speak for him" (italics in the original). In another instance, when Schuller reviewed the galleys to *Mountains into Goldmines*, he protested Voskuil's assertion that Peale, as "the Elijah of positive thinking," chose his successor: "The mantle has been placed on Robert Schuller." In response, Schuller contested Voskuil's notion that Peale

bequeathed the status, writing in the margins: "Not true. The mantle may have fallen, but Peale didn't choose it." Schuller also disputed the contention made by Ruth Peale, Norman's wife, that she had suggested the label of "Possibility Thinking." No matter the state of the relationship between the two RCA ministers, they would be forever linked as strong proponents of the integration of a positive attitude within the framework of Christian theology. See Bella Stumbo, "The Time Muhammad Ali Asked for Robert Schuller's Autograph," *Los Angeles Times*, May 29, 1983, http://www.latimes.com/local/california/la-me-schuller-1983-profile -20150330-story.html.

49 Jeet Heer, "The Power of Negative Thinking," *New Republic*, October 16, 2017, https://newrepublic.com/article/145311/power-negative-thinking-trump-lessons -democrats. Heer contends that much of President Donald Trump's business and political rhetoric resonates with the influences of Peale—his former pastor at Marble Collegiate Church in Manhattan. Moreover, Heet also notes a corresponding casting of the world in negative terms as the positive thinker asserts a primary role in surmounting such formidable challenges. In other words, the positive thinker finds it necessary to depict the larger context as a largely negative inhibitor that they have overcome. Therein, then, the power of positive thinking stands as strikingly potent.

50 Interview with Dennis Voskuil, April 2017.

51 Schuller, *My Journey*, 98.

52 Browne Barr, "Finding the Good at Garden Grove," *Christian Century*, May 4, 1977, 426–427.

53 Marti Ayres, "Minister Rejects Idea of 'Electronic Church,'" *Holland Sentinel*, March 5, 1982, 3.

54 Voskuil, *Mountains into Goldmines*, 128.

55 Voskuil, 129, 131.

56 Voskuil, 129.

57 Page proofs of Voskuil, file 16, galley 1 (DVP).

58 Draft mailer from GGCC to note holders, November 1974, GGCC Stewardship Materials, RHS/CC, box 6 (JAH).

59 Kenneth S. Kantzer and Paul W. Fromer, "A Theologian Looks at Schuller," *Christianity Today*, August 10, 1984, 23.

60 Kantzer and Fromer, "Theologian Looks at Schuller," 24.

61 Kantzer and Fromer, 22.

62 Ehrenreich, *Bright-Sided*, 79.

63 Ron Kirkpatrick, "Pastor Parlays Drive-in Sermon into National Fame," *The Register*, March 5, 1978.

64 "Door Interview: Dr. Robert Schuller," 12.

65 Joel A. MacCollum, "Self-Love: How Far? How Biblical? How Healthy?" *Eternity*, February 1979, 23–24.

66 Stumbo, "Time Muhammad Ali Asked."

67 Robert H. Schuller, interview with Dennis Voskuil, March 3, 1983 (DVP).

68 Jeffrey K. Hadden and Charles E. Swann, *Prime Time Preachers: The Rising Power of Televangelism* (Reading, MA: Addison-Wesley, 1981), 94–95.

69 Hadden and Swann, *Prime Time Preachers*, 95.

70 For more on the ascendance of rapture theology in the United States, see Matthew Avery Sutton, *American Apocalypse: A History of Modern Evangelicalism* (Cambridge, MA: Belknap Press of Harvard University Press, 2014).

71 *Larry King Live* transcript.

72 Deepa Bharath, "Schuller Sr. Speaks Out against Church's Anti-Gay Covenant," *Orange County Register,* March 17, 2011, https://www.ocregister.com/2011/03/17 /schuller-sr-speaks-out-against-crystal-cathedral-anti-gay-covenant/.

73 Quoted in Bharath, "Schuller Sr. Speaks Out."

74 Bharath.

75 Philip Gorski, *American Covenant: A History of Civil Religion from the Puritans to the Present* (Princeton, NJ: Princeton University Press, 2017), 179.

76 "Cracks in the Crystal Cathedral: Why We Are Better Off Letting God Make the Gospel Relevant," *Christianity Today,* January 10, 2011, http://www .christianitytoday.com/ct/2011/january/15.59.html.

77 Lois M. Joice, "The Glass Cathedral That Grew in an Orange Grove," *Church Herald,* April 16, 1971, 4–5.

78 Donner Atwood, "The Local Church's Edge," *Church Herald,* March 7, 1980, 11.

79 Martin D. Geleynse, "Review of *You Can Become the Person You Want to Be* by Robert H. Schuller," *Calvin Theological Journal,* November 1974, 252.

80 Letter from Norma Hertzog to Secretary, November 30, 1975, CC-Correspondence, 1975, RHS/CCM, H93-1188, box 4 (JAH).

81 Kramer, "Possibility Thinking."

82 Martin E. Marty, "Feeling Saved and Feeling Good," *New York University Educational Quarterly* 9, no. 3 (spring 1978), 5.

83 To view MacArthur's remarks, see https://www.gty.org/library/sermons-library /GTY150/inerrancy-under-attack.

84 Nathan Hatch, "Purging the Poisoned Well Within," *Christianity Today,* March 12, 1979, 15.

85 Hatch, "Purging the Poisoned Well," 16–17.

86 Michael R. Linton, "Smoke and Mirrors at the Crystal Cathedral," *First Things,* June 1997, https://www.firstthings.com/article/1997/06/002-smoke-and-mirrors-at -the-crystal-cathedral.

87 Ronald Yates, "From Outdoor Theater to 'Cathedral'—a Religious Success Story," *Chicago Tribune Magazine,* July 27, 1980, 23.

88 Christopher Lasch, *The Culture of Narcissism: American Life in an Age of Diminishing Expectations* (New York: W. W. Norton & Co.,1979), 7.

89 "Cracks in the Crystal Cathedral."

90 Quoted in Yates, "From Outdoor Theater to 'Cathedral.'"

91 Letter from Robert H. Schuller to Kenneth L. Woodward, June 16, 1987, Kenneth L. Woodward Papers, University of Notre Dame Archives, South Bend, IN (hereafter UNDA).

92 Letter from Schuller to Woodward.

93 Letter from Schuller to Woodward.

94 Letter from Schuller to Woodward.

95 Letter from Kenneth L. Woodward to Robert H. Schuller, April 25, 1997, Kenneth L. Woodward Papers, UNDA.

96 Letter from Robert H. Schuller to Kenneth L. Woodward, February 26, 1997, Kenneth L. Woodward Papers, UNDA.

97 Letter from Robert H. Schuller to Dennis N. Voskuil, May 6, 1985 (DVP).

98 Bruce Buursma, "Television Preacher Schuller Can Be Inspired by His Own Ego," *St. Paul Pioneer Press and Dispatch,* September 3, 1983.

99 Russell Chandler, *Understanding the New Age* (Dallas: Word Publishing, 1988), 205.

100 John Stapert, "A New Age Challenge," *Church Herald,* March 1990, 6.

101 Letter from Robert H. Schuller to Edwin G. Mulder, March 14, 1990 (SGCA).

102 Robert H. Schuller, letter to the editor, *Church Herald*, May 1990, 7. Some sociologists of religion have dismissed the prevalence of the New Age movement. Roger Finke and Rodney Stark contended that most converts to the movement understood it as more of an amusement and less of a religion. See Roger Finke and Rodney Stark, *The Churching of America, 1776–1990: Winners and Losers in Our Religious Economy* (New Brunswick, NJ: Rutgers University Press, 1997), especially p. 245. The authors described the movement as an "audience cult."

103 George D. Exoo and John Gregory Tweed, "Peale's Secret Source," *Lutheran Quarterly* 9 (summer 1995): 151–175. An earlier version of the article had been mailed to the Crystal Cathedral offices in 1992 with an alternative title, "The Purloining of Positive Thinking." A handwritten note on the manuscript from Schuller indicated that Exoo had actually attended the Institute for Successful Church Leadership in 1976. Moreover, Tweed had been a minister with Peale in New York City. Beyond the association with the occult, Exoo and Tweed accused Peale of plagiarism and cited numerous instances of similarity between his publications and those of Florence Scovel Shinn, a fairly obscure author affiliated with the Church of Religious Science. Exoo and Tweed also described Shinn as a teacher of "Occult science."

104 Exoo and Tweed, "Peale's Secret Source," 165.

105 Letter from Larry Sonnenburg to Edwin G. Mulder, December 15, 1992 (SGCA).

106 Elinor J. Brecher, "Inspired or Pirated? Two Question Peale's Works," *Miami Herald*, July 28, 1995.

107 Michael Horton, *Christless Christianity: The Alternative Gospel of the American Church* (Grand Rapids, MI: Baker Books, 2008), 67.

108 George A. Lindbeck, "The Church's Mission to a Postmodern Culture," in *Postmodern Theology: Christian Faith in a Pluralist World*, ed. Frederic B. Burnham (New York: Harper & Row, 1989), 45.

109 Dennis Voskuil coined this term in the early stages of preparing the papers and presentations that would eventually coalesce into *Mountains into Goldmines*.

110 Finke and Stark, *Churching of America*, 246.

111 Letter from Robert H. Schuller to Norman Vincent Peale, July 5, 1968, CC-Correspondence, 1968–1973, H93-1188, 4–32 (JAH).

112 Letter from Robert H. Schuller to Henry M. De Rooy, October 30, 1975, CC-Correspondence, 1975, RHS/CC, box 4 (JAH). The allusion to his "descendants" "splitting off" with the congregation is significant. Three decades later, this issue would prove destabilizing to the ministry (see chapter 8). For more on RCA classical control of church property, see Mark T. Mulder, *Shades of White Flight: Evangelical Congregations and Urban Departure* (New Brunswick, NJ: Rutgers University Press, 2015).

113 Development mailer, n.d., GGCC-Tower of Hope, 1966–1968, RHS/CC, box 6 (JAH).

114 Yates, "From Outdoor Theater to 'Cathedral.'"

115 Transcript of *The World of Religion*, January 3, 1975, included as an attachment in a letter from John Stapert to Robert H. Schuller, May 29, 1975, CC-Correspondence, 1975, RHS/CC, box 4 (JAH).

116 Letter from John Stapert to Robert H. Schuller, May 29, 1975, CC-Correspondence, 1975, RHS/CC, box 4 (JAH).

117 Letter from Robert H. Schuller to John Stapert (never sent), June 3, 1975, CC-Correspondence, 1975, RHS/CC, box 4 (JAH). The letter includes a hand-written instruction: "DO NOT MAIL" (capitalization in the original).

118 Memorandum from Tracy Hartman to Michael Nason, June 4, 1975, CC-Correspondence, 1975, RHS/CC, box 4 (JAH).

119 Letter from Tracy Hartman to John Stapert, August 4, 1975, CC-Correspondence, 1975, RHS/CC, box 4 (JAH).

120 Letter from Michael Nason to John Stapert, June 5, 1975, CC-Correspondence, 1975, RHS/CC, box 4 (JAH).

121 Letter from John Stapert to Robert H. Schuller, July 30, 1975, CC-Correspondence, 1975, RHS/CC, box 4 (JAH).

122 Letter from Robert H. Schuller to John Stapert, August 6, 1975, CC-Correspondence, 1975, RHS/CC, box 4 (JAH).

123 Schuller, interview with Voskuil.

124 For more, see Nicole C. Kirk, *Wanamaker's Temple: The Business of Religion in an Iconic Department Store* (New York: New York University Press, 2018). Kirk described "imagined communities" as those in which members may never meet and yet share similar values and ideals that allow them to recognize one another.

125 Letter from Robert H. Schuller to Dennis N. Voskuil, September 29, 1981 (DVP).

126 Quoted in Scott Fagerstrom, "Schuller Remarks Upset Reformed Church Officials: Minister's Claim of Accountability Called Misleading," *Orange County Register*, April 30, 1987.

127 Fagerstrom, "Schuller Remarks Upset Reformed Church Officials."

128 Wigger, *PTL*.

129 John Stapert, "Whose Cathedral?" *Church Herald*, June 19, 1987, 4.

130 Fagerstrom, "Schuller Remarks Upset Reformed Church Officials."

131 Letter from Mark A. Rozelle to Robert H. Schuller, May 13, 1987, CC-Correspondence, General, 1977–1991, RHS/CC, box 4 (JAH).

132 James Davison Hunter, *Evangelicalism: The Coming Generation* (Chicago: University of Chicago Press, 1987), 70–71.

Chapter 5   No Hippies in the Sanctuary

1 Memorandum from Robert H. Schuller to Head Ushers in Sanctuary, November 27, 1968, CC-Correspondence, 1968–1973, Robert H. Schuller/Crystal Cathedral (hereafter RHS/CC), box 4, Joint Archives of Holland, Holland, MI (hereafter JAH).

2 Larry Eskridge, *God's Forever Family: The Jesus People Movement in America* (New York: Oxford University Press, 2013).

3 Donald E. Miller, *Reinventing American Protestantism: Christianity in the New Millennium* (Berkeley: University of California Press, 1999).

4 Letter from Robert H. Schuller to Curt Roberts, December 4, 1968, CC-Correspondence, 1968–1973, RHS/CC, box 4 (JAH).

5 Gerardo Martí, *A Mosaic of Believers: Diversity and Innovation in a Multiethnic Church* (Bloomington: Indiana University Press, 2005); Gerardo Martí, *Hollywood Faith: Holiness Prosperity, and Ambition in a Los Angeles Church* (New Brunswick, NJ: Rutgers University Press, 2008); Darren Dochuk, *From Bible Belt to Sunbelt: Plain-Folk Religion, Grassroots Politics, and the Rise of Evangelical Conservatism* (New York: W. W. Norton & Co., 2011); Justin G. Wilford, *Sacred Subdivisions: The Postsuburban Transformation of American Evangelicalism* (New York: New York University Press, 2012); David V. Barrett, *The Fragmentation of a Sect: Schism in the Worldwide Church of God* (New York: Oxford University Press, 2013); Gastón Espinosa, *William J. Seymour and the Origins of Global Pentecostalism: A Biography*

and Documentary History (Durham, NC: Duke University Press, 2014); John G. Turner, *Bill Bright and Campus Crusade for Christ: The Renewal of Evangelicalism in Postwar America* (Chapel Hill: University of North Carolina Press, 2008).

6 Philip Gorski, *American Covenant: A History of Civil Religion from the Puritans to the Present* (Princeton, NJ: Princeton University Press, 2017), 140–141.

7 Robert H. Schuller and Paul David Dunn, *America's Declaration of Financial Independence* (Nashville: Rutledge Hill Press, 1995), 163.

8 Lydia Bean, *The Politics of Evangelical Identity: Local Churches and Partisan Divides in the United States and Canada* (Princeton, NJ: Princeton University Press, 2014), 30.

9 Bean, *Politics of Evangelical Identity*, 30.

10 Gerardo Martí, *American Blindspot: Race, Class, Religion, and the Trump Presidency* (Lanham, MD: Rowman & Littlefield, 2020); Gerardo Marti, "White Christian Libertarianism and the Trump Presidency," in *Religion Is Raced: Understanding American Religion in the 21st Century*, ed. Grace Yukich and Penny Edgell (New York: New York University Press, 2020; Darren E. Grem, *The Blessings of Business: How Corporations Shaped Conservative Christianity* (New York: Oxford University Press, 2016); Kevin Kruse, *One Nation under God: How Corporate America Invented Christian America* (New York: Basic Books, 2015); and Kim Phillips-Fein, *Invisible Hands: The Businessmen's Crusade against the New Deal* (New York: W. W. Norton & Co., 2009).

11 Kruse, *One Nation under God*, 28.

12 Bean, *Politics of Evangelical Identity*, 30. Bean also details how the founding of organizations that range from Campus Crusade for Christ to Pepperdine University could be traced to a conservative Christian effort to socialize university students to become political conservatives as a component of their religious identity.

13 Eileen Luhr, *Witnessing in Suburbia: Conservative and Christian Youth Culture* (Berkeley: University of California Press, 2009), 157–159.

14 Bruce Buursma, "Television Preacher Schuller Can Be Inspired by His Own Ego," *St. Paul Pioneer Press*, September 3, 1983.

15 Martí, *American Blindspot*, 115–145.

16 Robert H. Schuller, *Life's Not Fair, but God Is Good* (Nashville: Thomas Nelson, 1991), 17.

17 *Larry King Live*, January 23, 2006, http://transcripts.cnn.com/TRANSCRIPTS/0601/23/lkl.01.html.

18 Kruse, *One Nation under God*; Martí, *American Blindspot*; Martí, "White Christian Libertarianism and the Trump Presidency"; Lee Haddigan, "The Importance of Christian Thought for the American Libertarian Movement: Christian Libertarianism, 1950–71," *Libertarian Papers* 2, no. 14 (2010): 1–31, https://mises.org/library/importance-christian-thought-american-libertarian-movement-christian-libertarianism-1950–71; Benjamin T. Lynerd. *Republican Theology: The Civil Religion of American Evangelicals* (New York: Oxford University Press, 2014). For an argument related to Schuller's rejection of the commitments of the New Deal political order, see Richard Anderson, "'Super Successful People': Robert Schuller, Suburban Exclusion, and the Demise of the New Deal Political Order," master's thesis, University of Massachusetts Amherst, 2011, https://scholarworks.umass.edu/cgi/viewcontent.cgi?referer=https://www.google.com/&httpsredir=1&article=1783&context=theses.

19 Michael Emerson and Christian Smith, *Divided by Faith: Evangelical Religion and the Problem of Race in America* (New York: Oxford University Press, 2000).

20 Robert H. Schuller, "I Am the American Flag," 1972, Sermons, 1967–1977, RHS/CC, box 26 (JAH).

21 Martha Solomon, "Robert Schuller: The American Dream in a Crystal Cathedral," *Central States Speech Journal* 34 (fall 1983): 183.

22 Markku Ruotsila, *Fighting Fundamentalist: Carl McIntire and the Politicization of American Fundamentalism* (New York: Oxford University Press, 2016).

23 Daniel K. Williams, *God's Own Party: The Making of the Christian Right* (New York: Oxford University Press, 2010), 21. For more on the synergy of conservative politics and the shift of power to the Sun Belt, see Matthew D. Lassiter, *The Silent Majority: Suburban Politics in the Sunbelt South* (Princeton, NJ: Princeton University Press, 2006). For a better understanding of the political ramifications of suburbanization in the Northeast, see Lily Geismer, *Don't Blame Us: Suburban Liberals and the Transformation of the Democratic Party* (Princeton, NJ: Princeton University Press, 2015).

24 Williams, *God's Own Party*, 21.

25 Letter from Robert H. Schuller to Edith Gardner, November 4, 1960, CC-Correspondence, 1960, RHS/CC, box 4 (JAH).

26 Kruse, *One Nation under God*, 161. For more detail on Schwarz and his campaign, see pp. 148–161.

27 Letter from Robert H. Schuller to Henry Bast, November 23, 1960, CC-Correspondence, 1960, RHS/CC, box 4 (JAH).

28 Letter from Schuller to Bast.

29 Letter from Robert H. Schuller to GGCC members, October 19, 1960, CC-Membership Mailings, RHS/CC, box 6 (JAH).

30 Letter from Robert H. Schuller to GGCC members, November 16, 1960, CC-Membership Mailings, RHS/CC, box 6 (JAH).

31 Press release, "Will Communism Conquer America?" November 9, 1960, GGCC-News Releases, 1956–1965, RHS/CC, box 6 (JAH).

32 Robert H. Schuller, *My Journey: From an Iowa Farm to a Cathedral of Dreams* (San Francisco: HarperOne, 2001), 257.

33 Press release from GGCC, October 6, 1961, GGCC-News Releases, 1956–1965, RHS/CC, box 6 (JAH).

34 Press release from GGCC, May 23, 1961, GGCC-News Releases, 1956–1965, RHS/CC, box 6 (JAH).

35 Lisa McGirr, *Suburban Warriors: The Origins of the New American Right* (Princeton, NJ: Princeton University Press, 2001), 101.

36 McGirr, *Suburban Warriors*, 106.

37 Robert H. Schuller, "Tax Church Properties?!" *Church Herald*, March 13, 1964, 12.

38 Letter from Robert H. Schuller to Mr. and Mrs. Walter Knott, January 6, 1971, CC-Correspondence, 1968–1973, RHS/CC, box 4 (JAH).

39 John Dart, "Pastor Sees His Photo in Leningrad Museum," *Los Angeles Times*, October 7, 1972 (hereafter DVD).

40 Letter from Robert H. Schuller to Dick Cavett, November 15, 1972, CC-Correspondence, 1968–1973, RHS/CC, box 4 (JAH).

41 Letter from Hollis Green to Robert H. Schuller, November 5, 1976, CC-Correspondence, 1976, RHS/CC, box 4 (JAH).

42 Letter from Robert H. Schuller to Hollis Green, November 12, 1976, CC-Correspondence, 1976, RHS/CC, box 4 (JAH).

43 Mathis Chazanov, "The Rev. Billy Graham Said Today He Experienced 'Total Liberty,'" United Press International, May 12, 1982, http://www.upi.com/Archives /1982/05/12/The-Rev-Billy-Graham-said-today-he-experienced-total /8136390024000/.

44 Press release from Robert H. Schuller, May 14, 1982, CC-Correspondence, Mascom Public Relations, 1981, RHS/CC, box 4 (JAH).

45 Bella Stumbo, "The Time Muhammad Ali Asked for Robert Schuller's Autograph," *Los Angeles Times*, May 29, 1983, http://www.latimes.com/local/california/la-me -schuller-1983-profile-20150330-story.html.

46 Letter from Robert H. Schuller to Ruth Peale, January 11, 1971, CC-Correspondence, 1968–1973, RHS/CC, box 4 (JAH).

47 Ronald Yates, "From Outdoor Theater to 'Cathedral'—a Religious Success Story," *Chicago Tribune Magazine*, July 27, 1980, 23.

48 William Martin, *With God on Our Side: The Rise of the Religious Right in America* (New York: Broadway Books, 1996), 214–215.

49 Robert H. Schuller, notes on *Mountains into Goldmines*, file 15, galley 4 (DVP).

50 Schuller, notes on *Mountains into Goldmines*, galley 3.

51 Interview with Robert H. Schuller, March 31, 1983 (DVP).

52 Martin, *With God on Our Side*, 293.

53 John Beardslee III, "Who's against Communism?" *Church Herald*, April 20, 1962, 15.

54 Robert H. Schuller, letter to the editor, *Church Herald*, May 25, 1962, 20.

55 Letter from Robert H. Schuller to Norman Vincent Peale, November 19, 1973, CC-Correspondence, 1968–1973, RHS/CC, box 4 (JAH).

56 Browne Barr, "Finding the Good at Garden Grove," *Christian Century*, May 4, 1977, 427.

57 Jonathan Yardley, "Blessed Are the Self-Actualized," *Washington Post*, February 17, 1997, https://www.washingtonpost.com/archive/lifestyle/1997/02/17/blessed-are -the-self-actualized/af50a1ad-9256-4582-b298-51d3f3721e90/?utm_term= .39c1a25dca70.

58 Letter from Schuller to Cavett.

59 Robert Wuthnow, *The Restructuring of American Religion: Society and Faith since World War II* (Princeton, NJ: Princeton University Press, 1988), 198.

60 John M. Mulder, "The Possibility Preacher," *Theology Today*, July 1974, 158.

61 Mulder, "Possibility Preacher," 159.

62 Robert H. Schuller, "The Church's Prophetic Stance," October 23, 1975, 10–11, Shepherd's Grove Church Archive, Irvine, CA (hereafter SGCA).

63 Schuller, "Church's Prophetic Stance," 9–10.

64 Schuller, 15.

65 Robert H. Schuller, "What's Wrong with the World?" *Church Herald*, February 11, 1955, 16.

66 Schuller, "What's Wrong," 23.

67 See Emerson and Smith, *Divided by Faith*.

68 Schuller, *My Journey*, 267–269.

69 Wilfred Bockelman, "The Pros and Cons of Robert Schuller," *Christian Century*, August 20–27, 1975, 734.

70 Schuller, *My Journey*, 281–282.

71 Robert H. Schuller for the Consistory of Garden Grove Community Church, letter to the editor, *Church Herald*, August 26, 1966, 20–21.

72 In late March 1983, Dennis Voskuil flew out to Garden Grove to meet with Schuller about the galleys for *Mountains into Goldmines*. After reviewing the pages earlier in the week, Schuller had made a phone call on a Saturday evening threatening a lawsuit against Voskuil. In response, Voskuil and Schuller met to assess the minister's suggested edits of the book. The recorded meeting occurred in Schuller's office in the Tower of Hope and lasted three hours.

73 Schuller, interview with Voskuil (DVP).

74 Robert H. Schuller, interview with Dennis Voskuil, September 2, 1980 (DVP).

75 Pat Morrison, "Dedication Day for Crystal Cathedral," *Los Angeles Times* (Orange County edition), September 15, 1980.

76 Morrison, "Dedication Day."

77 Eileen Beyer, "Robert Schuller: Crystal Persuasion," *News from Hope College*, October 1980, 8 (DVP).

78 Beyer, "Robert Schuller."

79 For more on the manufactured linkages between conservative evangelicalism and modern consumer capitalism, see Timothy E. W. Gloege, *Guaranteed Pure: The Moody Bible Institute, Business, and the Making of Modern Evangelicalism* (Chapel Hill: University of North Carolina Press, 2015).

80 "Capitalism 'Basically Unjust,' Ecumenical Consultation States," September 27, 1975 (SGCA).

81 In fact, GGCC sent out a press release on church letterhead publicizing the resolution on October 1, 1975.

82 Resolution of the Classis of California, September 30, 1975 (SGCA).

83 Rich DeVos, "Free Enterprise," *Chemtech*, March 1980, 138–140, reprinted in "The Span of the Bridgebuilders," April 1980, Eugene Coffin Papers, RHS/CC, box 4 (JAH).

84 Community Church News, March 31, 1974, 1957, 1961, 1967–1969, 1972–1980, RHS/CC, box 5 (JAH).

85 Robert H. Schuller, *God's Way to the Good Life* (Grand Rapids, MI: Eerdmans, 1963), 84, quoted in Voskuil, *Mountains into Goldmines*, 158.

86 Robert H. Schuller, *Self-Love: The Dynamic Force of Success* (New York: Jove Books, 1969), 116.

87 Robert H. Schuller, *Success Is Never Ending, Failure Is Never Final* (Nashville: Thomas Nelson, 1988), 11–17, 23–24.

88 Nicole C. Kirk, *Wanamaker's Temple: The Business of Religion in an Iconic Department Store* (New York: New York University Press, 2018), 4.

89 T. D. Allman, "Jesus in Tomorrowland: Blessings to Go," *New Republic*, November 27, 1976, 7.

90 Kirk, *Wanamaker's Temple*, 12.

91 Dochuk, *From Bible Belt to Sunbelt*, 169.

92 Solomon, "Robert Schuller," 181–182.

93 Dochuk, *From Bible Belt to Sunbelt*, 183.

94 Dochuk, 184.

95 Letter from Robert Schuller to Jay Van Andel, May 27, 1976, CC-Correspondence, Howard Kelley, 1975–1990, RHS/CC, box 4 (JAH).

96 Letter from Robert H. Schuller to members of the Crystal Cathedral Consistory, December 28, 1982 (SGCA).

97 Robert H. Schuller, *Move Ahead with Possibility Thinking* (Old Tappan, NJ: Spire Books, 1967), 39–44.

98 Robert H. Schuller, *God's Way to a Good Life* (Grand Rapids, MI: Eerdmans, 1963), 85.

99 Robert H. Schuller, *Reach Out for New Life* (New York: Bantam Books, 1977), 29.

100 Robert H. Schuller, *You Can Become the Person You Want to Be* (Old Tappan, NJ: Spire Books, 1973), 91.

101 Edwin Diamond, "Should Government Crack Down on TV's Evangelicals?" *TV Guide*, November 14–20, 1981, 2.

102 Schuller and Dunn, *America's Declaration of Financial Independence*, 75.

103 "An Urgent Letter from the Ministers to All Friends and Members of Garden Grove Community Church," n.d., GGCC-Tower of Hope, 1966–1968, RHS/CC, box 6 (JAH).

104 Bella Stumbo, "Rev. Schuller Speaks Out on the Issues," *Los Angeles Times*, May 29, 1983.

105 Dennis E. Shoemaker, "Schuller Shooting," *Theology Today*, January 1975, 353.

106 Stumbo, "Time Muhammad Ali Asked."

107 Lynn Japinga, *Loyalty and Loss: The Reformed Church in America, 1945–1994* (Grand Rapids, MI: Eerdmans, 2013), 269.

108 Japinga, *Loyalty and Loss*, 270.

109 Solomon, "Robert Schuller," 182.

110 Letter from Robert H. Schuller to Jesse Jackson, June 13, 1975, CC-Correspondence, 1975, RHS/CC, box 4 (JAH).

111 Yardley, "Blessed Are the Self-Actualized."

112 Solomon, "Robert Schuller," 178.

113 Dochuk, *From Bible Belt to Sunbelt*, 187.

Chapter 6   Dig a Hole, Schuller

1 Robert H. Schuller, *My Journey: From an Iowa Farm to a Cathedral of Dreams* (San Francisco: HarperOne, 2001), 346.

2 Special Report from Robert H. Schuller to the Consistory, September 23, 1975, Shepherd's Grove Church Archive, Irvine, CA (hereafter SGCA).

3 Schuller, *My Journey*, 358–361.

4 Schuller, *My Journey*, 357–361.

5 John Crean continued his tremendous generosity to Schuller's projects, earning him a place of honor in the cemetery on the future grounds of the Crystal Cathedral—his gravesite would eventually sit just opposite that of Robert and Arvella Schuller's.

6 Schuller, *My Journey*, 364.

7 Schuller would eventually secure world-renowned Richard Neutra as the architect for the church. When eclipsed by the completion of the Crystal Cathedral in 1980, this original church on the campus would become known as the "Arboretum."

8 Schuller, *My Journey*, 243–252.

9 The tangible financial support of charismatic authority in Christian ministry is illustrated as early as the life of its founder. The start of the ministry of Jesus and his twelve apostles was supported by capital derived from three named women: Mary Magdalene; Joanna the wife of Chuza, Herod's steward; and Susanna (Luke 8:1–3).

10 Telephone interview, October 2016.

11 Schuller, *My Journey*, 163.

12 For a glimpse of the emotional connection between Schuller and Soviet president Mikhail Gorbachev, see *Hour of Power* episode 1603: https://www.youtube.com/watch?v=y3G5JOCokGU.

13 Katie E. Corcoran and James K. Wellman Jr., "'People Forget He's Human': Charismatic Leadership in Institutionalized Religion," *Sociology of Religion* 77, no. 4 (2016): 309–333.

14 Max Weber, *Economy and Society: An Outline of Interpretive Sociology* (Berkeley: University of California Press, 1978), 1113. For a fuller discussion of the relationship between charismatic authority and economic support, see pp. 212–213, 241–245, 1111–1157.

15 Sylvia Lavin, *Form Follows Libido: Architecture and Richard Neutra in a Psychoanalytic Culture* (Cambridge, MA: MIT Press, 2004), 122.

16 "A Commentary on the 'Schuller Family in Ministry Portfolio,'" 2007, Ronald Keener Papers, Chambersburg, PA (hereafter RKP).

17 Telephone interview, January 2018.

18 Larry W. Gates, *Dwelling in Schullerland* (Nashville: Winston-Derek, 1985), 62; emphasis added.

19 Interview with copastor, October 2016; Bella Stumbo, "Schuller: The Gospel of Success," *Los Angeles Times*, May 29, 1983.

20 Bella Stumbo, "The Time Muhammad Ali Asked for Robert Schuller's Autograph," *Los Angeles Times*, May 29, 1983, http://www.latimes.com/local/california/la-me -schuller-1983-profile-20150330-story.html.

21 Peter J. Schuurman, *The Subversive Evangelical: The Ironic Charisma of an Irreligious Megachurch* (Montreal: McGill-Queen's University Press, 2019), 139.

22 Erving Goffman, *The Presentation of Self in Everyday Life* (Garden City, NJ: Doubleday, 1959), 169; and Schuurman, *Subversive Evangelical*, 142.

23 As any reader of Max Weber's writings on the workings of charismatic authority knows, the routinization of personal charisma into a more stable organizational structure to support, regularize, and extend charisma is inherent in any successful attempt to sustain a leader's charisma over time.

24 Manfred Schwaiger, "Components and Parameters of Corporate Reputation— An Empirical Study," *Schmalenbach Business Review* 56 (January 2004): 46–71. On routinization of charisma, see Weber, *Economy and Society*.

25 John Curran Hardin, "Retailing Religion: Business Promotionalism in American Christian Churches in the Twentieth Century," PhD diss., University of Maryland, 2011, 289.

26 Letter from Robert H. Schuller to Wilbert Eichenberger, February 9, 1970, CC-Correspondence, 1968–1973, Robert H. Schuller/Crystal Cathedral (hereafter RHS/CC), box 4, Joint Archives of Holland, Holland, MI (hereafter JAH).

27 Letter from Schuller to Eichenberger.

28 "The Robert Schuller Institute Continues to Grow," *Cathedral Chronicle*, September 1981, 3. Dennis Voskuil Papers, Holland, MI (hereafter DVP).

29 "Schuller Institute Goes on the Road," *Cathedral Chronicle*, September 1981, 4 (DVP).

30 Browne Barr, "Finding the Good at Garden Grove," *Christian Century*, May 4, 1977, 425.

31 Barr, "Finding the Good," 426.

32 "Retail Religion: Robert Schuller, An Entrepreneur of Televangelism and Mega-churches, Died on April 2nd," *Economist*, April 11, 2015, https://www.economist .com/news/business/21647976-robert-schuller-entrepreneur-televangelism-and -megachurches-died-april-2nd-retail.

33 CD and cassette order forms, The Robert H. Schuller Institute for Successful Church Leadership, SGCA. Published in 2000, *The Prayer of Jabez* (Oregon: Multnomah) became especially popular within evangelical circles and a *New York Times* bestseller. The book's focus on "enlarging territory" also elicited criticism because of its similarity to "prosperity gospel."

34 George R. Plagenz, "'Church with Big Parking Lot' Called a Necessity," *Memphis Press-Scimitar*, August 19, 1978, Crystal Cathedral—News Clippings 1965, 1976, 1978, n.d., RHS/CC, box 30 (JAH).

35 *Christianity Today* advertisement, February 2, 1979 (DVP).

36 Sheila Strobel Smith, "Complexities of Pastoral Change and Transition in the Megachurches of the Baptist General Conference, Evangelical Lutheran Church in America, and Presbyterian Church (USA)," (PhD diss., Luther Seminary, 2010);

Hardin, "Retailing Religion," 95; Kimon Howland Sargeant, *Seeker Churches: Promoting Traditional Religion in a Nontraditional Way* (New Brunswick, NJ: Rutgers University Press, 2000); and Justin G. Wilford, *Sacred Subdivisions: The Postsuburban Transformation of American Evangelicalism* (New York: New York University Press, 2012).

37 Quoted in Sargeant, *Seeker Churches*, 196.

38 Quoted in Sargeant, 196.

39 Schuller, *My Journey*, 292.

40 Gerardo Martí, "New Concepts for New Dynamics: Generating Theory for the Study of Religious Innovation and Social Change," *Journal for the Scientific Study of Religion* 56, no. 1 (2017): 6–18; Gerardo Marti and Gladys Ganiel, *The Deconstructed Church: Understanding Emerging Christianity* (New York: Oxford University Press, 2014).

41 Smith, "Complexities of Pastoral Change and Transition," 93.

42 "Dr. Schuller Addresses Ministers on Final Day of Convocation," GGCC press release, February 22, 1975, CC-GGCC Press Releases, February 1975–June 1975, RHS/CC, box 29 (JAH).

43 "Church Leaders Gather at Convocation for Growth," GGCC press release, February 19, 1975, CC-GGCC Press Releases, February 1975–June 1975, RHS/CC, box 29 (JAH).

44 Scott Fagerstrom, "Trying Times: Schuller Ministry Beset by Problems," *Orange County Register*, August 9, 1987, M11.

45 Schuller, *My Journey*, 472; and Robert H. Schuller and James Coleman, *A Place of Beauty, a Joy Forever: The Glorious Gardens and Grounds of the Crystal Cathedral in Garden Grove, California* (Garden Grove, CA: Crystal Cathedral Creative Services, 2005), 25.

46 Herman J. Ridder, "How We Did It: The Schuller Film Workshop," *Church Herald*, January 23, 1981, 14–15.

47 "Film Workshop Workbook," Robert H. Schuller Institute for Successful Church Leadership, 1975–1980, RHS/CC, box 26 (JAH).

48 "Crystal Cathedral Academy," n.d., Academy, 1980–1981, RHS/CC, box 1 (JAH).

49 "A Weekend with Dr. Schuller," 1983, RHS/CC, box 2 (JAH).

50 C. Peter Wagner, "Recent Developments in Church Growth Understandings," *Review and Expositor*, December 1, 1980, 507–519, http://s.kwma.kr/kwma/archive/Recent%20Developments%20in%20Church%20Growth%20Understandings.pdf.

51 Letter from Marlin J. Van Elderen to Dennis N. Voskuil, April 24, 1980 (DVP).

52 Robert H. Schuller, *If It's Going to Be, It's Up to Me: Eight Proven Principles of Possibility Thinking* (San Francisco: HarperSanFrancisco, 1997), 145.

53 Robert H. Schuller, *Tough Times Never Last, but Tough People Do* (New York: Bantam, 1984), 130.

54 Darren E. Grem, *The Blessings of Business: How Corporations Shaped Conservative Christianity* (New York: Oxford University Press, 2016), 2.

55 Robert H. Schuller and Paul David Dunn, *America's Declaration of Financial Independence* (Nashville: Rutledge Hill Press, 1995), 159.

56 Letter from Robert Schuller to Jay Van Andel, May 27, 1976, CC-Correspondence, Howard Kelley, 1975–1990, RHS/CC, box 4 (JAH).

57 Letter from Schuller to Van Andel.

58 Letter from Robert H. Schuller to Jay Van Andel, February 9, 1989, personal papers of Duane E. Vander Brug, Grand Rapids, MI.

59 Transcript, Robert H. Schuller, "Message for Possibility Thinkers at the Meadow Spring Extravaganza '93," March 6, 1993, RHS/CC, box 30 (JAH); emphasis added.

60 Grem, *Blessings of Business*, 3–7.

61 Grem, 19. See also Kevin Kruse, *One Nation under God: How Corporate America Invented Christian America* (New York: Basic Books, 2015).

62 Michael Nason and Donna Nason, *Robert Schuller: The Inside Story* (Waco, TX: Word Books, 1983), 8–10.

63 Draft mailer from GGCC to note holders, November 1974, GGCC Stewardship Materials, RHS/CC, box 6 (JAH).

64 Memorandum from Barbara A. Taylor to Fred Southard, September 22, 1981, CC-Correspondence, Mascom Public Relations, 1981, RHS/CC, box 4 (JAH).

65 Memorandum from Barbara A. Taylor to Robert H. Schuller, May 18, 1982, CC-Correspondence, Mascom Public Relations, 1981, RHS/CC, box 4 (JAH).

66 Memorandum from Taylor to Schuller.

67 Letter from Robert H. Schuller to David Frost, July 1, 1971; letter from Robert H. Schuller to Hugh Downs, July 1, 1971; and letter from Robert H. Schuller to Johnny Carson, July 2, 1971. CC-Correspondence, 1968–1973, RHS/CC, box 4 (JAH). In 1972, Schuller did indeed appear on *The Tonight Show*. In a follow-up letter of gratitude, Schuller thanked Carson for the opportunity to be on his show—and allowing him to not receive a speeding ticket. It seemed the police officer who had stopped Schuller recognized him from his *Tonight Show* interview as "the minister of this big drive-in church." See letter from Robert H. Schuller to Johnny Carson, November 9, 1972. CC-Correspondence, 1968–1973, RHS/CC, box 4 (JAH).

68 Letter from Schuller to Van Andel, May 27, 1976.

69 Weber, *Economy and Society*.

70 Marion Goldman and Steven Pfaff, "Reconsidering Virtuosity: Religious Innovation and Spiritual Privilege," *Sociological Theory* 32, no. 2 (2014): 128–146.

71 Schuller and Coleman, *A Place of Beauty*, 25.

72 Grem, *Blessings of Business*; Timothy E. W. Gloege, *Guaranteed Pure: The Moody Bible Institute, Business, and the Making of Modern Evangelicalism* (Chapel Hill: University of North Carolina Press, 2015).

73 Charles Horton Cooley, "The Looking-Glass Self," in *Human Nature and the Social Order*, by Charles Horton Cooley (New York: Scribner's, 1902), 179–185; George Herbert Mead, *Mind, Self, and Society* (Chicago: University of Chicago Press, 1934); Goffman, *Presentation of Self*.

Chapter 7   Always a New Project

1 Bella Stumbo, "The Time Muhammad Ali Asked for Robert Schuller's Autograph," *Los Angeles Times*, May 29, 1983, http://www.latimes.com/local/california/la-me-schuller-1983-profile-20150330-story.html.

2 Susan Power Bratton, *ChurchScape: Megachurches and the Iconography of Environment* (Waco, TX: Baylor University Press, 2016), 125–126.

3 Robert H. Schuller, *Your Church Has a Fantastic Future!* (Ventura, CA: Regal Books, 1986), 306.

4 Ardis Whitman, "Four Remarkable Churches," *Reader's Digest* 117 (October 1980): 45–50.

5 Whitman, "Four Remarkable Churches," 47.

6 Stumbo, "Time Muhammad Ali Asked."

7 Molly Worthen, *Apostles of Reason: The Crisis of Authority in American Evangelicalism* (New York: Oxford University Press, 2014), 155.

8 Darren E. Grem, *The Blessings of Business: How Corporations Shaped Conservative*

Christianity (New York: Oxford University Press, 2016), 2; Steven P. Miller, *Billy Graham and the Rise of the Republican South* (Philadelphia: University of Pennsylvania Press, 2009). See also Kevin Kruse, *One Nation under God: How Corporate America Invented Christian America* (New York: Basic Books, 2015).

9 For example, Kate Bowler, *Blessed: A History of the American Prosperity Gospel* (New York: Oxford University Press, 2013), 102–103; Chris Lehmann, *The Money Cult: Capitalism, Christianity, and the Unmaking of the American Dream* (Brooklyn, NY: Melville House, 2016), 281, 307.

10 Scholarship on "the business turn" from historians of American religion continues to grow. We are particularly influenced by readings of certain widely cited works: R. Laurence Moore, *Selling God: American Religion in the Marketplace of Culture* (New York: Oxford University Press, 1994); N. J. Demerath III, Peter Dobkin Hall, Terry Schmitt, and Rhys H. Williams, eds., *Sacred Companies: Organizational Aspects of Religion and Religious Aspects of Organizations* (New York: Oxford University Press, 1998); D. Michael Lindsay, *Faith in the Halls of Power: How Evangelicals Joined the American Elite* (New York: Oxford University Press, 2007); Darren Dochuk, *From Bible Belt to Sunbelt: Plain-Folk Religion, Grassroots Politics, and the Rise of Evangelical Conservatism* (New York: W. W. Norton & Co., 2011); Timothy E. W. Gloege, *Guaranteed Pure: The Moody Bible Institute, Business, and the Making of Modern Evangelicalism* (Chapel Hill: University of North Carolina Press, 2015); Kruse, *One Nation under God*; Grem, *Blessings of Business*; Amanda Porterfield, John Corrigan, and Darren Grem, eds., *The Business Turn in American Religious History* (New York: Oxford University Press, 2017); Sarah Ruth Hammond, *God's Businessmen: Entrepreneurial Evangelicals in Depression and War* (Chicago: University of Chicago Press, 2017).

11 Raymond J. Elson, Casey Kennedy, and Mark Wills, "The Crystal Cathedral and Its Demise," *Journal of Business Cases and Applications* 18 (September 2017): 1–13, http://www.aabri.com/manuscripts/172634.pdf.

12 Porterfield et al., *Business Turn in American Religious History*, 2.

13 Schuller, *Your Church*, 27; and A Special Report from Robert H. Schuller to the Consistory, September 23, 1975, Shepherd's Grove Church Archive, Irvine, CA (hereafter SGCA).

14 On the promotion of a religious vision that could only be fulfilled through the generosity of wealthy businessmen, see Paul E. Johnson, *A Shopkeeper's Millennium: Society and Revivals in Rochester, New York, 1815–1837* (New York: Hill and Wang, 1978).

15 Letter from Robert H. Schuller to members and friends of Ivanhoe Reformed Church, n.d., Robert H. Schuller Correspondence, Robert H. Schuller/Crystal Cathedral (hereafter RHS/CC), box 30, Joint Archives of Holland, Holland, MI (hereafter JAH).

16 Robert H. Schuller, "Profitable Living," Ivanhoe RCA sermon text, n.d., Robert H. Schuller Correspondence RHS/CC, box 30 (JAH).

17 GGCC membership mailing, September 30, 1964, CC-Membership Mailings, RHS/CC, box 4 (JAH).

18 CC-Anniversary Celebration, 10th, 1965, RHS/CC, box 5 (JAH).

19 GGCC-CC Community Church News, October 27, 1965, RHS/CC, box 5 (JAH).

20 CC-Anniversary Celebration, 10th.

21 CC-Anniversary Celebration, 10th.

22 Letter from Robert H. Schuller to note holders, November 12, 1961, CC-Membership Mailings, RHS/CC, box 4 (JAH).

23 Robert H. Schuller, *My Journey: From an Iowa Farm to a Cathedral of Dreams* (San Francisco: HarperOne, 2001), 285–286.

24 Carol V. R. George, *God's Salesman: Norman Vincent Peale and the Power of Positive Thinking* (New York: Oxford University Press, 1993).

25 GGCC-CC Community Church News, October 27, 1965.

26 Schuller, *My Journey*, 294.

27 Robert H. Schuller, "Make Them Want to Give," *Church Herald*, November 22, 1968, 11.

28 Letter from Robert H. Schuller to Ferris Mack, January 26, 1968, CC-Correspondence, 1968–1973, RHS/CC, box 4 (JAH).

29 Garden Grove Community Church Yearbook, 1975, 128, GGCC, RHS/CC, box 6 (JAH).

30 Robert H. Schuller, *If It's Going to Be, It's Up to Me: Eight Proven Principles of Possibility Thinking* (San Francisco: HarperSanFrancisco, 1997), 162.

31 Ron Kirkpatrick, "Pastor Parlays Drive-in Sermon into National Fame," *Orange County Register*, March 5, 1978.

32 Ronald Yates, "From Outdoor Theater to 'Cathedral'—a Religious Success Story," *Chicago Tribune Magazine*, July 27, 1980, 26.

33 Letter from Robert H. Schuller to Harold L. Hiemstra, December 11, 1968, CC-Correspondence, 1968–1973, RHS/CC, box 4 (JAH).

34 Letter from Robert H. Schuller to Richard Detrich, November 27, 1968, CC-Correspondence, 1968–1973, RHS/CC, box 4 (JAH).

35 Robert H. Schuller, *Success Is Never Ending, Failure Is Never Final* (Nashville: Thomas Nelson, 1988), 160.

36 "Walk-in–Drive-in Church News," June 1969 (SGCA).

37 "Walk-in–Drive-in Church News."

38 "Walk-in–Drive-in Church News."

39 Draft mailer from GGCC to note holders, November 1974, GGCC Stewardship Materials, RHS/CC, box 6 (JAH).

40 Draft mailer from GGCC to note holders.

41 For more on the utility of "unworthy challengers," see Paul Joosse, "Countering Trump: Toward a Theory of Charismatic Counter Roles," *Social Forces*, May 2018, 1–24, https://doi.org/10.1093/sf/soy036.

42 Letter from Robert H. Schuller to Henry Kramer, July 23, 1968, CC-Correspondence, 1968–1973, RHS/CC, box 4 (JAH).

43 Mimi Zeiger, "Johnson Fain's Church Swap," *Architect: The Journal of the American Institute of Architecture*, October 31, 2016, http://www.architectmagazine.com /design/johnson-fains-church-swap_0.

44 Deyan Sudjic, *The Edifice Complex: How the Rich and Powerful Shape the World* (New York: Penguin Press, 2005), 315–316.

45 Robert H. Schuller and James Coleman, *A Place of Beauty, a Joy Forever: The Glorious Gardens and Grounds of the Crystal Cathedral in Garden Grove, California* (Garden Grove, CA: Crystal Cathedral Creative Services, 2005), 48.

46 CC-Anniversary Celebration, 20th, 1975, RHS/CC, box 5 (JAH).

47 Robert H. Schuller and Paul David Dunn, *America's Declaration of Financial Independence* (Nashville: Rutledge Hill Press, 1995), 34. Schuller indicated that he had been scarred by the debt his father had assumed in rebuilding the family farm in Iowa after it was destroyed by a tornado.

48 In one of his first books, Schuller confidently wrote, "You can build a fortune on borrowed money." See Robert H. Schuller, *Move Ahead with Possibility Thinking* (Old Tappan, NJ: Spire Books, 1967), 105.

49 In this statement, Schuller is likely adapting the well-known Methodist ethic "Do all the good you can, by all the means you can, in all the ways you can, in all the places you can, at all the times you can, to all the people you can, as long as ever you can."

50 A Special Report from Robert H. Schuller to the Consistory, September 23, 1975 (SGCA).

51 David M. Kotz, *The Rise and Fall of Neoliberal Capitalism* (Cambridge, MA: Harvard University Press, 2015) and Gerald F. Davis, *Managed by the Markets: How Finance Re-Shaped America* (New York: Oxford University Press, 2009).

52 Wayne Rice, "Big Spenders Department: How to Spend $15,000,000," *Wittenburg Door*, August/September 1978, 13.

53 John Dart, "Schuller's New Center Faulted for Its Secular Look," *Los Angeles Times*, November 25, 1989, http://articles.latimes.com/1989-11-25/entertainment/ca-304_1 _crystal-cathedral.

54 Dennis Voskuil coined the term "Schuller shooting" in the late 1970s.

55 "Retailing Optimism," *Time*, February 24, 1975, 23.

56 T. D. Allman, "Jesus in Tomorrowland: Blessings to Go," *New Republic*, November 27, 1976, 6.

57 Allman, "Jesus in Tomorrowland," 7.

58 Yates, 11.

59 Robert H. Schuller, *Your Church Has Real Possibilities!* (Glendale, CA: Regal Books, 1974), 27.

60 Development mailer, n.d. (SGCA).

61 American evangelist Dwight L. Moody used a similar technique in the 1850s to raise funds for his Sunday school class, designing and printing "shares" that mimicked stock certificates. See Gloege, *Guaranteed Pure*, 23.

62 CC-Anniversary Celebration, 20th.

63 By 1975, Schuller had founded the Inspiration Foundation to receive donations and invest them for profit, which included granting interest-bearing loans to churches. For example, a loan of $200,000 at 9 percent interest was provided to Robert A. Schuller toward his young church in San Juan Capistrano.

64 CC-Anniversary Celebration, 20th.

65 Schuller, *My Journey*, 392.

66 Schuller, 393.

67 Deepa Bharath, "'It Was a Life Well-Lived': The Reverend Robert Schuller, Leader of Crystal Cathedral and 'Hour of Power,' Dies at 88," *Orange County Register*, April 3, 2015, https://www.ocregister.com/2015/04/03/it-was-a-life-well-lived-rev -robert-schuller-leader-of-crystal-cathedral-and-hour-of-power-dies-at-88/.

68 GGCC-CC "Community Church News," October 27, 1965, RHS/CC, box 5 (JAH).

69 Stumbo, "Time Muhammad Ali Asked."

70 "Retail Religion: Robert Schuller, An Entrepreneur of Televangelism and Mega-churches, Died on April 2nd," *Economist*, April 11, 2015, https://www.economist .com/news/business/21647976-robert-schuller-entrepreneur-televangelism-and -megachurches-died-april-2nd-retail.

71 Schuller and Coleman, *Place of Beauty*, 48.

72 Lloyd Billingsley, "A Crystal Cathedral Spectacular: Christmas Pageant Is Reputed to Be the Country's Largest," *Christianity Today*, January 22, 1982, 34.

73 "Hotline: General Program Council/Reformed Church in America," January 22, 1982 (DVP).

74 Paul Goldberger, "Architecture: Johnson's Church," *New York Times*, September 6, 1980, C7.

75 Jim Hinch, "Where Are the People? Evangelical Christianity in America Is Losing Its Power—What Happened to Orange County's Crystal Cathedral Shows Why," *American Scholar*, Winter 2014, https://theamericanscholar.org/where-are-the-people/#.

76 Herman Wong, "Arts Plans Reflected Schuller's Optimism," *Los Angeles Times*, May 4, 1983, CC-Tax Situation, 1983, 1984, RHS/CC, box 29 (JAH).

77 Herman Wong and Richard C. Paddock, "Schuller Church Stripped of Its Tax-Exempt Status," *Los Angeles Times*, May 4, 1983, CC-Tax Situation, 1983, 1984, RHS/CC, box 29 (JAH).

78 Jerry Bowen, transcript of *CBS Evening News*, December 21, 1982, Luce Press Clippings, CC-Tax Situation, 1983, 1984, RHS/CC, box 29 (JAH).

79 Bowen, transcript of *CBS Evening News*.

80 Robert Lindsey, "Evangelist's Cathedral Loses Tax Exemption," *New York Times*, May 4, 1983; and Gary Hauna, "Schuller to Pay Cathedral Taxes," *Anaheim Bulletin*, July 29, 1983, CC-Tax Situation, 1983, 1984, RHS/CC, box 29 (JAH).

81 Press release, "Crystal Cathedral Borrows Money to Pay Taxes under Protest," August 30, 1983, CC-Tax Situation, 1983, 1984, RHS/CC, box 29 (JAH).

82 Radio broadcast transcript, KFWB news, August 30, 1983, CC-Tax Situation, 1983, 1984, RHS/CC, box 29 (JAH).

83 Press release, "Crystal Cathedral, under Protest, Borrows Money to Pay Taxes," August 31, 1983, CC-Tax Situation, 1983, 1984, RHS/CC, box 29 (JAH). For more background on conservative Christians in Orange County and their antistatism, advocacy for privatization, and favoring of low taxes, see Lisa McGirr, *Suburban Warriors: The Origins of the New American Right* (Princeton, NJ: Princeton University Press, 2001).

84 Robert H. Schuller, "Tax Church Properties?!" *Church Herald*, March 13, 1964, 12.

85 Letter from Robert H. Schuller to members of the Crystal Cathedral Consistory, December 28, 1982 (SGCA).

86 Leslie Berkman, "Church's Tax Dispute Reflects Trend," *Los Angeles Times*, May 4, 1983, CC-Tax Situation, 1983, 1984, RHS/CC, box 29 (JAH).

87 Robert H. Schuller, *Tough Times Never Last, but Tough People Do* (New York: Bantam Books, 1984), 120.

88 Letter from Robert H. Schuller to members and friends of the Crystal Cathedral congregation, May 10, 1983, Scrapbooks, 1971–1984, RHS/CC, box 25 (JAH).

89 Letter from Crystal Cathedral Festival of Concerts to Kathryn Lundquist, October 14, 1982, Scrapbooks, 1971–1984, RHS/CC, box 25 (JAH).

90 "Crystal Cathedral to Pay Back Taxes on Concert Receipts," *New York Times*, August 31, 1983, https://www.nytimes.com/1983/08/31/us/crystal-cathedral-to-pay-back-taxes-on-concert-receipts.html.

91 Clark Morphew, "Schuller's Dreams Crystal Clear," *St. Paul Pioneer Press and Dispatch*, September 21, 1985.

92 Ronald Campbell, "Trying Times: Empire Shows Signs of Financial Strain," *Orange County Register*, August 9, 1987, M2.

93 Yates, "From Outdoor Theater to 'Cathedral,'" 11.

94 Elson et al., "Crystal Cathedral and Its Demise."

95 Robert H. Schuller, "My Mission, My Ministry, My Methods," 1987, Promotional Material, RHS/CC, box 3 (JAH).

96 "Getting It Done in '91!," Stewardship Materials, 1980–1991, RHS/CC, box 3 (JAH).

97 Bylaws for the Positive Christian Singles, August 1978, CC-Nyematic, RHS/CC, box 4 (JAH).

98 Organizational sociologists have long known that greater organizational size

increases the infrastructure required to operate, supervise, and coordinate a more complex organization. See Peter M. Blau, "A Formal Theory of Differentiation in Organizations," *American Sociological Review* 35 (April 1970): 201–218.

99 "Crystal Cathedral Tax-Exempt Situation," January 16, 1983, CC-Press Clippings, RHS/CC, box 29 (JAH).

100 Internal memo from Paul Nunn to all Crystal Cathedral employees, November 16, 1989, Eugene Coffin Papers, RHS/CC, box 4 (JAH).

101 "Lay Ministers Training Center Opens Wednesday," *Community Church News*, January 18, 1976, GGCC-Community Church News, RHS/CC, box 5 (JAH).

102 Wilfred Bockelman, "The Pros and Cons of Robert Schuller," *Christian Century*, August 20–27, 1975, 732–735.

103 Crystal Cathedral Visitors Center Handbook, 1987, Eugene Coffin Papers, RHS/CC, box 4 (JAH).

104 Procedural rules are commonly found among revivalists. For example, Schuller likely knew about the Billy Graham Crusade handbooks, which included explicit details on interpersonal interactions for working with new converts. See Grem, *Blessings of Business*, 65–66.

105 Elson et al., "Crystal Cathedral and Its Demise."

106 Transcript, Robert H. Schuller, "Message for Possibility Thinkers at the Meadow Spring Extravaganza '93," March 6, 1993, RHS/CC, box 30 (JAH).

107 William Vanderbloemen and Warren Bird, *Next: Pastoral Succession That Works* (Grand Rapids, MI: Baker Books, 2014), 101.

108 Vanderbloemen and Bird, *Next*, 102.

109 Letter from Robert H. Schuller to Kathryn E. Lundquist, October 15, 1981, Scrapbooks, 1971–1984, RHS/CC, box 25 (JAH).

110 Letter from Robert H. Schuller to Kathryn E. Lundquist, October 30, 1981, Scrapbooks, 1971–1984, RHS/CC, box 25 (JAH).

111 Letter from Robert H. Schuller to Kathryn E. Lundquist, November 30, 1981, Scrapbooks, 1971–1984, RHS/CC, box 25 (JAH).

112 Year End Report of the Crystal Cathedral Ministries, December 31, 1988 (SGCA).

113 Dart, "Schuller's New Center."

114 Quoted in Dart.

115 Schuller and Dunn, *America's Declaration of Financial Independence*; and Robert H. Schuller and Paul David Dunn, *The Power of Being Debt Free: How Eliminating the National Debt Could Radically Improve Your Standard of Living* (Nashville: Thomas Nelson, 1985).

116 Schuller and Coleman, *Place of Beauty*, 120–127.

117 Schuller, *My Journey*, 474–476.

118 Vanderbloemen and Bird, *Next*, 101.

119 Kevin Sablan, "Action Picks Up for Filming in OC," *Orange County Register*, April 29, 2013, https://www.ocregister.com/2013/04/29/action-picks-up-for-filming-in-oc/.

120 Schuller and Coleman, *Place of Beauty*, 149.

121 Schuller and Coleman, 142.

122 Laurie Goodstein, "Dispute over Succession Clouds Megachurch," *New York Times*, October 23, 2010, https://www.nytimes.com/2010/10/24/us/24cathedral.html; and Deepa Bharath, "Rifts, Debt Tear at Crystal Cathedral," *Orange County Register*, October 24, 2010, https://www.ocregister.com/2010/10/24/rifts-debt-tear-at-crystal-cathedral/.

123 Bharath, "Rifts, Debt."

124 Schuller, *Your Church*, 158.

125 Bharath, "Rifts, Debt."

126 Bharath.

127 For more on ephemeral "products," see Kathryn Lofton, *Oprah: The Gospel of an Icon* (Berkeley: University of California Press, 2011), 21–25.

128 "Retail Religion: Robert Schuller, an Entrepreneur of Televangelism."

129 Kriston Capps, "Why Cities Should Be More Skeptical of New Cultural Centers and Expansions," *CityLab*, June 24, 2014, https://www.citylab.com/equity/2014/06/why -cities-should-be-more-skeptical-of-new-cultural-centers-and-expansions/373258/. See also Rowan Moore, "The Bilbao Effect: How Frank Gehry's Guggenheim Started a Global Craze," *Guardian*, October 1, 2017, https://www.theguardian.com /artanddesign/2017/oct/01/bilbao-effect-frank-gehry-guggenheim-global-craze.

130 Capps, "Why Cities Should Be More Skeptical."

131 Daniel Vaca, "Believing within Business: Evangelicalism, Media, and Financial Faith," in Porterfield et al., *Business Turn in American Religious History*, 26–27.

Chapter 8   When the Glass Breaks

1 "Homebuilders Questions for Dr. Sheila Schuller Coleman," n.d., Ronald Keener Papers, Chambersburg, PA (hereafter RKP).

2 Deepa Bharath, "Crystal Cathedral Asks Vendors for Forgiveness," *Orange County Register*, April 9, 2010, https://www.ocregister.com/2010/04/10/crystal-cathedral -asks-vendors-for-forgiveness/.

3 Bharath, "Crystal Cathedral Asks Vendors."

4 Deepa Bharath, "Crystal Cathedral to Be Sold to Pay Millions in Debt," *Orange County Register*, March 27, 2011, https://www.ocregister.com/2011/05/27/crystal -cathedral-to-be-sold-to-pay-millions-in-debt/.

5 "Cracks in the Crystal Cathedral: Why We Are Better Off Letting God Make the Gospel Relevant," *Christianity Today*, January 10, 2011, http://www .christianitytoday.com/ct/2011/january/15.59.html.

6 "Cracks in the Crystal Cathedral."

7 The RCA utilized "confessing members" for assessing quotas: the expected contributions from congregations per member. Interviewees reported that the Crystal Cathedral and the RCA had an arrangement by which the church reported only 1000 members as a method of limiting financial liabilities within the denomination.

8 Crystal Cathedral Annual Consistorial Report, 2005, Shepherd's Grove Church Archive, Irvine, CA (hereafter SGCA).

9 Deepa Bharath and Ronald Campbell, "Crystal Cathedral Plan: Lease Its Way Out of Debt," *Orange County Register*, May 27, 2011, https://www.ocregister.com/2011 /05/27/crystal-cathedral-plan-lease-its-way-out-of-debt/.

10 Robert P. Jones, *The End of White Christian America* (New York: Simon & Schuster, 2016), 21–28.

11 Laurie Goodstein, "Dispute over Succession Clouds Megachurch," *New York Times*, October 23, 2010, http://www.nytimes.com/2010/10/24/us/24cathedral.html.

12 Christian Copland, "The Demise of the Crystal Cathedral," *KCET*, December 20, 2017, https://www.kcet.org/shows/lost-la/the-demise-of-the-crystal-cathedral.

13 Copland, "Demise of the Crystal Cathedral."

14 Tom Vanderbilt, "The Gaudy and Damned," *The Baffler*, December 1995, https:// thebaffler.com/salvos/the-gaudy-and-damned-no-1.

15 Robert H. Schuller and Paul David Dunn, *America's Declaration of Financial Independence* (Nashville: Rutledge Hill Press, 1995). Beginning on page 35, Schuller and Dunn directly address the Orange County bankruptcy.

16 Tom Zoellner and Elaine Lewinnek, "Seeing Orange County," *Boom California*, February 13, 2018, 43, https://boomcalifornia.com/2018/02/13/seeing-orange-county/.

17 Joel Kotkin and Marshall Toplansky, "OC Model: A Vision for Orange County's Future," Chapman University Center for Demographics and Policy, October 1, 2016, https://www.chapman.edu/wilkinson/_files/oc-homefnc.pdf.

18 Susan Power Bratton, *ChurchScape: Megachurches and the Iconography of Environment* (Waco, TX: Baylor University Press, 2016), 130.

19 Deyan Sudjic, *The Edifice Complex: How the Rich and Powerful Shape the World* (New York: Penguin Books, 2005), 299.

20 Copland, "Demise of the Crystal Cathedral."

21 For more on Latino Protestantism, see Mark T. Mulder, Aida I. Ramos, and Gerardo Marti, *Latino Protestants in America: Growing and Diverse* (Lanham, MD: Rowman & Littlefield, 2017); and Aida I. Ramos, Gerardo Marti, and Mark T. Mulder, "The Growth and Diversity of Latino Protestants in America," *Religion Compass* (June 2018).

22 Juan Carlos Ortiz and Martha Palau, *From the Jungles to the Cathedral: The Captivating Story of Juan Carlos Ortiz* (Miami: Vida, 2011), 173–174.

23 Ortiz and Palau, *From the Jungles to the Cathedral*, 180.

24 Ortiz and Palau, 176.

25 Ortiz was not alone in his strategy of engaging in Roman Catholic liturgical practices within a Latino Protestant congregation. For more, see Mulder et al., *Latino Protestants in America*, 2017; Aida I. Ramos, Robert D. Woodberry, and Christopher G. Ellison, "The Contexts of Conversions among U.S. Latinos," *Sociology of Religion* 78, no. 2 (2017): 119–145.

26 Ortiz and Palau, *From the Jungles to the Cathedral*, 188.

27 Mitchell Landsberg and Nicole Santa Cruz, "At Troubled Crystal Cathedral, a Tale of Two Ministries," *Los Angeles Times*, June 19, 2011, http://articles.latimes.com/2011/jun/19/local/la-me-Crystal-Cathedral-20110619.

28 Landsberg and Santa Cruz, "At Troubled Crystal Cathedral."

29 Deepa Bharath, "Rifts, Debt Tear at Crystal Cathedral," *Orange County Register*, October 24, 2010, https://www.ocregister.com/2010/10/24/rifts-debt-tear-at-crystal-cathedral/.

30 Bharath, "Rifts, Debt."

31 Nicole Santa Cruz, "Crystal Cathedral May Lose Spanish-Language Ministry," *Los Angeles Times*, November 19, 2011, http://articles.latimes.com/2011/nov/19/local/la-me-crystal-cathedral-20111119.

32 Luiza Oleszczuk, "Dante Gebel's Hispanic Ministry to Leave Crystal Cathedral Campus," *Christian Post*, March 6, 2012, https://www.christianpost.com/news/dante-gebels-hispanic-ministry-to-leave-crystal-cathedral-campus-70899/.

33 Bharath, "Crystal Cathedral Asks Vendors for Forgiveness."

34 Year End Report of the Crystal Cathedral Ministries, December 31, 1988 (SGCA).

35 William Vanderbloemen and Warren Bird, *Next: Pastoral Succession That Works* (Grand Rapids, MI: Baker Books, 2014), 101.

36 Year End Report of the Crystal Cathedral Ministries.

37 "Door Interview: Dr. Robert Schuller," *Wittenburg Door*, no. 25 (June-July 1975): 19 (emphasis added).

38 John Dart, "Schuller's Glass Act: Passing the Baton at the Crystal Cathedral," *The*

Christian Century, April 10, 2002, https://www.christiancentury.org/article/2002
-04/schuller-s-glass-act.

39 Vanderbloemen and Bird, *Next*, 102.

40 "Crystal Cathedral: The State of Our Church and Global Ministry," May 2009, 14 (RKP).

41 Vanderbloemen and Bird, *Next*, 102.

42 Robert H. Schuller, *My Journey: From an Iowa Farm to a Cathedral of Dreams* (San Francisco: HarperOne, 2001), 448–463 and 478.

43 Abby Sewell and Nicole Santa Cruz, "Bankruptcy Filings Show Generous Pay for Relatives of Crystal Cathedral Founder," *Los Angeles Times*, December 3, 2010, http://articles.latimes.com/2010/dec/03/local/la-me-crystal-cathedral-20101203.

44 Interview with Robert A. Schuller, May 2017.

45 Interview with Robert A. Schuller, May 2017.

46 Robert H. Schuller, "The Schuller Family in Ministry," October 2001, and update October 2007, 2–3 (RKP); emphasis added.

47 Schuller, "Schuller Family in Ministry," 5–6.

48 Goodstein, "Dispute over Succession."

49 Goodstein.

50 Bharath, "Rifts, Debt."

51 Schuller, "The Trust of the Board of Trustees," 7–8.

52 Ronald Campbell, "Salaries of Principal Crystal Cathedral Employees," *Orange County Register*, November 17, 2010, https://www.ocregister.com/2010/11/17 /salaries-of-principal-crystal-cathedral-employees/.

53 Letter from anonymous pastor to Ronald Keener, n.d. (RKP).

54 Letter from anonymous pastor to Keener.

55 Robert A. Schuller, *When You Are Down to Nothing, God Is Up to Something: Finding Divine Purpose and Provision When Life Hurts* (New York: Faith Words, 2011), 119.

56 Goodstein, "Dispute over Succession."

57 "Crystal Cathedral: The Son Had It Right, but Siblings and Others Worked against Him, Says Source," *Christian NewsWire*, February 6, 2009 (RKP).

58 Deepa Bharath, "Family Dynamics at Heart of Schuller Resignation," *Orange County Register*, December 16, 2008, https://www.ocregister.com/2008/12/16 /family-dynamics-at-heart-of-schuller-resignation/.

59 Bharath, "Rifts, Debt."

60 Deepa Bharath, "Pianist Williams: Schuller Kids Spoiled Crystal Cathedral," *Orange County Register*, June 17, 2010, https://www.ocregister.com/2010/06/17 /pianist-williams-schuller-kids-spoiled-crystal-cathedral/.

61 Roxana Kopetman, "Three Schuller Family Members Fired from Crystal Cathedral," *Orange County Register*, March 6, 2012, https://www.ocregister.com/2012/03 /07/3-schuller-family-members-fired-from-crystal-cathedral/.

62 Browne Barr, "Finding the Good at Garden Grove," *Christian Century*, May 4, 1977, 426.

63 Dennis Voskuil, *Mountains into Goldmines: Robert Schuller and the Gospel of Success* (Grand Rapids, MI: Eerdmans, 1983).

64 Manuscript galleys of Voskuil, *Mountains into Goldmines*, file 5, galleys 1–3 (DVP).

65 Email from anonymous pastor to Ronald Keener, February 4, 2009 (RKP).

66 Deepa Bharath, "Lawsuit: Schullers Gained as Crystal Cathedral Lost," *Orange County Register*, October 6, 2011, https://www.ocregister.com/2011/10/06/lawsuit -schullers-gained-as-crystal-cathedral-lost/.

67 Matt Coker, "Has the Robert H. Schuller Family Been Running a Crystal Ponzi

Scheme Cathedral?" *OC Weekly*, October 4, 2011, https://ocweekly.com/has-the
-robert-h-schuller-family-been-running-a-crystal-ponzi-scheme-cathedral-6453360/.

68 "Homebuilders Questions for Dr. Sheila Schuller Coleman," n.d. (RKP).

69 "Homebuilders Questions."

70 Email from anonymous pastor to Keener.

71 Erika I. Ritchie and Deepa Bharath, "Saddleback Takes Control of Crystal
Cathedral Retreat," *Orange County Register*, May 11, 2010, https://www.ocregister
.com/2010/05/12/saddleback-takes-control-of-crystal-cathedral-retreat/.

72 Deepa Bharath, "Crystal Cathedral Was an Icon of Tradition," *Orange County
Register*, October 21, 2011, https://www.ocregister.com/2011/10/24/crystal
-cathedral-was-an-icon-of-tradition-2/.

73 Deepa Bharath, "Crystal Cathedral Cancels 'Glory of Easter,'" *Orange County
Register*, January 29, 2010, https://www.ocregister.com/2010/01/29/crystal
-cathedral-cancels-glory-of-easter/.

74 Gillian Flaccus, "Crystal Cathedral Makes Deep Cuts," *San Diego Union-Tribune*,
January 30, 2010, http://www.sandiegouniontribune.com/sdut-crystal-cathedral
-makes-deep-cuts-2010jan30-story.html.

75 Deepa Bharath, "Crystal Cathedral Members Launch Petition Drive," *Orange
County Register*, July 16, 2011, https://www.ocregister.com/2011/07/18/crystal
-cathedral-members-launch-petition-drive/.

76 Adelle M. Banks, "Schuller Loses Vote at Crystal Cathedral," *The Christian Century*,
July 5, 2011, https://www.christiancentury.org/article/2011-07/schuller-loses-vote
-crystal-cathedral. See also "Crystal Cathedral Not for Sale, Announces Church
Board," *Catholic News Agency*, August 1, 2011, https://www.catholicnewsagency.com
/news/crystal-cathedral-not-for-sale-announces-church-board.

77 Deepa Bharath, "Chapman Increases Offer to Buy Crystal Cathedral," *Orange
County Register*, November 1, 2011, https://www.ocregister.com/2011/11/02
/chapman-increases-offer-to-buy-crystal-cathedral/.

78 Deepa Bharath, "Food Request for Rev. Schuller's Wife Sparks Outrage," *Orange
County Register*, November 4, 2011, https://www.ocregister.com/2011/11/04/food
-request-for-rev-schullers-wife-sparks-outrage/.

79 Bharath, "Food Request for Rev. Schuller's Wife."

80 "Cathedral Denies Board Fired Schuller," United Press International, July 4, 2011,
https://www.upi.com/Cathedral-denies-board-fired-Schuller/80711309790882/.

81 Nicole Santa Cruz, "Crystal Cathedral's Senior Pastor Says She's Leaving to Start a
New Church," *Los Angeles Times*, March 12, 2012, http://articles.latimes.com/2012
/mar/12/local/la-me-schuller-reax-20120312.

82 Press release, "Crystal Cathedral Ministries Continues with Sunday Worship
Services, 'Hour of Power,'" A. Larry Ross Communications, March 13, 2012 (RKP).
See also Landsberg and Santa Cruz, "At Troubled Crystal Cathedral."

83 Roxana Kopetman, "Schuller Coleman Leaving: Crystal Cathedral Congregation
Faces Split," *Orange County Register*, March 12, 2012, https://www.ocregister.com
/2012/03/12/schuller-coleman-leaving-crystal-cathedral-congregation-faces-split/.

84 Kopetman, "Schuller Coleman Leaving."

85 Luiza Oleszczuk, "Crystal Cathedral's New CEO: Congregation, Donations
Doubled after Schuller's Departure," *Christian Post*, March 31, 2012, https://www
.christianpost.com/news/crystal-cathedrals-new-ceo-congregation-donations
-doubled-after-schullers-departure-72418/.

86 Ian Lovett, "Founding Family Decides to Leave Crystal Cathedral," *New York*

Times, March 11, 2012, https://www.nytimes.com/2012/03/12/us/robert-schuller
-family-cuts-ties-to-crystal-cathedral.html.

87 Oleszczuk, "Crystal Cathedral's New CEO."

88 Bharath, "Lawsuit: Schullers Gained."

89 Roxana Kopetman, "Crystal Cathedral: Schullers Lose in Court," *Orange County Register*, November 28, 2012, https://www.ocregister.com/2012/11/28/crystal
-cathedral-schullers-lose-in-court/.

90 Nicole Santa Cruz, "Church Family Loses Court Ruling," *Los Angeles Times*, November 27, 2012, http://articles.latimes.com/2012/nov/27/local/la-me-1127
-schuller-bankruptcy-20121127.

91 Michael Nason and Donna Nason, *Robert Schuller: The Inside Story* (Waco, TX: Word Books, 1983), 105.

92 Ian Lovett, "Lasting Tributes Meet Early End in Bankruptcy," *New York Times*, September 5, 2013, https://www.nytimes.com/2013/09/06/us/parishioners-find
-removal-of-memorial-stones-an-added-indignity.html.

93 Vanderbloemen and Bird, *Next*, 103.

94 "Crystal Cathedral: The State of Our Church."

95 Thanks to Scott Thumma for providing this vivid metaphor.

96 Letter from anonymous minister to Ronald Keener, November 21, 2011 (RKP).

97 Robert H. Schuller, *Success Is Never Ending, Failure Is Never Final* (Nashville: Thomas Nelson, 1988), 153–154.

98 Robert D. Putnam and Lewis M. Feldstein, *Better Together: Restoring the American Community* (New York: Simon & Schuster, 2003), 134.

99 Gerardo Marti, *A Mosaic of Believers: Diversity and Innovation in a Multiethnic Church* (Bloomington: Indiana University Press, 2005); Gerardo Marti, *Hollywood Faith: Holiness, Prosperity, and Ambition in a Los Angeles Church* (New Brunswick, NJ: Rutgers University Press, 2008).

100 Justin G. Wilford, *Sacred Subdivisions: The Postsuburban Transformation of American Evangelicalism* (New York: New York University Press, 2012), 55.

Coda: Ends and Beginnings

1 Deepa Bharath, "Chapman Increases Offer to Buy Crystal Cathedral," *Orange County Register*, November 1, 2011, https://www.ocregister.com/2011/11/02
/chapman-increases-offer-to-buy-crystal-cathedral/.

2 "Crystal Cathedral Gives Blessing to Catholic Bid," *North Country Times*, November 12, 2011, Ronald Keener Papers, Chambersburg, PA (hereafter RKP).

3 Deepa Bharath, "Diocese Increases Offer for Crystal Cathedral to $55.4 Million," *Orange County Register*, November 9, 2011, https://www.ocregister.com/2011/11/10
/diocese-increases-offer-for-crystal-cathedral-to-554-million/.

4 Deepa Bharath, "Future of Crystal Cathedral Uncertain," *Orange County Register*, November 18, 2011, https://www.ocregister.com/2011/11/18/future-of-crystal
-cathedral-uncertain/.

5 Barbara Bradley Hagerty, "Catholic Church to Buy Famed Crystal Cathedral," National Public Radio, November 18, 2011, https://www.npr.org/2011/11/18
/142518963/future-of-ministry-uncertain-after-cathedrals-sale.

6 Deepa Bharath, "Catholic Diocese of Orange County Will Buy Crystal Cathedral," *Orange County Register*. See also Nicole Santa Cruz, Ruben Vives, and Mitchell Landsberg, "Orange County Diocese to Buy Bankrupt Crystal Cathedral," *Los Angeles*

Times, November 18, 2011, http://articles.latimes.com/2011/nov/18/local/la-me
-crystal-cathedral-20111118.

7   At the time, the organization was known as Robert Schuller Ministries.

8   Ronald Campbell, "Judge: Crystal Cathedral Sale Will Go Through," *Orange
County Register*, January 30, 2012, https://www.ocregister.com/2012/01/31/judge
-crystal-cathedral-sale-will-go-through/.

9   Anthony Paletta, "How a Drive-in Megachurch became a Catholic Cathedral,"
CityLab, September 4, 2019, https://www.citylab.com/design/2019/09/crystal
-christ-cathedral-robert-schuller-philip-johnson/597022/.

10 Ivana Kvesic, "Bobby Schuller Talks Starting Over, Returning to Crystal Cathedral," *Christian Post*, May 17, 2012, https://www.christianpost.com/news/bobby
-schuller-talks-starting-over-returning-to-crystal-cathedral-75139/.

11 Anugrah Kumar, "Bobby Schuller Encourages Crystal Cathedral to Press On,"
Christian Post, June 11, 2012, https://www.christianpost.com/news/bobby-schuller
-encourages-crystal-cathedral-to-press-on-76406/.

12 Interview with board member, February 2017.

13 Mary Louise Schumacher, "The Crystal Cathedral was a Monument to Televangelism. It's about to become a Catholic Church," *The Washington Post*, July 17, 2019,
https://www.washingtonpost.com/religion/2019/07/17/crystal-cathedral-was
-monument-televangelism-its-about-become-catholic-church/.

14 Heather Adams, "Crystal Cathedral, Home to 'Hour of Power,' Transforms into
Catholic Seat," Religion News Service, November 28, 2018, https://www.ocregister
.com/2010/04/10/crystal-cathedral-asks-vendors-for-forgiveness/.

15 Robert P. Jones, *The End of White Christian America* (New York: Simon &
Schuster, 2016), 28.

16 Jim Hinch, "Where Are the People? Evangelical Christianity in America Is Losing
Its Power—What Happened to Orange County's Crystal Cathedral Shows Why,"
American Scholar, Winter 2014, https://theamericanscholar.org/where-are-the
-people/#.

17 For more on these changes, see Jones, *End of White Christian America*.

18 Deepa Bharath, "Vietnamese Shrine in Cathedral Plans," *Orange County Register*,
December 8, 2016, http://www.ocregister.com/2016/12/08/vietnamese-shrine-in
-cathedral-plans/.

19 "Schuller's Tree of Life Community Church to Merge into Shepherd's Grove,"
Religion News Service, February 16, 2015, https://religionnews.com/2015/02/16
/schullers-tree-life-community-church-merge-shepherds-grove/.

20 Maurice Hoogendoorn, "A Thousand Times 'You Are Loved,'" *Dutch Daily*,
April 6, 2018, 2.

21 Deepa Bharath, "It's a New Time," *Orange County Register*, October 10, 2014,
https://www.ocregister.com/2014/10/10/its-a-new-time/.

22 Warren Cole Smith, "Bobby Schuller on the Crystal Cathedral Exodus," *World*,
March 25, 2015, https://world.wng.org/2015/03/bobby_schuller_on_the_crystal
_cathedral_exodus.

23 Interview with Bobby Schuller, May 2017.

24 Accessed June 28, 2018: http://www.shepherdsgrove.org/bettertogether/. See "Will Any
of Our Theological Views Change?"

25 Ruth Graham, "Church of the Donald: Never Mind Fox. Trump's Most Reliable
Media Mouthpiece Is Now Christian TV," *Politico Magazine* (June 2018), https://
www.politico.com/magazine/story/2018/04/22/trump-christian-evangelical
-conservatives-television-tbn-cbn-218008.

26 Deepa Bharath, "It's a New Time," *Orange County Register*, October 10, 2014, https://www.ocregister.com/2014/10/10/its-a-new-time/.

27 Ronald Keener, "Interview with Bobby Schuller: Reaching New Generations in Emerging Ways for Christ," *Church Executive*, November 2005, 22.

28 Keener, "Interview with Bobby Schuller."

29 Deepa Bharath, "Former Crystal Cathedral Leader Robert H. Schuller in Critical Condition," *Orange County Register*, April 1, 2015, https://www.ocregister.com/2015/04/01/former-crystal-cathedral-leader-robert-h-schuller-in-critical-condition-his-family-says/.

30 Kimberly Winston, "Crystal Cathedral Founder's Memorial Covered by Crowdfunding Campaign," *Washington Post*, April 21, 2015, https://www.washingtonpost.com/national/religion/crystal-cathedral-founders-memorial-covered-by-crowdfunding-campaign/2015/04/21/134073cc-e86b-11e4-8581-633c536add4b_story.html?utm_term=.b77287ef7a08.

Appendix: Research Methodology

1 The Joint Archives of Holland is a cooperative institution established by Hope College and Western Theological Seminary. Schuller graduated from both, and they both remain affiliated with the RCA—as did both Crystal Cathedral and, until April 2018, Shepherd's Grove Church.

Bibliography

Adams, Courtenay. "The Peak of Possibility Thinking: Robert H. Schuller's Crystal Cathedral in Orange County, California, during the 1980s." PhD diss., University of Calgary, 2012.

Adams, Heather. "Crystal Cathedral, Home to 'Hour of Power,' Transforms into Catholic Seat." Religion News Service, November 28, 2018. https://religionnews.com/2018/11/28/crystal-cathedral-home-to-the-hour-of-power-transforms-into-catholic-seat/.

Ammerman, Nancy Tatom. *Congregation and Community.* New Brunswick, NJ: Rutgers University Press, 1997.

Anker, Roy. *Self-Help and Popular Religion in Modern American Culture.* Westport, CT: Greenwood Press, 1999.

Archer, John. *Architecture and Suburbia: From English Villa to American Dream House, 1690–2000.* Minneapolis: University of Minnesota Press, 2005.

Atwood, Donner. "The Local Church's Edge." *Church Herald*, March 7, 1980.

Balmer, Randall. *Evangelicalism in America.* Waco, TX: Baylor University Press, 2016.

———. "The Genius of Robert Schuller." *Valley News*, April 12, 2015. https://www.vnews.com/opinion/16416917-95/coumn-the-genius-of-robert-schuller.

Banks, Adelle M. "Schuller Loses Vote at Crystal Cathedral." *The Christian Century*, July 5, 2011. https://www.christiancentury.org/article/2011-07/schuller-loses-vote-crystal-cathedral.

Barron, Jessica M., and Rhys H. Williams. *The Urban Church Imagined: Religion, Race, and Authenticity in the City.* New York: New York University Press, 2017.

Bean, Lydia. *The Politics of Evangelical Identity: Local Churches and Partisan Divides in the United States and Canada.* Princeton, NJ: Princeton University Press, 2014.

Beardslee, John, III. "Who's against Communism?" *Church Herald*, April 20, 1962.

Benes, Louis H. "Community or Reformed Churches." *Church Herald*, November 10, 1950.

———. "New Hope for the Church." *Church Herald*, April 16, 1971.

Bharath, Deepa. "Chapman Increases Offer to Buy Crystal Cathedral." *Orange County Register.* November 1, 2011. https://www.ocregister.com/2011/11/02/chapman-increases-offer-to-buy-crystal-cathedral/.

———. "Crystal Cathedral Asks Vendors for Forgiveness." *Orange County Register.* April 9, 2010. https://www.ocregister.com/2010/04/10/crystal-cathedral-asks-vendors-for-forgiveness/.

———. "Crystal Cathedral Cancels 'Glory of Easter.'" *Orange County Register.* January 29, 2010. https://www.ocregister.com/2010/01/29/crystal-cathedral-cancels-glory-of-easter/.

———. "Crystal Cathedral Choir Asked to Sign Anti-Gay Covenant." *Orange County Register*. March 16, 2011. http://www.ocregister.com/2011/03/16/crystal-cathedral-choir-asked-to-sign-anti-gay-covenant/.

———. "Crystal Cathedral Members Launch Petition Drive." *Orange County Register*. July 16, 2011. https://www.ocregister.com/2011/07/18/crystal-cathedral-members-launch-petition-drive/.

———. "Crystal Cathedral to Be Sold to Pay Millions in Debt." *Orange County Register*. March 27, 2011. https://www.ocregister.com/2011/05/27/crystal-cathedral-to-be-sold-to-pay-millions-in-debt/.

———. "Crystal Cathedral Was an Icon of Tradition." *Orange County Register*. October 21, 2011. https://www.ocregister.com/2011/10/24/crystal-cathedral-was-an-icon-of-tradition-2/.

———. "Diocese Increases Offer for Crystal Cathedral to $55.4 Million." *Orange County Register*. November 9, 2011. https://www.ocregister.com/2011/11/10/diocese-increases-offer-for-crystal-cathedral-to-554-million/.

———. "Family Dynamics at Heart of Schuller Resignation." *Orange County Register*. December 16, 2008. https://www.ocregister.com/2008/12/16/family-dynamics-at-heart-of-schuller-resignation/.

———. "Food Request for Rev. Schuller's Wife Sparks Outrage." *Orange County Register*. November 4, 2011. https://www.ocregister.com/2011/11/04/food-request-for-rev-schullers-wife-sparks-outrage/.

———. "Former Crystal Cathedral Leader Robert H. Schuller in Critical Condition." *Orange County Register*. April 1, 2015. https://www.ocregister.com/2015/04/01/former-crystal-cathedral-leader-robert-h-schuller-in-critical-condition-his-family-says/.

———. "Future of Crystal Cathedral Uncertain." *Orange County Register*. November 18, 2011. https://www.ocregister.com/2011/11/18/future-of-crystal-cathedral-uncertain/.

———. "It's a New Time." *Orange County Register*. October 10, 2014. https://www.ocregister.com/2014/10/10/its-a-new-time/.

———. "'It Was a Life Well-Lived': The Reverend Robert Schuller, Leader of Crystal Cathedral and 'Hour of Power,' Dies at 88." *Orange County Register.*, April 3, 2015. https://www.ocregister.com/2015/04/03/it-was-a-life-well-lived-rev-robert-schuller-leader-of-crystal-cathedral-and-hour-of-power-dies-at-88/.

———. "Lawsuit: Schullers Gained as Crystal Cathedral Lost." *Orange County Register*. October 6, 2011. http://www.ocregister.com/2011/10/06/lawsuit-schullers-gained-as-crystal-cathedral-lost/.

———. "Pianist Williams: Schuller Kids Spoiled Crystal Cathedral." *Orange County Register*. June 17, 2010. https://www.ocregister.com/2010/06/17/pianist-williams-schuller-kids-spoiled-crystal-cathedral/.

———. "Rifts, Debt Tear at Crystal Cathedral." *Orange County Register*. October 24, 2010. https://www.ocregister.com/2010/10/24/rifts-debt-tear-at-crystal-cathedral/.

———. "Schuller Sr. Speaks Out against Crystal Cathedral Anti-Gay Covenant." *Orange County Register*. March 17, 2011. http://www.ocregister.com/2011/03/17/schuller-sr-speaks-out-against-crystal-cathedral-anti-gay-covenant/.

———. "Vietnamese Shrine in Cathedral Plans." *Orange County Register*. December 8, 2016. http://www.ocregister.com/2016/12/08/vietnamese-shrine-in-cathedral-plans/.

Bharath, Deepa, and Ronald Campbell. "Crystal Cathedral Plan: Lease Its Way Out of Debt." *Orange County Register*. May 27, 2011. https://www.ocregister.com/2011/05/27/crystal-cathedral-plan-lease-its-way-out-of-debt/.

Billingsley, Lloyd. "A Crystal Cathedral Spectacular: Christmas Pageant Is Reputed to Be the Country's Largest." *Christianity Today*. January 22, 1982.

———. "The Gospel according to Robert Schuller." *Eternity*, March 1983.

Biography: Robert Schuller. A&E, 1998. https://www.youtube.com/watch?v=U4nYEf8F-9g.

Bird, Warren. "How Robert H. Schuller Shaped Your Ministry." *Leadership Network*. April 2, 2015. http://leadnet.org/how-robert-h-schuller-shaped-your-ministry/.

Bottles, Scott L. *Los Angeles and the Automobile: The Making of the Modern City*. Berkeley: University of California Press, 1987.

Bowler, Kate. *Blessed: A History of the American Prosperity Gospel*. New York: Oxford University Press, 2013.

———. "Why Are There So Few Mainline Celebrities?" *Faith and Leadership*. May 30, 2017. https://www.faithandleadership.com/kate-bowler-why-are-there-so-few-mainline -celebrities.

Bowler, Kate, and Wen Reagan. "Bigger, Better, Louder: The Prosperity Gospel's Impact on Contemporary Christian Worship." *Religion and American Culture: A Journal of Interpretation* 24, no. 2 (2014): 186–230.

Bratton, Susan Power. *ChurchScape: Megachurches and the Iconography of Environment*. Waco, TX: Baylor University Press, 2016.

Brecher, Elinor J. "Inspired or Pirated? Two Question Peale's Works." *Miami Herald*. July 28, 1995.

Brenneman, Todd M. *Homespun Gospel: The Triumph of Sentimentality in Contemporary American Evangelicalism*. New York: Oxford University Press, 2013.

Butterfield, Stephen. *Amway: The Cult of Free Enterprise*. Boston: South End Press, 1985.

Campbell, Ronald. "Judge: Crystal Cathedral Sale Will Go Through." *Orange County Register*. January 30, 2012. https://www.ocregister.com/2012/01/31/judge-crystal -cathedral-sale-will-go-through/.

———. "Salaries of Principal Crystal Cathedral Employees." *Orange County Register*. November 17, 2010. https://www.ocregister.com/2010/11/17/salaries-of-principal-crystal -cathedral-employees/.

Capps, Kriston. "Why Cities Should Be More Skeptical of New Cultural Centers and Expansions." *CityLab*, June 24, 2014. https://www.citylab.com/equity/2014/06/why -cities-should-be-more-skeptical-of-new-cultural-centers-and-expansions/373258/.

"Cathedral Denies Board Fired Schuller." United Press International. July 4, 2011. https:// www.upi.com/Cathedral-denies-board-fired-Schuller/80711309790882/.

Chandler, Russell. *Understanding the New Age*. Dallas: Word Publishing, 1988.

Chazanov, Mathis. "The Rev. Billy Graham Said Today He Experienced 'Total Liberty.'" United Press International, May 12, 1982. http://www.upi.com/Archives/1982/05/12/The -Rev-Billy-Graham-said-today-he-experienced-total/8136390024000/.

Christerson, Brad, and Richard Flory. *The Rise of Network Christianity: How Independent Leaders Are Changing the Religious Landscape*. New York: Oxford University Press, 2017.

Cooley, Charles Horton. "The Looking-Glass Self." In *Human Nature and the Social Order*, by Charles Horton Cooley, 179–185. New York: Scribner's, 1902.

Copland, Christian. "The Demise of the Crystal Cathedral." *KCET*. December 20, 2017. https://www.kcet.org/shows/lost-la/the-demise-of-the-crystal-cathedral.

Corcoran, Katie E., and James K. Wellman Jr. "'People Forget He's Human': Charismatic Leadership in Institutionalized Religion." *Sociology of Religion* 77, no. 4 (2016): 309–333.

Cox, Claire. *The New-Time Religion: What Is Really Happening in Our Churches and Among Churchgoers in America Today*. Englewood Cliffs, NJ: Prentice-Hall, 1961.

"Cracks in the Crystal Cathedral: Why We Are Better Off Letting God Make the Gospel Relevant." *Christianity Today*. January 10, 2011. http://www.christianitytoday.com/ct /2011/january/15.59.html.

"Crystal Cathedral to Pay Back Taxes on Concert Receipts." *New York Times*. August 31, 1983. https://www.nytimes.com/1983/08/31/us/crystal-cathedral-to-pay-back-taxes-on-concert-receipts.html.

Cuniff, Meghann N. "Age, Income, Ethnicity: Latest Census Data Reveals All Facets of O.C." *Orange County Register*. December 29, 2014. https://www.ocregister.com/2014/12/29/age-income-ethnicity-latest-census-data-reveals-all-facets-of-oc/.

Curwen, Thomas. "Robert Schuller's California Brand of Christianity." *Los Angeles Times*. April 2, 2015. http://beta.latimes.com/local/lanow/la-me-ln-robert-schullers-california-brand-christianity-20150402-story.html.

Dart, John. "Schuller's New Center Faulted for Its Secular Look." *Los Angeles Times*. November 25, 1989. http://articles.latimes.com/1989-11-25/entertainment/ca-304_1_crystal-cathedral.

Davis, Douglas, Jonathan Kirsch, and Maggie Malone. "The Crystal Cathedral." *Newsweek*, October 6, 1980.

Davis, Gerald F. *Managed by the Markets: How Finance Re-Shaped America*. New York: Oxford University Press, 2009.

Diamond, Edwin. "Should Government Crack Down on TV's Evangelicals?" *TV Guide*. November 14–20.

Do, Anh. "Crystal Cathedral Enters a New Era as It Transforms into Christ Cathedral." *Los Angeles Times*. September 17, 2016. http://www.latimes.com/local/lanow/la-me-ln-orange-county-catholics-adv-snap-story.html.

Dochuk, Darren. *From Bible Belt to Sunbelt: Plain-Folk Religion, Grassroots Politics, and the Rise of Evangelical Conservatism*. New York: W. W. Norton & Co., 2011.

Droog, Chester. "The RCA: Growing in the Southwest." *Church Herald*, June 7, 1985.

Ehrenreich, Barbara. *Bright-Sided: How Positive Thinking Is Undermining America*. New York: Picador, 2009.

Ellingson, Stephen. *The Megachurch and the Mainline: Remaking Religious Tradition in the Twenty-First Century*. Chicago: University of Chicago Press, 2007.

Elson, Raymond J., Casey Kennedy, and Mark Wills. "The Crystal Cathedral and Its Demise." *Journal of Business Cases and Applications* 18 (September 2017): 1–13. http://www.aabri.com/manuscripts/172634.pdf.

Emerson, Michael, and Christian Smith. *Divided by Faith: Evangelical Religion and the Problem of Race in America*. New York: Oxford University Press, 2000.

Enroth, Ronald. "A Self-Styled Evangelist Stretches God's Truth: Terry Cole-Whittaker Uses Television to Advance Her Own Version of the Gospel." *Christianity Today*. September 21, 1984.

Eskridge, Larry. *God's Forever Family: The Jesus People Movement in America*. New York: Oxford University Press, 2013.

Exoo, George D., and George Tweed. "Peale's Secret Source." *Lutheran Quarterly* 9 (summer 1995): 151–175.

Fagerstrom, Scott. "Schuller Remarks Upset Reformed Church Officials: Minister's Claim of Accountability Called Misleading." *Orange County Register*. April 30, 1987.

Ferré, John P. "Searching for the Great Commission." In *American Evangelicals and the Mass Media: Perspectives on the Relationship between American Evangelicals and the Mass Media*, edited by Quentin J Schultze, 99–117. Grand Rapids, MI: Zondervan, 1990.

Finke, Roger, and Rodney Stark. *The Churching of America, 1776–1990: Winners and Losers in Our Religious Economy*. New Brunswick, NJ: Rutgers University Press, 1997.

Fishman, Robert. *Bourgeois Utopias: The Rise and Fall of Suburbia*. New York: Basic Books, 1987.

FitzGerald, Frances. *The Evangelicals: The Struggle to Shape America*. New York: Simon & Schuster, 2017.

Frame, Randy. "Surviving the Slump: Can Religious Broadcasters Overcome Rising Costs, Competition, and the Lingering Effects of Scandal?" *Christianity Today*. February 3, 1989.

Frankl, Razelle. *Televangelism: The Marketing of Popular Religion*. Carbondale, IL: Southern Illinois University Press, 1987.

Gates, L. *Dwelling in Schullerland*. Nashville: Winston-Derek, 1985.

Geismer, Lily. *Don't Blame Us: Suburban Liberals and the Transformation of the Democratic Party*. Princeton, NJ: Princeton University Press, 2015.

Gloege, Timothy E. W. *Guaranteed Pure: The Moody Bible Institute, Business, and the Making of Modern Evangelicalism*. Chapel Hill: University of North Carolina Press, 2015.

Goffman, Erving. *The Presentation of Self in Everyday Life*. Garden City, NJ: Doubleday, 1959.

Goldman, Marion, and Steven Pfaff. "Reconsidering Virtuosity: Religious Innovation and Spiritual Privilege." *Sociology Theory* 32, no. 2 (2014): 128–146.

Goodstein, Laurie. "Dispute over Succession Clouds Megachurch." *New York Times*. October 23, 2010. https://www.nytimes.com/2010/10/24/us/24cathedral.html.

Gorski, Philip. *American Covenant: A History of Civil Religion from the Puritans to the Present*. Princeton, NJ: Princeton University Press, 2017.

Graham, Ruth. "Church of the Donald: Never Mind Fox. Trump's Most Reliable Media Mouthpiece Is Now Christian TV." *Politico Magazine*. June 2018. https://www.politico.com/magazine/story/2018/04/22/trump-christian-evangelical-conservatives-television-tbn-cbn-218008.

Grem, Darren E. *The Blessings of Business: How Corporations Shaped Conservative Christianity*. New York: Oxford University Press, 2016.

Gribben, Crawford. "Holy Nation: America, Born Again." *American Interest*, November 22, 2015. http://www.the-american-interest.com/2015/11/22/holy-nation-america-born-again/.

Haas, J. Eugene, and Thomas E. Drabek. *Complex Organizations: A Sociological Perspective*. New York: Macmillan, 1973.

Hadden, Jeffrey K. "The Rise and Fall of American Televangelism." *Annals of the American Academy of Political and Social Science* 527, no. 1 (May 1993).

Hadden, Jeffrey K., and Charles E. Swann. *Prime Time Preachers: The Rising Power of Televangelism*. Reading, MA: Addison-Wesley, 1981.

Haddigan, Lee. "The Importance of Christian Thought for the American Libertarian Movement: Christian Libertarianism, 1950–71." *Libertarian Papers* 2, no. 14 (2010): 1–31. https://mises.org/library/importance-christian-thought-american-libertarian-movement-christian-libertarianism-1950–71.

Hagerty, Barbara Bradley. "Catholic Church to Buy Famed Crystal Cathedral." National Public Radio. November 18, 2011. https://www.npr.org/2011/11/18/142518963/future-of-ministry-uncertain-after-cathedrals-sale.

Hardin, John Curran. "Retailing Religion: Business Promotionalism in American Christian Churches in the Twentieth Century." PhD diss., University of Maryland, 2011.

Harris, Elizabeth A. "Tattoos, Bieber, Black Lives Matter, and Jesus." *New York Times*. October 26, 2017. https://www.nytimes.com/2017/10/26/books/hillsong-church-carl-lentz-book-justin-bieber.html.

Heer, Jeet. "The Power of Negative Thinking." *New Republic*. October 16, 2017. https://newrepublic.com/article/145311/power-negative-thinking-trump-lessons-democrats.

Hinch, Jim. "Where Are the People? Evangelical Christianity in America Is Losing Its Power—What Happened to Orange County's Crystal Cathedral Shows Why." *American Scholar*. Winter 2014. https://theamericanscholar.org/where-are-the-people/.

Hines, Thomas S. *Richard Neutra and the Search for Modern Architecture*. Berkeley: University of California Press, 1982.

Hoogendoorn, Maurice. "A Thousand Times 'You Are Loved.'" *Dutch Daily*. April 6, 2018.

Horton, Michael. *Christless Christianity: The Alternative Gospel of the American Church*. Grand Rapids, MI: Baker Books, 2008.

"How Schuller Shaped Your Ministry: A Conversation with Robert Schuller." *Leadership Journal*. Accessed March 16, 2016. http://www.christianitytoday.com/pastors/1997 /spring/7l2114.html.

Hudnut-Beumler, James. *Looking for God in the Suburbs: The Religion of the American Dream and Its Critics, 1945–1965*. New Brunswick, NJ: Rutgers University Press, 1994.

Hunter, James Davison. *Evangelicalism: The Coming Generation*. Chicago: University of Chicago Press, 1987.

Hutchison, William R., ed. *Between the Times: The Travail of the Protestant Establishment in America, 1900–1960*. Cambridge: Cambridge University Press, 1989.

Jackson, Kenneth T. *Crabgrass Frontier: The Suburbanization of the United States*. New York: Oxford University Press, 1985.

Japinga, Lynn. *Loyalty and Loss: The Reformed Church in America, 1945–1994*. Grand Rapids, MI: Eerdmans, 2013.

Joice, Lois M. "The Glass Cathedral That Grew in an Orange Grove." *Church Herald*. April 16, 1971.

Jones, Robert P. *The End of White Christian America*. New York: Simon & Schuster, 2016. http://www.simonandschuster.com/books/The-End-of-White-Christian-America /Robert-P-Jones/9781501122293.

Kantzer, Kenneth S., and Paul W. Fromer. "A Theologian Looks at Schuller." *Christianity Today*. August 10, 1984.

Kay, Jane Holtz. *Asphalt Nation: How the Automobile Took Over America and How We Can Take It Back*. Berkeley: University of California Press, 1997.

Kerstetter, Todd M. *Inspiration and Innovation: Religion in the American West*. Malden, MA: Wiley-Blackwell, 2015.

Kilde, Jeanne Halgren. *Sacred Power, Sacred Space: An Introduction to Christian Architecture and Worship*. New York: Oxford University Press, 2008.

———. *When Church Became Theatre*. New York: Oxford University Press, 2002.

Kirk, Nicole C. *Wanamaker's Temple: The Business of Religion in an Iconic Department Store*. New York: New York University Press, 2018.

Kirkpatrick, Ron. "Pastor Parlays Drive-in Sermon into National Fame." *Orange County Register*. March 5, 1978.

Kopetman, Roxana. "Crystal Cathedral: Schullers Lose in Court." *Orange County Register*. November 28, 2012. https://www.ocregister.com/2012/11/28/crystal-cathedral-schullers -lose-in-court/.

———. "Schuller Coleman Leaving: Crystal Cathedral Congregation Faces Split." *Orange County Register*. March 12, 2012. https://www.ocregister.com/2012/03/12/schuller -coleman-leaving-crystal-cathedral-congregation-faces-split/.

———. "Three Schuller Family Members Fired from Crystal Cathedral." *Orange County Register*. March 6, 2012. https://www.ocregister.com/2012/03/07/3-schuller-family -members-fired-from-crystal-cathedral/.

Kotkin, Joel and Marshall Toplansky. "OC Model: A Vision for Orange County's Future." Chapman University Center for Demographics and Policy, October 1, 2016. https://www .chapman.edu/wilkinson/_files/oc-homefnc.pdf.

Kotz, David M. *The Rise and Fall of Neoliberal Capitalism*. Cambridge, MA: Harvard University Press, 2015.

Krippner Greta R. *Capitalizing on Crisis: The Political Origins of the Rise of Finance*. Cambridge, MA: Harvard University Press, 2011.

Kruse, Kevin. *One Nation under God: How Corporate America Invented Christian America*. New York: Basic Books, 2015.

Kumar, Anugrah. "Bobby Schuller Encourages Crystal Cathedral to Press On." *Christian Post*. June 11, 2012. https://www.christianpost.com/news/bobby-schuller-encourages -crystal-cathedral-to-press-on-76406/.

Kvesic, Ivana. "Bobby Schuller Talks Starting Over, Returning to Crystal Cathedral." *Christian Post*. May 17, 2012. https://www.christianpost.com/news/bobby-schuller-talks -starting-over-returning-to-crystal-cathedral-75139/.

Landsberg, Mitchell, and Nicole Santa Cruz. "At Troubled Crystal Cathedral, a Tale of Two Ministries." *Los Angeles Times*. June 19, 2011. http://articles.latimes.com/2011/jun/19 /local/la-me-Crystal-Cathedral-20110619.

Lane, Christopher. *Surge of Piety: Norman Vincent Peale and the Remaking of American Religious Life*. New Haven, CT: Yale University Press, 2016.

Larry King Live. January 23, 2006. http://transcripts.cnn.com/TRANSCRIPTS/0601/23 /lkl.01.html.

Lasch, Christopher. *The Culture of Narcissism: American Life in an Age of Diminishing Expectations*. New York: W. W. Norton & Co., 1979.

Lassiter, Matthew D. *The Silent Majority: Suburban Politics in the Sunbelt South*. Princeton, NJ: Princeton University Press, 2006.

Lavin, Sylvia. *Form Follows Libido: Architecture and Richard Neutra in a Psychoanalytic Culture*. Cambridge, MA: MIT Press, 2004.

Lee, Shayne, and Phillip Luke Sinitiere. *Holy Mavericks: Evangelical Innovators and the Spiritual Marketplace*. New York: New York University Press, 2009.

Lindbeck, George A. "The Church's Mission to a Postmodern Culture." In *Postmodern Theology: Christian Faith in a Pluralist World*, edited by Frederic B. Burnham, 35–55. New York: Harper & Row, 1989.

Linton, Michael R. "Smoke and Mirrors at the Crystal Cathedral." *First Things*. June 1997. https://www.firstthings.com/article/1997/06/002-smoke-and-mirrors-at-the-crystal -cathedral.

Lippy, Charles H., ed. *Twentieth-Century Shapers of American Popular Religion*. New York: Greenwood Press, 1989.

Lobdell, William, and Mitchell Landsberg. "Rev. Robert H. Schuller, Who Built Crystal Cathedral, Dies at 88." *Los Angeles Times*, April 2, 2015. http://www.latimes.com/local /obituaries/la-me-robert-schuller-20150403-story.html.

Lovett, Ian. "Founding Family Decides to Leave Crystal Cathedral." *New York Times*. March 11, 2012. https://www.nytimes.com/2012/03/12/us/robert-schuller-family-cuts -ties-to-crystal-cathedral.html.

———. "Lasting Tributes Meet Early End in Bankruptcy." *New York Times*. September 5, 2013. https://www.nytimes.com/2013/09/06/us/parishioners-find-removal-of-memorial -stones-an-added-indignity.html.

Luhr, Eileen. *Witnessing in Suburbia: Conservatives and Christian Youth Culture*. Berkeley: University of California Press, 2009.

Lynerd, Benjamin T. *Republican Theology: The Civil Religion of American Evangelicals*. New York: Oxford University Press, 2014.

Mariani, John. "Television Evangelism: Milking the Flock." *Saturday Review*. February 3, 1979.

Martí, Gerardo. *American Blindspot: Race, Class, Religion, and the Trump Presidency*. Lanham, MD: Rowmand & Littlefield, 2020.

———. *Hollywood Faith: Holiness, Prosperity, and Ambition in a Los Angeles Church*. New Brunswick, NJ: Rutgers University Press, 2008.

———. *A Mosaic of Believers: Diversity and Innovation in a Multiethnic Church*. Blooming-ton: Indiana University Press, 2005.

———. "New Concepts for New Dynamics: Generating Theory for the Study of Religious Innovation and Social Change." *Journal for the Scientific Study of Religion* 56, no. 1 (2017): 6–18.

———. "White Christian Libertarianism and the Trump Presidency." In *Religion Is Raced: Understanding American Religion in the 21st Century*, edited by Grace Yukich and Penny Edgell. New York: New York University Press, 2020.

Martí, Gerardo, and Gladys Ganiel. *The Deconstructed Church: Understanding Emerging Christianity*. New York: Oxford University Press, 2014.

Martin, William. *With God on Our Side: The Rise of the Religious Right in America*. New York: Broadway Books, 1996.

Marty, Martin E. "Feeling Saved and Feeling Good." *New York University Educational Quarterly* 9, no. 3 (spring 1978): 2–8.

McCoy, Esther. *Richard Neutra: Masters of World Architecture Series*. New York: George Braziller, 1960.

McGirr, Lisa. *Suburban Warriors: The Origins of the New American Right*. Princeton, NJ: Princeton University Press, 2001.

Mead, George Herbert. *Mind, Self, and Society*. Chicago: University of Chicago Press, 1934.

Mehta, Seema, Christopher Goffard, and Anh Do. "Hillary Clinton Turned Orange County Blue. Minorities and College-Educated Women Helped Her." *Los Angeles Times*. November 9, 2016. http://www.latimes.com/politics/la-me-oc-clinton-20161109-story .html.

Meyer, Donald. *The Positive Thinkers: Popular Religious Psychology from Mary Baker Eddy to Norman Vincent Peale and Ronald Reagan*. Middletown, CT: Wesleyan University Press, 1988.

Miller, Donald E. *Reinventing American Protestantism: Christianity in the New Millennium*. Berkeley: University of California Press, 1999.

Miller, Holly. "Living on the Edge." *Saturday Evening Post* 273, no. 2 (April 2001): 36–39, 78.

Monsma, Stephen V. "What Is an Evangelical? And Does It Matter?" *Christian Scholars Review* 46, no. 4 (spring 2017): 323–340.

Mooney, Michael. "Why Joel Osteen Is the Most Popular Preacher on the Planet." *Success*. January 11, 2016. http://www.success.com/article/why-joel-osteen-is-the-most-popular -preacher-on-the-planet.

Moore, Rowan. "The Bilbao Effect: How Frank Gehry's Guggenheim started a Global Craze," *The Guardian*, October 1, 2017. https://www.theguardian.com/artanddesign /2017/oct/01/bilbao-effect-frank-gehry-guggenheim-global-craze.

Mulder, John M. "The Possibility Preacher." *Theology Today* 31 (July 1974): 157–160.

Mulder, Mark T. *Shades of White Flight: Evangelical Congregations and Urban Departure*. New Brunswick, NJ: Rutgers University Press, 2015.

Mulder, Mark T., Aida I. Ramos, and Gerardo Martí. *Latino Protestants in America: Growing and Diverse*. Lanham, MD: Rowman & Littlefield, 2017.

Nagourney, Adam, and Robert Gebeloff. "In Orange County, a Republican Fortress Turns Democratic. *New York Times*. December 31, 2018.

Nason, Michael, and Donna Nason. *Robert Schuller: His Story*. Waco, TX: Word Books, 1983.

———. *Robert Schuller: The Inside Story*. Waco, TX: Word Books, 1983.

Neutra, Richard. *Survival through Design*. New York: Oxford University Press, 1954.

Oleszczuk, Luiza. "Crystal Cathedral's New CEO: Congregation, Donations Doubled after Schuller's Departure." *Christian Post*. March 31, 2012. https://www.christianpost.com

/news/crystal-cathedrals-new-ceo-congregation-donations-doubled-after-schullers
-departure-72418/.

———. "Dante Gebel's Hispanic Ministry to Leave Crystal Cathedral Campus." *Christian Post*. March 6, 2012. https://www.christianpost.com/news/dante-gebels-hispanic
-ministry-to-leave-crystal-cathedral-campus-70899/.

Ortiz, Juan Carlos, and Martha Palau. *From the Jungles to the Cathedral: The Captivating Story of Juan Carlos Ortiz*. Miami: Vida, 2011.

Paletta, Anthony. "How a Drive-in Megachurch became a Catholic Cathedral." *CityLab*, September 4, 2019. https://www.citylab.com/design/2019/09/crystal-christ-cathedral
-robert-schuller-philip-johnson/597022/.

Peale, Norman Vincent. *Enthusiasm Makes the Difference*. Englewood Cliffs, NJ: Prentice-Hall, 1967.

———. *The Power of Positive Thinking*. New York: Prentice-Hall, 1952.

———. *Stay Alive All Your Life*. Englewood Cliffs, NJ: Prentice-Hall, 1957.

Penner, James. *Goliath*. Anaheim, CA: New Hope Publishing Co., 1992.

Phillips-Fein, Kim. *Invisible Hands: The Businessmen's Crusade against the New Deal*. New York: Norton, 2009.

Pritchard, Gregory A. "The Strategy of Willow Creek Community Church: A Study in the Sociology of Religion." PhD diss., Northwestern University, 1994.

———. *Willow Creek Seeker Services: Evaluating a New Way of Doing Church*. Grand Rapids, MI: Baker Books, 1996.

Putnam, Robert D., Lewis M. Feldstein, and Don Cohen. *Better Together: Restoring the American Community*. New York: Simon & Schuster, 2003.

"Retail Religion: Robert Schuller, An Entrepreneur of Televangelism and Megachurches, Died on April 2nd." *Economist*. April 11, 2015. https://www.economist.com/news
/business/21647976-robert-schuller-entrepreneur-televangelism-and-megachurches-died
-april-2nd-retail.

Richardson, Kip. "Gospels of Growth: The American Megachurch at Home and Abroad." In *Secularization and Innovation in the North Atlantic World*, edited by David Hempton and Hugh McLeod. New York: Oxford University Press, 2017.

———. "The Spatial Strategies of American Megachurches." *Oxford Research Encyclopedia of Religion*. May 2017. http://religion.oxfordre.com/view/10.1093/acrefore/9780199340378
.001.0001/acrefore-9780199340378-e-473.

Ridder, Herman J. "How We Did It: The Schuller Film Workshop." *Church Herald*. January 23, 1981, 14–15.

Ritchie, Erika I., and Deepa Bharath. "Saddleback Takes Control of Crystal Cathedral Retreat." *Orange County Register*. May 11, 2010. https://www.ocregister.com/2010/05/12
/saddleback-takes-control-of-crystal-cathedral-retreat/.

"Robertson: Sharon's Stroke Is Divine Punishment." *USA Today*. January 5, 2006. http://
usatoday30.usatoday.com/news/nation/2006-01-05-robertson_x.htm.

Robles-Anderson, Erica. "The Crystal Cathedral: Architecture for Mediated Congregation." *Public Culture* 24, no. 3 (2012).

Roorda, Jan. "A Call to Live Joyously: Dr. Robert H. Schuller, TV's Powerhouse of Spirituality, Inspires Legions of Possibility Thinkers with His Vision of God's Belief in Man." *Saturday Evening Post* 250, no. 3 (April 1978): 54–57, 120.

Ruotsila, Markku. *Fighting Fundamentalist: Carl McIntire and the Politicization of American Fundamentalism*. New York: Oxford University Press, 2016.

Rybczynski, Witold. "An Anatomy of Megachurches: The New Look for Places of Worship." *Slate*. October 10, 2005. http://www.slate.com/articles/arts/architecture/2005/10/an
_anatomy_of_megachurches.html.

Sablan, Kevin. "Action Picks Up for Filming in OC." *Orange County Register*. April 29, 2013. https://www.ocregister.com/2013/04/29/action-picks-up-for-filming-in-oc/.

Santa Cruz, Nicole. "Church Family Loses Court Ruling." *Los Angeles Times*. November 27, 2012. http://articles.latimes.com/2012/nov/27/local/la-me-1127-schuller-bankruptcy-20121127.

———. "Crystal Cathedral May Lose Spanish-Language Ministry." *Los Angeles Times*. November 19, 2011. http://articles.latimes.com/2011/nov/19/local/la-me-crystal -cathedral-20111119.

———. "'Crystal Cathedral's Senior Pastor Says She's Leaving to Start a New Church." *Los Angeles Times*. March 12, 2012. http://articles.latimes.com/2012/mar/12/local/la-me-schuller-reax -20120312.

Sargeant, Kimon Howland. *Seeker Churches: Promoting Traditional Religion in a Nontraditional Way*. New Brunswick, NJ: Rutgers University Press, 2000.

Schuller, Robert A. *When You Are Down to Nothing, God Is Up to Something: Finding Divine Purpose and Provision When Life Hurts*. New York: Faith Words, 2011.

Schuller, Robert H. "The Drive-in Church—A Modern Technique of Outreach." *Reformed Review* 23, no. 22 (1969).

———. "Dr. Schuller Comments." *Christianity Today*. October 5, 1984.

———. *God's Way to the Good Life*. Grand Rapids, MI: Eerdmans, 1963.

———. *If It's Going to Be, It's Up to Me: Eight Proven Principles of Possibility Thinking*. San Francisco: HarperSanFranciso, 1997.

———. *The Inspirational Writings of Robert H. Schuller*. New York: Inspirational Press, 1986.

———. *Life's Not Fair, but God Is Good*. Nashville: Thomas Nelson, 1991.

———. "Make Them Want to Give." *Church Herald*. November 22, 1968.

———. *Move Ahead with Possibility Thinking*. Old Tappan, NJ: Spire Books, 1967.

———. *My Journey: From an Iowa Farm to a Cathedral of Dreams*. San Francisco: HarperOne, 2001.

———. *Reach Out for New Life*. New York: Bantam Books, 1977.

———. *Self-Esteem: The New Reformation*. Waco, TX: Word Books, 1982.

———. *Self-Love: The Dynamic Forces of Success*. New York: Jove Books, 1969.

———. *Success Is Never Ending, Failure Is Never Final*. Nashville: Thomas Nelson, 1988.

———. "Tax Church Properties?!" *Church Herald*, March 13, 1964.

———. *Tough Times Never Last, but Tough People Do*. New York: Bantam Books, 1984.

———. "Turn Your Scars into Stars." *Saturday Evening Post* 250, no. 3 (April 1978): 58–59, 98.

———. "We Can Be Strong." *Church Herald*. June 6, 1969.

———. "What's Wrong with the World?" *Church Herald*. February 11, 1955.

———. *You Can Become the Person You Want to Be*. Old Tappan, NJ: Spire Books, 1973.

———. *Your Church Has a Fantastic Future! A Possibility Thinker's Guide to a Successful Church*. Ventura, CA: Regal Books, 1986.

———. *Your Church Has Real Possibilities!* Glendale, CA: Regal Books, 1974.

Schuller, Robert H., and James Coleman. *A Place of Beauty, a Joy Forever: The Glorious Gardens and Grounds of the Crystal Cathedral in Garden Grove, California*. Garden Grove, CA: Crystal Cathedral Creative Services, 2005.

Schuller, Robert H., and Paul David Dunn. *America's Declaration of Financial Independence*. Nashville: Rutledge Hill Press, 1995.

———. *The Power of Being Debt Free: How Eliminating the National Debt Could Radically Improve Your Standard of Living*. Nashville: Thomas Nelson, 1985.

Schuller, Robert H., Kenneth S. Kantzer, David F. Wells, and V. Gilbert Beers. "Hard Questions for Robert Schuller about Sin and Self-Esteem." *Christianity Today*. August 10, 1984.

Schuller, Robert H., and H. Smart. "The Crystal Cathedral Hymn." *Crystal Cathedral News*. September 6, 1992.

"Schuller's Tree of Life Community Church to Merge into Shepherd's Grove." Religion News Service. February 16, 2015. https://religionnews.com/2015/02/16/schullers-tree-life -community-church-merge-shepherds-grove/.

Schultze, Quentin J., ed. *American Evangelicals and the Mass Media: Perspectives on the Relationship between American Evangelicals and the Mass Media*. Grand Rapids, MI: Zondervan, 1990.

Schumacher, Mary Louise, "The Crystal Cathedral was a Monument to Televangelism: It's About to Become a Catholic Church." *Washington Post*, July 17, 2019. https://www .washingtonpost.com/religion/2019/07/17/crystal-cathedral-was-monument -televangelism-its-about-become-catholic-church/.

Schwaiger, Manfred. "Components and Parameters of Corporate Reputation—An Empirical Study." *Schmalenbach Business Review* 56 (January 2004): 46–71.

Sewell, Abby, and Nicole Santa Cruz. "Bankruptcy Filings Show Generous Pay for Relatives of Crystal Cathedral Founder." *Los Angeles Times*. December 3, 2010. http://articles .latimes.com/2010/dec/03/local/la-me-crystal-cathedral-20101203.

Sinitiere, Phillip Luke. *Salvation with a Smile: Joel Osteen, Lakewood Church, and American Christianity*. New York: New York University Press, 2015.

Smith, Sheila Strobel. "Complexities of Pastoral Change and Transition in the Mega-churches of the Baptist General Conference, Evangelical Lutheran Church in America, and Presbyterian Church (USA)." PhD diss., Luther Seminary, 2010.

Smith, Warren Cole. "Bobby Schuller on the Crystal Cathedral Exodus." *World*. March 25, 2015. https://world.wng.org/2015/03/bobby_schuller_on_the_crystal_cathedral_exodus.

Solomon, Martha. "Robert Schuller: The American Dream in a Crystal Cathedral." *Central States Speech Journal* 34 (fall 1983): 172–186.

Stadtlander, John H. "Schuller Shows the Way." *LCA Partners*, April 1983, 11–14.

Stapert, John. "Lessons from RCA Church Growth: An Interview with Chester Droog." *Church Herald*. May 1, 1987.

———. "A New Age Challenge." *Church Herald*. March 1990.

———. "Robert Schuller Is from La Mancha." *Church Herald*. October 17, 1980.

———. "Whose Cathedral?" *Church Herald*. June 19, 1987.

Stark, Rodney, and Roger Finke. *Acts of Faith: Explaining the Human Side of Religion*. Berkeley: University of California Press, 2000.

Stephens, Randall J. "Culture, Entertainment, and Religion in America." *Oxford Research Encyclopedia of Religion*. October 2017. http://religion.oxfordre.com/view/10.1093 /acrefore/9780199340378.001.0001/acrefore-9780199340378-e-446.

Stout, Henry S. *The Divine Dramatist: George Whitefield and the Rise of Modern Evangeli-calism*. Grand Rapids, MI: Eerdmans, 1991.

Stumbo, Bella. "The Time Muhammad Ali Asked for Robert Schuller's Autograph." *Los Angeles Times*. May 29, 1983. http://www.latimes.com/local/california/la-me-schuller-1983-profile -20150330-story.html.

Sudjic, Deyan. *The Edifice Complex: How the Rich and Powerful Shape the World*. New York: Penguin Press, 2005.

Sutton, Matthew Avery. *American Apocalypse: A History of Modern Evangelicalism*. Cambridge, MA: Belknap Press of Harvard University Press, 2014.

Thompson, James D. *Organizations in Action: Social Science Bases of Administrative Theory*. New York: McGraw-Hill, 1967.

Thumma, Scott, and David Travis. *Beyond Megachurch Myths: What We Can Learn from America's Largest Churches*. San Francisco: Jossey-Bass, 2007.

Tweed, Thomas. *America's Church: The National Shrine and Catholic Presence in the Nation's Capital*. New York: Oxford University Press, 2011.

Vanderbilt, Tom. "The Gaudy and Damned." *The Baffler.* December 1995. https://thebaffler.com/salvos/the-gaudy-and-damned-no-1.

Vanderbloeman, William, and Warren Bird. *Next: Pastoral Succession That Works.* Grand Rapids, MI: Baker Books, 2014.

Voskuil, Dennis. *Mountains into Goldmines: Robert Schuller and the Gospel of Success.* Grand Rapids, MI: Eerdmans, 1983.

Warner, Sam Bass, Jr. *The Urban Wilderness: A History of the American City.* Berkeley: University of California Press, 1995.

Weber, Max. *Economy and Society: An Outline of Interpretive Sociology.* Berkeley: University of California Press, 1978.

Wellman, James K., Jr. *The Gold Coast Church and the Ghetto: Christ and Culture in Mainline Protestantism.* Urbana: University of Illinois Press, 1999.

———. *Rob Bell and a New American Christianity.* Nashville: Abingdon Press, 2012.

Wellman, James K., Jr., and Katie E. Corcoran. "'People Forget He's Human': Charismatic Leadership in Institutionalized Religion." *Sociology of Religion: A Quarterly Review* 77, no. 4 (2016): 309–332.

Wellman, James K., Jr., Katie E. Corcoran, and Kate Stockly-Meyerdirk. "'God Is Like a Drug...': Explaining Interaction Ritual Chains in American Megachurches." *Sociological Forum* 29, no. 3 (September 2014): 650–672.

Whitman, Ardis. "Four Remarkable Churches." *Reader's Digest* 117 (October 1980): 45–50.

Whyte, William H. *The Organization Man.* New York: Simon & Schuster, 1956.

Wigger, John. *PTL: The Rise and Fall of Jim and Tammy Faye Bakker's Evangelical Empire.* New York: Oxford University Press, 2017.

Wilford, Justin G. *Sacred Subdivisions: The Postsuburban Transformation of American Evangelicalism.* New York: New York University Press, 2012.

Williams, Daniel K. *God's Own Party: The Making of the Christian Right.* New York: Oxford University Press, 2010.

Winston, Kimberly. "Crystal Cathedral Founder's Memorial Covered by Crowdfunding Campaign." *Washington Post.* April 21, 2015. https://www.washingtonpost.com/national/religion/crystal-cathedral-founders-memorial-covered-by-crowdfunding-campaign/2015/04/21/134073cc-e86b-11e4-8581-633c536add4b_story.html?utm_term=.b77287ef7a08.

Worthen, Molly. *Apostles of Reason: The Crisis of Authority in American Evangelicalism.* New York: Oxford University Press, 2014.

Wuthnow, Robert. *The Restructuring of American Religion: Society and Faith since World War II.* Princeton, NJ: Princeton University Press, 1988.

Yardley, Jonathan. "Blessed Are the Self-Actualized." *Washington Post*, February 17, 1997. https://www.washingtonpost.com/archive/lifestyle/1997/02/17/blessed-are-the-self-actualized/af50a1ad-9256-4582-b298-51d3f3721e90/?utm_term=.39c1a25dca70.

Zeiger, Mimi. "Johnson Fain's Church Swap." *Architect: The Journal of the American Institute of Architecture*, October 31, 2016. http://www.architectmagazine.com/design/johnson-fains-church-swap_o.

Zoellner, Tom, and Elaine Lewinnek. "Seeing Orange County." *Boom California.* February 13, 2018. https://boomcalifornia.com/2018/02/13/seeing-orange-county/.

Index

About the Authors

MARK T. MULDER is a professor of sociology at Calvin College. Mulder's scholarship focuses around urban congregations and changing racial-ethnic demographics. He is the author of *Shades of White Flight: Evangelical Congregations and Urban Departure* (Rutgers University Press, 2015), *Congregations, Neighborhoods, Places*, and coauthor of *Latino Protestants in America: Growing and Diverse* (2017). In addition, Mulder has published numerous peer-reviewed articles in academic journals, including *Social Problems* and *The Journal of Urban History*. He has also published pieces for church audiences and won awards from the Evangelical Press Association and the Associated Church Press for his writing.

GERARDO MARTÍ is L. Richardson King Professor of Sociology at Davidson College. Active in several research collaborations, he publishes broadly on religion and social change. He is the author of *A Mosaic of Believers: Diversity and Innovation in a Multiethnic Church* (2005), *Hollywood Faith: Holiness, Prosperity, and Ambition in a Los Angeles Church* (Rutgers University Press, 2008), *Worship across the Racial Divide: Religious Music and the Multiracial Congregation* (2012), *American Blindspot: Race, Class, Religion and the Trump Presidency* (2020), and coauthor of *The Deconstructed Church: Understanding Emerging Christianity* (2014) and *Latino Protestants in America: Growing and Diverse* (2017). He also served for many years as the editor in chief of the peer-reviewed journal *Sociology of Religion: A Quarterly Review*.